SOMEONE TO WATCH OVER ME

JAZZ PERSPECTIVES
Lewis Porter, Series General Editor

Open the Door: The Life and Music of Betty Carter
By William R. Bauer

Jazz Journeys to Japan: The Heart Within
By William Minor

Four Jazz Lives   By A. B. Spellman

Head Hunters: The Making of Jazz's First Platinum Album
By Steven F. Pond

Lester Young   By Lewis Porter

The André Hodeir Jazz Reader
By André Hodeir   Edited by Jean-Louis Pautrot

Someone to Watch Over Me: The Life and Music of Ben Webster
By Frank Büchmann-Møller

OTHER BOOKS OF INTEREST

Before Motown: A History of Jazz in Detroit 1920–1960
By Lars Bjorn with Jim Gallert

John Coltrane: His Life and Music   By Lewis Porter

Charlie Parker: His Music and Life   By Carl Woideck

The Song of the Hawk:
The Life and Recordings of Coleman Hawkins
By John Chilton

Let the Good Times Roll:
The Story of Louis Jordan and His Music
By John Chilton

Twenty Years on Wheels
By Andy Kirk as Told to Amy Lee

SOMEONE TO WATCH OVER ME

The Life and Music of **Ben Webster**

Frank Büchmann-Møller

UNIVERSITY OF MICHIGAN PRESS   Ann Arbor

I dedicate this book to my wonderful wife Emmy

who encouraged me to go ahead

and was a constant supporter during the long process

Copyright © by the University of Michigan 2006
All rights reserved
Published in the United States of America by
The University of Michigan Press
Manufactured in the United States of America
⊗ Printed on acid-free paper

2009   2008   2007   2006   4   3   2   1

A CIP catalog record for this book is available from the British Library.

Library of Congress Cataloging-in-Publication Data

Büchmann-Møller, Frank.
   Someone to watch over me : the life and music of Ben Webster /
Frank Büchmann-Møller.
      p.   cm. — (Jazz perspectives)
   Includes bibliographical references (p.   ), discography (p.   ),
and index.
   ISBN-13: 978-0-472-11470-2 (cloth : alk. paper)
   ISBN-10: 0-472-11470-0 (cloth : alk. paper)
   1. Webster, Ben.   2. Jazz musicians—United States—
Biography.   I. Title.   II. Jazz perspectives (Ann Arbor, Mich.).
ML419.W39B83   2006
788.7'165092—dc22   2005028459

CONTENTS

PREFACE

I owe the inspiration for this book to two fortuitous incidents. In 1997, the Ben Webster Collection—records, tapes, photos, and other memorabilia—was transferred from the Danish Jazz Centre to the Music Department of the University Library of Southern Denmark, where I work. I had the good fortune to be placed in charge of cataloguing Webster's records and tapes, and in the process I came across a trove of material never before documented.

Around this time, I also met Heinz Baumeister, who has collected Ben Webster's music for decades, and he gave me access to all of his research, which revealed a great deal of information not previously compiled.

Having thus been given an opportunity to fill in some of the holes left by previous studies of Ben Webster's life, I took it.

In many ways, this book is a continuation of work begun by Jeroen de Valk in *Ben Webster: His Life and Music* (Berkeley, Calif.: Berkeley Hills Books, 2001), originally published in Dutch in 1992, and by Peter Langhorn and Thorbjørn Sjøgren, compilers of *Ben: The Music of Ben Webster: A Discography* (Copenhagen: JazzMedia, 1996), both of whose contributions to this book I gratefully acknowledge.

When one listens to as much of Ben Webster's music as I have, it becomes clear that Webster was fairly consistent in his playing: not inspired on every track, he nevertheless produced noteworthy solos on virtually every recording session, broadcast, and private recording. Thus, in the text of this book, I have had to limit myself to discussing only those solos of exceptional quality, or those that help to shed light on Webster's development as a musician. However, a complete list of Webster's musical activities from 1925 to 1973 will be made available on the Internet by the University of Michigan Press, and a complete sessionography of Ben Webster's music compiled by Heinz Baumeister will be made available on the Ben Webster Foundation's website.

ACKNOWLEDGMENTS

I could not have written this book without the help of many people and institutions. I managed to contact many musicians, friends, and others connected with Ben Webster, and it was a constant delight to discover how interested in the project everyone became. Many people went out of their way to help. First of all, I am grateful to Heinz Baumeister for his never failing support as a collector and discographer of Ben Webster. Without him my knowledge about the musician's music would have been much narrower. He and Lars Boie Christiansen offered valuable comments on the contents of the manuscript. It was a pleasure to receive the understanding and support of the management and staff of the University Library of Southern Denmark and the Carl Nielsen Academy of Music, Odense. Without a grant from the Ministry of Cultural Affairs that allowed me to work part-time at home on the book for one and a half years, and also provided funding for a month's stay in New York, the work would have taken much longer to finish. In the United States I enjoyed help from everyone on the staff at the Institute of Jazz Studies— Dan Morgenstern, Ed Berger, Vincent Pelote, Tad Hershorn, John Clement, Annie Kuebler, and Esther Smith—and I am pleased to say that I returned to Denmark with much more information than I had ever dreamed of when I left. I also received much help from the jazz archives in Sweden, Norway, Finland, Germany, and the Netherlands.

I acknowledge my great debt to the following persons for agreeing to be interviewed: Harold Ashby, Ben Besiakov, Egbert de Bloeme, Billy Brooks, Benny Carter, Al Casey, John Darville, Richard Davis, Hans Dulfer, Roman Dylag, Dave Frishberg, Dave Green, Mona Hinton, Jens Jefsen, Bent Jædig, Herluf Kamp-Larsen, Dick Katz, Bent Kauling, Torben

Kjær, Lawrence Lucie, Arnvid Meyer, Dan Morgenstern, Birgit Nordtorp, Hans Nymand, Horace Parlan, Hugo Rasmussen, Ove Rex, Alex Riel, Hans Jacob Sahlertz, Harvey Sand, Tore Sandnæs, Lars Sjösten, Cees Slinger, Niels Jørgen Steen, Anders Stefansen, Bo Stief, Billy Taylor, Clark Terry, Ed Thigpen, Jesper Thilo, Bert Vuijsje, Marlene Widmark, Jenny Wilkins, Henrik Wolsgaard-Iversen, Finn Ziegler, and Niels-Henning Ørsted Pedersen.

Also, a big thank you to the following persons who supported me with information, photos, and other help: Björn Alterhaug, Anthony Barnett, Johs Berg, Peter Broadbent, Tom Buhmann, Paul Bynens, John Chilton, Bill Crow, Jan Bruér, Otto Flückiger, John Jeremy, Poul Jørgensen, Chris Krenger, Seppo Lemponen, Per Møller Hansen, Klaus Nägeli, Jan Persson, Doris Gahner Petersen, Ulf Renberg, Han Schulte, Thorbjørn Sjøgren, Jack Towers, Jeroen de Valk, Al Vollmer, Nils Winther, and Theo Zwicky. In this respect Arild Wideröe was outstanding, constantly finding new information from Ben Webster's tours in Switzerland in the form of concert dates, advertising and promotion materials, concert reviews, and so forth.

Nellie Manford translated Italian articles to Danish for me, while I translated the quotations from Swedish, Norwegian, Dutch, German, and French. Finally, the translation into English has been possible only because of generous grants from the Ben Webster Foundation, the Carl Nielsen Academy of Music, and the University Library of Southern Denmark. Special thanks to Paul Banks for his great translating job, and to my editors Chris Hebert and Lewis Porter for their valuable support in all matters related to the publication of the book.

Grateful acknowledgment is given to Theo Zwicky, mr.jazz Photo Files, Zurich, Switzerland, for permission to reproduce the following photos (in order of appearance).

Jap Allen and His Orchestra, by W. Bert
Blanche Calloway and Her Joy Boys, Stiger Photo
Andy Kirk's 12 Clouds of Joy
Willie Bryant and His Orchestra
Teddy Wilson's Big Band
Ben Webster Quartet 1946

Al Hall Quintet
Part of Count Basie All Stars
Jimmy Witherspoon, Albert Nicholas, and Ben Webster

Grateful acknowledgment is also given to the Ben Webster Collection, University Library of Southern Denmark, Odense, for permission to reproduce the following photos (in order of appearance).

Ben Webster, Alan Dawson, Larry Richardson, and
    Horace Parlan
Ben Webster skiing
Ronnie Scott at Chelsea Bridge
Grethe Kemp
Pori Jazz Festival 1967
"Hi Eddie" score
"Jaw is Bookin' Now" score
Ben Webster in the studio 1968
Ben with friends 1970

Grateful acknowledgment is also given to Jan Persson, www.janpersson.dk, for permission to reproduce the following photos (in order of appearance).

Ben Webster Quartet, 1965
Frontline of Arnvid Meyer's Orchestra
Danish Radio Big Band
Jazzhus Montmartre, 1971
Meeting Benny Carter, 1971
In Danish TV Studio, 1973
In Danish Radio Building, 1973

Grateful acknowledgment is also given to the following for permission to reproduce the following photographs.

Timme Rosenkrantz Collection, University Library of Southern
    Denmark, Odense, for the photograph of Duke Ellington and
    His Orchestra
Heinz Baumeister, Ingå, Finland, for his photographs of Dum
    Dum Jazzklub and Downtown Jazzkeller
Chris Krenger, Jona, Switzerland, for his photograph of Ben feed-
    ing the male giraffe

Birgit Nordtorp for her photographs of Tivoli Gardens; Ben with Russell Procope, Paul Gonsalves, and Cootie Williams in his apartment; Ben demonstrating stride piano

John Jeremy Productions for the photograph of Ben Webster's last gig, by Maria Wierdsma

INTRODUCTION

Ben Webster occupies a special place in my heart because the night I first heard him in person was a night of several firsts: It was my first visit to the world-renowned Jazzhus Montmartre in Copenhagen, the first time I witnessed an impromptu jam session with professional jazz musicians, and the first—and only—time I was arrested.

I lived in Roskilde, a little town situated at the bottom of a beautiful inlet twenty miles west of Copenhagen, famous for its cathedral. It was January 31, 1965, and I was in high school. My friends and I played in an amateur jazz band, and that particular Sunday we had two options: Duke Ellington and His Orchestra, or Ben Webster, both playing in Copenhagen. None of us had much pocket money, so we could afford only one concert. As Ellington used to visit Denmark every year, I threw in my vote for Webster, who reportedly was in great form. It was the last night of his two-week engagement at Montmartre—his first visit to Denmark—and no one knew if he would ever return. At that time I knew Webster only from his records with Ellington, and from the splendid LP *King of the Tenors*, which I had bought very cheap from a friend next door the previous year, but I was anxious to hear him, and my friends agreed.

We took the train to Copenhagen and walked through the city to Jazzhus Montmartre at Store Regnegade 19. Inside, the nightclub had a wooden lattice under the roof and a series of large relief plaster masks on the wall to the left of the stage. We were disappointed to find that every seat in the house was already occupied, which meant we'd have to stand up all night. Harvey Sand, the stocky, red-bearded waiter, was pushing his way through the chairs and tables with trays loaded with beer, spring rolls, baked mussels, and tuna sandwiches.

As Webster came on stage accompanied by Kenny Drew, Niels-Henning Ørsted Pedersen, and Alex Riel, a burst of applause filled the smoky room. As soon as the music began, I forgot about not having a seat. The steady beats of Drew's improvisations were like pearls on a string. Webster's huge sound filled the room like a golden light. Every phrase swung, and his lines in up-tempo numbers were more rhythmically complex than anything I've heard before.

We had planned to return to Roskilde on the last train out of Copenhagen at a quarter past midnight, which meant that we would have to leave Montmartre after the first of the two sets. But at intermission, a rumor began circulating that some of the musicians from the Ellington orchestra had arrived and were celebrating their reunion with Webster in the kitchen. We decided to stay on.

When Webster returned to the stage in a cheerful mood after a one-hour intermission, he was accompanied by Cat Anderson, Ray Nance, Paul Gonsalves, and Billy Strayhorn, a short fellow with large horn-rimmed spectacles. I remember that Strayhorn played excellently. Webster and Nance, on the other hand, seemed more interested in joking around and talking than in the music.

Usually the hours allotted the main attraction at Montmartre were from ten to one, while the night band, usually a trio, played from two to five, but on this particular night the Ellingtonians played for more than an hour. When we finally arrived at the Copenhagen Central Station, the gates were closed. We went around the building and saw a mail train, which we knew would leave soon. We opened a small gate, crossed the tracks—which of course was strictly forbidden—entered the platform, and strolled right into the arms of a train guard. We were marched off to an office where another guard questioned us and wrote a report, after which we were discharged, having paid a fine of ten kroner ($1.50). Back on the platform, we realized that the mail train had already left, and decided to share a taxi all the way home. We arrived in Roskilde four hours before school, broke, but with vivid memories for the rest of our lives.

I visited Jazzhus Montmartre dozens of times before it closed in 1976, and I heard Webster frequently in other jazz clubs as well, but my initial encounter with that intimate, Kansas City–like atmosphere at the Jazzhus Montmartre is the experience I treasure the most.

I.

Kansas City Childhood
(1909–1927)

Kansas City, Missouri—to the jazz aficionado the name rings as romantic and sweet as New Orleans, Chicago, and New York. One imagines jam
sessions and small, smoke-filled rooms, where jazz is played till early morning by legendary musicians like Bennie Moten, Andy Kirk, Count Basie,
Lester Young, Mary Lou Williams, Dick Wilson—and Ben Webster.

The real Kansas City of the early twentieth century was more
mundane. It was an enterprising town, situated where the Kansas River—
also called Kaw River—meets the Missouri. It became a junction for Mid-
western trade, traffic, finance, and industry. A small trading station in the
1820s, by 1860 the town had grown to forty-five hundred inhabitants, and
when a railway bridge over the Missouri was completed in 1869, development intensified even more. By the end of that year, seven railroads led to
Kansas City, a number that was to double over the next ten years. As a
result, trade with livestock from Texas and grain from the North blossomed. The city's livestock market grew to become the country's second
largest after Chicago, as did its meat industry. In the humid summer heat,
a heady stench from the livestock markets and industrial chimneys clung
to the city.

The grain market and flour production grew to become the
nation's third largest. Work was plentiful, and the population exploded.
The Kansas City of 1880 had a population of 55,000. By 1890 that number
had multiplied to 132,000, to 164,000 in 1900, to 250,000 in 1910, and to
325,000 in 1920. By 1930, 400,000 people lived in the city. From 1910 to
1930, the black population stayed at a fairly constant 10 percent.

Around 1900, the black population, initially spread over the city,
became concentrated in an area bordered by Independence Avenue to the

north, Prospect Avenue to the east, Twenty-seventh Street to the south, and Oak Street to the west. Most blacks were employed as industrial workers, waiters, janitors, or assistants of some sort.

On March 27, 1909, at 12:02 P.M., at 2441 Highland Avenue, on the south side of the black ghetto, Mayme Barker gave birth to a boy baptized Benjamin Francis Webster.[1]

In the early nineteenth century, one of Ben's great-grandmothers was brought as a slave from Guinea in West Africa to a Kentucky plantation. Her son fled from slavery and settled in Liberty, Missouri. He called himself Missourian Sallé. His wife bore him four daughters, one named Alice, another Agnes. Alice married into the Barker family and gave birth to five children, among them one girl, Mayme, born in 1872. Mr. Barker died early and Alice remarried George Ruff, but had no more children.

Alice's sister Agnes (1864–1963) came to play an important part in Ben's and Mayme's lives, helping to raise Mayme and her sister Blanche, as Alice and George Ruff worked to make ends meet. Agnes Johnson was a woman of principle and strong will, a puritan with a good heart. When Blanche left home to marry Harley W. Robinson Sr., Mayme stayed on with Agnes in Kansas City and attended teacher's college, just as her older sister had.

When she was thirty-five, Mayme went to Chicago to take a course at the University of Chicago. At a party in Bob Mott's Pekin Temple at 2700 South State Street she met a tall, handsome man six years her senior. His name was Walter Webster. They were married on Sunday, September 17, 1907, in the hometown of the bride. The ceremony was held at West Point Baptist Church, and Mayme's eleven-year-old niece, Joyce Cockrell, was bridesmaid. The newly married couple moved to Chicago, where Walter was employed as a waiter on the Pullman Company's dining cars.

The marriage was a disaster. Reality proved to be much less poetic than Walter's promises had been. They lived in a one-room apartment on the southeast side of the Windy City's Black Belt, where they shared utilities with three other families. What was worse, the mild-tempered Mayme soon discovered that Walter was a crude, violent, and alcoholic womanizer. In September 1908, a visiting family member found Mayme pregnant, undernourished, and weak. Agnes decided to intervene. In January 1909 she arrived in Chicago, and through her resolution and authority managed to take Mayme back home to Kansas City, where she once again moved into the house on Highland Avenue.

Mayme and Walter were not yet officially divorced when Ben was born, which is why he was given his father's name. Mayme took back her maiden name after the divorce. Shortly after Ben's birth, the three of them moved to a two-story house at 1222 Woodland Avenue close to the corner of Twelfth Street,[2] and after summer vacation Mayme resumed teaching. Agnes presumably gave up her job to raise Ben until he was old enough for school.

Ben was spoiled equally by his mother, whom he called "Mayme," and by Agnes, whom he called "Mom." He always got his way: "I was pretty lucky when I was a kid, very lucky. I should say fortunate," he recalled later in life. "If I wanted a bicycle, my mother would buy it for me. If I wanted a wagon, she would buy it, and if I wanted skates, my mother would buy that for me."[3] Apparently the family had no financial worries; pianist Mary Lou Williams, later Ben's girlfriend and lifelong friend, recounts that Ben "came from a very wealthy, wonderful family of doctors and lawyers and teachers," and that he always dressed in the most expensive clothes.[4]

Spoiling Ben might have been one way of keeping peace in the household. His temper was known to fluctuate from one extreme to the other. "Mayme, his mother, was a very intelligent, quiet, lovely person of high morals," Joyce Cockrell remembered. "And his father was earthy, and he had a high temper, so that was responsible for him [Ben] being a dual personality. Ben could be just as lovely and sweet as he possibly could be, but if you made him angry, he could be violent and almost brutal."[5]

While Ben was still a small boy, Mayme married Frank W. Love, an army officer six years her senior,[6] but Ben never developed a close relationship with his stepfather, nor with his biological father, whom he allegedly visited for the first and only time in Chicago in January 1932.

Not much is known of his father's family, except what Ben himself told. He saw his paternal grandfather only once, when he was still a small child. He recalled lying in bed when suddenly a man appeared in the doorway with hair down to his shoulders. "That was my grandpa," Ben recalled. "It was the only time we saw each other. He was a Cherokee. Back then, it was unheard of for us blacks and redskins to be together, if it was a decent family, which we were."[7] In the nineteenth century, it wasn't uncommon for runaway slaves to be accepted into Native American societies, and even to live with or marry into the tribe. Both minorities stood on the bottom rung of the ladder to acceptance in American society and shared a mutual interest in sticking together. Many other well-known black jazz musicians also had Native American ancestors, among them bassist Oscar Pettiford, pianists Horace Silver and John Lewis, saxophonists Benny Golson and Earle Warren, trumpeters Doc Cheatham, Harry "Sweets" Edison, and Art Farmer, trombonists Kid Ory, Eddie Durham, and Trummy Young, and drummer Ed Thigpen.

Mom—Ben's great-aunt Agnes—was an enterprising and proud woman, actively interested in politics and religion. She arranged meetings against racism, and participated in demonstrations for women's suffrage. She was a member of the Allen Chapel, an African Methodist Episcopal church.[8] The family attended service regularly with her, and this is where Ben discovered Methodist sermons and songs, with their rich African American oral traditions. The AMEC was probably a conscious choice of Mom's, since it fit in better with her assimilation of white, middle-class values than did the Baptist Church. Mayme and Mom raised Ben to be proud of his race and impressed upon him principles of decent behavior, a code of dress, punctuality, a good work ethic, self-discipline, and the ability to defend his views. They intended for Ben to grow up to be a respectable and successful man.

Although Ben didn't attend church much in adult life, he retained a religious view in his own quiet way, as did many other musicians of his generation. "Ben Webster was kind of an introvert, always respectful when he was sober," said pianist Jimmy Rowles, who knew Ben for thirty-five years. "He would never say anything like 'Jesus Christ' or 'Goddammit.' He would use 'MF' a lot. But he would never allow anybody to say 'Jesus Christ' or 'Goddammit' in his apartment or in his presence. Whenever they did it, he was ready."[9] Tenor saxophonist Don Byas found out just how far Ben would go when Ben picked him up and threw him across the White Rose bar in New York because he was saying "Lord" this and "God" that.[10]

Mom taught music at school, and she played the piano at home.

Ben showed signs of a marked musicality at an early age, but it was Joyce Cockrell, who lived on the second floor for a while, who discovered his talent. "I was taking piano lessons, and Ben would annoy me all the time," she recalled.

> Sometimes he even walked across the piano keys to keep me from playing. So I said to myself that the best thing to do is to start teaching him how to play the piano so he wouldn't annoy me. So I learned him how to play C, B, D, F, you know, and for some reason he had a keen ear for music. He listened to the radio, and he came back and picked the right notes. I said, "That's fine," so that's the way he really developed his ear. I taught him to play the piano for a couple of years, but Mayme did not know that I was teaching him. So when he would come home and he would bang on the piano she said, "Well, I better have to do something for this boy, because he shall not play by ear." So she started him to take violin lessons.[11]

When Ben began taking violin lessons with a teacher called Charles Watts, he was attending Attucks Elementary School, in the farthest southeastern corner of the black neighborhood, which made it possible for Mom, who had found employment there at about the same time, to escort him.

Ben didn't enjoy violin lessons; he would have preferred continuing on the piano. "When I was quite young, I had to study violin," he told an interviewer. "My mother, she wanted me to be a little Lord Fauntleroy, with that big Buster Brown collar, and take violin lessons. But I hated that thing. I had to take my violin lessons, and all my friends, every time I'd go—he [the teacher] lived two and a half, three blocks from our house—they'd call, 'Sissy with the violin! Sissy with the violin!' . . . My mother, God bless her, said, 'Practice, practice!' . . . As soon as she'd left the house to go and teach school, I was at that piano."[12] Ben had perfect pitch, which must have made it easy for him to play the violin, despite his dislike for the instrument. "Sometimes I think back," he said, "and maybe I was tone conscious even then, because I would never get the sound of that violin."[13]

Pete Johnson lived at 1215 Woodland Avenue; he was five years

Ben's senior and would later become one of the major boogie-woogie pianists. When Ben met him, he was a drummer in several orchestras and didn't play piano professionally until 1926.[14] Johnson remembered Ben's visits and recalled that he "lived on the other side of the same street where I lived in Kansas City and before he became a very good tenor man he played piano and used to come over to my home to ask me to teach him bass on the piano. I guess he was more sure of his right than of his left."[15]

In 1921 Ben left Attucks for Lincoln High School, and around the same time he smashed the violin on Joyce's piano in a fit of rage, and thus five years of violin lessons came to an end.[16]

At Lincoln High Ben's interest in music increased. He found a new violin and joined the school band, where he played with two Ashby brothers, whose younger brother Harold, born in 1925,[17] would play with Ben later in life. One of Ben's classmates at Lincoln High was the slightly older John Williams,[18] who would later play with Ben in Andy Kirk's orchestra.

But when Ben was in his teens, it was another future member of Andy Kirk's orchestra, pianist Mary Lou Williams (née Scruggs), who was of the greatest importance to Ben. They first met some time after 1925, when she arrived in Kansas City with the Syncopators, in which her future husband, saxophonist John Williams, played. Certainly it was at a time when Ben was still concerned with improving his piano skills, because he remembered that "Mary Lou Williams taught me quite a bit about the piano, too."[19]

In his teenage years, Ben and his friends began exploring their neighborhood, and there is no doubt that he felt attracted to the many possibilities and temptations surrounding him. After the Volstead Act was passed in 1920—a law that prohibited sale and manufacture of intoxicating liquors—nightlife in Kansas City exploded. The town council, with its close gangster affiliations under the leadership of Tom Pendergast, happily looked the other way in matters concerning prohibition. The town was always full of visiting businessmen and tradespeople with money in their pockets, looking to be entertained. Bars, cabarets, and nightclubs offering music and other forms of entertainment shot up all over town, not least in the black section, which housed the Subway Club, the Sunset Club, the Novelty Club, the Reno Club, Lucille's Band Box, the Cherry Blossom, the Lone Star, Elk's Rest, and Amos and Andy. Ben lived right in the middle of all these temptations. He began to frequent the Sunset Club around the corner, not only for the music supplied by his friend Pete Johnson, but also to play pool, a game for which he discovered a natural talent. He spent a lot of time in a pool hall on the corner of Twelfth and Paseo, which was owned by one of his uncles. The seasoned players taught him so well that he eventually became capable of challenging even the sharpest pool sharks. When he was low on pocket money, he would take a little from his mother's purse to start him up at the pool hall.[20]

It must have been quite a culture shock for Ben, but he quickly learned to appreciate the freewheeling life in the cabarets and bars, among the offbeat—and sometimes dubious—characters. It was a welcome challenge, and a contrast to the puritan matriarchal life at home. However, he had some brutal experiences as well: In a notebook, he later wrote of seeing a man shot and beaten by the police on Fifteenth or Sixteenth Street. The man survived and fled, zigzagging his way down the street. The same notebook discloses that Ben and his cronies enjoyed hanging out at Lee's Drug Store, and that he heard James P. Johnson perform in town in 1925.

Ben hid his impressionable and sensitive mind—in part responsible for shaping the fine musician in him—behind a blunt and macho mask that fit in better with the harsh surroundings. He learned the language and behavior of the street, but he never quite forgot his decent upbringing. Without his mother's knowledge, he was already drinking, and later told his Danish lady friend Birgit Nordtorp that he "once had a bottle of booze stowed away in the clothes closet. One day, when secretly sneaking over to take a sip, Mom called from the kitchen, 'Are you going to share that with me, Ben!'"[21] Another childhood memory was seeing cowboys drive cattle toward the markets and slaughterhouses. You knew they were coming long before you could see them, because the cattle stamped up great clouds of dust that filled the air in Kansas City. "There was dust all over," he remembered.[22]

According to Mary Lou Williams, Ben was wild at the time, and before long he was forced to change schools. "He was called Little Peck's Bad Boy because they couldn't keep him in college. He'd been sent to several colleges. One day Ben was telling us a story. He said the girls were dressing in the dormitory and he was peeping through the window and fell through the window. He has a cut on his arm now."[23]

The geography and chronology of Ben's high school years are somewhat uncertain. Joyce Cockrell said that he "graduated from Sumner High School, K.C., Kansas & then from Western University in Quenemo, Kansas June 2, 1927, also was awarded the Major Letters for positions in football of guard & tackle on Varsity squad. . . . He was sent to Wilberforce University in Ohio, and stayed two years."[24]

There is no doubt that Ben attended Sumner High School in Kansas City. Among his papers is a postcard with a picture of the school, sent to him by one of his teachers, and he also told an interviewer that he went to a high school on the other side of the river.[25] In the same interview he tells of playing violin in the school band, and—much to the consternation of the bandleader—trying to jazz up the music they played. There is no Western University in Kansas, and Quenemo is so tiny that it doesn't even have a school, but perhaps Joyce mistook it for Southwestern College in Winfield, Kansas. Established in 1885, and with Methodist affiliations, it could well have appealed to Mom and Mayme. While Ben's attendance at Southwestern College is uncertain, there is no doubt that from 1925 to 1926 he was enrolled at Wilberforce University, just outside Xenia, Ohio, the oldest private African American college in the nation.

Ben and pianist Horace Henderson arrived at Wilberforce at the same time. It was a popular college for young musicians, and Henderson started an orchestra called the Wilberforce Collegians. Ben wasn't in the orchestra, but he was affiliated. As Henderson recalled, "We had a little fella there that later went on to fame. He was our valet in the band, Ben Webster. All he played was a little F-sharp piano [using only the black keys]. He didn't think anything about the saxophone or anything. He was our valet. He used to go around, set the band up and everything, help."[26]

In March 1926, while at Wilberforce, Ben went to Cincinnati to hear Fletcher Henderson's orchestra.[27] "It was my last year there and we were interested in the music," recalled Ben.

I'd never heard Smack [Fletcher Henderson] but always wanted to. You see, I was interested in piano then. This must have been early in 1926, when I was just seventeen. I know [Russell] Pops Smith was on trumpet, and I think Joe Smith, too, and Rex Stewart was in the band. If I'm not mistaken, he was playing a silver trumpet then. Also I remember Hawkins was there, and Don Redman. [Charlie] Big Green was on trombone and Kaiser Marshall, drums. But I went to hear Fletcher, and I don't think I even listened to Hawkins or Rex or anybody else. I wanted to be a piano player so I concentrated on Fletcher.[28]

Ben continued to develop his stride style, modeled after idols such as Fats Waller and Duke Ellington, and he frequented bars and cabarets, listening and learning from the many visiting pianists. Soon he began performing in some of the clubs around Twelfth Street and Vine as a solo act or with his own band, Rooster Ben and His Little Red Hens. O. D. Thompson, one of the musicians in the band, remembered that they started out playing dances after school, and later became good enough to compete for jobs with established orchestras like George E. Lee's band.[29]

Mayme and Mom surely would have preferred that Ben stay at school, but he was drawn toward the free and independent life, and convinced that his future was in music. Following graduation he stayed on in Kansas City for a while, and some time in 1927 he ran into a pianist named William "Bill" Basie. Basie played with Gonzelle White and Her Jazz Band, part of a touring vaudeville show performing at the Gaiety Theatre in Kansas City. Back then jazz was still mainly entertainment and show music. Said Basie of his time with White, "Everybody played standing up except the drummer. The upright piano was turned so that your side was to the audience, so I played looking out over the footlights, and I turned around and played behind my back, and then I turned back around and stood on one foot and then the other, and put my leg all up on the piano and did all kinds of fancy tricks with my arms and hand."[30]

"Basie was in Kansas City and I wanted to learn playing the piano," Ben recounted.

I found Basie, at that time I called him Mr. Basie, and I asked him to teach me to play the piano, because I had heard him play downtown in Kansas City. At that time Basie really stopped the show playing stride piano. We would talk and he told me quite a few things, and he said that if I ever got the chance to go to New York, I should find Willie "The Lion" Smith, because he knew everybody in New York. He also said, "There's a little short fellow that comes from New Jersey, Donald Lambert, and twice a year he comes over to New York and busts off all the piano players." When he said "busts," it meant to cut them up, to outplay them.[31]

Ben remembered every word, but it would be another four years before he had the chance to go to New York and look up "The Lion." Apparently Ben was a better pianist at the time than he realized. A few days later he and Basie were in the same line in front of a Kansas City cinema, looking for a job playing for silent movies. Ben landed the job.[32]

2. From Piano to Saxophone
(1927–1931)

It's uncertain when the chance arose for Ben to stand on his own two feet, but it was probably in late 1927 or early 1928. A few isolated sources mention him leaving Kansas City with violinist Clarence Love,[1] an improbable claim, since Ben never mentioned any connection with Love. But he did often speak of the leader of a territory band named Brethro Nelson from Enid, Oklahoma, about whom nothing is known, and whose greatest contribution to music, it seems, was to have offered Ben his first professional job. In Ben's own words, "He heard me play piano and asked me to join his band. I didn't think that my people would let me leave home, so I invited him over to my house. He came and met my mother and my grandmother [aunt], and he promised that he would look out for me. My mother told him that 'Ben knows the telephone number if he gets in trouble.'"[2]

Ben left with him and went to Oklahoma, and then on to Amarillo, Texas. Ben himself said that Nelson's band was small,[3] probably no more than four or five musicians, so they were able to travel in one car. In Amarillo, Ben quit Nelson's band and joined another band led by Dutch Campbell. We know little about Campbell and the lineup of his band, but an article a few years later reported that he played drums and was also the band's manager.[4]

When oil and natural gas was discovered around Amarillo in the early 1920s, the town grew to become the industrial center of the region. There Ben found much of the same lively nightlife he knew from Kansas City, although on a smaller scale. We don't know how long Ben stayed on with Campbell, but after a while he began looking for other work, either because Campbell found a more competent pianist or because Ben quit.

Whichever the case, the spring of 1928 found him playing piano for silent movies in the neighborhood cinema.

When saxophonist Budd Johnson, one year Ben's junior, arrived in Amarillo with Eugene Coy and His Original Black Aces, it proved a turning point for Ben. It was Budd's first professional job. Fresh out of high school, Coy had hired him and his older brother, trombonist Keg Johnson, for his twelve-piece orchestra. Budd Johnson booked into a little hotel where Ben happened to be staying. They met, and Ben got so interested in Johnson's saxophone that he asked him how to play a scale. "So I proceeded to show Ben how to play the saxophone that way," Johnson recalled, "and he always gives me credit, but I mean, this is all I really did.

> Well, one thing I did sort of teach him how to play was Frankie Trumbauer's [recorded solo on] *Singin' the Blues,* and you know, all those saxophone players were playing *Singin' the Blues* sort of note for note. We thought this was so beautiful. And I showed Ben a little about this, so we became great friends."[5]

Ben also had fond memories of those days with Budd and Keg Johnson, when none of them had much money. "We used to play pool together every day, and I had to win that pool game, because the three of us used to go to a restaurant called 'Scott,' and for twenty-five cents you could eat."[6]

Budd and Keg soon left Amarillo, while Ben stayed on, playing in the movie house. However, the saxophone had captured his interest. "I then borrowed a horn from an old man. It was his daughter's alto, and I used to practice every day, all day."[7] "Oh, I worried people to death in that neighborhood," Ben went on. "Up in the morning at six o'clock blowing, and you can imagine what a saxophone player sounds like just starting out! And then I just got stuck with it, and I came back to this old man 'Pops' Smith and started trying to do gigs with him. I can imagine what I sounded like then!"[8]

Ben's life continued much in this fashion until well into the summer of 1929, when Lester Young's father, Willis Handy Young, arrived in Amarillo from Albuquerque, New Mexico, to hire pianist Harry Nelson for his band. Ben happened to be with Nelson at the time, and he took the opportunity to see if Young had any use for him as well. "I asked him if he needed a saxophone player. He said, 'Yes, I need a saxophone player.' I had to tell him something, so I said, 'I can't read.' So he laughed a little and said, 'I'll teach you how to read, son,' and I said the other thing I would tell him, 'I don't have an instrument!' He cracked up and said, 'Come on, get in the car!' And I did, and Harry did too."[9]

Lester Young's father had a band with Lester's brother Lee on drums and his sister Irma on saxophone. Valdo Romano played trumpet and Lester played tenor. Ben stayed in their house. Willis Handy Young and his family lived in a two-story house at 216 Stover Street on the south side of Albuquerque. Aside from running the band, he and his wife Sarah ran Young's Music Store at 115½ West Gold, close to the center of town.[10]

Willis Young was a talented musician. He could play any instrument, and he demanded discipline and decency from everyone around him. His family belonged to the AMEC congregation and were regular churchgoers, so for Ben it must have been almost like coming home. Lester and Ben were the same age; they both had very high musical aspirations, liked the same music, and soon became inseparable. "I used to ask Lester," Ben recalled, "'Please come and practice with me,' and you can imagine what I sounded like, having played saxophone for a few weeks! But he said, 'OK' and started to practice with me. He showed me different things, you know, like to read the correct note. I had completely forgotten what I learned while playing the violin."[11]

He spent the summer practicing and listening to many of Lester's records with soloists like Bix Beiderbecke, Frankie Trumbauer, Louis Armstrong, Red Nichols, Benny Goodman, Prince Robinson, Stump Evans, and Ben Pollack,[12] and playing several local jobs with the family orchestra or in a trio with Harry Nelson and Lester. In the beginning Lester played all the solos; Ben played an alto saxophone, borrowed from Irma. Once Lester pushed him off the deep end. "We played a gig one night," Ben remembered. "Harry played the piano, and Lester just held off and said, 'Hey, Ben!' 'Yeah,' I had the sax, I just had it. I could not play, I just had it here. 'Come on!' And I just felt a little embarrassed because of Harry's feelings, you know. Harry dragged his head like that, 'Hey Ben, come on!' So I started playing."[13] At this time, Lester was already a full-fledged professional on the instrument, and Ben remembers that "Lester sounded great then. But he started young. I didn't start till I was twenty.

Maybe he wasn't playing as much then as he was when he joined Basie, but that was quite a time later. He had a lot of fire, though."[14]

The young men had a lot of free time, so they supplemented their income by working at the local sawmill. However, they had some relaxation time as well, which they often spent cooling off in the Rio Grande. Once, Ben helped secure the development of jazz history as we know it by saving Lester from drowning. "We used to go swimming every day in [the] Rio Grande," he recalled,

> and when you think back to that, it was very treacherous. I was not a good swimmer, I would rather say a lucky swimmer. Theodore Brinson, the banjo player—later he turned to the guitar—was an excellent swimmer, and one day we pulled Lester out of that river, and one day I pulled Lee out myself. He had just jumped in a sand hole. The way around it there was maybe two, three, four feet of water, and then you stepped off into a hole twenty, maybe thirty feet deep, and Lee went down. I had told him, "If you come up, just call and I'll come and get you." Then one day he called me, his eyes were like saucers, and down he went again. He didn't move a muscle and I just pulled him out, he lay perfectly still. And then he went right back into the water![15]

At this time, Ben was a handsome, strong twenty-year-old with his father's broad shoulders and his mother's beautiful brown eyes. His eyes were somewhat protruded, a feature that became more pronounced over the years and caused musician friends to nickname him "Frog." His copper hue came from his Native American grandfather.

Toward the end of 1929, Ben went to Phoenix, Arizona, for an extended booking in East Lake Park with the Young Family Band. While there, he received a telegram from Eugene Coy, asking him to return to Amarillo and play alto saxophone with his band. Ben accepted the offer and left immediately. "Coy bought me an alto from a pawnshop and put me to work," he recounted. "It was the first horn I ever owned and the first big band I ever played with. I'll never forget it."[16] The three or four months with Young had been well spent, for his saxophone abilities had apparently improved greatly. "He was all right from the word go," Coy commented years later.[17]

Eugene—usually just called Gene—Coy was a drummer, and had led his own band, The Original Black Aces, since the mid-1920s. His wife, Ann, was an excellent pianist, and the band toured most of the United States on an endless string of one-nighters. The late 1950s found him performing in a Monterey club with a trio. He died in Fresno, California, in the autumn of 1962.[18]

In the spring of 1930, tenor saxophonist Harold Coleman left the band, and Ben saw this as his chance to change over to the larger instrument.[19] The change to tenor suited Ben. As he himself explained later, "I think I couldn't express myself on alto. The tenor had a bigger sound."[20]

The Original Black Aces arrived in Oklahoma City toward the end of February 1930 to perform at Market Square Garden for a crowd of thousands. The engagement was mentioned in the *Chicago Defender*, which listed the lineup as follows: "Alton Moore, trombone; Joe Keep [Keyes], trumpet; Roderick Thompson, trumpet; Bennie Webster, sax; Odell West, sax; Tad Maney [Manning], sax; Eugene Coy, drums and manager; Mrs. Coy, piano; Clyde Durham, bass; Forest [Forrest] Conley, banjo; Bat Johnson, singer."[21] Coy didn't record until 1949, so we have no way of knowing what the band sounded like in 1930, but they were well respected among other musicians, and Ann Coy in particular made a favorable impression with a powerful style reminiscent of Mary Lou Williams's.

In Oklahoma City, Ben reunited with Lester Young, who was playing the Ritz Ballroom with Walter Page's Blue Devils. A favorite hangout among the young musicians was Hallie Richardson's shoeshine parlor in the black section of town, and Ralph Ellison remembers that it was here he heard Lester Young and Ben jamming.[22] Ben was proud of his progress on the saxophone, and he sought out Budd Johnson, who also was in town, to show him how good he had become.[23] The band stayed on in Oklahoma City for several weeks, because the census of 1930 mentions Ben still living there at East First Street, no. 422.

The variety of tour life suited Ben's natural curiosity. "It was quite an experience for me and I enjoyed it," he recalled of these early years.

I always like seeing different places. I was fortunate in getting along because I've never seen it really hard. Not like some I know.

Luck plays a great part in this. Life was tough and there was a lot of travelling. You didn't make much money but, if you understand me, in those days you didn't need much money anyway. There were times when you made a few dollars, but it really didn't amount to much. Then you would get tips. People would ask you for a request and if you played these requests they would give you maybe a dollar. The band had what they called a kitty and all the money went into this kitty. After the game you would divide it up, you know. But a lot of the time we earned hardly anything. It was just managing to survive. We played dances and things like that. The audience weren't mixed or anything, not in Texas.

But they had one hall, they used to call it Hooks, a little way out of Amarillo. It was a coloured place and we used to play dances out there. If we had a crowd we used to split the money up and that was OK. It was fun then.[24]

Ben toured with Coy till autumn 1930. While in Tulsa, Oklahoma, he met a Kansas-based band under the leadership of bassist and tuba player Jasper "Jap" Allen. His Cotton Club Orchestra had recently finished a summer booking at the Casa Loma Ballroom in Tulsa, and was ready to return to Kansas City. Some replacements in the lineup were under way, and as Ben was homesick at the time, he joined the saxophone group.

Back in Kansas City, the orchestra posed for promotional photographs that showed the following lineup: Joe Keyes, Dee "Prince" Stewart, Eddie "Orange" White, trumpets; Alton "Slim" Moore, trombone; Booker Pitman, Alfred Denny, alto saxophones; Ben, tenor saxophone; Clyde Hart, piano; James "Jim Daddy" Walker, guitar; Jap Allen, bass; Raymond Howell, drums; and O. C. Wynne, vocalist. It was a talented band, and especially Hart played a prominent role. Like Ben, he had perfect pitch, and he wrote the band's arrangements, many of them copied from the recordings of McKinney's Cotton Pickers.[25]

On route to a tour of the West Coast early in January 1931, McKinney's Cotton Pickers passed through Kansas City. Budd Johnson tells the following story: "They [Allen's orchestra] played a battle of music with McKinney's Cotton Pickers at Paseo Hall on Fifteenth and Paseo. McKin-

ney's Cotton Pickers had been traveling through the east, and their reper-
tory had been stolen, and when they heard Jap Allen from the arrangements that Clyde had, they went and called the police, because they
thought they had their music. But Clyde had actually copied it off the
record, transcribed their music and Jap Allen's band was playing this
music. They thought they had stolen the book."[26]

Hart was not the only musician to copy McKinney's music. At that
time, original scores were not published, only stock arrangements of popular tunes of the day. As a consequence, bands that didn't commission
arrangements would "steal" what they could use from recordings by other
orchestras. One of the musicians in the Cotton Pickers to whom Ben
undoubtedly listened intensely was tenor saxophonist Prince Robinson. He
had a rich, dark tenor sound, very much like that of the most influential
tenor man of the day, Coleman Hawkins, who became Ben's model as well.

In February 1931 Allen's Cotton Club Orchestra toured South
Dakota, Iowa, and Nebraska.[27] Despite this success, the depression made
it difficult for Allen to find sufficient bookings. In March 1931 he was
forced to let six members of his orchestra go when they received an offer
from trumpeter Edgar Battle to join a band backing the popular vocalist
Blanche Calloway at the Pearl Theatre in Philadelphia. Among the depart-
ing musicians were Joe Keyes, Alton "Slim" Moore, Ben, Booker Pitman,
and Clyde Hart.

The many well-respected as well as unknown territory bands
criss-crossing the States during this period were instrumental in bringing
knowledge of jazz music to even the most remote rural districts. These
bands didn't make very much money. If they were lucky, they made ends
meet, a new experience for Ben, who hadn't given much thought to money
at home. Given these circumstances, many musicians made friendships
that lasted for the rest of their lives. This was the case with Ben as well. During his years in Europe, he often mentioned missing his "way backs," as he
called them. For a young musician like Ben, the long tours and the bonds
with other musicians contributed to his personal maturity and helped turn
a pampered young man into a responsible person, enhancing his self-
assurance and imbuing him with a pride of his profession.

3. From Kansas City to New York
(1931–1934)

Blanche Calloway (1902–1978) was a singer, dancer, and bandleader. Her career in show business began in local revues in her hometown, Baltimore. Upon her arrival in New York in 1921, she joined the cast of Eubie Blake and Noble Sissle's musical *Shuffle Along* with Josephine Baker and Paul Robeson.

Like her more famous little brother Cab, she was more of an entertainer than musician, but her stage presence won the hearts of the black population. In 1931 an advertisement announced that in Chicago she had performed at the Regal Theatre for three years, the longest engagement there of any performer.[1]

In early 1931 she played the Pearl Theatre in Philadelphia with Andy Kirk's Twelve Clouds of Joy. The Pearl's manager, Sam Steiffel, tried to persuade several of Kirk's musicians to join a permanent backing band for her, but when Kirk heard of the plans, he quickly accepted an offer back in Kansas City. All of Kirk's musicians followed him with the exception of trumpeters Clarence Smith and Edgar Battle, nicknamed "Puddinghead," who had contacted six musicians from Jap Allen's band and enticed them to join up with Calloway. Other musicians were hired, and in March, Steiffel was able to book Calloway accompanied by a band in which Ben became a member.

Of his time with Calloway Ben remembered that "we more or less played for her to sing. We played both for dances and in theatres."[2] Apparently Ben's solo opportunities were slim, but Cozy Cole gives us the following description of the music and of Calloway, drawing an accurate picture of the circumstances and the ensuing musical conflicts of interest:

We had a fairly nice band, a good band, but it wasn't a standard good band like McKinney's Cotton Pickers or Chick Webb or something like that. All we had was about three or four arrangements that we played. The rest were heads, you know, and we enjoyed it. We were young and enjoyed playing. I think our best arrangement was on *Trees.* Clyde Hart made the arrangement of that.

Blanche would be in front of the band dancing. If Ben had a solo or any one of the musicians had a solo to play, Blanche would still be out there dancing, selling the band. Well, while she's dancing and kicking her legs up in the air, I had to catch her on the cymbals. Well, that's very unprofessional with Ben Webster taking a solo and you're up there trying to catch Blanche Calloway when she's kicking her legs up in the air on the cymbal. You know, that was one of the troubles. Ben couldn't do anything about it, because it was Blanche's band.[3]

Ben's musical development on the tenor saxophone can be traced fairly accurately through his recordings, as he started recording quite early, on his twenty-second birthday, after only two years on the instrument. It would have been interesting to hear his piano playing at this time, but the first recordings of him on this instrument were not made until ten years later.

On March 27, May 8, and June 11, 1931, he recorded with Blanche Calloway's Orchestra. Rhythmically, his playing is fine, but his tone is rough and amateurish, and most of his solos are much too staccato and primitively articulated, marred by rigid phrasing. However, the staccato playing was the style of the day. Prince Robinson's solos with McKinney's Cotton Pickers on *Crying and Sighing, Will You, Won't You Be My Baby, Talk to Me* and *Okay, Baby,* and Coleman Hawkins's solos with Fletcher Henderson on *King Porter Stomp, Oh Baby! Feelin' Good, Hop Off,* and *Blazin'* are all played in the same staccato manner, and they both produce a likewise uncultivated and rough sound.

Of the four songs from the first session, Ben is heard on three, but his sixteen-bar solo on *I'm Getting Myself Ready for You* is the only solo that can be categorized as actual improvisation. On *Just a Crazy Song,* he performs the A-parts of the theme in call-and-response with a trumpet. He is even out of tune here and there, and the same can be said of his eight bars on *Misery* from the next session. His sixteen bars on the three takes of *Sugar Blues* are structured so schematically and so similarly that the solo must have been worked out beforehand. On *It Looks Like Susie* from the last session, he plays an excellently expressed two-bar key change, bridging Calloway's vocal and an arranged ensemble chorus, while on the following tune, *Without That Gal,* his eight bars are quite primitively stated. At this time, he was a young and immature musician, lacking original and experimental ideas, content to tread well-known territory.[4]

Ben performed with Blanche Calloway and Her Joy Boys in many of the large theaters on the East Coast. His first trip to New York was in the beginning of April for a booking at the Lafayette Theatre in Harlem.

Ben hadn't forgotten Basie's advice about listening to Willie "The Lion" Smith at the Rhythm Club in New York. As soon as he had the chance, he and Clyde Hart, or "Buzzard" as Ben called him, visited the club. The Rhythm Club was right around the corner from the Lafayette Theatre, and Ben recalled that

> we went to the club, Clyde and myself and found "The Lion." Basie had told us, "Get him some cigars, and if he wants some 'taste' give him a little taste and maybe he will play for you, and what he will do is to make you acquainted with everybody." And "The Lion" is the first man that I met in New York. Exactly like Basie said, he made us acquainted with everybody, Coleman [Hawkins], Johnny [Hodges], Benny Carter, everybody. Then we walked out of the Rhythm Club to the corner to the cigar store and bought him some cigars. At that time as big as his thumb, three for fifty cents. So we asked him, Clyde and I called him Mr. Lion, "Will you like a little 'smile' [liquor], Mr. Lion?" "Yes, you kids are nice kids!" So we went to a place across the street directly in front of the club, if I remember correctly, where you could get a little smile in the daytime, and we said, "We sure would like to hear you play, Mr. Lion." So he played for three or four hours, just for Clyde and myself, you know, and that was a great thrill.[5]

At that time, there were many small clubs in Harlem with just a pianist on the payroll, and Ben loved to frequent them, listening and learning as the masters showed off their stride piano skills.

New York was every bit as exhilarating as Ben had expected, and he visited other places as well, listening to jam sessions involving horns. Later, Ben loved partaking in jam sessions, but at this time he felt far from ready.

Autumn saw Blanche Calloway and Her Joy Boys on the road again, this time touring the eastern states. In September, the orchestra played Philadelphia's Pearl Theatre, sharing the bill with Duke Ellington. Cozy Cole remembered that "everybody knew us around Philly and liked us. The audience wouldn't let us get off the stand. And Duke came on, but they kept applauding, you know, for us to come back and do an encore."[6] At the end of 1931, the *Pittsburgh Courier* held a reader's poll on the most popular bands. Duke Ellington came in first, and Calloway placed number six, before Louis Armstrong.[7]

At this time, show business was beginning to feel the effects of the depression, but Blanche Calloway said, "The Joy Boys are still able to produce joy with the saxes and flutes, even if the basso may grumble deep in the throat when certain places are reached. It'll take a long, hard fall in everything to make us lose our pep. My boys will be singing songs of joy when the depression reaches rock bottom. The salvation lies in the fact that there are several bankers in the band."[8]

One attempt at fighting the depression was sending several of the most popular orchestras on a package tour. Associated Coloured Orchestras arranged one such rolling "battle of music" over four weeks in October. Five orchestras were booked for the package tour, Blanche Calloway and Her Joy Boys, Bennie Moten and His Victor Recording Orchestra, Zack Whyte's Chocolate Beau Brummels, Roy Johnson's Happy Pals, and Chick Webb and his Chicks. Cozy Cole remembered that they traveled by bus and that "one time we made a jump from Kansas City to Baltimore, Maryland. And we got in Baltimore just in time to change clothes on the bus. We had five different buses. The audiences loved it. Bennie Moten and Chick Webb were the best bands."[9]

When the tour visited Kansas City, Ben had the opportunity to see his family and old friends, and on tour he renewed his friendship with

Basie, who played in Bennie Moten's orchestra. But most importantly, these weeks brought him together with several other saxophonists with whom he could exchange experiences and ideas, and who could teach him tricks. They were Clarence Paige and Fred Jackson from Zack Whyte's orchestra, Woodie Walder and Jack Washington from Bennie Moten's orchestra, Elmer Williams from Chick Webb's band, and Harold Griffon and Emmett Johnson from the Happy Pals. The tour ended in New York, but Ben's visit in Kansas City had made him realize how much he missed his home. "New York seemed to be too fast for me," he remembered. "So I wanted to go home, you know. So Bennie Moten asked me to join his band when I told him so, and I left Blanche Calloway."[10]

Moten (1894–1935) had led his own bands in Kansas City since 1918. His local Mob connections ensured him many of the best bookings in town, and since he was a popular bandleader as well, he attracted many of the best musicians. His orchestra was instrumental in developing what later was to be known as Kansas City jazz. At that time it was common for rhythm sections to play a two-beat rhythm, but around the time when Ben was in the band, Moten's orchestra began using a more even pattern, accentuating all four beats in the bar equally. Other characteristics included the many horn riffs and the blues-based compositions.

However, Ben didn't see his hometown for a while, because Moten's orchestra spent the next months touring. In January 1932, they were in Chicago.[11] While in town, Ben found his father's address and paid him a surprise visit. One of Walter Webster's brothers was there, and right away Ben got the feeling that his visit was inconvenient. The two of them were drinking and trying to get Ben to leave, but he stayed on. Suddenly the doorbell rang, and two prostitutes strolled in, laughing and talking. That was the last time Ben saw his father. A year later, he died of a combination of nephritis and blood poisoning.[12]

Soon after, Eddie Barefield joined the band, and together he and Walter Page enhanced the orchestra in several ways. Barefield was a fine saxophonist, clarinetist, soloist, and arranger; Page's walking bass contributed to the development of the evenly accented beats in the rhythm section. At this time, tuba was still the most common bass instrument because it projected far better than the bass fiddle in the dance halls, but Page's powerful playing cut through without amplification, lending a lightness and lucidity to the rhythm section and generating a better swing. Basie also appreciated the changes in the lineup and remembered that "with Eddie Barefield playing lead on alto, we had a man who could set riffs in the reed section like we had in the trumpet section, and he was also a real swinging solo man. And so was Ben Webster. The Frog, as we called him, was definitely one of the best tenorsax men I ever heard anywhere. Everybody in that territory knew what he could do."[13]

The orchestra followed a somewhat strange course at this time, alternating musical success and financial catastrophe. During that summer, they played the Graystone Ballroom in Detroit, where the young guitarist Junior Warren heard them and was visibly impressed. "I had never heard anything like the Moten band in my life," he said. "Every chorus they set a different style of rhythm. You know, pushing rhythms where they pushed the soloists. They played riffs as background rhythm on every chorus. We didn't dance even though we had brought our girls to the Graystone; we forgot all about the girls! No band in Detroit played that well."[14]

That fall the orchestra's bookings were poorly coordinated, and the ghost of the depression turned the trips into a financial disaster. Often the musicians were forced to wait in the city of their latest engagement until the next booking showed up, and sometimes they even lost their pay. "Sometimes, the promoters would run off with the money after the intermission and leave us. Oh, a lot of things happened," remembered Barefield.

> We were stranded in Zanesville, we were stranded in Columbus, Ohio, we were stranded in Cincinnati, and we were stranded in Philadelphia. The story of Philadelphia is a crack-up. We had played all these places and stranded from place to place. Finally we're getting into Philadelphia and we're going to play the Pearl Theatre that was run by Sam Steiffel. Now, we're going to play there a week, and we'd never had a week stand anyplace. We were so happy that we were going to get a week's salary at the end of the week, we just had a ball. We tabbed our room, we tabbed food, tabbed whiskey. We had a ball the whole week.
>
> At the end of the week we were lined up to get paid and Bennie

tells us that the last time they had been out there in Philly working, Sam Steiffel had lent them money to buy uniforms and he
owed him that money. So they attached the box office and took
all the money. So we stood there, the whole band out in front of
the Pearl Theatre, with our bags and our horns but no bus. They
took the bus and everything.

Finally Bennie goes off and he finds a guy named Archie
[Robinson] who's a colored guy, promoter. They got a big old
bus and took us over to Camden, New Jersey. They took us to a
pool hall and this guy took a tub and took one rabbit and made a
big stew. We got bread, and stood around and sopped up this
stew and ate this gravy. I always called it cat stew because I didn't
figure out where this guy got this rabbit. I always kid Basie and
say that we ate cat stew that day![15]

Basie, too, remembered many details from that tour. As usual on
the road, they stayed in a variety of lodgings: Cheap hotels, rooming
houses, or two or three at a time in private homes. But he never enjoyed
the times when pay was overdue, and it was difficult, at times impossible,
to pay their hosts. "When you got stuck in a situation like that in one of
those places where you were rooming with a private family, it could get to
be very embarrassing. But not always. Because people who took in traveling musicians and entertainers were usually pretty reasonable about
things like that, especially when they were old show-biz people themselves."[16] He recalled the time when Archie Robinson fed the band in the
pool hall. "Everybody was there except Jimmy Rushing and Ben Webster.
Those two low-down dirty dogs had sneaked off to a restaurant around
the corner somewhere. They always kept one or two dollars stashed away
somehow or another."[17]

On the day of this historical meal, December 13, 1932, Moten's
orchestra recorded no less than ten sides during a marathon session in a
church in Camden, New Jersey. These recordings are the very best by the
band, and are widely considered among the finest early big band swing
recordings. Despite financial turbulence and much hardship, friendship
and solidarity among the musicians persevered, ensuring the orchestra's
musical success. The musicians were not hampered by scores, giving them

room to concentrate on the musical expression and the beat, giving the band a powerful swing, regardless of tempo. "A lot of our stuff was done by ear and by head," Barefield explained, "and I used to set all of the rhythmic patterns for the saxophone section, which they didn't do previous to that."[18]

While the Calloway recordings are mainly of historical interest to us, Ben has much more to offer on these recordings. Ben, Hot Lips Page, Barefield, and Basie do most of the soloing, and Ben performs with far more self-assurance, independence, and enthusiasm. His tone is still rough and unpolished, but he controls it better, expresses himself more lucidly than previously, and displays far more interesting ideas. He reveals a fine overview and excellent sense of structure on *Blue Room* and especially *New Orleans,* perhaps because the tempi are slower than on most of the other tunes. He concludes his solo nicely on *Blue Room* with a two-note phrase given a powerful vibrato, an imitation of a trumpet or trombone shake. *Topsy, Milenberg Joys, Lafayette,* and *Prince of Wails* are set at such a fast pace that Ben occasionally has problems fingering. Today, one might say that his solos overflow with far too many notes, but it is important to remember that he was a young man of twenty-three, an age at which one is eager to show off accomplishments.

Shortly before Christmas the orchestra arrived in Columbus, Ohio, and many of Moten's musician's left to spend the holiday with their families. Ben was among the first to leave. It seems very probable that he did not return after the New Year, because on February 18, 1933, the *Chicago Defender* mentions a lineup of the band in which Barefield and Ben are substituted with Earl Bostic and Herschel Evans, respectively. It was probably around this time that Ben found employment at the Sunset Club, which was managed by Piney Brown. Here he became part of a small outfit including trumpeter Irving "Mouse" Randolph, pianist Pete Johnson, vocalist and bartender Joe Turner, and drummer Murl Johnson. "I lived down the block from the Sunset then," said Ben. "They had a mike on the bandstand and one of the speakers was out on the street. If the joint was empty, Piney Brown would say, 'Better call 'em, Joe.' Then we'd blow the blues for 45 minutes and Joe would sing 'em. The place filled up and then Piney would say, 'Cut it back, Joe,' so he could serve some drinks."[19]

In January 1933, Ben's employment situation changed once again, when he was hired by Andy Kirk and his Twelve Clouds of Joy, with whom Mary Lou Williams played the piano. Ben was hired right before the band set off on a three-month tour.[20]

At this time in Williams's life, her relationship with John Williams was over, and she was seeing another of the musicians in the band, saxophonist John Harrington. However, Ben's arrival changed this. She soon became fascinated by his personality and his playing, and before long, the two of them had become inseparable. The fascination was mutual, and he remembered that "one great thing about being with Andy Kirk: It was a chance to play with Mary Lou Williams. We used to practice together, I'd say four or five times a week. She'd show me different things. I really enjoyed that and I learned so much."[21]

"From the moment I met him," said Williams of Ben,

> I was fascinated because he was always up to something. Then, too, I liked his tenor. If he felt over-anxious, Ben would play roughly, distorting a style which was already full of vitality. It seemed to me he played best when he was either sick or tired.
>
> Ben was really bad boy pick [peck], always wrong. Sometimes John Williams yelled at him on the stand to stop experimenting and play. But after being around with the guys a while Ben became less boisterous, which made me like him better. We used to walk for miles together, and he always took me to jam sessions.[22]

John Williams didn't realize that Ben was in a process of developing, and in order to do that, to find his own voice, his own style, he had to experiment. And the only place to do this was on the bandstand.

Another time Williams said, "Ben Webster was really my first love. We used to be together all the time. I loved him. Things that he did in the band would shame the boys and after he was with us about a year he was just as nice and calm, because the guys were so nice in the band and they always helped wild musicians like Ben and he was really a wild one. He was really a wild man and he was really too wild for me."[23] Her last remark alludes to Ben's physical wildness and tendency toward violence, something she later discussed with bassist Hugo Rasmussen while visiting Denmark in 1968.[24] Although Ben wasn't quite right for Williams, their fondness for one another continued, and they kept in touch and wrote each other till the last year of Ben's life. "All the time Ben and I were together, he'd see another girl and tell me about a desire to be with her and I'd tell him I'd see him later," she recalled. "I never was jealous of him, because of being around guys all my life. I knew they always felt they still loved their wives even if they cheated once in a while."[25]

Andy Kirk and his Twelve Clouds of Joy were one of the best orchestras in Kansas City, in part due to Williams's compositions and arrangements. The orchestra toured often in the Midwest and was a popular dance band in Kansas City. Kirk says that "the Clouds played their share of black society affairs at Labor Temple at 15th and Paseo. There were so many social clubs giving dances and parties—break-a-day dances, breakfast dances, matinee dances, grand balls—that all the bands worked all the time. Every group in Kansas City's segregated black society— teachers, nurses, doctors, school principles, politicians—had its club."[26]

In Kansas City, Ben took Mary Lou Williams along to jam sessions. On December 18, 1933, Fletcher Henderson's orchestra came to town, and after their job Coleman Hawkins and bassist John Kirby went over to the Cherry Blossom to listen to an ongoing jam session involving several of the best tenors in town, including Lester Young, Herschel Evans, Dick Wilson, Herman Walder, and Ben. They invited Hawkins to sit in, and much to Kirby's surprise he went back to his hotel to get his saxophone. At that time Hawkins would never join jam sessions. Apart from Lester Young, who had a style all his own, Hawkins was an idol for the other saxophonists, and they were all anxious to show him how much they had learned from him. According to Basie, nobody challenged Hawkins, but he remembers that once he was warmed up, Hawkins began calling the tunes in difficult keys such as B major. "I don't know anything about anybody challenging Hawkins in the Cherry Blossom that night," he says. "Maybe that is what some of those guys had on their minds. But the way I remember it, Hawk just went on up there and played around with them for a while, and then when he got warmed up, he started calling for them bad keys. That's the main thing I remember."[27]

Mary Lou Williams had gone to bed, but at some point during the night Ben came over and woke her up, so she could take over the piano.

I opened the window on Ben Webster. He was saying, "Get up, pussycat, we're jamming and all the pianists are tired out now. Hawkins has got his shirt off and is still blowing. You got to come down."

Sure enough, when we got there, Hawkins was in his singlet, taking turns with the Kaycee men. It seems he had run into something he didn't expect.

Lester's style was light, and as I said, it took him maybe five choruses to warm up. But then he would really blow; then you couldn't handle him on a cutting session.

That was how Hawkins got hung up. The Henderson band was playing in St. Louis that evening, and Bean knew he ought to be on the way. But he kept trying to blow something to beat Ben and Herschel and Lester. When at last he gave up, he got straight in his car and drove to St. Louis. I heard he'd just bought a new Cadillac and that he burned it out trying to make the job on time. Yes, Hawkins was king until he met those crazy Kansas City tenor men.[28]

This legendary jam session has been interpreted as a competition—mostly based on Williams's recollection—between Lester Young and Coleman Hawkins, between a new and a traditional saxophone style, with Hawkins losing and Young winning. According to Basie, reality was not quite as dramatic, and not much different from any normal, peaceful jam session in those days, except for the fact that it may have lasted a little longer. Just the fact that Basie went home at one point indicates that he didn't feel that anything sensational was afoot. Still Hawkins must have felt pressured, since he chose to challenge the local musicians by playing in difficult keys, and since he stayed on so long. Ben, too, remembered it as a special night on which Lester Young was particularly hot. "That was the night 'Prez' blew over his head. Sometimes you can blow over your head, that means you play something maybe you never thought of before, like blowing over your head. That was the night, that was a really funny night that night."[29] As for Lester Young, his performance that night earned him the reputation of a rising star among musicians. When Hawkins left for Europe four months later, and Young took his chair in

Henderson's orchestra, the papers wrote that he was "one of the most celebrated tenor sax players in the music world" and "rated by many to be
the equal of the old master."[30] The night was important for Ben as well,
because the visitors from Henderson's orchestra noticed him, and noticed
how much he had emulated Hawkins's style at the time. Like Hawkins,
Ben had developed a big sound, and as both he and Hawkins were tem-
peramental soloists, he also emulated Hawkins's way of using altissimo
notes, often in sudden outbursts into the high register. He didn't have
Hawkins's solid musical background, though, so when Hawkins chose to
explore the harmonies of the songs in his solos, often adding passing
notes, Ben told his stories in lyrical phrases, which Lester Young also preferred, and often built up to a climax by dramatic outbursts of altissimo
notes.

However, Young's light phrasing and slender sound did not fit
into Henderson's orchestra, and a few months later in 1934 Henderson
contacted Kirk, complaining about Young, and they agreed to trade tenor
saxophonists. The time of this exchange can be pinpointed very precisely
to mid-July, because a couple of articles by John Hammond mention that
"Fletcher has brought back his marvellous new second trumpet, Irving
'Mouse' Randolph, and during the latter part of the week there'll be a new
tenor man."[31] A month later, he wrote that "Fletcher now has a new tenor
saxophonist, Lester Young having returned to the Andy Kirk band in
Kansas City. This new saxophonist is Ben Webster, and I hold him in very
high esteem. Beautiful tone and high musicianship."[32] The last remark
indicates that Ben had developed enormously since his recordings with
Moten. The result of the exchange was that Young returned to Kansas
City, while Ben had the opportunity to prove himself mature enough at
the age of twenty-five to travel to New York and take over the coveted and
challenging place as Coleman Hawkins's successor in one of the nation's
best black orchestras.

4. From Smack to Duke
(1934–1940)

According to Ben, he was probably chosen to replace Hawkins because at the time he sounded very much like his idol. A few of Henderson's musicians were at the legendary jam session at the Cherry Blossom in December 1933. Basie recalls bassist John Kirby being there, and trombonist Claude Jones was probably there as well. Ben has said that "it was Claude Jones, the trombone player, who told Fletcher: 'You've overlooked the fellow who's always admired Hawk and tries to play like him all the way.' That was me, and I got the job."[1]

Upon his arrival in New York, Ben—just as Lester Young before him—stayed with Fletcher Henderson and his wife Leora in their spacious white house on 139th Street in Harlem. Henderson's orchestra played the Savoy Ballroom in the week of July 14, which suggests that Ben played his first job with the band at that venue, and that Hammond may well have heard him on that occasion.

Fletcher "Smack" Henderson (1897–1952) led an outfit that had experienced a transition from an ordinary dance band in the mid-1920s to the most influential of the early big bands. In the beginning Henderson did no arranging himself, but relied on Don Redman and later Henderson's brother Horace. However, when it became necessary to try his hand at it, he revealed a natural talent. In their arrangements of popular music, both Henderson brothers set a standard imitated by more or less every other big band. Fletcher Henderson had a fine ear for new talent as well, and his orchestra always featured some of the best soloists and sidemen of the day.

Ben's encounter with Henderson's music was something of a culture shock, for he was forced headlong into fairly advanced reading. "Frankly, Fletcher Henderson was the only band I was afraid to join, when

I heard how difficult his music was," he recalled. "You see, his practice then was to play in every key of the keyboard. Maybe starting off playing in B-flat nice and easy, and when you looked down at the middle of the chorus, you looked at six sharps!"[2]

Russell Procope was of great help to Ben during that first hard period. The orchestra didn't rehearse before the Savoy Ballroom or during the run, but as Ben said, "He [Procope] would tell me to take my book home and the next day he would come around and help me with the arrangements."[3]

The band on the whole, and the saxophone section in particular, welcomed the exchange of Lester Young and Ben. Procope recalled that

> Lester's sound left a big void, a big hole in the sound of the band. After Lester left, you know, everybody agreed that Ben Webster had the big sound, he had the tone. Ben could play pretty, and he had a tone which Coleman had and Lester didn't have. Lester's style was sort of new, but we weren't paying too much attention to his style as we did to how he sounded. It wasn't what he played, it was how he played it, you see, and Ben actually had the big sound of Coleman Hawkins. Because you must remember then that a reed section was just a tenor and two altos. Then Lester made it sound like three altos. All due respect to Lester Young. Yeah. That was the difference in sound.[4]

Guitarist Lawrence Lucie offers an explanation as to why Henderson's orchestra sounded so good. "The music was in all the hard keys, like A major and E major. Most of the other bands played in F, B-flat and E-flat, but Fletcher made his band sound better. He gave it a more brilliant sound [by using sharp keys that other bands didn't use]. And it was easy for Fletcher because he was a natural musician. But it required top players to play that music. Ben had so much trouble, so he worked really hard with the arrangements. He never would be drinking, he would be thinking all the time on the music."[5]

While Ben was welcomed to Henderson's orchestra and accepted the musical challenge, he was sorely missed in Kansas City, not least by Mary Lou Williams. "Until he had gone I didn't realize how much I would miss him," she said. "Then I lost 25 lb., as I couldn't eat for some time."

"Lester Young replaced Ben [in July 1934], and sensational as he was, never fitted the band like that big Webster sound had. In truth, Ben could blow more in two bars, so far as soul and 'story' are concerned, than most can in a chorus."[6] "Lester could play 12 or 15 choruses and each one of them would sound different," she continued, "but with a man in the band like Ben, you'd miss him."[7]

In Henderson's orchestra Ben was in the company of a long list of experienced, top-notch musicians, and he absorbed what he could from them all. One of the musicians whose advice meant most to Ben was trumpet player Russell "Pops" Smith. In Ben's words: "He watched me when I first joined the band, and I played so loud. After ten days, I guess, he said, 'Jeff [Hilton Jefferson] plays the lead.' I said, 'Yes.' He said, 'It's impossible to blend with the lead if you can't hear it.' I got the message! I played so loud he couldn't hear it. Incidentally, he was the man who made me tone conscious. He told me, 'Now you have been in the band a little while, and you try to play fast like (Russell) Procope, Buster (Bailey) and Jeff. See, you've got a nice little tone. Work on your tone and leave the fast notes alone.' And that's when I started to slow down."[8]

On another occasion, Ben recalled, the other musicians pulled a hoax on him in order to test his reading abilities. "Red Allen had a solo, in a tune called *Yeah, Man!*" he remembered,

> and the sax had a background for Red, you understand. And that tune was so fast, so they made a plan for me, because they knew I was jiving my parts. They'd play the first four bars loud, drop out, and listen to Ben scuffle. And that's what they did, and I hit one note into the fifth bar, and Pops Smith, Russell, the first trumpet player, he had said, "Always follow the leader!" So I dropped out. So I said, "I need the lead!" And they couldn't play. They laughed so hard they cried. Everybody was crying. I followed the leader, Hilton Jefferson played the lead then. The band just stopped. They laughed so hard they didn't hear anything. I said, "Why, I listened to the leader, I listened to Jeff!" It took about ten minutes before they could get back.[9]

The depression years were hard on Henderson, and 1934 in particular brought many booking problems that forced the orchestra into periodic inactivity, especially in the early summer of that year, while Lester Young was still with the band. After the job with Ben at the Savoy Ballroom, the band calendar was empty until the beginning of August, when the orchestra toured briefly, playing in Pittsburgh before continuing south to perform at dances in a number of tobacco warehouses. Ben took advantage of the spare time, frequenting small clubs in Harlem, listening and occasionally joining a jam session. Among the musicians he met was Roy Eldridge, himself always an avid participant in jam sessions. Eldridge introduced Ben to Billie Holiday, who was singing at the Hot-Cha Bar and Grill on Seventh Avenue. For someone like Ben, recently arrived in New York, the exposure at these jam sessions was important. They provided an opportunity for him to show his talent and become known in the community. Ben was much more self-assured than three years previously and had no reservations about sitting in.

During the last week of August, the band played at the Harlem Opera House close to the Apollo Theatre on 125th Street, followed by a week at Palais d'Or in Montreal, Canada. The last two weeks of September were spent performing at Lincoln Theatre in Philadelphia and New York's Roseland Ballroom on Broadway, one of the city's most popular dance halls. "With Fletcher we played a lot of dance music," says Lawrence Lucie. "It was a dance band too, so at Roseland we played waltzes, tangos, popular tunes of the day, etc. The musicians then could play everything. We had to play all kinds of music."[10] The band did not record that part of its repertoire.

In August, Henderson signed a contract with a new label, Decca, to record twelve sides and fulfilled the contract in three recording sessions, on September 11, 12, and 25. The Decca recordings show the band in fine form. *Big John's Special,* with its catchy rhythmic theme, became particularly popular and was later recorded by both Chick Webb and Benny Goodman. "Horace wrote that one out of his head," says Lawrence Lucie. "He just sat on the bus and wrote it. We never rehearsed it, we just went on the band stand and played it. Big John's was a club, a bar near the Lafayette Theatre on the corner of 132nd Street and 7th Avenue where all the musicians used to go and drink."[11]

The recordings also show Ben in excellent form. His tone has improved, and his playing is more mature and reveals a larger overview.

The influence from Hawkins is obvious, but a budding personal style is apparent, revealing a more melodic approach. Although he is too busy on the B-parts of *Tidal Wave* and *Hotter Than 'Ell,* he is learning to play more relaxed, to straddle on top of the rhythm and let it carry him, as documented by his contributions on *Limehouse Blues* and *Happy as the Day Is Long.* The two takes of *Memphis Blues* contain very different solos from Ben. He plays two choruses on both takes, sandwiching Keg Johnson, but on the second solo on take A he plays more freely, whereas take B shows him repeating in the high register the brass group figures in a call-and-response that seems prearranged rather than spontaneous. In the middle of his solo on *Rug Cutter's Swing,* he plays two shakes that very well could have been inspired by the previous soloist, Claude Jones, and on *Hotter Than 'Ell,* he picks up Red Allen's concluding figure, using it as his own starting point.

In the beginning of November, after a month at the Cotton Club in Cleveland, followed by a week at Detroit's Graystone Ballroom, Henderson's orchestra disbanded. For some reason, the band wasn't paid in Detroit. Henderson already owed the musicians back pay, and upon their arrival in New York the band resigned collectively. Most of them, including Ben, were recruited by Benny Carter, who had a booking at the Apollo Theatre in the week of November 16, and this was followed by an engagement at the Arcadia Ballroom in Detroit.

Carter, only two years Ben's senior, was an exceptionally gifted musician, equally competent on piano, clarinet, alto saxophone, and trumpet, and a fine arranger and composer as well. He had played with Henderson as early as 1926, and later he landed a job as musical director for McKinney's Cotton Pickers, replacing Don Redman. In 1932 he formed his own band, but toward the end of 1934, he lost several of his musicians, which is why he was able to take over most of Henderson's band and reshape his orchestra.

The friendship and mutual respect between Webster and Carter, which lasted until Ben's death, started at this time. Ben performed with Carter on several occasions later in his life, and in admiration of Carter's versatility and competence he titled him "King." Carter says, "I met Ben Webster for the first time in 1934. I always loved his playing, also at that time. He was a very dear friend of mine, and spiritually we were very close."[12]

On December 13, 1934, Carter brought his band to the recording studios. He was the first to see Ben's abilities as a ballad interpreter, and Ben fulfills expectations nicely on *Dream Lullaby,* just as he delivers solid work on the other three tracks from the session, all composed and arranged by Carter. He plays an excellent, if impersonal, solo over a B-part of *Shoot the Works,* but plays with far more authority, ease, and melodic substance, building his solo well in his sixteen bars on *Everybody Shuffle.* However, *Dream Lullaby* is the first pearl in Ben's long string of ballad interpretations. Carter's theme is built on a slightly unusual harmonic structure, but Ben gives it a convincing treatment, playing with majestic calm and maturity, and already one senses his remarkable lyrical vein, and ability to imbue a solo with warm emotions. His vibrato is now controlled and utilized to give his phrases a lovely, rounded conclusion. The last eight bars exemplify how elegantly he was able to construct meaningful lines out of one simple idea and conclude them in a natural manner. For the first time on record, Ben's tenderness comes to light.

Carter, however, had no more financial luck than Henderson, and shortly after a booking at New York's Webster Hall on New Year's Eve, with no future engagements in sight, he too was forced to disband. Toward the end of January, Willie Bryant recruited several of his musicians, among them Ben and Carter himself, in an effort to shape his own big band.

Willie Bryant (1908–1964) was an entertainer. He had toured with vaudeville shows since 1926 as a dancer and vocalist. He was very popular among the black population, and had a natural gift for show business. As with Blanche Calloway, the primary function of Bryant's band was to create a backdrop for his own performance. In the band, Ben had occasion to renew his friendships with Edgar Battle and Cozy Cole, and another important member was the pianist, Teddy Wilson. Battle, Carter, and Wilson wrote arrangements of the orchestra's material, which included several excellent compositions from Bryant's hand.

The band enjoyed immense popularity in New York and received jubilant press coverage before every booking, especially when playing the

Apollo, such as: "No band has had a more spectacular rise in public favor than Willie Bryant and his orchestra. Bryant is regarded as one of the finest master of ceremonies on the stage and his orchestra ranks with the greatest of colored bands."[13]

Ben recorded twice with Willie Bryant's orchestra. The first session took place on May 8, 1935, and Ben takes a sixteen-bar solo on *Rigamarole* and *The Sheik,* both excellent but devoid of special characteristics. However, *The Sheik,* one of the orchestra's very best recordings, gives us the opportunity to make an interesting comparison, because Ben shares a chorus with the orchestra's other tenor saxophonist, Johnny Russell. Whereas Russell follows in Hawkins's footsteps, mainly structuring his phrases on the chords, Ben's solo is far more melodic and epically progressive; consequently it is much more timeless. On the next session, on August 1, Ben solos on three tunes. On *The Voice of Old Man River,* his solo is well expressed, full of ideas, and with a sound that improves in personality and clarity with each new recording. *Steak and Potatoes* shows Ben swinging nicely and forcefully, commencing with relaxed phrases, gradually intensifying, but concluding with a couple of far too eager double-time runs that end up tripping of themselves, while his eight bars on *Liza* are unremarkable.

For a recording session on February 25, 1935, vocalist and pianist Bob Howard gathered a group consisting of, among others, Benny Carter, Ben, Teddy Wilson, and Cozy Cole. Like Bryant, it was his habit to call out encouragingly to the soloists, such as his "Blow it, Frog!" on *The Ghost of Dinah;* but although Ben swings well, he seems a little uncomfortable and deviates very little from the theme. He seems more at ease on the second track, *Pardon My Love,* however, but he is only featured for eight bars.

On July 2, 1935, Ben made his first recording work with Billie Holiday. John Hammond produced the session, which was the first of a long line of recordings for Brunswick featuring Holiday and Wilson. Among the other musicians that day were Roy Eldridge, Benny Goodman, and Cozy Cole. "When we first recorded with Billie Holiday," explains Lawrence Lucie, "John Hammond was afraid she wouldn't sell. So he got all the top soloists to help the records sell, because the soloists were popular at the time."[14]

What a Little Moonlight Can Do is set at a breakneck tempo, but dealt with superbly by the rhythm section as well as Holiday, and Ben solos after Holiday's vocal. His first two phrases bear a remarkable resemblance to those with which Lester Young introduced his famous *Lady Be Good* solo the next year. The key—A major on the tenor saxophone—is even the same, but where the last of the three notes of Ben's upbeat E-F#-A ends on the tonic, Young's three notes C-C#-E end on the fifth of the scale. Ben's phrasing is a little off here and there, but his ideas are excellent, and he concludes very well, passing the solo on to Wilson via a few descending figures, starting a step higher with each repetition. On this session, his best contribution is on *A Sunbonnet Blue,* where he delivers the theme with great taste till the end of the B-part, where Wilson takes over. He plays with a richer, relaxed tone, enhancing the melody with just the right small personal details that make everything more interesting to listen to, at the same time setting the mood for Holiday.

A few days after the July 2 session, Willie Bryant's orchestra commenced a week's booking at the Apollo Theatre, and twenty-year-old Billie Holiday performed as one of the advertised "juvenile stars." The Danish jazz writer Timme Rosenkrantz took a famous photograph that week that shows Ben and Johnny Russell each with an arm around Holiday; pianist Ram Ramirez stoops in front of them. In the background, Bryant's band boy, "Shoebrush," has a guitar on his shoulder. All but Ben look straight at the camera, smiling. He glances indifferently to the side, his saxophone under his free right arm. Nothing in the photo reveals the budding affair between Holiday and Ben.

They became a pair; it is easy to see why Billie was attracted to Ben. Although a country boy from the Midwest, he had turned into a man about town. Charming and debonair, good looking and elegantly dressed, he was modern in every way.

Like Ben, Billie was something of an epicurean and already quite experienced in the consumption of marijuana and liquor, and Ben wasn't far behind. While Billie had her habits under control at the time—nobody remembers seeing her drunk during the thirties—Ben had less discipline and was occasionally even known to get violent when drinking. Once, after an evening spent with Ben—it was probably in 1936, at a time when he could afford a car—Billie returned with a black eye to the apartment she shared with her mother on 9 West Ninety-ninth Street. Billie tried to shrug it off, but her mother, Sadie Harris, was outraged, and next time Ben came by to pick up his girlfriend in his new Buick, he was wise enough to remain seated and blow his horn. But Sadie tiptoed down the stairs behind Billie, and when Ben chivalrously got out to open the car door, she sprang forth and beat him with an umbrella, a warning never to hit her daughter again. Later Ben said of the episode, "Naturally I could see that Billie's ma was really mad, but what made it worse was that Billie was just busting with laughter at the sight of me being whipped, that made me mad, but we all ended up friends."[15]

At one point the two of them went to Kansas City so Billie could meet Ben's family, but the visit was a catastrophe. Billie's straightforward approach and her big-city behavior and language were not what Ben's mother and grand-aunt hoped for in a daughter-in-law, and Ben and Billie left early. Eventually their relationship ended, and when Billie joined Count Basie's orchestra in March 1937, she soon found a new beau in the band's guitarist, Freddie Green. Billie and Ben remained friends, though, right up till Billie's death.

Ben had dreamed of playing with Duke Ellington's orchestra for a long time, and later that August the chance arrived. "Barney Bigard took a little vacation two or three weeks in 1935," he recalls, "and I joined Duke when the opportunity popped up."[16]

Ben left Willie Bryant around the middle of August and participated in an Ellington recording date on August 18, although he may have joined the orchestra a few days before. Bigard, Ellington's clarinetist and tenor saxophonist, is heard soloing on clarinet on the recordings, so he couldn't have gone on vacation before the session. Ben plays a solo on *Truckin'*, one of the popular dances of the day. The arrangement integrates the soloists with the ensemble in an outstanding manner, and the orchestra plays with great drive and commitment in the up-tempo tune. Ben solos over a whole chorus, and does so with authority and confidence, including the frisky break in the last two bars of the B-part. The solo is structured well; after a soft start with a phrase nestling nicely on the ninth of the chord, he plays more outwardly in the second A-part, playing repetitive figures up to the tonic note, the high D on the saxophone. The following B-part consists of lyrical phrases, once again concluding with figures peaking on the high D.

Though Ben enjoyed playing Ellington's music and sitting with Johnny Hodges and Harry Carney, whom he held in particularly high esteem, he was forced to leave the orchestra again in the beginning of September when Bigard returned.

Over the following years, Ben never neglected to call attention to how much he wanted to play in the band again, going as far as getting a clarinet, just in case the opportunity arose to sit in for Bigard again. However, he never became really satisfied with his ability on the instrument: "I could never get the sound that Barney got, and get that was what I wanted to do."[17] He made a few private recordings on the clarinet in 1941, and they show an excellent, if not finished technique, and a tone very close to Bigard's.[18]

Since Ben couldn't stay on with Ellington, he needed a job with another band. Ellington and Cab Calloway were both managed by Irving Mills, and it is probable that Ellington mentioned to Mills that Ben was out of work; he may even have put a word in with Calloway. At any rate, Ben was offered the chair when tenor saxophonist and clarinetist Arville Harris left Calloway late that summer. He accepted, and in September 1935 he flew to Toronto to meet with the band.[19]

Upon joining Calloway, Ben was employed in the most popular and best-paid black orchestra of the day. He went from thirty-five dollars a week with Fletcher Henderson, and probably not much more with Willie Bryant, to a weekly one hundred dollars. The band toured in its own Pullman car with a private luggage car, and there were four band boys to take care of everything, including handling the large wardrobe trunks, which had been given to each musician. "When we arrived at a theatre, we'd be assigned our dressing rooms," says trumpeter Doc Cheatham, who played with Calloway at the same time as Ben. "Usually each man had a room to himself. You'd go up there and your trunk would be there. You didn't have to do anything but open it. We had uniforms . . . and they went from our neckties down to our shoes. We had jackets, socks, pants, shirts to change for every show."[20] It was a life in luxury. Not bad, considering that six years ago, Ben was playing at silent movies in a little Texas town.

Calloway, but two years Ben's senior, became popular for his stage performance, which often involved a sort of call-and-response, as in his famous *Minnie the Moocher*. His habit of scatting in the fast tunes earned him the nickname "the Hi-De-Ho Man," and he was an amazing dancer and good actor as well. The music was usually built around his stage show, and Ben recalled that "Cab was so popular then, and we mostly played backgrounds for him to sing. There wasn't much opportunity to play a solo, even though he had great musicians in the band."[21]

The orchestra left Toronto for California with stops in Detroit and Chicago. After several engagements in theaters in Hollywood and San Francisco and bookings at the San Diego Fair Exposition and Frank Sebastian's Cotton Club in Culver City, they were hired to appear in *The Singing Kid,* a movie starring Al Jolson. The shooting started January 12, 1936, and lasted for the rest of the month. At one point, the orchestra was involved in a heated discussion with the studio, who wanted the musicians painted whiteface for a promotional photo. As the press wrote, "Resenting the insinuation and utter disregard for their rating as artists, Cab Calloway and the members of his band refused to don 'whiteface' makeup and appear with Al Jolson, who was to appear in blackface for contrast, as a publicity stunt."[22]

Although Calloway's big band is seen performing in the movie, the music heard is not played by the band. At that time, it was standard practice to record the soundtrack separate from the filming, and Warner Brothers chose to have the music recorded by white session musicians instead.

On their way back to New York in February, two new musicians joined the band. Eddie Barefield and bassist Al Morgan both stayed on in Los Angeles and were replaced by Garvin Bushell in Indianapolis and Milt Hinton in Chicago. Born in 1902, Bushell was one of the most experienced members of the band. He recalls, "When I joined Cab, I didn't notice Ben Webster's playing too much because he wasn't as good as he became later on, in the 1940s and '50s. He was still developing. Besides, there weren't many solo opportunities in the band; Cab took up all the extra space in an arrangement, and every number always featured him as a singer or dancer. Ben may have had an unusual style, but it wasn't enough to upset anybody in those days."[23] Bushell also comments on Ben's behavior and need to impress, offering the opinion that it was related to his adolescence. "I got to know Ben very well. He was an unusual character, very humorous, also very tough. He didn't get along with the girls at all because he'd knock them down if they said the wrong thing to him. He was a typical product of Kansas City at that time. . . . I think Ben was influenced by the hustlers and pimps—he had their mannerisms."[24]

Ben and Calloway became good friends. "Ben called Cab 'Twist,'" Milt Hinton said,

> I guess because he was always shaking. They were good friends. They hung out together 'cause they were both the kind of cats that kind of liked a little roughing up and things like that. Ben would hang out in the whorehouses and drinking all night with Cab. They would wrestle and sometimes it got really hairy there. They would go over with big guys and they'd get to wrestling in the dressing room and one would throw the other one or slap the other one a little too hard, and we thought it was going to wind up in a fight. We'd have to separate them, but they were of the same nature and they liked one another.[25]

In April 1936, Calloway was back in New York playing the Apollo Theatre, among other places, before leaving for another long tour to the South in June and July. They anticipated the southern tour with mixed emotions for, as Doc Cheatham recalls,

> It's impossible to understand some parts of the black enter-tainer's life. Like the fear we had of going to Alabama. The feeling you got when the bus pulled into that state, or Mississippi, or Georgia, or Florida. The fear came over everybody in the band. But we knew we had to play. We had to work, to earn our living.
> And they wanted us. But, in most of those places, they resented us too. Isn't that something? They wanted us to play, and then get the hell out of there. They did everything they could to harass us while we were there. A lot of musicians felt their whole life had been hurt or damaged by going there.[26]

Cheatham, Milt Hinton, and Bushell each offer examples of problems, violence, and shooting at venues during Calloway's tours in the South, sometimes involving musicians. Once Ben got in serious trouble, accord-ing to Bushell.

We were playing at the Howard Theatre in Washington. Claude Jones and I were coming around the corner in front of the theatre when we saw Ben Webster backed up against a wall, and a guy getting ready to throw a ball at him. It turns out Ben had been throwing the ball back in the alley with someone and it had missed and hit one of the thugs that was hanging around. The guy was telling Ben, "You hit me, now I'm gonna hit you!"

Ben was frightened—but if you turned Ben loose, he was vicious, very vicious. At that moment, Keg Johnson came down the alley with his .45. He said, "Don't throw that ball, you mother-fucker," and he shot up in the air. That cleaned everybody out. But then someone called the cops. The manager of the Howard took Keg's gun and put it in his office, so the cops never did find it.[27]

The New Orleans booking was Calloway's first visit to Louisiana. The band got a sensational reception and played for eleven thousand dancers at the Fairground at an event presented by the Gypsy Tea Room, one of the finest black nightclubs in the South. Calloway was mainly pop- ular among the black population, which is apparent from a review of two concerts for war veterans in Johnson City, Tennessee.[28] However, despite the band's musical and financial success on this tour, the tension and unfortunate experiences were so great that Calloway decided to tour as seldom as possible in the South.

The band was back in New York by late July, and Ben moved in to the Dewey Square Hotel. Following a few local bookings, Calloway was hired for a six-month engagement at the Cotton Club, considered the most famous of New York nightclubs in the 1920s and 1930s, catering to the city's white upper class.

On July 29, 1936, Ellington used Ben on another recording ses- sion. Once again, Ben is featured in one tune only, *In a Jam,* and here the influence of Johnny Hodges is evident. Hodges solos before Ben in call- and-response with Rex Stewart, and Ben imitates Hodges's calm phrasing and vibrato to the extent that in the beginning, one thinks Hodges is still playing. Apparently, Ben is more self-conscious than at the last session because he plays a correct but much too safe solo over a chorus in which Ellington solos on the B-part.

On his recording debut with Cab Calloway on January 27, 1936, Ben presents the theme in the first two A-parts of *You're the Cure for What Ails Me* with a large and nice tone, but without taking any liberties in his solo. On *Save Me Sister* he is heard in two arranged passages. He was allowed more space on May 21, 1936, where he plays a sixteen-bar solo on *Love Is the Reason.* He seems somewhat overly zealous and busy, asserting himself too much to achieve a really good result, whereas his performance on the B-part of *Are You in Love with Me Again?* is played with controlled energy. A session on September 15, 1936, shows Ben in two short solos. His eight bars in *Copper-Colored Gal* are a lovely, lyrical, and melodic oasis after Bushell's somewhat hectic clarinet solo, and on *The Wedding of Mr. And Mrs. Swing* he performs nicely but impersonally. His best contributions with Calloway stem from his next-to-last session with the entertainer, on March 3, 1937. He solos on five out of six tunes. On *My Gal Mezzanine,* he is wonderfully relaxed and plays with great swing, starting off with a theme quotation and concluding with a funny and original figure slightly expanding the harmonic structure. His playing is energetic on *That Man Is Here Again,* on which he ends his solo in a flight up to the high register. *Peckin'* is performed in a slow medium tempo, and Ben follows Claude Jones, beginning his solo with a quotation from Jones's final figure. *Congo* is one of the few instrumental tunes played by the band without the leader, and Ben is allowed to stretch out, demonstrating authority, genuine pleasure, and good ideas. He shares a solo with Bushell and swings well from the very beginning with a good melodic phrase that moves upward to climax after a few repetitive figures, before Bushell enters for the B-part. The last eight bars are performed in the middle register with great swing, vitality, and propulsion. He initiates with a large, full sound and a relaxed phrase on *Swing, Swing, Swing,* and concludes with livelier figures. Ben plays but one eight-bar solo on *Wake Up and Live* from his last session with Calloway two weeks later, on March 17, 1937. His performance has ease and clarity, but lacks imaginative ideas.

Ben recorded four times with Billie Holiday and Teddy Wilson during this period; the last of the sessions was in Holiday's name. He plays what is needed on all four sessions, but his performance is somewhat restrained. His best contribution from the session on October 21, 1936, is on *With Thee I Swing,* on which he plays on the A-parts of the first chorus.

The two first A-parts find him presenting the theme with a soft, unpressured tone; the last is performed more freely. He solos on the B-part of the final chorus, still relaxed, peaking in a series of finely balanced descending triplets in the last couple of bars. A week later, only one track was recorded, *Who Loves You?* with Ben playing an interesting solo in the last sixteen bars of a chorus. His melodic lines are full of original, large intervals, but they are logical. From recordings on November 19, 1936, he is best on *I Can't Give You Anything but Love,* with a solo radiating ease and restrained passion. Two sixteen-bar solos from January 12, 1937, reveal Ben swinging nicely, but phrasing a little rigidly on *I've Got My Love to Keep Me Warm* and *Please Keep Me in Your Dreams.*

He plays with far more inspiration on November 9, 1936, at a session with vocalist Mildred Bailey. *For Sentimental Reasons* and *More Than You Know* are played in a medium slow tempo; on the first tune Ben continues the mood of the song wonderfully with a deeply emotional and grandly structured solo. This is the first time he demonstrates how sensitively he is able to match a vocalist, an ability that later made him first choice for numerous similar sessions. His eight bars on the latter track are close to the same distinguished standard, concluding with a series of fine, original figures. It is interesting that many discographers have thought that Johnny Hodges participated on this session, because a two-bar break on *It's Love I'm After* sounds as if it is he playing. The break is played by Ben, but the comparison would have made him proud. It would have been extremely difficult for Hodges to be present anyway. At the time of the recording session, he was in Dallas with Ellington's orchestra.

In January and February 1937, Ben played on several commercial radio broadcasts from a cellar studio in the Biltmore Hotel in New York. Four big-band transcriptions are preserved; from January 6, 15, 18, and 22, and two undated recordings of the smaller band under Teddy Wilson. Ben isn't featured in every tune, but a lyrical eight-bar solo in *Stardust* from the first transmission deserves attention for its majestic composure. The January 15 broadcast offers a fabulous version of *Put On Your Old Grey Bonnet,* in which Ben begins his twelve-bar solo with a descending line starting in altissimo notes and subsequently swinging along with power and intensity. *Honeysuckle Rose* from January 18 features a somewhat unusual solo from Ben. He shares a chorus with Clyde Hart, who is featured in the B-part, but Ben seems tense, expressing himself in heavy-handed phrases. His best ideas are in the last A-part, which he begins with harmonically interesting ascending sequences. He is much more relaxed on *Make Believe Ballroom* from January 22, playing a looser and more melodically successful solo with two fine incorporated breaks.

Ben plays two solos with the smaller group led by Wilson. *I Got Rhythm* is performed at a suicidal pace, but Ben manages to shape his ideas well and connect them into a well-structured climax. However, the next tune, *Did You Mean It?* is a gem. The tempo is medium, and he is heard in the last half of a chorus with well-connected and lovely tripleted phrases, shaping one of his best solos of the period.

Ben was always interested in visiting jam sessions, developing musically, listening to other players, and generally keeping in touch with whatever was going on in jazz. The long evenings in Calloway's orchestra didn't present him with enough challenges as a soloist, so after a job he would tuck his horn under his arm and go out looking for a place to play. The other musicians in the band preferred going to nightclubs and restaurants, but when young Milt Hinton joined, Ben saw him as a possible ally. He had noticed Hinton's talent, and since the local bassists in the towns they visited were seldom of his standard, this was but one more advantage. Hinton enjoyed going out with Ben, and they began working out musical routines at the theater in breaks between shows. "So I got his style," Hinton said. "I learned from Ben to research the artist I was playing with, to study his antics, what he likes, the type of rhythm he likes. If you're playing for this guy, and he likes that type of thing, you can hear it in his playing. Then you give him that. I learned that from Ben."[29]

Another thing Hinton learned from Ben was the slang particular to black musicians. Hinton tells of being introduced to it shortly after joining Calloway's band. "Some of the newer guys in the band used a hip language, the way a lot of jazz musicians always have. Ben was really the one who introduced me to it. He seemed to know the latest expressions and liked using them, especially when we were out of town in a club or restaurant, around strangers who we thought were square. After a while it got to be a natural way of speaking for him and a group of other guys, including me." The slang kept certain people from understanding what was being said, and it created a bond between the musicians using it.

"A girl was 'soft,'" Hinton explained, "a guy was 'lane.' 'Pin' meant dig or look or see. A 'rough' was a quarter, fifty cents was a 'line.' 'Line two' was a dollar, 'line four,' two dollars, and so on. We called fifty dollars a 'calf,' and a hundred, a 'cow.' Ben might say, 'Pin the frame on that lane. It's a possible calf and a cow.' That meant 'Look at the suit that guy's wearing. It must have cost a hundred and fifty dollars.'"[30]

Although Ben had dated Billie Holiday, he still nourished warm feelings for Mary Lou Williams, and they had never lost contact. Ben had long tried to persuade her to move to New York and stay with him, but she had been hesitant. However, opportunity arose in the autumn of 1936, when the Clouds of Joy landed a week's booking at the Apollo Theatre, starting November 13. She moved in with Ben at Dewey Square Hotel. She wanted to divorce her husband, John Williams, and had told him that Ben would take care of it once the two of them had been separated for a year. John had replied that if that was the case, they might as well get divorced right away. But he had also warned her against Ben, who didn't have a favorable reputation among women. That gave her something to think about, and when the Apollo Theatre booking was over, she moved on with Andy Kirk's orchestra.

The long engagement in New York left Ben with plenty of spare time in the day. In the summer, he often drove up to the Lido Pool on Harlem's Lenox Avenue to cool off and pass the time with other musicians such as Rex Stewart, Buster Bailey, J. C. Higginbotham, Bud Freeman, and Sidney Catlett. When evening closed in and it was time to go to work, Ben would drive them all home in his Buick. Many afternoons were spent recording as well, with Calloway or with pickup bands. Calloway didn't approve of his musicians recording with other bands. At a session with Billie Holiday on October 21, Teddy Wilson wanted to use Ben, Irving "Mouse" Randolph, and Milt Hinton, but when Calloway heard about it, he became jealously angry. Hinton recounts that he said, "'I'm not gonna have the guys in my band makin' somebody else great.' So Ben had a lotta clout, 'cause he was a star, gettin' bigger all the time. Ben said, 'Well, if I can't make records with other people, I might as well leave the band. Get outta here.' And Cab didn't want that, so the next thing I hear he says, 'I'm glad we got guys in our band that everybody else wants.'"[31]

On March 18, 1937, after more than half a year at the Cotton Club with attendance surpassing two hundred thousand,[32] Calloway's orchestra began a four-month tour taking them to theaters in Philadelphia, Washington, D.C., Montreal, Toronto, Detroit, Cleveland, Kansas City, Chicago, and Minneapolis. One evening after the show, during their stay in Minneapolis, Hinton and Ben went to a nightclub in St. Paul where they heard a fourteen-year-old bassist named Oscar Pettiford. They were so impressed that they invited him to the theater the next day to let the other musicians from Calloway's band hear his gifted playing. It was also here that Ben, Hinton, Calloway, and Bushell became Freemasons, joining at Pioneer Lodge No 1, Prince Hall, St. Paul. It wasn't easy for a touring musician to participate regularly in lodge meetings, but there were enough Freemasons in the orchestra for them to have their own meetings on the road. At the meetings they discussed how freemasonry and the moral rules built on teachings from the Bible could help them in their daily life.[33] Later Ben became a Freemason of the First Degree.[34]

Ben began to tire of the meager solo opportunities with Calloway, and when the band arrived in Chicago for a booking at the Savoy Ballroom, he told Calloway that he was quitting. When asked if he could find a good replacement, Ben answered affirmatively. Fletcher Henderson's orchestra was playing the Grand Terrace in Chicago, and his tenor saxophonist, Chu Berry, was one of the best soloists of the day. Ben asked Berry if he would be interested in exchanging jobs, and he responded positively, not least attracted by the substantial raise in prospects with Calloway's band. To make the transition easier, Ben offered to help him, when his two weeks' notice was over. At that time, Calloway was in Cleveland, so "Chu came over to Cleveland and sat in the band with Ben," Hinton said. "And Ben showed him the book. They sat side by side. He showed Chu the book till he got acquainted with it for a couple of nights. Then Ben disappeared and went to Chicago [to join Henderson]."[35] According to Walter C. Allen, Chu Berry left Fletcher Henderson on July 22,[36] which means that Ben joined the band a few days later.

The booking at the Grand Terrace finished on August 18, after which the band headed east. In New York the band was booked at several venues. After a week at the Apollo Theatre, they left for a long tour, and Ben didn't see New York for the next half year. Lawrence Lucie, who was still with the band, remembers that "during the winter of 1937–38 we toured all the way to the West Coast and back to Chicago. We traveled all by bus. We did the whole thing by bus. It was more convenient, because it was one-nighters. Sometimes we couldn't sleep in the little towns, because there were no hotel rooms, so we used to sleep on the bus. Sometimes the bus would stop so the driver could take a nap himself. That was a long tour, four, five months."[37]

With the exception of four weeks at the Vogue Ballroom in Los Angeles starting December 11, and ten days at the Trianon Ballroom in Seattle starting January 27, the orchestra played an endless stretch of one-nighters. Two days before their Vogue Ballroom booking, the band played for five thousand dancers at the Shrine Auditorium in Los Angeles, and they were quite successful at the Vogue, where they followed Louis Armstrong. "Henderson is practically unknown to the dance fans on the West Coast," wrote *Metronome*, "and as his appearance at The Vogue marks his initial engagement in Los Angeles very little could be expected merely from his name. The combo was well received, however, and was accepted as a good colored dance aggregation."[38] Traveling back east, Ben visited his hometown for a short spell when Henderson played the Pla-Mor Ballroom on April 2, before continuing toward Chicago. They were to open at the Grand Terrace on May 12 and arrived a couple of days early. After some days at the Grand Terrace, Ben suddenly left the band without warning. As for the cause of his sudden departure, saxophonist Franz Jackson, who replaced Ben in the orchestra, said that he "had debts or some trouble, and he left the band, just cold—bam!"[39] This theory isn't improbable, because Ben had developed very expensive habits, and as his income had dropped drastically in comparison to his days with Calloway, he had to make extra for himself and the other musicians playing pool. Years later he told Bent Kauling in Copenhagen that they would pool whatever money they had, and then go out to play. Ben was supposed to lose a little at first, until they started playing for money, and then he was supposed to win.

Ben left for New York, where he found Stuff Smith performing at the Onyx Club on Fifty-second Street in a small band with trumpeter Jonah Jones, Clyde Hart, guitarist Bobby Bennett, bassist Mack Walker, and Cozy Cole. Smith, recently reorganized after a bankruptcy, had returned to the Onyx Club with renewed strength, and welcomed Ben, hiring him straight off. Smith's band was hard-swinging, and like Fats Waller, his stage presence was carefree and humorous, and his unorthodox style set a new standard for just how much a fiddle could swing. Vibraphonist Lionel Hampton visited the Onyx Club in April, a month before Ben arrived in town, and he said, "The Onyx fairly jumps. You can't get near the door, front or back, and everybody's either happy or drunk."[40] Stuff Smith hired Ben in May.[41]

1938 was a meager recording year for Ben; he worked on but one session, on July 29, with vocalist Nan Wynn, for which Teddy Wilson had put together a septet including such fine musicians as Jonah Jones, Benny Carter, John Kirby, and Cozy Cole. Wynn was a decent vocalist with a pretty, dark alto register, but it is Benny Carter who makes these recordings special, playing with outstanding inspiration on all four tracks.

Ben deals excellently with the B-part of the final chorus of *On the Bumpy Road to Love,* and begins his sixteen bars on *A-Tisket, A-Tasket* well, with sound, catchy figures, but continues in busy lines. *Laugh and Call It Love* contains his best contribution from this session. The first twenty-four bars of the theme are presented with a big, soft, and pleasant tone without deviating much from the melody with the exception of one descending double-time run, probably inspired by Benny Carter. His varied sound, supple phrasing, and restrained vibrato add life and controlled passion to a solo that matches the message of the song.

In the beginning of August, Ben and Clyde Hart left Smith's band. Ben and Smith probably parted as friends, because they often met later in life, especially in the middle of the 1960s when both of them were living in Copenhagen. Ben and Hart were hired by Roy Eldridge, whose small orchestra had arrived from Chicago for a four-week booking at the Savoy Ballroom starting August 6, and was sorely in need of a couple of musicians. The press gave them fine advance publicity.[42]

Two years Ben's junior, Eldridge had led his own band at the Three Deuces in Chicago since the end of 1936. Saxophonist Scoops Carry and pianist Ted Coles had chosen to stay in Chicago, so for the booking at the Savoy, Eldridge's band consisted of the following musicians: Roy's older brother Joe, violin and alto saxophone; Ben; Clyde Hart, piano; John Collins, guitar; Truck Parham, bass; and Harold "Doc" West, drums.

Ben and Eldridge spent a lot of time together offstage, and Eldridge said of the time, "See, me and Ben Webster around here, we were the only two cats in our set that used to save our money, man. Post Office it, you know. On our day off, we'd always draw out a little money and put on our best suits, and we'd hang out, you know."[43]

After the engagement at the Savoy Ballroom, which finished September 2, Ben and "Fur," as he called Eldridge, went on a tour of New England booked by the Falk-Kibbler Agency in Detroit. But by the end of October, Eldridge had tired of the roaming life of a musician, with its humiliating discrimination and agency hassles. He disbanded his orchestra, dropped the trumpet for a while, and started studying radio engineering. Back in New York, Ben suddenly found himself without steady work or employer, but he found freelance jobs in small bars and bistros in Harlem, and for the first time in his career as a saxophone player, he was able to choose his own repertoire.

Compared with previous recordings, Ben's sound on recordings from this autumn is larger, softer, and prettier, probably due to a new saxophone. The brand of his old saxophone is unknown, but in 1938 he purchased a slightly used French Selmer "Balanced Action," of which he was extremely fond and later named "Ol' Betsy." Ben's saxophone has the serial number 25418, which indicates that it was built in late 1936, the same year Selmer introduced the model.[44] Ben used the same mouthpiece all his life, a metal Otto Link with a fairly large opening, size 8 (the largest is 10), and he used hard reeds, often Rico no. 5, the heaviest. The large opening in the mouthpiece, combined with the reed, the quality of the horn, and his embouchure, contributed to his rich tone. While many saxophonists continue to experiment with different combinations of mouthpieces and horns throughout their careers, it is remarkable how conservative Ben was in that respect. Apparently he felt that he had found the ideal combination from the start.[45]

Ben was still developing musically, and one night while playing with Stuff Smith at the Onyx Club, Clyde Hart gave him a push in the right direction. "One day," said Ben,

he came to me and said, "Well, you finally did it!" I said, "Did what?" "You sound just like Hawk!" He was a funny cat, so he just looked at me after he made the statement. He just gave me a funny look, turned and walked off. Right away I got the message. I took all of my Coleman Hawkins records and my record player and left them in Kansas City with my people. Then I tried to go for myself, tried to establish something, you know, because I understood what he meant. If you sound just like another fellow and his style is established, when people hear you play you only boost the cat you're trying to imitate. So I got the message, and that's really what turned me around.[46]

One of the ways Ben found his own style was by letting himself be inspired by other musicians. "I've always gone to hear as many different musicians as I could," he said. "Maybe you can pick up what he was trying to do, take it and put it in your own bag, and then it is yours. And in nine out of ten chances he wouldn't know it if he heard it again."[47] As seen when examining his solos, he was already busy incorporating ideas and figures from saxophonists other than Coleman Hawkins, people like Johnny Hodges, Lester Young, and Benny Carter.

In the spring of 1939 a new big band was born. Teddy Wilson moved out from under Benny Goodman's shadow to start his own orchestra. He left Goodman on March 2 at the conclusion of a booking in Detroit, and stayed in town for a week afterward visiting with relatives. He heard trumpeter Karl George, trombonist Jake Wiley and drummer J. C. Heard playing around venues in the city, and brought them back with him to New York. The rest of his orchestra were as follows: trumpeter Harold Baker, trombonist Floyd Brady, saxophonists Rudy Powell, Pete Clark, Ben, and George Irish, guitarist Al Casey, and bassist Al Hall. The majority of the orchestra's arrangements were written by Wilson and Buster Harding, who also played piano when Wilson was conducting. Their vocalist was Thelma Carpenter, in September replaced by Jean Eldridge.

Everyone who had contact with the band has since complimented it for its great musicianship, and surely it deserved a longer existence than one year. It was a good dance band with fine soloists, but the orchestra's Achilles' heel was Wilson's lack of showmanship, which from the very start caused the discontinuation of a six-week engagement at the Famous Door on Fifty-second Street after only two weeks.[48]

Wilson was aware of his lack of showmanship, but he had hoped that the dancers and audiences would come mainly for the music. "I had imagined that I could make it on my name—famous then due to my appearances with Goodman's small groups and the many records that had come out under my own name—without any commercial concessions repertory-wise and without any jumping around the stage and making faces."[49]

The orchestra's first job was on April 15, 1939, at the Rockland Palace in Harlem. Following their unfortunate experience at the Famous Door, they tightened their grip, and the band had a fairly successful period, performing for a couple of weeks in Boston and touring New England and Pennsylvania, with jobs in Detroit and Washington, D.C., as well.[50] A job at the Apollo Theatre in the week of July 28 resulted in good reviews and a new booking.[51] Ben liked the band, and he liked the solo space allotted him.

The orchestra's guitarist, Al Casey, remembers that

> there was a place up on 127th Street and Lenox Avenue which had a studio downstairs. We rehearsed with Teddy there. The room had a good sound, but we also rehearsed at the Apollo Theatre downstairs, and we also rehearsed on gigs. Everyone could read, so it came easy that way.
>
> Teddy wrote some of the arrangements for the band, and Buster Harding, who was a piano player, wrote many arrangements, too. Sometimes he would feature the trombones, or Harold Baker on trumpet, and he wrote special arrangements for Teddy with the band playing behind.[52]

After playing the Roseland Ballroom in September, Wilson's orchestra and Andy Kirk and His Clouds of Joy were hired as the two regular dance bands at the refurbished Golden Gate Million Dollar Ballroom on Harlem's 142nd Street and Lenox Avenue. It opened on October 19 with a party special that included guest performances by, among others, Louis Armstrong and His Orchestra, and Buddy Wagner and His Elektro-Swing Orchestra. Wilson's booking lasted until January 13, and the new dance hall was a great success for all involved.[53]

With an eight-piece horn section, Wilson's orchestra was somewhat smaller than other big bands, where twelve or thirteen horns were standard. Wilson was often asked why he didn't expand his orchestra to a full big-band size, to which he replied, "We have a reason—we want a balanced tone in the whole band. As it stands now we have two of each instrument. We use two trumpets, two trombones, two altos and tenors. We found that there was a secret in knowing how to voice correctly. We never use four brass in any way where five or six would sound better."[54] In other words, they would use voicings that sounded best with four brass, and avoid voicings where one would miss the additional brass players.

Nevertheless, Wilson doubled the trumpet section during the engagement at the Million Dollar Ballroom. First Gene Prince was added, and shortly after, thanks to Webster's persuasive talents, Doc Cheatham. Cheatham had recently arrived in New York following more than six months of reconvalescence at his parents' home in Nashville, and was in need of a job. "I was so weak when I joined Teddy, after being ill, there was some discussion about what I was going to play," he recalls. "After all, in my condition I couldn't play lead, and I wasn't up to playing many solos as I just wasn't strong enough. So what Teddy did, out of the kindness of his heart, he wrote out a whole set of special parts for me, doubling up what the lead player would play, but an octave lower. That gave the band a special sound, a different sound, by doing that."[55]

During the ten months Ben spent with Wilson's orchestra, they recorded several times. Apart from the bandleader himself, Ben was one of the most regularly featured soloists. He plays two noteworthy solos at a session on June 28, 1939. On *The Man I Love* he gives the first sixteen bars of the theme a beautiful and sensitive interpretation, staying close to the melody but allowing himself small detours. His longest solo is on *Exactly Like You,* where he is given an entire chorus. He starts out with a simple figure, developing his ideas throughout the first eight bars, and swinging through the next eight with majestic force. The solo climaxes in the following B-part, built of lyrical figures in the high register and performed with great emotion and beauty. He brings the solo to a perfect conclusion with yet another excellently structured phrase, before allowing the ensemble to take over.

Four weeks later, the introduction to *This Is the Moment* is a fine example of the lovely sound Ben had developed, especially in the high register, where his figures are crystalline and played with great lyrical sense and authority. His sixteen bars on *Early Session Hop* are excellent, logical, and performed with a heavy swing, but lacking the spark that could have produced something extraordinary.

On August 10, the band cut several tracks in CBS's studio for a subsequent radio broadcast. On *Exactly Like You* Ben plays authoritatively in ascending phrases moving higher and higher, finally reaching a climax, before concluding—once again with an expert sense of structure—with a descending line. *The Man I Love* is almost identical to the recording from June 28 with well-structured improvisations played beautifully and with just enough vibrato, without becoming sentimental. *I Know That You Know* is set at a quick pace, which doesn't seem to bother Ben, because he plays a wonderfully melodious solo, even finishing off with a sophisticated and elegant four-bar break. After the introduction to *Lonesome Road* the tempo is doubled, and Ben's solo reveals a new side of his talent, in that this is the first time we hear him growl. He starts his solo growling, apparently inspired by the growl-filled phrase in the trumpet group, which virtually fires him off like a rocket. He seems very inspired and continues with a fine, dynamic solo where the contrasting, lyrical B-part creates a delightful breathing space. He continued to use growl for the rest of his life, especially in medium tempi or faster. At that time, growl was an effect usually reserved for brass and some blues vocalists such as Bessie Smith, and it was still unusual to hear the effect used by a saxophonist.

Ben plays two eight-bar solos at a session on September 12, 1939. On *Jumpin' on the Blacks and Whites* he is repeating a two-bar phrase, adjusting it to the harmonies; not a great solo, but delivered with confidence and great swing. *Some Other Spring* is a very beautiful tune written by Wilson's wife, Irene. Ben became very fond of it, and recorded it later with strings in the United States and in Denmark. On this recording, he interprets the A-part of the final chorus emotionally, and with all the beauty of tone and phrasing he can muster. Ben plays eight bars on *Wham* from December 11, 1939, swinging well, but producing quite ordinary phrases. However, the same session offers a solo on *Sweet Lorraine* that is quite a gem, consisting of simple, lovely phrases performed with unequalled calm and plenty of time to perfect the expression of his lines.

He has now lost the fear of pauses that had followed him up to the previous year, and replaced it with a befitting mature approach.

From Ben's last session with the orchestra, January 18, 1940, he is heard in several remarkable solos. He builds a lovely solo on the slightly unusual harmonic structure of the B-part of *Crying My Soul Out to You*, and he utilizes growl on *In the Mood*. Once again, he swings optimally, and despite the simplicity of his lines, the growl effect improves the listening quality by lending the solo a far more emotional energy. Most noteworthy from this session, however, is *71*, written and arranged by Ben, and named simply for its number in the band book. The tune is played in medium tempo, and the theme of the A-parts is based on one two-bar riff, while the B-part is improvised by trombonist Jake Wiley. This is followed by a chorus played perfectly by the saxophone group with Ben taking lead. What makes this arrangement so special is the voicing. "The melody is on the bottom," explained saxophonist Rudy Powell, "and the harmony is built above the melody like this: 4th voice (alto), Rudy Powell; 3rd voice (alto), Pete Clark; 2nd voice (tenor), George Irish; lead (tenor), Ben Webster. The harmony is built from the bottom up (lead is bottom). The next tenor (George) is above Ben, the next sax—which is alto (Pete)—is above George and the next alto (yours truly) is above Pete. This is in reverse to the way a chorus is usually written, the lead being normally on top, while the rest of the harmony is built from top to bottom."[56] Following this chorus, Ben and Wilson share the next, and here Ben truly plays with inspiration and an exceptionally solid swing. The solo peaks in the last A-part with an octave leap up to altissimo notes, from which he descends growling. This is followed by the concluding chorus, arranged and written by Ben for the entire ensemble in the A-parts, with trumpeter Karl George improvising the B-part, and the tune closing with a drum coda.

The recordings bear witness of the orchestra's great musicianship. Like Wilson himself, the band plays tastefully, well balanced, disciplined, and in tune, in a repertoire based on the popular songs of the day and aimed toward a dancing audience. The arrangements are generally of a high standard with many sophisticated details, and time-wise, the band keeps within the prescribed framework in the radio transcriptions, never yielding to the temptation of stretching out in longer or more numerous solos, as Count Basie's orchestra was in the habit of doing. In time their interplay became exemplary, and the saxophone group, especially, worked to perfection. It seems as if they phrase, think, and breathe identically. It is easy to understand why the musicians remembered the period with veneration. The maturity and breadth in Ben's contributions give an impression of what was to come, and he never betrays the confidence bestowed on him as the band's featured saxophonist.

Ben played on two sessions under Lionel Hampton's name, first on September 11, 1939, in fine company with, among others, Dizzy Gillespie, Benny Carter, Chu Berry, and Coleman Hawkins. Ben solos on only one tune, *Early Session Hop,* and, perhaps because he is self-conscious, his phrasing is stilted and he does not seem to be in very good form. Although he enters with an excellent phrase, he soon runs out of ideas, and the B-part is a technical disaster of stumbling figures, out of time. He is in far better form on the next session on October 30, 1939, given two solos; on *Four or Five Times* he plays relaxedly, once again swinging well in excellent phrases reaching a growling peak toward the conclusion. *Gin for Christmas* is a blues in breakneck tempo with each solo introduced with a four-bar break. Ben takes the second chorus and plays an inspired solo imbued with growl and a trip into altissimo notes.

Four days later, on November 3, 1939, Ben recorded with Mildred Bailey again. Apart from Teddy Wilson, no one else in the ensemble is identifiable, but it would seem natural if some of the other musicians were borrowed from Wilson's orchestra. Three tracks were recorded, and Ben's only long feature is in a fine ballad, *Blue Rain.* He solos for sixteen bars, modestly kept in the saxophone's middle register, but delivered with a lovely, full sound in pleasant, relaxed phrases.

On January 21, 1940—just three days after Ben's last recording date with Wilson—Duke Ellington had a booking at the Savoy Ballroom in New York, and the same day he sent his band boy Jonesy—whose real name was Richard Bowden Jones—with a most welcome invitation.

5. Golden Years with Ellington
(1940–1943)

Later Ben would clearly remember the occasion when Ellington sent for him, because it meant the fulfillment of his wildest wishes and highest ambition. "Jonesy came over one day to tell me that Ellington wanted to see me," he recalls. "I immediately felt twenty years younger. I was drunk at the time, but the news sobered me up in a second. I went to see Ellington in the dressing room of the theatre he was playing at the time. He said, 'Why don't you come to the rehearsal tomorrow morning?' Then I realised I had to tell Teddy Wilson that I was leaving him. To be able to do that, I had to get drunk all over again."[1] It was with mixed emotions that Ben broke the news to Wilson. He liked the band and his own prominent role in it, but he had also heard rumors that the band would never get close to a major breakthrough. "So I spoke to Teddy and told him I had the chance to join Duke Ellington, and I also told him that that was the only band that I would leave his band to join. Every time I'd run across some of Duke's men I would ask for a job, because it was my ambition to join Duke. And it did happen, and I just got so excited, it was a dream come true. I wasn't the first tenor player he had. Barney Bigard played tenor, but he hated it, he just wanted to play the clarinet, so I think Barney became really glad when I joined the band."[2]

If Ben's long-cherished wish had come true, the same was true for Ellington. "After he had made a record date with us in 1935, I always had a yearn for Ben," he said years later.

> So as soon as we thought we could afford him, we added him on, which gave us a five-piece saxophone section for the first time. Although Barney Bigard used to play tenor saxophone, clarinet

was his main instrument, so Ben Webster was really our first tenor specialist and soloist. His splendid performances on *Cottontail* [*Cotton Tail*], *Conga Brava, Just a-Settin' and a-Rockin'* and *What Am I Here For?* were a sensation everywhere, and he soon became a big asset to the band. His enthusiasm and drive had an especially important influence on the saxophone section.[3]

Ben's arrival in Ellington's orchestra most probably hurried the disintegration of Wilson's band, because he did not find a replacement of Ben's stature. But for Ben, prospects were good, and in fact many lucky circumstances coincided at this time in the Ellington orchestra. In late October 1939, Ellington had hired twenty-one-year-old bassist Jimmie Blanton, whose revolutionary bass-playing came to his attention during a booking at the Coronado Hotel in St. Louis. His perfect timing, brilliant technique and intonation, strongly developed melodic and harmonic sense, his natural ear for counterpoint, and fine swing and powerful drive were of great importance not only to Ellington's orchestra, but for the further development of the bass. After Slam Stewart, he was the first soloist on the instrument to leave the principle of walking bass and begin playing imaginative melodic solos. Because Ellington never fired musicians, the band had two bassists until January 1940, when Billy Taylor suddenly got fed up during a gig at the Southland Café in Boston.[4]

Ben and Blanton were welcome additions to an orchestra suffering under the burden of having played together too long. The newcomers were of great inspiration to Ellington as well, and the period shows his compositions and arrangements revitalized and virtually bubbling over with creativity and innovation, often in collaboration with Billy Strayhorn, substitute pianist and arranger, lyricist, and composer for the band since 1938. Over the next couple of years, the orchestra released a long series of outstanding recordings in rapid succession, defining the orchestra of this period as the Blanton-Webster band. With Ben's arrival, the sound of the saxophone group became fuller and richer, and, along with Carney, he added a power, vitality, and potency unmatched by any other saxophone section of the day. But more than this, Ellington must have seen the possibilities in Ben as a soloist, with his large range of expression and sound, from soft, warm, and lyrical to powerful and virile. When writing music, Ellington's mind worked in sound pictures; consequently he always made sure to have musicians around him who could fulfill his wishes in this regard. At this time the brass section included Wallace Jones and Cootie Williams, trumpets; Rex Stewart, cornet; Joe "Tricky Sam" Nanton and Lawrence Brown, trombones; and Juan Tizol, valve trombone. Ben's new colleagues in the saxophone group were Barney Bigard, Johnny Hodges, Otto Hardwick, and Harry Carney, and the rhythm section comprised Fred Guy, guitar; Jimmie Blanton, bass; Sonny Greer, drums; and the bandleader himself on piano. Ivie Anderson and Herb Jeffries were the vocalists.

Ben's style, with its powerful swing and drive, fit perfectly with Blanton's. Ben had this to say about his style at the time, and who had inspired him most:

> By this time I had just about developed my own style. There are four guys that I've always listened to and admired and have great respect for. I think they're just about the greatest for what they're doing. That's Benny Carter, Coleman Hawkins, Johnny Hodges and Hilton Jefferson. Jeff sounds beautiful. The way he treats a note—he plays so pretty.
>
> If I have a kind of alto approach to the tenor, I guess that's because I like Johnny, Jeff and Benny so much. I've listened to them for so long, you know. I take each guy for what he does.
>
> I wouldn't want to sound just *like* somebody else. But I think it's kind of healthy to listen to these guys, because I consider all four of them bosses. They all have definitely different styles, and you know them as soon as you hear them.[5]

Ben's first job with the Ellington orchestra was probably at the Roseland State Ballroom in Boston on January 26, 1940 following a few days rest in New York. He spent the first months with the band acclimatizing, not only socially but musically as well. As he was an extra member of the saxophone group, there were no lines written for him; he had to figure out what to play on his own, and that wasn't always easy. If he played a note from one of the other saxophone parts, they would sneer, "Get off my note!" Mercer Ellington recalled, "and Ben would just turn around and say, 'I'll find something.' And he kept listening until he found a note that nobody played, and it eventually became the five-part sound that identified the Ellington reed section."[6] Ben remembered how hard a time it was, and how he had to grow accustomed to the orchestra's sound:

> I think I was in the band for more than three months without any music, so I tried to find a fifth part myself. When I got my music, I used to look at some notes and play some notes, and I would say to myself that the guy that copied this did it wrong! The next night I hit that note soft, so Juan Tizol called me and said, "You got some notes and you played them soft." And I said, "Yes, they don't sound right to my ear." He said, "Blow them out. That's what Duke wants!" And then I noticed when I started to play these notes out, that when I glanced at Duke he even smiled. It was so strange to sit in that band, it was so different from any other band.[7]

Ben played saxophone in the orchestra, but Ellington wrote a few new arrangements, for example, *The Flaming Sword*, requiring that Ben and the other musicians in the saxophone group double on clarinet.

Many of Ellington's musicians were reputedly hard to get to know; some were loners, others conceited, and usually they would keep to themselves after a job. Mercer Ellington says that this changed when Ben joined the band. "Ben wouldn't accept the fact that these people stayed apart and stayed aloof and would say nothing to him. He drew them out, and I think, if anything else, he established a camaraderie within the band and made them more sociable to themselves."[8]

Of his time with the band, the musicians, and Ellington, Ben recounted,

> It seems that the longer I have been out of that band, the more I got to really understand what was going on. Duke would call a tune and the band would play it, and maybe he would think that the band wasn't ready to make a recording of it. I wasn't thinking of that when I was in the band. And then sometimes the band had a recording date about nine o'clock in the morning, sometimes at night, and the band was ready for these particular tunes that Duke wanted to record.

Sometimes he passed out arrangements on the bandstand that we've never seen before. We played them and he would say, "Pass them back again!" He would then change some notes, because it wasn't really what he wanted, you know. And then, maybe the next night, he would pass it out again to see what it now sounded like. Then we played the tune maybe four, five, or six nights, and then you could feel it come into shape. He constantly tried different things until he got it where he thought it was right. We didn't only try things on the bandstand, though. We also rehearsed sometimes, but we did quite a bit of rehearsing on the gig. On a record date, the first time you run a tune is the best time. When you run a tune down five times, six times, you get sick of hearing the tune. I had a lot of good solo spots in the band. *Rain Check,* I like that, *Bojangles,* I like that. Frankly, it was really a pleasure to go to work and get a chance to hear the band so much.

For a dance or maybe a theater gig there was more time to stretch out, which means you could get an extra chorus, maybe two extra choruses, but the time limit on a record cut that down. Maybe you could only play one chorus, or half a chorus. As far as I remember Duke never asked you to repeat a solo from a record. It was up to your better judgment.

Duke knows something about music that no one else knows. From the sound of the band, people for years have been trying to find the key to what Duke was doing, the secret way to write and voice like him. He writes for you. I have seen a new man come into the band, and just in the course of two weeks Duke had judged the man and his possibilities and written a concert for him. It's fantastic, but I mean, he is a great judge.

When I was in the band I couldn't differentiate between the music of Ellington and the music by Billy Strayhorn. It was a closely knit thing. But since I've been away from the band, I think that I can recognize a difference sometimes.

Chelsea Bridge wasn't written especially for me. There is so much more going on in that arrangement, so even though I had the solo, no, I can't say that it was for me.

Strayhorn wrote so beautifully, and he wrote so much. I can't name another writer with his format to write a tune. It is completely different from what else is heard—things like *Lush Life.* Take a tune like *Rain Check*—brilliant, he was very brilliant.

I sat beside "Rab"—Johnny Hodges—for four years, and he had so much feeling. To sit beside a man for four years must rub off on you. I can thank Harry Carney for the power I try to get on the horn. To me Harry Carney is *the* baritone player. He had so much power, and I tried to blend with him. He was on the left end and I was on the right end, and I was trying to blend with him. I guess we had Duke pretty upset sometimes because it got so loud in the band. The altos were between Harry Carney and myself, so it was not the easiest way to blend.

Jimmie Blanton was so smart. It was so much fun to play with him because he had quite a bit of knowledge. You could really tell that from his playing, which was no ordinary way of playing the bass violin. I used to ask him about a few things about chords, things like that, and right away he would explain it to me. So I asked him where he did gather this knowledge, and he told me from his uncle. I don't remember his name, but I was fortunate to meet him one day at Blanton's house. I met his mother, I met all his family, and his uncle was there, too. I looked at his uncle, and I imagine I was at the house 3½ to 4 hours, we talked and everything, but I don't think I heard his uncle say two words! And that's what really confused me. How could this man know so much music and say nothing!

I could talk about Sonny Greer for ages, and I remember one thing, he used to love to really kick the drums. When I say kick, I mean to really play loud on the drums. But Duke didn't want that kind of thing, so he would tell Greer to soften down. And I would stop right in the middle of a solo at the mike, you know, and I'd say, "Kick it out!" We were buddies, so he kicked it out![9]

Just as Milt Hinton became Ben's best friend in Calloway's orchestra, Ben and Blanton became inseparable in Ellington's. Ben was quick to see Blanton's potential, and he took him along to jam sessions just as he had Hinton. He took Blanton under his wing and protected him as a father, and Blanton would take care of Ben when he had too much to drink. They shared a great mutual empathy, respect for each other's playing, and a musical curiosity and eagerness to learn and improve. Blanton's upbringing in a musical home had given him a thorough musical education. Like Ben, he had started on violin; his theoretical foundation was in place, and he was pleased to share his knowledge with Ben. "Blanton was always with Ben," says Hinton.

> Blanton didn't drink, didn't smoke. And he was a handsome young man. He was a good-looking cat. Lithe and tall and thin, with very long fingers. Beautiful hair and clothes, and the girls just went mad about him, and he didn't bother with participation with them. He, you know, was just a very cool cat. He was just wrapped up completely with music.
> And I can remember one case, Ben was always borrowing my money. He paid back, if he had it. He always paid his debts when he had it, but he didn't have it too often, and everybody just loved to give it to him. I know I did. He'd come and say, "Give me twenty dollars," and I'd reach in my pocket and give it to him, and he'd buy everybody a drink.
> So when he left Cab's band, Lord knows how much Ben owed me, but that wasn't important. So he did the same thing with Blanton. They went around together, and Blanton always had the money.
> And I remember one time I had a big argument with my first wife, and I was splitting and I'd left home, and I didn't have any money at all. Ben was staying at the Braddock Hotel, and I called him and told him that I was broke and I had to leave town. So he said, "Well, come on down to the Braddock." So I showed up, and Ben was still in the bar, him and Blanton. He said, "What's happening?" So I told him, and if he had some money, you know, I could use a little because I'm kind of short.
> He had spent all his money, so he turned to Blanton and said, "Bear, you got any money?" So Blanton says yeah. So he says, "How much you got?" Blanton went into his watch pocket and he

had a wad of one-hundred-dollar bills. So Ben said, "Well, give
Milt a hundred, I'll give it back to you." So Blanton gave me a
hundred dollars. So Ben said, "Okay, have this. Come on and
have a drink." So he took me back in the bar and bought me a
drink. And I thanked him and I went on down to Pennsylvania
Station to catch my train.

But Ben was like that, he wouldn't let anybody down. Anything
he had, you could have. I can assure you.[10]

Rex Stewart offers another example of Ben's unreserved generosity:

Ben was generous and would give you the shirt off his back.
Actually, he did just that for me when, early one morning in
Detroit, my Margie got her dander up and decided to carve a
totem out of me [threaten him with a knife]. I guess I wouldn't
have panicked if I hadn't been asleep at the time and groggy
from drinking. Plus that I always slept in the raw and didn't
have a stitch on. She and I waltzed around that room for ten or
so minutes. Then, when the room clerk came to see what all of
the commotion was about, I broke for the door, went to Ben's
room at the other end of the hall and borrowed money, underwear, suit, hat, coat, shoes and overcoat! Within a few hours, I
was in Chicago, thanks to Ben.

I know I must have presented a strange sight in these ill-fitting
garments, as Ben was a burly fellow about four inches taller than
me.[11]

Stewart has this to say about Ben's friendship with Blanton:

Ben was a different man as he watched over Blanton like a mother
hen. For the first time since I'd known Ben, he cut way down on
his whisky and would sit by the hour counseling young Jimmie
on the facts of life. It is mere speculation—and I may be wrong—
but I can't help feeling that if Blanton had followed Ben's advice,
he might still be with us. A humorous bit of the association
between Blanton and Ben comes to mind:

The Ellington band was up in the far northern part of the
country playing a theatre, and just as we finished our last show,

we noticed that it had begun to snow like mad. Everybody decided to head for home immediately, instead of making one of the jam sessions that was our customary after-work amusement. I recall going to bed without stopping to eat, only to be awakened by hunger pangs a few hours later. I got up and stumbled through the blizzard to a nearby restaurant. As I drew near, I saw a strange sight. At first there appeared to be a group of primitive monsters trudging through the snow. But it was Ben carrying Blanton piggy back, with Jimmie's bass fiddle under one arm. Jimmie was doggedly hanging onto Ben's neck with one arm, while the other clutched Ben's saxophone.

I don't believe I ever have seen any two musicians closer to each other than those two.[12]

Ben and Blanton may have been inseparable, but Strayhorn became part of a threesome when Ben took him under his wing as well. They were newcomers in an orchestra where most musicians had been members for several years, and they were considered outsiders, which gave them extra motivation to stick together. As the oldest of the three, Ben more or less adopted the other two, making sure that they made the band bus on time, and so on, and Strayhorn took to calling him "Uncle Benny."

Blanton's enormous talent and youthful ardor didn't go unnoticed. Barney Bigard mentioned that

> his teacher from St. Louis thought so much of Jimmie that he gave him a whole list of teachers so he could take a lesson anywhere in the country. When we'd play theatres, they'd be looking for Jimmie and he'd be down in the basement, practicing. He played that bass anywhere, any time of night, wouldn't care how cold; if it was a blizzard and there was a jam session, he'd be there, he and Webster.
>
> We saw him develop before our very eyes. The best thing about it was, if you were taking a solo, he would keep you happy. He wouldn't interfere with your solo—playing riffs behind your riffs—he would play a good, solid beat for you; not some funny time thing, but when it came down to his part, that was another

story. A lot of the girls went crazy about Jimmie and bothered him. We'd be in a room talking and they'd call him; he'd answer the phone and say, "Yeah, sure, wait a minute, I'll be right back." He'd just leave the phone dangling and never go back because he didn't care about anything but his bass.[13]

Blanton, Strayhorn, and Ben had many opportunities to go out together. The week after Ben joined, the Ellington orchestra went on tour to California via a series of theater bookings. During a job in Tacoma, Washington, March 29–31, 1940, the three musical friends ran into pianist Jimmy Rowles, at the time a twenty-one-year-old student. Rowles and Ben instantly became friends. They often played together professionally in years to come, and their friendship lasted till Ben's death. Rowles has the following to say of their first encounter:

> I went up and introduced myself to Ben Webster during the first intermission the band took in Tacoma. I was enthralled. I heard him warming up. "There he is, there he is. My guy." I went up and said, "I know where you're going to be next. You're going to be at the 411 Club on Jackson Street." And he said, "Probably." That's the first thing he ever said to me. He shook hands with me, those big eyes looking around. We're right in the middle of the dance floor. And he said, "How do you do? Which way to the shithouse?" So I pointed out the men's room to him. He came back and we started talking. Ben and I played together that night in Tacoma.
>
> The feeling I got from playing with Ben right there with that big, beautiful sound. And Jimmie Blanton. Holy God, you can't imagine. I was only eighteen or nineteen years old, and they let me play. Even tenor saxophonist Corky Corcoran came in. Ben liked the way he played. All of a sudden, Ben would turn around to us. We were playing *I Got Rhythm* or something in B flat, and he'd say, "Take it up half a tone. Put it in B natural." And I immediately panicked, but I went anyway. I said, "I'll do my damnedest." And Corky was stuck, too. But we got through. Finally, Ben says, "That's just . . . I only did that to teach you a les-

son. The best thing to do is to learn to play in all keys. All the great, great players could play in all keys."[14]

Rowles also recalls an evening in Seattle in late spring when Ben, Blanton, and Strayhorn dropped into a club and began playing. "It was amazing—the most beautiful trio I'd ever heard in my life. They had perfect taste. Every note was just right. And they could swing. I mean, they really swung."[15]

"One night, I saw Duke take Ben upstairs, fill him with coffee, and make him sit up there for about an hour," Rowles continues.

> Ben had jumped off the bandstand to dance with some lady he saw on the floor. He was trying to take this woman away from this guy she was with and dance with her. That was when Duke went down and got him. He said, "Come here." Jesus, God, he was mad! When Ben came back down, Duke played *Cotton Tail* at a tempo you would not believe. That was the way Duke used to get Ben. There was Ben stepping all over it. Everyone would be laughing, Johnny Hodges would be laughing. Nobody would be playing. It was just ridiculous. Then Duke turned around and gave Ben a ballad, just to say, "I just did that to give you some shit. Now I want to hear you play something pretty." Ben would look at him and say, "You son of a bitch." Duke started playing *All Too Soon* or something like that. And the people in the audience would be looking at him like, "He didn't play shit a few minutes ago. Listen to him now." And he'd make four or five people fall in love.[16]

Many critics have claimed that Ben changed his style in his first Ellington recordings. However, this is not the case. It is more a case of changing context, in that Ellington, or Strayhorn for that matter, wrote arrangements to fit Ben's means of expression. In the years to come, Ben would still develop and hone his style, and particularly his playing in slow tempi matured and became deeper, but in faster tempi as well his solos gained expression. Ben never developed the speed and ease of a Don Byas. To the contrary; he traveled another road and, like Lester Young, proved that less is more. He became a master in the art of nuance, like Duke Ellington and Count Basie. Like Lester Young he had the ability to capture and sustain the mood of a tune. But he went even further than Young, utilizing a greater arsenal than perhaps any other saxophonist to express his emotions. In addition to this, the development of his sound took a unique direction. The colorings he used were like an imitation of the human voice, ranging from caress and ingratiation to violence and roar, in addition to which he developed the ability to play with a timbre close to that of a cello. The sound of strings had always intrigued him, and probably no saxophonist came closer than he to imitating the sound of a bowed instrument. He was amply helped in this direction by almost four years of daily influence from Johnny Hodges, whose characteristic, lovely, lyrical sound on the alto saxophone and whose emotional approach to playing he admired greatly. The influence from Hodges may be heard in Ben's way of ornamenting ballads, where he likewise begins imitating Hodges's use of glissando. He was born with the ability to swing, and his phrasings were simple and with perfectly placed accents. Through the years, Ben's trademark became beauty, emotion, and simplicity.

On February 13, 1940, barely three weeks after Ben joined, three titles in slow tempo were recorded. Ben is heard on all three. On *Solitude* he plays a four-bar solo, using a soft tone in original and very beautiful lines in the middle register of the instrument, as is the case in the concluding eight bars of *Mood Indigo*. Only one chorus is played of *Stormy Weather,* sung by Ivie Anderson, and accompanied by Ben's somewhat sleepily executed and overly embellished obbligato.

In February, Ellington's contract at Columbia expired, and a new contract was initiated with RCA Victor. As soon as March 6, the orchestra began recording a series of masterpieces with *Jack the Bear* and *Ko-Ko.* On this session, Ben's contribution was limited to a nice presentation of the B-part of *You, You, Darling.*

At the next session, on March 15, the band recorded *Conga Brava,* composed by Juan Tizol using a twenty-bar structure consisting of two ten-bar halves on an African-inspired rhythmic pattern. During Ben's solo the orchestra returns to the traditional swing rhythm; he plays two choruses accompanied by the rhythm section. The solo is unusual, because Ben ignores the form, shaping his melodic lines across the structure. He manages to keep a steadily growing intensity, a logical context, and the sensation of concentrated energy. In actual fact, Ben might be lost during his solo, but in a very creative way. He stays fairly close to the tonic note at all times, and Ellington helps him home to the progression by marking the transition in every chorus.

It was an inspiring period for Ben in many ways. After only a couple of weeks in the band, he had composed a tune for the orchestra, just as he had done for Teddy Wilson's big band. Milt Hinton remembered the circumstances well, because he and Ben met coincidentally when Ellington's and Calloway's orchestras happened to be touring the West at the same time and traveled together in their Pullman wagons for a while. "The trains hooked our two cars together. And it was from Chicago to Omaha," Hinton recalled. "And what a great time we had, you know, with two cars together, the two bands sittin' around drinkin' and talkin' and ridin' the train. And he said to me, 'I just wrote this tune, and Duke is gonna record it.' And he starts playin' to me and says, 'I call it *Shuckin' and Stiffin'*. Now, that's the name that Ben gave *Cotton Tail*."[17]

At a session on May 4, the orchestra recorded *Cotton Tail*— which Ellington renamed, finding Ben's too suggestive—and two tracks that were originally rejected and recorded again at the next session: *Bojangles* and *Blue Goose*. With the exception of the saxophone chorus, also Ben's idea, the arrangement of *Cotton Tail* is Ellington's. The harmonic structure of *Cotton Tail* builds on *I Got Rhythm*, and the theme begins without introduction, which is uncommon on Ellington recordings. From the very start, Blanton's and Greer's contagious playing radiates a freshness and energy caught by the rest of the band for the whole performance. Following the introductory chorus, Ben solos over two choruses, beginning with relaxed and logically connected phrases, but taking a more dramatic turn in the second chorus with a series of ascending figures in a broken diminished-seventh chord, ignoring the harmonic basis and reaching a climax in altissimo notes. Blanton yields magnificent support with a pedal note, while Ellington sustains the tension with powerful chords. From here, the intensity is gradually released in lines containing long notes with powerful vibrato and great variation in tonal coloring, sometimes employing growl. The solo works very well as a whole, in a combination of the expected and the unpredictable. The epic, progressing melody lines of the saxophone chorus may point all the way to Jimmy Giuffre's arrangement of *Four Brothers* for Woody Herman's orchestra seven years later.

Despite his successful solo, Ben felt later that he could have done even better, had he only played what he had intended. Normally they would record two takes of every track, but on this occasion, Ellington surprised Ben. "We'd go in the studio," Ben explains. "And no one saw this, I think, maybe some of the older guys did, but I didn't. Duke had slipped into the control room and told that engineer, 'Shoot for the master the first time down!' Then he came back out and said, 'Fellows, let's just run this one down, just the notes.' So everybody was easy, you know, and when we finished the last note, I would call it a lackadaisical solo I played. He turned around and said, 'Lock it up!' And man, I flipped! I got so mad at Duke!"[18] Despite his dissatisfaction with the solo, it has become a classic, and when the record was released that June, a reviewer in *Down Beat* commented, "*Tail* is taken at a fast tempo and allows Webster to get off royally. Interesting is the manner in which Ben sounds off a la Hawkins— a recent development which has been noted before in this column."[19]

Bojangles is Ellington's portrait of the tap dancer Bill "Bojangles" Robinson, and Ben swings nicely and naturally in his sixteen bars, whereas his four bars in *Blue Goose*, named after a bus company, is but a paraphrase of the melody. Both titles were rerecorded on May 28 with more success. On *Bojangles*, the interplay is much tighter and energetic, and Ben's solo is far more inspired. On *Blue Goose*, he retains the paraphrasing approach without changing much from the previous session.

However, *Cotton Tail* was the only tune Ben wrote for the orchestra. Perhaps he stopped writing when he discovered that Ellington took all the credit. Although *Cotton Tail* was Ben's tune, Ellington's name is on the composition, which must have annoyed Ben, especially since he missed out on other royalties as well. "Well, the thing that I think bothered most of the guys that worked with the Duke was that, like all the band leaders in his generation, he took credit for everything the band did." Milt Hinton remarked, "Well, it was his band, it was his concept, and that was the conditions under which you worked. And that rankled a lot of guys. I mean, a lot of guys didn't know that *In a Mellotone* is Ben Webster's tune."[20] Another of Ben's themes used by Ellington is *Dearie*. In 1941 and

1942 Ben recorded privately at a friend's house in Los Angeles. Among the tunes is *Dearie,* on which Ben is heard singing and playing piano. The unadulterated theme pops up as the conclusion to *Emancipation Celebration* in the *Black, Brown and Beige* suite. Rowles has yet another example of how Ellington was inspired by his musicians. "Duke was always stealing things from what the guys were playing so he could jot them down and write a new tune, see? He used to do that. He could hear a guy play something and take a pencil and scribble a little thing. The next night there would be an arrangement of that thing the guy played. And nobody knew where it came from."[21]

Ben's breakthrough as a soloist came with Ellington. Just as Lester Young had made his name with Basie three years previously, the same thing happened for Ben now. Ellington introduced him frequently and used him well on the band's recordings, released on a steady basis; consequently his name became well known—not least among other musicians. And there was always an opportunity to see and hear him, for the orchestra spent the next years criss-crossing the nation in an endless combination of one-nighters and weeklong bookings at theaters and ballrooms. The booking agent Holmes "Daddy-O" Daylie vividly recalled one of the Ellington orchestra's visits to Chicago and the impression Ben's playing made on him and a couple of the young tenor saxophonists. Ellington's musicians were staying at the DuSable Hotel.

"Although there was always something going on at the DuSable Lounge," Daylie recounts, "the most memorable event was the morning that Ben Webster, Chu Berry and Roy Eldridge got fired up on their horns. I will never forget Ben 'The Brute' Webster playing *All Too Soon* and *Cotton Tail,* and sending the joint into a musical high. Ben Webster was called 'The Brute' because he was always looking for a rumble, and he walked around talking about it. But, inwardly, he was a very soft-hearted, sensitive man. How else could he have played *All Too Soon,* in such a hypnotic, tender fashion. Gene 'Jug' Ammons, Claude McLinn, and Tom Archer, who were the young musical tenor sax 'Turks' in Chicago at that time, would sit at Webster's feet and drink up his solos with their minds and eyes."[22]

On June 12, 1940, Ben soloed on *Blue Goose* and *Cotton Tail*, recorded in the CBS Studio in New York for the radio show *America Dances*. The first is given a routine treatment, but the latter offers several quite interesting new details. The arrangement has been prolonged since the session in May, with a B-part, an A-part, and a coda. Ben varies the expression of his solo less than on the record, playing more dynamically from the very start and displaying more raw power than refinement. Nevertheless, he swings well, and he throws in some strategically magnificent accents in the first bars. The ascending figures in the beginning of the second chorus are a repetition of the first recording, before he finishes the solo with several excellent ideas. He solos in the prolongation of the arrangement as well, entering with several chromatically ascending lines. The brass repeat their riff in the last eight bars with Ben playing on top before bringing the tune to conclusion alone with a slightly hectic coda, but landing on his feet.

July 22 brought another masterpiece with the recording of *All Too Soon,* a ballad also titled *I Don't Mind*. The tune is performed over two choruses with a very tasteful and masterful theme interpretation by Lawrence Brown, followed by a full chorus from Ben after an abrupt ascending half note modulation. He is extremely relaxed, starting out with a paraphrase of the melody in the high register. His solo progresses epically with Ben staying within the mood of the tune. In the final bars of the second A-part, he delivers one of his trademarks, a repetitive figure, ascending with each repetition. The solo peaks in the B-part with relaxed and lyrically performed lines in the high register, interrupted by occasional quick ornamentations, giving associations to Coleman Hawkins or Chu Berry, and he concludes with relaxed, singable melodic lines. The whole solo radiates majestic serenity and overview, and is performed with the loveliest tone he could muster at the time. There was no extra take. That was unnecessary.

Two days later, the orchestra recorded *My Greatest Mistake* and *Sepia Panorama*. On the first track, Ben interprets the B-part in balanced, soft lines, before heading into a four-bar solo at the end of the chorus, played with equal beauty. *Sepia Panorama* has a palindromic structure, unusual even for Ellington, as the tune is constructed of four sections that are repeated in reverse order. Ben solos on the second of the middle blues parts. Beginning with a short lyrical phrase, he pursues it in the loveliest fashion until peaking in a powerful shake-type vibrato, before slowly returning to relaxed lines, finishing with a couple of trilled figures. Ben displays great sense of structure and expression, demonstrating controlled, restrained energy while still giving the impression that anything may happen. He uses the same formula on the second take, but his approach is more restrained, bereaving the solo of its pent-up passion.

From September to October 1940 a series of radio transcriptions are preserved from the Panther Room at the Hotel Sherman in Chicago. On opening night, September 6, the band performed a version of *Sepia Panorama* including a beautiful and emotional blues chorus played by Ben. He starts out with soft phrasing, building midway to a climax with a powerful shake. On September 10, he is potent in a tight, swinging *Bojangles* where he builds a fine solo with rising intensity. Two days later he is in equally fine form. On *Madame Will Drop Her Shawl* his creativity and sense of structure celebrate a small triumph. His wonderful one-chorus solo starts out with eight bars of paraphrasing on the theme, developing into unruly phrases and lines toward the conclusion. His contribution to *All Too Soon* is not as imaginative and abundant, and the conclusion of his solo seems to cruise in neutral gear. However, he expresses great beauty and emotion in the B-part. In conclusion, a couple of undated recordings of *Cotton Tail* and the ballad *It's the Same Old Story* deserve mention. There is but one version of the latter, with Ben playing sixteen easygoing bars with certain repetitive phrases, whereas *Cotton Tail* is exuberant with Blanton and Greer in solid teamwork generating a wonderful drive and egging Ben on to greater creative peaks than usual in a solo that already takes unexpected turns from the second A-part. The second chorus begins with the well-known ascending broken diminished-seventh chord, but from then on he plays runs and lines that may not all be pretty, but nevertheless lend the performance a wonderful freshness and energetic feeling. The same is true of the coda, which virtually bubbles with sheer joy of playing.

On October 28, the orchestra recorded again; this time Ben was a soloist on two tracks, *Chloe* and *I Never Felt This Way Before*. On the first, he is heard in extremely beautiful melodic lines, well connected, among other reasons, because the first eight bars consist of four phrases that are variations of each other. There is fine detail a couple of bars later, when a perfectly executed descending line is resolved in a couple of phrases naturally leading to the solo's concluding deep note. On two takes of *I Never Felt This Way Before*, his contribution is limited to paraphrasing the theme's B-part over eight bars. He plays the theme straight on the first take, while he feels less restricted on the next, however, without producing great music.

Ben's next studio session was in Chicago on November 2, as a member of a small Ellington ensemble led by Rex Stewart. Of the four tunes recorded, Ben solos on *Mobile Bay* and *Linger Awhile*, both in two takes. *Mobile Bay* is in a medium slow tempo, with Ben improvising on a blues structure. On the first take, he once again performs in controlled phrases with a few surprising figures—to himself as well—while potency lurks barely under the surface like a tiger ready to jump. The following take sees him proceeding more energetically, playing a few fine chromatic figures in ascent and descent, and his conclusion is especially successful.

The next live recordings of the Ellington orchestra consist of a different sort of repertoire than they usually played, the first ever recording of them playing a dance, and for that reason they are historically interesting. The recording also happened to be made on one of those magic evenings when the orchestra played its best; the atmosphere is tangible with enthusiasm and a wonderful, informal repartee between the musicians and audience. The setting was the Crystal Ballroom in Fargo, North Dakota, on November 7, 1940.

Certain myths from this evening must be rectified. In an interview, Ben said that "it was so cold there that night, we played in our overcoats, and some of the guys kept their gloves on!"[23] Ben must have confused the Fargo date with another job, because the evening was in fact unusually warm for the season, as Jack Towers remembers that he was sweating after carrying the recording equipment,[24] and a photograph from the booking shows the musicians in nothing but their usual band uniforms.[25] Another myth claims that the Fargo booking was Ray Nance's debut with the orchestra. This is not quite true either, because he was hired in the very beginning of November in Chicago, where he was playing at the De Luxe Club and consequently probably joined the band at their subsequent booking in East Grand Forks, Minnesota, on November 5.[26]

Jack Towers, one of the men making the recordings, had this to say: "We had earphones, but when the band began we couldn't tell what kind of recording we were getting. So at intermission we played back some of the numbers and listened on a speaker. Many of the band guys got interested in what we were doing, and asked us to play certain numbers. Ben Webster and Johnny Hodges each listened to each other's solos."[27] Towers and Ben began a lifelong friendship that night, and over the years, Towers sent many tapes to Ben; not only copies of this evening's recordings, but other music as well, and often with Ellington.

Out of the almost fifty recorded tracks, Ben is featured on eleven. He is heard in eight bars of the opening tune, *It's Glory*, but is almost drowned out by the ensemble. His energetic playing surfaces only sporadically. He plays a one-chorus solo in *The Sheik of Araby*, which is dynamic and emotional with plenty of growl, but disappointing in its lack of structure, whereas his contribution to Strayhorn's arrangement of *There Shall Be No Night* is more ornamented but every bit as beautiful as on the studio recording two months before. A disk is changed just as Ben begins his solo on *Chloe*, so that is lost, but the following *Bojangles* features a double length solo, with Ben starting in an easygoing mood, playing a few phrases identical with the studio version, but building up to a climax in the beginning of the second chorus. His swing is extremely effective, and his growling phrases in the last half of his solo are very expressive, culminating in altissimo notes. Ben plays two choruses on *Sepia Panorama* as well. The first chorus covers well-known ground, but in the last bar, we hear Ellington yell, "Go ahead, Ben!" after which he jumps to the high register, continuing with beautiful lines, intense and lyrical at the same time, until concluding, as expected, with trills. *Cotton Tail* is set at a slightly faster pace than the studio version, but the last half chorus and coda are lost, as disks are changed just as Ben enters for the second time. His solo follows more or less the pattern we have come to recognize, but aside from his introductory phrases, the ascending lines in the beginning of the second chorus, and the structure of the B-part in this chorus, the rest is new. He seems very inspired, performing with contagious vitality, great drive, and personality, earning applause from the audience. However, he doesn't seem particularly enthusiastic about *Conga Brava*, playing more out of duty than joy it seems, although he sounds as if he feels more at home in the unusual structure than in the studio version. On *I Never Felt This Way Before,* he is once again in a lyrical mood. His eight bars are possibly even prettier and more sensitive than previously heard, and his conclusion, ascending into the high register, is extremely beautiful, played with a tone perfectly matching the paraphrase.

In one of the breaks, Ben told Jack Towers to be ready with a fresh disk for a tune he and Jimmie Blanton had arranged. "It was *Star Dust* [*Stardust*]," Towers remembered. "When they finally played it towards the end of the evening, the band was hearing it for the first time too, yet they chimed in real well."[28] However, when the rhythm section began, Towers wasn't quite ready, and he missed the first twelve bars of Ben's interpretation—a pure declaration of love to Hoagy Carmichael's tune. Two improvisational choruses follow with the saxophone group supporting with long notes in the first chorus, and the horns following suit in the last. This is the first time Ben is heard playing a whole tune on his own, but *Stardust* demonstrates that he already has a fine understanding of structure, because his solo has an inner logic and balance, appearing as a whole, with each new phrase a natural consequence of the previous phrase. The solo builds up with rising intensity, peaking at the onset of the third chorus, gradually waning, and finishing in the same calm, beautiful phrasing it began with. Ben caresses his interpretation of the melody with a soft and rich tone in beautiful and placid lines, but in the second chorus he relies on more energy and dynamic effects to express his emotions. His double-time lines show that he still is somewhat influenced by Hawkins, just as he emulates his idol's habit of making an occasional short excursion in altissimo notes. But other than that, he is well on his way to a personal style, and his solo is a masterpiece of perfect structure, unique combination of emotional content, controlled energy, and majestic performance. His sound and phrasing keep it on the right side of sentimentality and banality. It is fully understandable that Ben, upon hearing the recording afterwards, asked Towers to send a copy to Casa Mañana in Culver City, California, where the orchestra was booked for seven weeks starting in early January 1941.

After this amazing effort, his last solo on the Fargo recordings is a little disappointing. He follows Ivie Anderson's vocal on *St. Louis Blues* with five choruses, beginning with a promising easygoing phrase on which he builds the rest of the chorus. He intensifies his energy and dynamics over the next three choruses, peaking at the beginning of the fourth chorus, but from here on he loses his grasp, and the rest of his solo consists of a bunch of more or less coincidental and incoherent lines.

The orchestra was back in Chicago a few days later, and November 11 was spent in part in a RCA studio, where Ben performed on several recordings with a contingent from the orchestra under the auspices of Barney Bigard. Ben solos on two of the four recorded tunes, *Charlie the Chulu* and *Lament for Javanette*. *Chulu* is Spanish for pimp, and Charlie was the name of a pimp operating in New York at the time. *Charlie the Chulu* is set at a medium fast tempo. Two whole takes exist where Ben's contributions are limited to, respectively, four and six bars at the end of the second chorus. *Lament for Javanette* is much more interesting as far as Ben is concerned. A "Javanette" is a beautiful coffee-colored girl; the tune has an Asian minor mood, and is written by Bigard and Strayhorn. On the unnumbered take, most probably the first to be recorded, Ben is unsure of where to fall in, and as he finishes slightly before time, his solo lasts eleven bars. He plays very nicely, if somewhat searchingly, and never really builds anything. He plays with far more authority on the official take, imbuing his solo with more emotion and playing more in accord with the melancholy mood of the theme. He uses a soft and pleasant sound throughout, swinging elegantly, likewise with a good ear for the mood, and not too aggressively.

The orchestra was in New York most of December, playing theaters. Ben was invited to participate in a recording session on December 15 at which trombonist Jack Teagarden was the leader and Rex Stewart and Barney Bigard also played. The session was late at night after the job at the Apollo Theatre, but Stewart and Bigard showed up without Ben; they hadn't succeeded in getting him to come, but some people went up to the Apollo in a cab to get him.[29]

As demonstrated by the music, Ben's contributions are first rate, and he is inspiring to the other musicians. On *St. James Infirmary,* his sixteen-bar solo immediately after the theme presentation is well articulated and warm with many references to the melody. The ascending figure is made up of large intervals in the solo's first half and a powerful shake in its last half. His one-chorus solo on the fast *The World Is Waiting for the*

Sunrise is excellent without being particularly catchy, whereas his sixteen bars in the final chorus reveal far more virility and dynamics. Utilizing growl and a fantastic drive, he eggs everyone on—and not least Stewart—to a great and inspired finale. *Big Eight Blues* is performed in a slow medium tempo. It is not a traditional twelve-bar blues. The title is a play on words, as it refers to the recording band's name—Jack Teagarden's Big Eight—as well as the eight-bar blues structure of the tune. Ben solos over two choruses performed with the same tenderness and ease as *St. James Infirmary,* imbued with an earnest, gentle sound. The session is concluded with a quick version of *Shine.* Ben plays one chorus following Teagarden's theme interpretation. He distributes his energy well, establishing a rising intensity. Just as you think he is going to play another chorus, he stops, passing the ball on to pianist Billy Kyle with a two-bar break. The last sixteen bars of the final chorus consist of inspired collective improvisation in which Ben's powerful phrases contribute to the culmination of the tune.

As of January 1941, Ellington began recording for Standard Transcriptions, and these disks are interesting for their focus on tunes unknown from the orchestra's commercial releases. The recordings were made in RCA Victor's New York studio, and at the first session, on January 15, ten tracks were recorded, out of which Ben solos on four. On the ballad *I Hear a Rhapsody,* he first plays sixteen bars that do not deviate very much from the theme and feature an excellent melodic conclusion. In the final chorus he returns with another sixteen bars, likewise containing fine, romantic lines, never turning sentimental, after which he concludes the tune with a short coda. *Madame Will Drop Her Shawl* was a popular tune of the day, and a real swinger. The theme is a rumba, but upon Ben's solo the orchestra reverts to a swing rhythm, and Ben responds to the challenge with forceful playing and wonderful drive, keeping right on the beat. He seems inspired, building his solo to a climax over the last eight bars of his chorus, even finding time to round off his statement logically with a few very nice figures. *Frenesi* is reminiscent of the previous tune in its mixture of rumba and swing rhythms. Here, Ben's eight bars comprise one of his more ordinary solos. The ballad *Until Tonight*—also called *Mauve*—is a feature tune for Ben. He plays two choruses; first one in which he interprets the theme faithfully, followed by a chorus improvised in soft lines. The contrast to *Stardust,* recorded only two months earlier, is large. He has freed himself greatly from the influence of Hawkins. There are none of Hawkins's sudden outbursts of altissimo notes, and the double-time runs are kept at a minimum. The embellishments are played with a steady hand, and the whole story is told with a soft and beautiful tone, a wonderful, calm pulse, and a few original phrases during the last sixteen bars. A lovely, classic solo to be heard over and over again.

One month later, on February 15, during an engagement at Casa Mañana in Culver City, California, the orchestra recorded five tunes for RCA on which Ben is heard only on Mercer Ellington's beautiful sound poem, *Blue Serge*. His twelve bars are a study in compressed expression. The first four bars are performed in restrained lines with a lovely, soft sound, but from the fifth bar he shoots upward, continuing with two growl-filled dynamic phrases, after which he reduces the intensity gradually until he concludes the solo lyrically with a couple of perfectly balanced phrases toward the lower register. At first, Ben's solo seems too rough for the otherwise lovely and richly faceted arrangement, but upon hearing it again, the listener recognizes that he brings far more life and presence to the tune than the other soloists.

Ellington's musician's were known to be sloppy about their stage attitude. It was a rare occasion when the whole band entered the stage at the same time, and it was not uncommon for the music to begin before everyone had found their seat. After the intermission, Ellington would usually improvise over a short syncopated theme titled *The Band Call* to draw the musicians to the stage, but now he would often use Ben instead, because he knew that Ben loved performing on the piano. "If Duke maybe had an interesting conversation going maybe somewhere in the place," Ben recalls, "then he would say, 'Ben, call the band.' And, I would say after around one or two minutes the whole band would be at the bandstand."[30] Sometimes Ben would be the last one to take his seat, because he would tease Ellington by playing on, even after being asked repeatedly to take his place in the sax group. This behavior didn't please the band leader and didn't benefit their relationship.

The orchestra was in California throughout the summer and autumn of 1941. For three weeks in June, Ellington was booked at the Trianon Ballroom in Los Angeles, after which the orchestra played the show

Jump for Joy at the Mayan Theatre in Los Angeles from July 10–September 27. The music was written by Ellington with help from his son Mercer, Billy Strayhorn, and composer Hal Borne. The well-known tunes from the show include Ellington's *The Brown Skin Gal in the Calico Gown,* the title tune, *Jump for Joy, Bli-Blip, I Got It Bad and That Ain't Good,* and *Subtle Slough,* which was supplied with lyrics a few years later and reemerged as *Just Squeeze Me.* The musical sketch in the second act featured Duke Ellington and Ivie Anderson, and Ben played *Concerto for Clinkers* with Rex Stewart, "Tricky Sam" Nanton, Ray Nance, Barney Bigard, and the rhythm section. A slow tempo movement from *Concerto for Clinkers,* featured as a solo for Ben, was later used as *The Blues* in Ellington's *Black, Brown and Beige.*

On June 5, the orchestra recorded four tracks in Los Angeles, including Juan Tizol's *Bakiff,* on which Ben's musical ear caused a change in the arrangement of the riff under the theme, played by the saxophone group with the clarinet voice on top. Mercer Ellington explains: "Ben was demonstrating the feeling *Bakiff* should have, but

> the guys kept playing it in a certain fashion and he said, "No, that's not the way it goes, it goes like this (hums)." And he would hum that to them. The old man listened to him, he said, "Wait a minute!" He called a break, brought back and gave the music to them again. This time Ben was playing the lead, Johnny Hodges and the rest of them were playing the parts under him and that was the first time he came up with the idea of a tenor playing the lead above the rest of the section, rather than double it underneath, he came up with what is recognized as a "tenor lead."[31]

Ben does not solo on *Bakiff;* he steps forward on only one tune at this session, *Just a-Settin' and a-Rockin',* where he plays the first two choruses with the exception of the first B-part. In terms of improvisation, nothing much happens here, but Ben creates a tranquil mood through his ability to precisely place his phrases and small embellishments. He perfectly plays up to the orchestra's backing, and he swings with wonderful ease, in an almost sly manner without forcing. A contemporary review provides this assessment of Ben: "How this man phrases and breathes, and what expression he obtains from his designs! Gorgeous stuff."[32]

In November and December 1941, the Ellington orchestra recorded five soundies, the music videos of the day. Soundies were popular in the 1940s, and each one lasted approximately three minutes, corresponding with the length of a 78 record. First the music was recorded, and subsequently the orchestra was filmed. The soundies were used in a sort of viewable jukebox. Upon inserting a coin, you were allowed to see the movie projected on a screen in eye level while the music was played through a loudspeaker below. Eight soundies were collected on a reel in which they were sorted by genre, and each soundie cost ten cents per view. Ellington's soundies were recorded in Hollywood, and they were all ready for release in January and February 1942. The five soundies were *Bli-Blip, Flamingo, I Got It Bad and That Ain't Good, Hot Chocolate,* and *Jam Session.* Ben solos on the last two; the music is *Cotton Tail* and *C Jam Blues.* On the former, his solo is limited to one chorus, and the phrases in the two first A-parts add nothing to our perception of his playing at the time. His solo climaxes in the B-part, and the dynamic and expressive level is sustained throughout the rest of his solo, but without producing anything remarkable. During the last bars of the theme, Ellington introduces Ben, saying, "Ben Webster!" after which Ben is seen in a close-up while playing the first two A-parts. He appears to be quite unimpressed, almost devoid of emotion and nonchalant. A short sequence later on in his solo shows him in front of the orchestra. *C Jam Blues* begins with a series of theme choruses, first by the rhythm section and later by the orchestra, after which there are solos by Ray Nance on violin, Rex Stewart, Ben, "Tricky" Sam Nanton, Barney Bigard, and Sonny Greer, each for one chorus, before the track closes with a ride-out with the whole orchestra. All horns solos are introduced with a four-bar break, and Ben's is nicely made up of calm and soft phrases. His solo is structured very nicely with rising intensity. He swings tightly to a climax, barely rounding off with a couple of fine figures before Nanton takes over.

Between recording sessions, theater and ballroom bookings, and five soundies, Ben found time to visit some of the clubs in town. When in Los Angeles, Ellington's orchestra always stayed at the Dunbar Hotel on Central Avenue. The area around the hotel housed many clubs where musicians would relax or jam after their jobs: the Memo Club, the Ritz Club, Club Alabam, the Downbeat, and Honey Murphy's, a favorite hangout of Art Tatum and Lester Young. A short distance from down-town, in Hollywood, there was the Club Capri, where Ben often sat in with Lee and Lester Young's band, of which Jimmy Rowles now was a member. Often there was a jam session on Sundays, and a particularly famous session took place at Club Capri on June 22, 1941, when Ben, Rex Stewart, and Jimmie Blanton from Ellington's orchestra, tenor saxophon-ist Joe Thomas from Jimmie Lunceford's orchestra, and Lester Young, Bumps Myers, Lee Young, Nellie Lutcher, and the duo Slim Gaillard and Slam Stewart all joined in. A reviewer of this musical battle had certain reservations about Ben, writing that he "as always went six stories below the basement to dish up his particular brand of dirty tone."[33] Ben proba-bly felt pressured in this company, because when he was nervous he had a tendency to use a lot of growl.

During his stay in Los Angeles, Ben heard of a man who owned a machine to cut records, and he took the opportunity to make several records of himself alone on piano, clarinet, and tenor saxophone, and with a quartet and quintet with Ray Nance on violin and trumpet. The rhythm section consisted of a guitarist, a drummer playing with brushes, and on some tracks a bassist. No musicians are mentioned on the record-ings, but Nance is easily recognizable, just as the great drive and solo abil-ity of the bassist leaves no doubt that he is Jimmie Blanton. The other musicians in the rhythm section may be Fred Guy and Sonny Greer, but it is hard to discern because their playing is fairly neutral. Greer was one of Ben's best friends in the Ellington band, so it seems likely that he was invited to the session. The presence of Jimmie Blanton may well date these recordings to the autumn of 1941. The other side of one of the acetates on which he is featured contains the first part of President Roosevelt's speech to the nation following the Japanese attack on Pearl Harbor, December 7, 1941. This indicates that these private recordings with Blanton are the very last he made, recorded just before he was hospitalized at the Los Angeles General Hospital in early November 1941. The three quintet and four quartet recordings all follow almost the same formula. Following a guitar introduction and the theme choruses, Ben and Nance play a few rounds alternating one-chorus solos, after which one or two members of the rhythm section are given space before finishing off the tune, usually with a collectively improvised chorus.

The quintet plays *I Never Knew, The Sheik of Araby,* and *I Can't Believe That You're in Love with Me.* The first two are performed in a medium fast tempo, the latter in a medium tempo. Nance plays trumpet and Ben plays tenor saxophone on the first track. He is inspired, building his solo well with growing intensity in each of his choruses. Blanton follows Nance's second solo with one chorus, before Ben takes over again full tilt with original lines, especially in the B-part. Then it is Nance's turn again, and during the conclusion of the chorus, the plugs are pulled for an eight-bar ride-out. On *The Sheik of Araby,* the trumpet is replaced by the violin and the saxophone with the clarinet. Ben plays the lead and Nance is the first soloist; both play two rounds of solos, followed by two choruses from Blanton, beginning with a nice variation on Ben's concluding figure. Ben's solos follow the same pattern of growing intensity as the previous solos. The first solo offers singable phrases, in which the figures are reminiscent of what he plays on the saxophone. The second solo is growling and dynamic, and each figure is timed expertly, creating an outstanding swing. On *I Can't Believe That You're in Love with Me,* Ben has returned to the saxophone. He interprets the theme, supported by Nance, still on violin and taking the first solo. Then Ben takes his turn, and in the transition, Blanton demonstrates his great understanding of counterpoint. Knowing that Ben usually opens with phrases somewhere between the middle and low range, he chooses to accompany in the high register during the first bars of Ben's solo. The tune has an incredible drive and viscous swing right from the start, which makes Ben hold back on the dynamic effects and concentrate on sustaining the swing instead. His simple phrases are delivered with authority, and contrary to his custom, there is no buildup to climax. One senses a little confusion as to form in the two concluding choruses as Ben can't bring himself to stop. He continues into another chorus which is played collectively with Nance on top, finally finding a natural ending with a leading phrase from Ben. The energy and powerful swing of the rhythm section, and the simple, but effective playing on the part of the two soloists produces a take that can be heard again and again.

Three of the four tunes without Blanton are improvisations over the harmonic structure of *I Got Rhythm: A Flat Swing, E Flat Swing,* and *Swingin' in 4.* The latter tune is played at a fast pace; the two first are set at the same medium fast tempo as *I Never Knew.* Ben plays clarinet and

Nance plays violin on all three tracks, and Ben starts off the first two with a riff-based chorus, commented by Nance's violin. On *A Flat Swing*, Nance and Ben take turns soloing for three rounds before Ben leads on to conclusion in an ensemble chorus in which Nance takes over in the B-part. Ben's first two solos feature growing dynamics, and he finishes the first with excellent ascending phrases. The second A-part of his next solo starts out with a nice melodic line in the high register, repeated an octave lower. He concludes this solo with growling riffs. His last solo is initiated with restrained phrases in the low register, whereas he builds the B-part in chromatically ascending figures, some of which unfortunately are difficult to follow due to the bad condition of the disk.

On *E Flat Swing* Ben is more inspired than on the previous tune. He builds his solo with rising intensity, peaking in the last A-part with animated double-time runs. After Nance, he takes off for his next turn with a couple of riffs. The guitar offers a stop chorus in the B-part, and Ben rounds things up with energetic figures with growl. The subsequent ensemble chorus is played collectively, but Ben does not stop here, but plays on, providing excellent lines in the concluding chorus.

The form of *Swingin' in 4* is just as loose, but the fast tempo allows the soloists to alternate two choruses each. Ben sets out with inspired phrases, but here and there the quick pace seems to obstruct his efforts. His second solo is initiated in the low register of the clarinet, working its way up as he goes along, and from the second chorus, he plays inspired and with growl. After yet another Nance solo, the tune is concluded with two ensemble choruses with riffs. Once again, the rest of the band wants to end after one chorus, but when Ben continues playing new, inspired riffs, they follow him. The content seems a bit thin, and the playing more hectic than the rest of the tunes, whereas the ballad *Memories of You* produces a nice, calm atmosphere. Following two introductory bars of guitar, Nance interprets the tune beautifully on the violin, accompanied by low notes from Ben's clarinet, after which Ben plays a lovely solo, keeping to the middle register and imbuing his tone with maximum beauty. The last bars are performed in the high register as a paraphrase on the theme.

One side of another private recording—titled *Barney*—is a Barney Bigard clarinet solo; the other side is called *Me* and features Ben on clarinet, accompanied by a drummer playing tap-drum. Ben improvises over an Oriental scale on a rhythm where only bars 1, 2, and 3 are indicated. He utilizes the whole register of the clarinet and is very sound conscious. The form is excellent; he begins and finishes in the low register, building excellently to a climax in the high register along the way. We also hear a short fragment from another recording—which he has chosen to call *Tricky Me*—of Ben playing a clarinet solo, and practicing, among other things, a few blues phrases.

Ben recorded four tracks on piano: The above-mentioned *Dearie*, on which he sings lyrics of his own making, *Hallelujah, Untitled Blues,* and *Sweet Lorraine. Dearie* must be for his new girlfriend, a pretty black woman named Eudora Williams. Eudora was a statistician in a government office and a friend of Joyce Cockrell's daughter, Clara Lewis, who was a pianist in Washington, D.C. Among the private recordings in Ben's collection is one on which Ben does not appear; we hear Eudora speaking with a man and a woman—possibly Clara Lewis—about Ben, Barney Bigard, Sonny Greer, and other musicians. One of the items is a mock interview on her views on saxophonists. In this interview, it is obvious that she and Ben are engaged.

The disk was almost certainly recorded shortly before Ellington's orchestra left California in December 1941. Ben's cousin, Joyce Cockrell, had moved from Kansas City to Los Angeles, and Ben had probably taken the opportunity to visit his family while he was in town, and met Clara Lewis and Eudora Williams on the same occasion. Whatever the circumstances, he and Eudora fell in love and decided to marry later. *Dearie* has a catchy theme, but unfortunately the recording makes it a little difficult to understand the lyrics sung by Ben in his curious falsetto. A couple of verses go something like this:

> I know what you're begging of
> You my honey dear
> Don't you (need?) to wait for me
> You will be in here
>
> I know what you're begging of
> You my sweetie pie

Don't you ever fool with me
(Getting?) on my side

The simple chorus is as follows:

Oh, dearie, dearie
Dearie, you my honey dear
Oh, dearie, dearie
Dearie, you my honey dear

He starts the recording with this statement: "I am going to play an odd number, haven't named it yet." He plays a melody chorus followed by the vocal, and finishes it off with a stride piano chorus. The other side's *Hallelujah* is even better proof of Ben's accomplished stride playing at the time, because he plays his spellbinding interpretation powerfully in a fast tempo without faltering the least. It is more difficult to assess *Untitled Blues* because the acetate is in such bad condition that the needle either jumps or sticks in the same track time after time throughout the tune. Ben introduces it with a short speech, perhaps once again to Eudora, because he says, "Hi! How do you feel? I am sorry. Never mind. A friend of mine in Los Angeles, he has a little recording machine, so I've made a record up there. You take it easy." After this, he plays a few choruses of medium tempo blues, breaking the stride rhythm in his left hand midway to play a good walking bass line. The disk of *Sweet Lorraine* is in almost as bad condition, but one senses Ben's emotional focus in this well-organized rendition in which the first chorus is performed rubato with a few Tatum-influenced runs.

Another interesting recording is an almost five-minute long *Body and Soul*, played as a tenor saxophone solo. It is not far from being just as outstanding as the *Stardust* recording from Fargo. The way Ben plays over the harmonic structure and creates an inner logic, we never miss the accompaniment. His sound is exquisite and soft, and he never becomes overly emotional. He paraphrases the first two A-parts, and begins improvising from the B-part. In the transition between the first and second choruses, he plays Hawkins-inspired chromatic figures, then continues in long lines. The conclusion of the next B-part includes a series of descents in double time that sound just like Hawkins. He plays in double time throughout most of the last chorus, until he returns to the original ballad tempo with an interpretation of the theme in the last A-part with a beautifully expressed ending. It is obvious that he feels at home and comfortable, and with the exception of the few references to Hawkins, he is totally himself. Many outstanding details pop up along the way, not least in the double-time sequence in the final chorus. This recording can probably be dated to early summer 1942, at which time the Ellington orchestra featured him in the tune.[34]

Although time has been unkind to several of these private recordings, they are noteworthy in that they reveal a couple of Ben's otherwise undocumented accomplishments. He shows an equal care with his sound on the clarinet as on the saxophone. He modeled his playing closely on Barney Bigard's, although he lacked the latter's fullness in the top and broad "wood" sound in the low register. However, he was completely his own when improvising, playing with the same originality and use of vibrato and growl as on the saxophone. He had a good technical foundation, although he has a little trouble in fast tempi. Many musicians remember him as a fine stride pianist, and the private recordings from Los Angeles support their claim. There are later recordings of Ben playing piano, but on most of them, especially the European, he is rusty, revealing that he has not kept his piano chops honed over the years.

Ben and Eudora met again during the band's booking at the Howard Theatre in Washington, D.C., in early March 1942, and Ben persuaded Eudora to come to Baltimore, where the orchestra had an engagement the following week. They were married in the town hall on March 11. Barney Bigard was best man, and afterward the newlyweds celebrated with the whole orchestra.[35] Later, Eudora accompanied Ben to California, where the orchestra was booked for the next four months.

It would be an exaggeration to claim that Ben was the perfect husband. Jazz was his whole life, his best friends were jazz musicians, and consequently Eudora was dragged from concert to jam session to jazz clubs, wherever Ben happened to spend his free time when not at their hotel. During their four-month stay in Los Angeles, they rented an apartment close to Central Avenue, but they never had a real home. It didn't fit in with tour life, and Ben's life was not much different from most other jazz musicians'. If Eudora had hoped to find a little newlywed romance on their "honeymoon" or just be alone, the two of them, for any extended time, she must have been disappointed. Ben had no intention of asking for leave or giving up his close friendships, even for a short while. This is how Eudora remembered the first weeks in California: "Some honeymoon! First thing I'd see when I opened my eyes in the morning was Jimmy Rowles."[36]

On the West Coast during the spring and early summer of 1942, Ben once again took part in a number of jam sessions, now systemized by a young Norman Granz. From mid-June, there was a session at the Trouville Club in Hollywood every Sunday from four to seven, and each musician received nine dollars. The rhythm section at these jam sessions consisted of Nat "King" Cole on the piano, Johnny Miller on bass, and Lee Young on drums; the guitarist was either Les Paul or Oscar Moore. Lee Young remembers that the horns were often four of a kind. "One Sunday, we had Lester (Young), Ben (Webster), Bumps (Myers), and I don't know whether it was Don Byas or whoever, but we had four tenor players. And the next Sunday we had Willie Smith, Johnny Hodges, and two alto players. And then we would have the trumpet players Lloyd Reese, Rex Stewart, and Red Mack (Morris), who was a real good trumpet player in town, and someone else."[37] June 28, 1942 was hot in more than one sense; *Down Beat* reported that "At his Sunday jam session of this week, (June 28) Norman Granz had what he claimed were the three greatest tenor men of the day on the same stand, and literally carving each other into strips— Ben Webster, Les Young and Joe Thomas."[38]

A couple of days after the arrival of the orchestra in California, Ben was hired by vocalist and guitarist Slim Gaillard for a recording on April 4, 1942. Four tunes were recorded, but none were released on 78, and only three have since been released. It is optimistic and humorous music, with a fine, swinging rhythm section including Gaillard, Jimmy Rowles, bassist and vocalist Slam Stewart, and drummer Leo Watson, who seems very inspiring to Ben. *Palm Springs Jump* is introduced in four bars by Ben, and he solos after Gaillard and Stewart's duet. Ben starts up with phrases that latch onto each other logically and gradually increase in energy, and he swings wonderfully. *Ra-Da-Da-Da* is set at a fast pace, and his solo is perfectly structured; vital and melodic at the same time, climaxing before handing the baton to Rowles with a couple of well-accented figures. *Groove Juice* finds him swinging solidly in simple melodic lines that lack nothing in dynamics. The tempo is medium, once again, and his first phrases are wonderfully logical. He peaks in the B-part, jumps to the high register, plays a powerful shake, repeated a few bars later, before coming to a perfect conclusion. All in all, these sessions are uplifting with plenty of good music from all participants. It is strange that these recordings had to wait for so long before they were judged worthy of release.

In early July 1942, the Ellington orchestra moved east, and shortly before they left, Jimmy Rowles drove Ben and Eudora in his car to visit Jimmie Blanton, who had been committed to a sanatorium with tuberculosis. While playing *Jump for Joy* the previous year, it was discovered that he was ill, and a few months later, he was so weak that Ellington hired Alvin "Junior" Raglin in San Francisco to play bass along with him. Ellington soon had him hospitalized at the Los Angeles General Hospital, where tuberculosis specialists had promised to help him. After the orchestra had left town, Lee Young visited Blanton and had him instead transferred to the Dore Sanatorium in Monrovia, on the outskirts of Los Angeles. He was given a single room and spent most of his time alone. His condition did not improve, and he kept losing weight. "I remember the cottage Jimmie was in," Rowles recounts. "White sheets, white room. All he had in this little room was a picture of Ben Webster. I drove Ben and Eudora way out there to the San Gabriel Valley to see Blanton. Eudora waited in the car. I went in to pay my respects to Jimmie. When Ben got down on his hands and knees and put his head on Jimmie's chest, I had to leave the room. That was the last time I saw Jimmie Blanton. When Ben came out of that little cottage, he was a wreck, because he knew. Ben was in Chicago when Blanton died a short time later. Ben really raised hell then. He tore Chicago up."[39] Like many other musicians, Rowles is of the opinion that Blanton fell ill out of carelessness—that he didn't take care of himself. "After hours, Blanton went around with his shirt collar open, all covered with sweat," he remembers. "He used to in these clubs in Seattle; he'd play and work up a terrible sweat. He'd put on his overcoat and walk out the door with it hanging open. And Ben would tell him, 'Button it. It's chilly out here. Windy. Button up.' But he'd never do it."[40] Ben surely agreed, because in the mid-1960s he did some trick recording of himself playing piano and trap drums. One of the tunes is called *Button Up Your Overcoat,* an obvious tribute to Blanton.

Blanton's death on July 30, 1942, affected Ben deeply. He never got over it; even thirty years later tears would come to his eyes when he thought back. When he received the news, he broke down and was unable to play. His drinking increased and he began to gain weight. His behavior became more violent, at times so much so that he would scare people when he was drunk.

His marriage to Eudora went sour and, late that summer, broke down. "When they went on the road, and I think they were going back to New York," says Joyce Cockrell, "Ben found out that she had been involved with one of the men in the orchestra. Now, Ben's mother was a very decent type of person, so he thought that when he married, he would get the same type of person as his wife. But when he found out that she was not that type, he became enraged and very brutal, and I understand that many times he did beat her because it was something he just couldn't take."[41] Ben and Eudora remained friends, even after their divorce in 1953, and Ben visited her several times, first in Los Angeles and later in Washington. She remarried, and in the late 1960s, when she and her new husband were vacationing in Europe, they met shortly with Ben in Amsterdam.

Ben never remarried, although he had various lady friends throughout his life. Occasionally his relationships turned violent, and consequently were short-lived. Mercer Ellington got to know Ben quite well. Of the violence in his character he remarked, "Ben said that a woman never interested him if she was conducive to what he wanted to do. He only got the real feeling and a real call to have her when he sort of could force her into action. I think that this sensuousness and this beauty of Ben Webster was a cover that was meant not to let you discover the monster until it was too late."[42] These remarks fit in well with the experiences both Billie Holiday and Mary Lou Williams had with him. Thus Ben often looked for more commitment-free affairs with prostitutes, but here, too, he almost crossed the line once, barely avoiding a lawsuit. "When his wife lived here and he was at the Dunbar Hotel on Central Avenue in Los Angeles," Cockrell explained, "he and a woman friend had an argument, and he threw her out of the window. That was a terrible thing, but because he was connected with Duke Ellington and was in the band, they were able to get him out, and especially not to go to jail. So he never did go to jail. But those things hurt him, and his reputation followed him."[43] One possible reason that he avoided prison was that he and the prostitute were both black. The judicial system often closed its eyes to the affairs of blacks as long as white people weren't involved.

It is remarkable that Ben's hard living during these and subsequent years was not detrimental to the quality of his music. To the contrary, he kept improving. The recordings speak their own language, and a review of a radio transmission from the Sherman Hotel's Panther Room in Chicago August 13, 1942, states that "*Perdido* was the elaborately embroidered centrepiece, featuring the superb solos of Ray Nance and Ben Webster."[44] In the first edition of *Down Beat* from 1943, he and Tex Beneke were chosen as the tenor saxes in the magazine's "All American Swing Band 1942."

During a week at the Palace Theatre in Cleveland, the musicians discovered that Mary Lou Williams and her band were playing at a place called Mason's Farm in Solon, ten to fifteen miles from Cleveland, and one evening they all drove out to surprise her. "We did our show and we had a jam session," Williams recalled,

> and I think Baby Lee Laurence the great tap dancer was with them, so we really had a ball that night. Ben Webster took out his horn, he came up and jammed with us, and I discovered that Orlando Wright, whose name is now Musa Kaleem, was just about one of the greatest tenor men going. He was around seventeen or eighteen years old. So Ben got up on the stand and he was blowing *Body and Soul,* so when it came time for Orlando to take his solo, he said, he stuttered, "Miss-miss-miss Williams, E natural." I said, "Oh, my goodness." He played it in E natural and before he finished he said, "B natural." He played in all these keys, and Ben Webster looked at him with his big eyes and said, "Well, man, that's too much for me!"[45]

That evening Ellington hired Williams's boyfriend, Harold Baker, and two weeks later he joined the band. Williams disbanded her own orchestra that fall and subsequently traveled with Baker on his tours with Ellington. On December 10, they were married in Baltimore, and soon Ellington realized that he might as well utilize Williams's talents, and she began composing and arranging for the orchestra.

In late September and early October 1942, Ellington's orchestra performed in two Hollywood film productions, *Cabin in the Sky* and *Reveille with Beverly*. The credits in *Cabin in the Sky* feature several famous show business people, including Ethel Waters, Lena Horne, Buck & Bubbles, and Louis Armstrong, and Ellington's orchestra performs in a short dance sequence, playing *Goin' Up*, in which Ben shares solo space in the last chorus with Ray Nance. Leading up to this scene, the orchestra is heard in an abridged version of *Things Ain't What They Used to Be*. *Reveille with Beverly* is a kind of musical revue with orchestras led by Count Basie, Bob Crosby, Duke Ellington, and Freddie Slack, and including performances by the Mills Brothers and Frank Sinatra. Ellington's contribution, *Take the "A" Train*, was produced on October 8. In the movie, the orchestra plays standing, and Ben is placed directly next to the grand piano, behind Ellington. Following the orchestra's theme presentation, Betty Roché sings a chorus accompanied by a vocal trio consisting of Ray Nance, Rex Stewart, and Harry Carney. The subsequent chorus is split between solos by Ellington, bassist Junior Raglin, and Ben. The short tenor sax solo is extroverted, with growl in the upper register, and it swings wonderfully.

On January 23, 1943, Ellington played his first concert in New York's prestigious Carnegie Hall as a benefit performance for the Russian War Relief. During the three-hour concert, the middle set consisted of Ellington's forty-five-minute *Black, Brown and Beige*.

The recording of the concert indicates that Ben played a somewhat smaller role than he may have expected, as he was reduced from one of the orchestra's featured soloists to a supporting role, playing but one solo in each of the three sets. However, he plays two choruses on *Bojangles* instead of the usual one, steadily building the intensity of his solo. The soft starting point may be seen as a paraphrase over his usual solo in this tune, whereas he gets rougher in his second chorus. Swinging aggressively and utilizing growl and high-register phrases, he climaxes midway before concluding with slightly less dynamic lines. His next solo is in the slow *The Blues*, the last movement of *Black, Brown and Beige*, following *Emancipa-*

tion Celebration, in which Ellington used Ben's theme *Dearie* as a feature for Rex Stewart and in his own concluding solo. Ben enters after Betty Roché's vocal, playing sixteen bars that are pure pleasure and a perfect display of how beautiful tone and interpretation can be united. He imbues his presentation with all his feeling and emotive force. Although it is part of a tight arrangement, his playing is fairly free, and wrapped in the sweetest and most lyrical tone imaginable. In the concert's third set, Ben solos on a breakneck-paced *Cotton Tail.* He plays two choruses, the first in legato lines, the second more virile and explosive. A sixteen-bar coda follows the last ensemble chorus, and here Ben once again expresses himself energetically with growl. The performance of the orchestra as a whole is in no way memorable; the fast tempo creates a hectic feeling in the ensemble as well as the solos.

During the four years Ben spent with Ellington at this time, there were a few changes in the lineup, which should be mentioned here. Cootie Williams left the orchestra for Benny Goodman's band in November 1940 and was replaced by Ray Nance, who became Ben's close friend and roommate on tours, with the exception of the period Ben and Eudora were together. Bigard left Ellington in June 1942 and was eventually replaced by twenty-five-year old Jimmy Hamilton. Ben had given Bigard his nickname, "Steps." The story is that the Ellington orchestra had played before one of heavyweight champion Joe Louis's title matches. The band performed in the ring, and when they were on their way down, Bigard stumbled over the first step and slid all the way down on his backside.[46]

On April 1, 1943, after many months of touring, the Ellington orchestra settled into a long and well-deserved engagement at New York's Hurricane Club on Broadway and 49th, lasting till September 27. Ben was pleased to be back in New York, and happy to spend time and play with many of his old friends at the many jam sessions on 52nd Street—not to mention his favorite hangout, Minton's Playhouse on 210 West 118th Street, in the same building as the Cecil Hotel, where Ben stayed.

At this time, Jimmy Rowles had arrived in New York, which proved just as hectic and overwhelming an experience for him as it had been for Ben twelve years earlier. "I caught up with Ben in New York, too," Rowles recalled. "He took me clear up to Harlem one time, to Minton's. It was the first time I ever saw Thelonious Monk. I don't remember anyone else who was up there. I remember Monk. I didn't know what to think of it. I was from California. I was scared to death in New York. I don't even remember the kind of music they were playing. It was jazz and all that, but it was kind of unrecognisable to me. Thank God, I didn't have to sit in and play. Ben kept me in the back. We just sat there. I didn't meet anybody I can remember. My impressions of Minton's are real hazy."[47]

Among others, the house band at Minton's included tenor saxophonist Kermit Scott, drummer Kenny Clarke, and bassist Nick Fenton. Like Ben, saxophonist Budd Johnson dropped by regularly, and according to him, Scott was hard to beat in jam sessions. "And then I remember when Ben Webster and Prez were there together, and they're gonna go up there and cut this guy Scotty, you know. Scotty knew that music backwards. He used to sound like Hawk, too. But all the guys used to go up there and sit and play. And I mean they would get a good lesson when they sat in."[48]

Ben had fond memories of the time.

I used to live at the Cecil Hotel, which was next door to Minton's. We used to jam just about every night when we were off. Lester, Don Byas and myself—we would meet there all the time and like, exchange ideas. It wasn't a battle, or anything. We were all friends.

Most of the guys around then knew where I lived. If someone came in Minton's and started to play—well, they'd give me a ring, or come up and call me down. Either I'd take my horn down, or I'd go down and listen. Those were good days. Had a lot of fun.[49]

There was a lot happening in jazz back then; the young musicians were developing bebop at jam sessions, and jobs were plentiful for small combos in the clubs. Among the most innovative were trumpeter Dizzy Gillespie, pianists Thelonious Monk and Tadd Dameron, and saxophonist Charlie Parker, whose soaring, vivid, and unhampered playing in even the fastest tempi took Ben completely by surprise at their first encounter.[50] Ben recalled, "That was quite a thrill. The guy scared me to death!"[51] Afterward he would rave about Charlie Parker. However, he had one reservation. "Around this time someone asked me about Charlie Parker," he remembered. "And I said, 'This kid will mess up a gang, a real big gang of saxophone players. He won't disturb me, because I'm only trying to play the little that I know how to play, but you watch! He will really destroy a lot of saxophone players!' And he did."[52] Apparently Parker did not scare Ben that much, because a couple of years later, he hired him for his quintet.

Apart from Minton's, Ben went to jam sessions at other places as well. Teddy Reig arranged a Sunday afternoon jam session at Kelly's Stable on Fifty-second Street. In his memoirs, he recounts that Ben told him,

> "I want Hawk!" I said, "Okay, we'll get you Hawk." I begged Hawkins to do it and he agreed, but for $20 which was double what we usually paid. Sunday came, and Ben went up to the mike, all big, bad and bold. He growled out a chorus and Hawk egged him on, saying "C'mon, take some more." Ben looked at him a little suspiciously but went ahead. And then Hawk took over where he left off and buried him. When we looked around, there was no more Ben Webster. He didn't even finish the set, never mind the gig. That night, we were back at Minton's, lining up the acts for next week, when in walks Ben, completely crocked. He's waving a clarinet in his hand, yelling, "Get me Barney Bigard!"[53]

During the booking at the Hurricane Club, something happened involving Ben and Jimmy Hamilton. "Ben took a liking to me and he always liked to talk to me and help me in whatever way he could," Hamilton says.

> That was during the time of the war and there was a lot of prejudice going on. There used to be many servicemen marching up and down the streets. One night, when we had our intermission, I was standing on the street. I was just a little guy, you know, and there used to be these sailors and soldiers that used to come along, and it was a prejudiced kind of people. We talked to everybody, we had many friends, and some of the girls, you know, they were white, and we talked to them, but it was no big thing, it was

New York City. But one time I was talking to this girl that I knew pretty good, and this sailor came along and he didn't like it, and he wanted to beat me up for it. But Ben Webster happened to be standing on the side, and Ben Webster came over and knocked him out on the street. And that ended that, you know!![54]

Ben once told a story also involving Hamilton to trumpeter Clark Terry. Ben and Terry later became close friends and performed together often, including the time after Ben had moved to Europe. "I don't really remember the first time I met Frog," Terry recalls.

It seems that I have known him all my life, but the first time I saw him was probably when he was with the Duke Ellington band and was hanging out with Jimmie Blanton in my hometown, St. Louis. When Frog was with the Ellington band, Jimmy Hamilton, the clarinetist who also played the tenor sax, played in the reed section with him. They were rehearsing a tune in A-flat, and every time they came to an A-flat, Ben would play an A-natural, a wrong note. After two or three times Jimmy Hamilton with his funny sense of humor says, "Hey Ben, you're a favorite of that note, aren't you?" I cracked up when Ben told me that story, and I started calling him "Fav'rin" all the time, and that's how we started calling each other "Fav'rin."[55]

Just as he had with Nance and Hamilton, Ben took vocalist Al Hibbler under his wing when he joined the band at the Hurricane Club. "Ben Webster told me a lot about singing," Hibbler says. "Ben always wanted me to sing the low notes. I would sit by him and he would take that horn and blow the low notes right in my ear, 'Get *down* there, way *down*.' Ben Webster was a favourite of mine."[56]

Quite a few transcriptions are preserved from the band's six month engagement at the Hurricane Club, from which the radio trans-mitted every evening except Monday, the band's night off. In addition to these transmissions, the orchestra took part in other radio shows as well, including *Treasury Star Parade*.

On the April 3 transcription, Ben is heard in an inspired version of *Hayfoot, Strawfoot,* playing an elegant and surprising descending line in the middle of his eight bars. He enters his solo on *What Am I Here For?* with a short paraphrase on the theme, subsequently building logically up to his conclusion sixteen bars later with fine phrasing, rounding it off with a trill. The next tune, *Main Stem,* is played with great drive, and Ben's solo is no less intense, although it is lacking in beauty and inner logic. *Goin' Up* is somewhat hectic, and despite dedicated playing on Ben's part, his solo never really takes off. The following evening's version of *Main Stem* shows Ben equally inspired, although his solo, again, is not very interesting melodically.

There are many radio transcriptions from the following month. Ben's contributions start with a couple of ballads from June 6. *You'll Never Know* and *Tonight I Shall Sleep* are both performed with ease and beauty and without frills. He offers solid craftsmanship, no more. However, he had a very good night on June 17, playing one inspired solo after another. As on the Carnegie Hall version, he plays two choruses on *Bojangles,* swinging wonderfully, an excellently structured solo with a particularly exquisite conclusion. *Five O'clock Drag* is set in a relaxed medium slow tempo, and Ben is featured twice. First he plays calm obbligato to the ensemble theme presentation, finishing off with an elegant break leading into the trumpet solo. In his next solo, his performance has a much more powerful swing, leading up to a climax with a series of catchy staccato figures. From there on, he gradually reduces his dynamic grip in call-and-response with the orchestra for the final sixteen bars. Billy Strayhorn's *Johnny Come Lately* is performed in a delightful, swinging version, inspiring Ben to use a little too much growl, whereas he gives *Tonight I Shall Sleep* a far more beautiful and empathetic treatment than eleven days previously. His last feature on this transcription is *Blue Skies,* yet another fine medium tempo swinger. Ben gives it all he has in the final sixteen bars, using shake, growl, and several original phrases, creating a more emotional than pretty solo.

June 20 gives us Ben's best version of *C Jam Blues* with Ellington, performed in wonderfully melodic and relaxed lines, introduced with a break consisting of exquisite phrases. The last commercially released solo Ben played with Ellington is a flawless and emotional version of *Blue Serge* from July 11. The overall structure and performance is very close to previous versions of this wonderful tune—a worthy and elegant sortie from an important period in Ben's career.

In the spring of 1943, Ellington and Ben were growing tired of each other. Ben's excessive drinking, his bragging, and occasional uncontrolled behavior had long irritated Ellington, who once felt Ben's sudden temper himself. "He wasn't always 'Gentle Ben,'" recalls Clark Terry. "He loosed his temper sometimes, you know, and he slapped Duke one time in the spur of the moment."[57] Another time, Ben arrived early for a concert and went into Ellington's dressing room to try on some of his fancy clothes. While trying a jacket, he straightened up to look at himself, but as he was too broad, the jacket ripped all the way down the back. Naturally, Ellington, who happened to walk in right then, was furious. Once Ben humiliated Ellington in front of an audience, which certainly did not help their tense relationship. Somewhat drunk after the break, Ben played *The Band Call* as he had done so often, to rally the musicians for the next set, but this evening Ben didn't leave the piano bench when Ellington entered the stage. Ellington tried to push Ben away, but received such a heavy shove in return, that he fell over on stage in front of the audience.[58]

Rather than fire him, "The Guv'nor," as Ben called Ellington, used the music to punish him. He knew how much Ben wanted to show off as a soloist, so he gradually took away more and more of his solos. He gave him but one solo in each of the three sets at the Carnegie Hall concert, and the same meager harvest came Ben's way at Boston's Symphony Hall the next week. Ben, on the other hand, knew that he was an asset to the orchestra, and bartered for more than the $150 a week he received at the time. "Duke," he said, "why don't you pay me more money? You're working me to *death*." "Ben," replied Ellington in his usual diplomatic fashion, "I can't afford to pay you what you're worth. Nobody can."

This psychological warfare ended in the summer, when Ben decided to look into job possibilities in one of the clubs on Fifty-second Street with a band of his own. Jazz was blossoming on the street as never before or since, and Ben landed a booking at the Three Deuces at 72 West Fifty-second for a weekly wage of $315. Ben played his last job with Ellington on Sunday, August 8, at the Hurricane Club. They parted without bitterness, and later Ben would recall his time with Ellington as some of the happiest years of his life. His admiration of "The Guv'nor" as a person and bandleader never waned. "When Duke gets ready for that band to play," he recalled, "I still don't understand how he does it. He turned that band on like you turn that faucet on. There is just one Ellington. He does not say, 'Do this, do that.' That's the reason I say that it was the biggest thrill of my life sitting in that band. And you miss them. You miss the band, you miss the sound, you miss Duke's music, and it never gets out of your system. Never, never gets out of your system."[59] Ben remained an Ellingtonian for the rest of his life, as was reflected later in his choice of repertoire and in his sitting in with the orchestra at every possible opportunity. Of his own reason for leaving the band—and the one Ellington cited later—he said, "I quit Duke at the Hurricane because I had the opportunity to make a little more bread and have my own band. It wasn't because of the traveling, because Duke was always traveling in style, and to be with Duke, there was never a dull moment. Every day was a fête. I had just the chance to get my own band."[60]

6. From Fifty-second Street to Kansas City
(1943–1949)

Music thrived during the war years. In 1943, jazz and other music was played on New York's Fifty-second Street in a number of clubs, usually situated in the cellar of residential buildings. A great many musicians were employed in these clubs, as they all had at least two alternating bands. "Everybody was playing on Fifty-second Street," reminisced Ben.

> Art Tatum, Clyde Hart, Billie Holiday, Dizzy Gillespie, Coleman Hawkins, Stuff Smith. Bop wasn't my style. I liked it, but I just tried to play what I knew. I think they had about six different clubs right on Fifty-second Street between Sixth Avenue and Fifth Avenue, and just about everybody in the music business was down on the Street at some time. We usually played a half hour on and a half hour off, and everybody used to hang around a place called the White Rose, just around the corner of Sixth Avenue. At the White Rose you could see Lady Day and Tatum, Slam Stewart, Dizzy Gillespie, Charlie Parker, and I can go on and on. And even when the guys didn't work on the Street, that was their office. Those were happy days.[1]

Bands with extended bookings would play the clubs from Tuesday through Sunday. Monday was the musicians' regular night off. However, many clubs were open seven days a week, and they booked other bands on Mondays. It has been stated that Ben left Ellington August 13,[2] a Friday, but this does not coincide with usual club policy or the newspaper announcements of Ben's new job, which read, "The Three Deuces, 52nd Street nitery, told the *Beat* at press time that Ben Webster, with a trio, had been signed to open at that spot on August 10, replacing Joe 'Flip' Phillips and his crew."[3] August 10 was a Tuesday, and the same notice mentioned that Art Tatum was scheduled to start a booking the same place on August 17, likewise a Tuesday. Everything points toward August 10, 1943 as the date of Ben's debut as bandleader.

The exact lineup of Ben's rhythm section at the beginning of the engagement is unknown, but drummer Sidney Catlett and bassist Al McKibbon were in Ben's new rhythm section from the start, but it is unknown whether Johnny Guarnieri was the original pianist or if someone preceded him. In any case, Guarnieri was replaced by Billy Taylor in November 1943. "I had just come to New York and I wanted to meet people and get a job," says Taylor,

> so if I went to one of the very well known places, perhaps I could meet musicians there. Anyway, I went up to Minton's and I asked a young member of the house group there if I could sit in. At that time it was possible for everybody to sit in, one way or the other. Unfortunately for me it was a Friday night, and several people showed up whose work he was familiar with, and he called them up to play, so I sat around and sat around. Finally, on the very last set of the evening he called me up and let me sit in with the band. There were quite a few people on the bandstand by that time, because many musicians had gotten off from work, it was two o'clock in the morning. So I got to sit in, but I didn't get to solo much because all the horn players had to play.
>
> While I was playing, Ben Webster came in. I knew Ben, because I had seen him perform many times in Washington, D.C., where I was from. He was one of my all-time favorites. Anyway, he came over and stood by the piano, and when the set was over he asked what my name was, and said that he liked what he could hear and that he was interested in me. He said, "If you are available, you can come down to the Three Deuces where I am performing, and you can play with my group. You can audition, and we can see how it works out." He said that it was not a good idea to come on Saturday because it was so crowded, but I could come Sunday.
>
> So I came back two days later on Sunday and sat in with the

quartet and got the job. The drummer was Sidney Catlett, and the bassist was Charlie Drayton, who I didn't know at the time, and I was replacing Johnny Guarnieri, who was leaving to go with Raymond Scott. As a sideman I didn't get paid that much, maybe a hundred dollars a week. The people who ran the Three Deuces paid the musicians in the quartet individually, so Ben was getting his salary, and I was paid union scale. I'm sure I was not making near what Guarnieri had been paid.[4]

Up till now, Ben's rhythm section was a dream lineup. Guarnieri was already a well-established musician. His playing was influenced equally by Count Basie, Teddy Wilson, and Art Tatum; he was a virtuoso with plenty of drive, and a stride master. Sidney Catlett was no less formidable. Ben remembered him as "one of the greatest drummers. We used to call him 'The All-Season Drummer,' you know. If you were fortunate enough to have him, you never had to worry about the drum department because the tempo was *there,* including everything else that went along with swing. He could swing on the drums. I named him 'Farm Hand' because he was such a huge cat, broad shoulders and everything. But Sid was far from being a country boy. He had such time and swing, oh man!"[5] Next to these giants, Charlie Drayton was a novice. However, he was an excellent and steady bassist, and he had previously played with Louis Jordan and Benny Carter. Some time that autumn he had replaced McKibbon, who had been hired by Lucky Millinder.

Joining Ben's quartet was a huge kick for Taylor, and Ben encouraged him to continue developing his piano skills. Taylor had heard Ellington's band at the Howard Theatre several times, and had traveled to New York to hear Wilson's orchestra. ""Ben was outrageous in that band," he recalls. "He was fantastic. But everybody in that band was remarkable. For the time the band was unusual. It was very musical, and I can't think of another band at that particular time that impressed me in that way."[6]

"The way that I play a ballad is very much influenced by listening to Ben Webster playing the saxophone," Taylor says.

I learned from him by playing in his combo. He was one of the very few musicians at that particular time of my career who encouraged me to play in a style that later became a vivid part of the manner of which I play the piano, which was based on something I had learned from Ellington. In the introduction to *In a Mellotone*, Ellington played a ninth chord in his left hand, and on top of the ninth chord he was playing a note that was the fifth of the chord. If you play in A-flat the ninth is B-flat, and the note on top of that, the fifth of the chord, will be E-flat. I just loved the sound of that, and I began to do other variations of that, so at the time I joined Ben Webster and his group I was playing a little like that. Ben was the first one that I worked with who liked it and encouraged me to do that. He just liked the sound of what I was doing and said, "Why don't you do some more of that?"[7]

Musicians would regularly sit in on each other's gigs, and Taylor remembers that the Three Deuces was no exception. "Usually the people that sat in at the Three Deuces at the time would be someone who was extremely well known, like Roy Eldridge or someone like that. It would never be someone like me coming in off the street, so it was quite an experience for me and much more than I hoped for when I came to New York."[8]

One of the musicians to sit in was the young, newly married drummer Shelly Manne, who lived next door to the Three Deuces and had recently been drafted.

When I was shipped out, my wife was working at Radio City Music Hall. Our apartment was on 52nd, and Ben Webster would make sure that she got home safely. He'd manage to take five just about the time when she was walking home. He'd see her to the door of our place. But was I miserable while I was away! Not only missed my wife. I missed The Street. The first night after I returned, I was down at the Three Deuces sitting in. It was a Ben Webster trio, with Big Sid Catlett on drums and Al McKibbon on bass. I didn't even bother to take off my Coast Guard uniform. Two shore patrolmen came in and dragged me off the stand. Said I had no right to perform in my uniform. Believe me, these guys were nervous when Ben and Al and Sid followed us out into The Street. They didn't call Ben The Brute for nothing. And Al and Sid weren't small either. Those shore patrol guys sure took off in a hurry—me with them. Nothing came of it. When we got to headquarters and I made my explanation about being home on leave and living on the block, the CO told those shore patrol guys off.[9]

The booking at the Three Deuces did not last long for Taylor. In December trumpeter Dizzy Gillespie began a booking at the Onyx Club across the street, and he needed a pianist. Since Ben's quintet played the first set at the Three Deuces and Art Tatum played second, whereas Al Casey opened the evening at the Onyx, followed by Gillespie's band, Taylor was able to run across the street and sit in during his breaks. But finally the proprietors at the Three Deuces tired of it and fired Taylor. Even though he only played with Ben for a couple of months, it was an important period for him, and he clearly recalls Ben's playing, which "epitomized the kind of ballad playing that became his signature. He moved people. It was like a concert hall. I mean, Ben was playing things that were so swinging when he was playing up tempo, and so very lovely when he decided to play a ballad. It was a wonderful experience for me, and the audience responded to it."[10]

The considerate behavior toward Manne's wife was typical of Ben. He was always protective of women he was not involved with, just as he always made sure that the young musicians in his group didn't drink too much or begin taking drugs. The young drummer Stan Shaw replaced Sidney Catlett in 1944, and he explains that Ben "talked to me like an uncle. He used to tell me, do this, don't do that, this is good for you, stay away from so and so. . . . Ben had no objections to me drinking, as long as he supervised it."[11] Shaw witnessed several jazz musicians with drug problems, and says that it was Ben's influence that kept him away from such temptations.[12]

Ben thrived on Fifty-second Street, enjoying the freedom away from the straitjacket of a big band, making his own decisions regarding repertoire and how much he himself would play. "With a group, you have more of an opportunity to play—and I've always *liked* to play. This gave me a real chance to play just about as much as I'd want to."[13] In the same interview, he explains his approach to his music. "I like to play things that people understand, or maybe tunes that they could recognize. And so—I play for the people just as much as for myself."[14]

Ben still stayed at the Cecil Hotel, and at one point Milt Hinton and his wife Mona moved in on the first floor, three stories below Ben. The two friends spent as much time together as possible. Once Ben gave the couple an experience they never forgot.

"Well, Ben had chicks, you know," Hinton recalled.

Man, Ben had chicks on top of chicks, ladies of the evening. He was a great sportsman, and he loved it and we loved him. Ben was single, and he loved it. I never remember seeing Ben with too many white girls. They were mostly colored girls.

Ben would get drunk and he would knock on the door. I'd open the door, and here's a whore with Ben. And he'd say, "Milt, Mona, I want you to meet Lucille." And here this chick was with eyelashes six inches long, and out of her nut, right off the block. Mona's in the bed, you know, trying to pull the covers up. No way to get up to put a robe on. And Ben says—well, he's probably got a bottle—"Let's have a drink." And Mona's sitting there, and he sits down at the table, and Mona's got to still stay in bed because she can't even get up to get her robe.

And we would sit, and it would probably be hours. We would sit there and kill this fifth of whiskey talking, you know. And poor Mona would be caught in bed. And Ben would be out of his hut, so he'd finally say, "Okay, I'll see you" And he would split, go up to his room.

That's maybe two-thirty in the morning, three o'clock in the morning. All right, we'd try to go back to sleep. And about seven-thirty, eight o'clock, there's a knock on the door, and this chick's come around. "You'd better go up there and get Ben. I'll kill that son of a bitch. He's got my shoes, and I can't find my shoes, and I've got to go home." She's been out on the street hustling, and she's got a pimp that she's supposed to have a certain amount of money for, and if she shows up by nine or ten o'clock in the morning with no money, this pimp is going to kill her.

So here she's screaming, "Tell that son of a bitch to find my shoes! He's got my shoes!" And Mona says, "Well, honey, you didn't leave them down here." Well, we're looking all over the room to see if the lady's shoes were down here, and she's performing because she can't go back out on the street to finish her evening. Ben is upstairs in the bed stone drunk.

So I put on my robe and I go to Ben's room and I look, and I look, and I can't find this girl's shoes any places.

This chick weighed about 200 pounds and Mona weighed about 105. And Mona says, "Well, darling, keep peace. Here's a pair of my shoes." This chick could only get her toes in one of Mona's shoes. So she trots out of this hotel with Mona's shoes on, you know, to go back to her business.

Well, about ten-thirty in the morning, there's another knock on the door, and I'm sleepy, so I stumble to the door. And here's the bell captain, the bellhop of the hotel. On the way up in the elevator this girl has stumbled and broke a heel on the shoe, and Ben had given the shoes to the bellhop to take them to a shoe repairman to get them repaired. In the meantime, he's gotten drunk and gone to sleep. The chick has got to go, and now the guy can't wake up Ben, so he knocks on my door, says, "Can you give me a dollar and a half for these shoes?" So by noon I got Ben up, gave him the shoes, left the shoes up in his room.[15]

After his break with Ellington, Ben's first recordings were with clarinetist Woody Herman's big band. He was called in three times, and soloed on almost every tune. All of these recordings were made for World Transcriptions for sale to radio stations. The first session took place on November 8, 1943, and Ben is heard on *The Music Stopped* in a warmly articulated eight-bar solo with a supple and soft tone. The solo contains many fine double-time runs, which were typical in his playing in this period. His longest solo is on *I Couldn't Sleep a Wink Last Night*, where he begins with a soft paraphrase on the theme. In following passages, in which he is backed by the orchestra, his tone becomes more aggressive, but never really rough.

On the following session of November 17, Ben solos on *Basie's Basement* and *Who Dat Up Dere?*, both medium tempo tracks. On the former, a blues, Ben is allotted one chorus. Beginning with a simple five-note figure that could have been played by Lester Young, he follows up with several excellent, original, and very well articulated phrases completely devoid of blue notes. On the latter tune, he plays sixteen bars of call-and-response with the other musicians, who back him with a vocal riff. With gradually building intensity, Ben goes from charming to growl-filled figures with both feet solidly on the ground, rounding the solo off excellently.

The last Woody Herman session on January 8, 1944, was quite a marathon in which all of nine popular tunes were recorded. However, only five were later released commercially. On the humorous *Noah*, Ben is heard in an outstanding eight-bar solo of double-time runs in rising intensity, peaking exactly as the orchestra reenters. On *I've Got You under My Skin*, his high-register introduction is so gentle and sensitive that one initially mistakes it for an alto saxophonist, but a few bars later, there is no doubt as to the identity of the player. Ben performs with great commitment, a lovely controlled vibrato, beautiful tone, and very lyrical lines, alternating nicely between double-time runs and calmer figures of long notes. He is at his best and in his most romantic mood in an eight-bar presentation of part of the theme in *Cryin' Sands,* and later in the tune, a solo consists of very elaborate and ornate phrases, concluding with a surprising ascending figure of large intervals.

On February 8, 1944, Ben made his first recording as a bandleader. He was joined by his rhythm section from the Three Deuces, Clyde Hart, Charlie Drayton, and Sidney Catlett in addition to Hot Lips Page. The quintet recorded eight tracks, of which the first five were composed by Ben—all in an AABA form, and curiously, there is not one blues among them. As was the case with Woody Herman, all the recordings were made for radio airplay only. With the exception of *I Surrender Dear,* all tunes were recorded in several takes.

The autobiographical *Woke Up Clipped,* befittingly in a minor key, is in a slow medium tempo. After the theme, Page and Hart share a chorus before Ben closes the tune playing over sixteen bars. His solos are very similar on the two takes. Staying in the middle register, he plays softly and in relaxed, singable phrases. In the second take he expresses himself more freely in the high register to fine effect, still in lyrical lines with restrained phrasing. *Teezol* is an up-tempo tune dedicated to Juan Tizol. Ben presents the singable theme in the high register with a lovely, singing tone. On the three complete takes, Ben's solos are quite similar, although he is more dynamic in the last one, using growl. The rhythm section swings wonderfully, and take 5 differs from the rest in that Ben seems restless, there is more bite in his phrases from the very first note, and his drive is fantastic throughout. *'Nuff Said* is very much like *Woke Up Clipped* in mood and tempo, and in the very lyrical theme. Of the two takes, Ben's solo is most homogenous and emotional on the last. *The Horn* is a quick-paced paraphrase of *I Got Rhythm,* and exists in two takes. Once again, the first take is a sort of test take, as the next take sees him playing far more freely and with more edge from the start. The transition between his first and second choruses consists of a powerful shake, and from then on he is extremely expressive without exaggerating it. Seen from the viewpoint of Ben's contribution, *Dirty Deal* is the least interesting track, as the tune is mainly a feature for Drayton. However, Ben allows himself a solo over the last B-part, playing nicely but without noteworthy details. A ballad, *Don't Blame Me,* was recorded in two complete takes, each consisting of two choruses; the first is a theme presentation shared by Ben and Page. Ben follows with a solo, and Page enters in the last A-part with the theme while Ben improvises on top to conclude the tune. Both of Ben's solos are well articulated, but neither reach a climax, as he plays straightforwardly, using lyrical phrases with a pinch of Hawkins in the eighth-note figures. *I Surrender Dear,* a ballad, offers a lovely theme presentation by Ben; the B-part especially is a gem of mood creation. He shares the last chorus with Page, following the latter's sixteen bars, and utilizing the same singable pattern as before, although failing to reach remarkable peaks. The last tune from the session is *Tea for Two,* also recorded in two complete takes. Performed at a medium fast tempo, the second take is faster and also more expressive. Ben interprets the theme quite freely, after which Page, Hart, and Ben each play a chorus before concluding with a riff chorus. Ben plays excellently on the slower take, whereas he is more expressive and extroverted in the second, growled solo. All in all, a fine debut for the new bandleader.

Ben was busy in the studios over the next two months. On March 4, 1944, he recorded for Blue Note as a member of a group put together by pianist James P. Johnson. Ben plays a fine blues chorus on the slow *Blue Mizz,* performing similar solos on both takes. The moderately up-tempo *Victory Stride* is in a minor key, and likewise exists in two takes. Ben seems to feel comfortable in the key and tempo, because he creates two excellent solos. *Joy-Mentin'* is yet another medium slow tempo blues. Ben plays a warm chorus, but his best contribution that day was the fast *After You've Gone*. In two choruses, he demonstrates a great rhythmic and melodic surplus, not least in a series of breaks. It is surprising that Ben restrains his temperament here. He refrains from building his solo from the second chorus with rising intensity and growl, as was his usual custom. However, one senses smoldering energy just below the surface, waiting to burst free. This is indeed an excellent solo, and one with which Ben was pleased, as he taped it on several of his reels.

There is much more from him on his own Savoy session from April 17, 1944. Teddy Reig was employed by Savoy and remembered this session for its touch of panic. Ben "was working with Raymond Scott's house band at CBS; we had a date set for 9 A.M. with [pianist Johnny] Guarnieri and [bassist Oscar] Pettiford and a drummer. Ben showed at 11:40 and we cut four sides in 20 minutes."[16] The time schedule is probably somewhat exaggerated, because they recorded alternative takes, but there is no doubt that they worked fast, as Ben was due back with Raymond Scott at 1:00 P.M. With the exception of *Blue Skies* and *Kat's Fur*— the theme of which is identical to *'Nuff Said* from February 8, 1944—the tracks are released in two takes. *Honeysuckle Rose* is performed in a comfortable medium tempo; the alternative take being slightly slower than the official take. Ben deals with the first two choruses, played in relaxed phrases, and is followed by a shared chorus from Guarnieri and Pettiford, before Ben swings the tune to its conclusion in a chorus that raises the temperature a few degrees. The two takes are of the same high quality. The form of *I Surrender Dear* is the same as the take from the session on March 25 except for the fact that Ben is the only soloist. Both versions start with a silky, caressing theme interpretation, followed by a shift to double-time via a drum break, after which Ben finishes the tune with a chorus in which the bars are doubled. The two takes differ very little in the first choruses, but Ben's method of building tension in the last A-part is more successful in the alternative take, just as his lines are generally more logical, but also more predictable. The formula and tempo from *Honeysuckle Rose* is repeated in *Blue Skies*. Ben plays excellently, building nicely and using growl in the last chorus without getting too rough. *Kat's Fur* is performed

at a medium pace, and as in the previous tune, broad strokes are not utilized, but due consideration is taken to the minor key mood of the theme.

Through no fault of his own, Ben became the indirect cause of
Lester Young reuniting with Basie's orchestra. Basie was playing at the
Lincoln Hotel, and one evening around December 1, 1943, Ben went over,
probably just to hear the band, which had Don Byas on tenor. The other
tenor saxophonist in the band, Buddy Tate, described what happened.

> I don't know why Basie asked Don to get up and let Ben play. But
> Ben sat down. Now nobody in the world could touch Don Byas at
> that time. Nobody. Not nobody I know. He had everything—
> speed, sound—you couldn't play too fast for him. He was ahead
> of everybody. Well, in the middle of the hotel, you could go down
> to an underpass and across to a bar called Martin's that had
> three-for-ones—three drinks for the price of one. . . .
>
> So, Ben's playing, and Don went over there and he must have
> had about nine or 12 of those drinks. And he couldn't drink
> much—he got crazy when he'd drink. He came back and the guys
> were bragging on Ben. He just sat in the back and listened, and the
> guys were going, "Ohhh, never heard anything like this" and so-
> and-so talking about Ben. He couldn't handle it, man. The way it
> started is Basie said something to him. . . . One word brought
> another and they got to arguing. Then he pulled out this little .22,
> the size of your palm, and said, "All of you, up against the wall."
> I'm telling you, the whole band got against the wall. Basie said,
>
> "Go get him, Buddy."
>
> I said, "Come on, Don."
>
> "You get back there, too."
>
> I did—I got back there with them. So the house dick and the
> valet [of the Basie band] eased up behind him and they pinned
> him, and we brought him uptown [to his hotel]. The next day,
> Basie sent him his salary—two weeks [severance pay]. He raised
> out of the bed, looked at it, and said, "It's about time Basie gave
> me a raise." He didn't remember what had happened the night
> before. The valet said, "He raised you all right, he raised you right
> out of the band."[17]

The outcome was that Lester Young, who was playing the Onyx Club with Dizzy Gillespie's quintet, and Don Byas switched jobs. Although Ben probably would have liked to avoid it, the event boosted the tension between Byas and himself. They still ran into each other at jam sessions at Minton's Playhouse and elsewhere, and even performed together often, not least in Europe, but from then on there seemed to be a rivalry between them that did not always benefit the music.

The spring of 1944 had brought many changes in Ben's quartet. Marlowe Morris replaced Billy Taylor, and in turn was replaced by Clyde Hart in April, while John Simmons joined on bass when Charlie Drayton was employed elsewhere. At some point the quartet became a sextet with the addition of Roy Eldridge and his brother Joe on alto saxophone. It seems that Ben tired of the role of bandleader because he relinquished the job to Sidney Catlett, and in early May he left the Three Deuces for a job with John Kirby's orchestra, which played at the Aquarium Restaurant.

As of April, Ben had doubled with Raymond Scott's big band, which broadcast a fifteen-minute show every afternoon. Stan Shaw was part of the orchestra for a while, and he remembers that

> Raymond Scott had a deal with CBS that was absolutely unique because at that time they hired conductors and then they assigned the musicians to go and play with them. Raymond Scott's deal was that they hired him and I don't know whether he had free rein to hire everybody in the orchestra or if he had to use a certain percentage of staff musicians, but he had the freedom to hire a lot of people. So, he hired *a lot* of jazz musicians. He had these guys on the band. Charlie Shavers and Ben Webster I gravitated to because they were Black, because they were giant jazz musicians, because I loved their music. As a matter of fact, when Charlie Shavers and Ben Webster put together a quintet in the Three Deuces I was the drummer.[18]

At the time radio stations would not hire blacks as regular orchestra members, but Scott jumped this obstacle by hiring his musicians for a week at a time. Ben and Shavers enjoyed each other's company and remained friends until Shavers's death in 1971. "Charlie and I have been friends for years," said Ben.

We've had a lot of fun together all through the years we've known each other. We used to work with Raymond Scott at the radio, you know. And we used to have a lot of fun on that, too, on the intermissions. I could never keep up with Charlie when it came to drinking. We started at one o'clock to rehearse, and then around four, four-fifteen, four-thirty we would record. And then we would take another fifteen-minute break until a quarter to five, and at five we would do the second recording. And I remember many a day that I've been so stoned. I would try to get to the mike, the mike would be over here, but I would be blowing away over there at the right, and the band would crack up, everybody, except Raymond Scott.[19]

Scott was very serious about his work as bandleader, composer, and arranger. He could not tolerate this excessiveness for very long, and Shavers's and Ben's employment was terminated at the end of May.

John Kirby probably hired Ben on Shavers's recommendation. In Kirby's small orchestra Ben was reunited with his old friend "Buzzard," pianist Clyde Hart. Shavers had played with Kirby since 1937 and contributed many arrangements and compositions. With its tight and precise ensemble parts in unison, intricate polyphonic arrangements, and its light swing, the orchestra was a forerunner of the coming cool groups. The repertoire included a number of arrangements of light classical pieces, treatments of children's songs, and popular tunes of the day. With the addition of Ben, the band became a septet, and the many preserved radio transmissions from the Aquarium Restaurant indicate that Ben fit into the many difficult arrangements with surprising ease. During Ben's four months with the band, there were many changes in the lineup. Shavers left in the middle of May, and his place went in rapid succession to Dizzy Gillespie, Hot Lips Page, and Emmett Berry, while drummer Bill Beason was replaced by Cliff Leeman.

That spring Ben performed in Carnegie Hall at a memorial concert for Fats Waller, who had died in December 1943. The concert was held on April 2, but many discographies misdate it as from May 2. A review of the concert mentions that Andy Razaf, who had collaborated with Waller on many tunes, composed a tune especially for the affair, *Big*

Boy, which was sung by Edith Sewell.[20] Ben played with a small group that included, among others, clarinetist Mezz Mezzrow, trombonist Dickie Wells, and Catlett, performing a run-of-the-mill version of *Lady Be Good.*

Ben's next recording session, on May 17, 1944, was as part of the Auld-Hawkins-Webster Saxtet. In general, Hawkins pulls the longest straw, putting his two students in their place. On this first commercial recording of *Salt Peanuts,* Ben follows Auld in a mediocre, growl-filled solo, after which Hawkins enters, bringing the tune to a masterful conclusion. The title of the tune, *Pick-Up Boys,* refers to the fact that bands put together for a special occasion are called pickup bands. Taking the first solo, Ben enters powerfully, but seems uncomfortable and finishes his chorus with disconnected and disjointed phrases. Ben and Auld supply support for Hawkins on, respectively, clarinet and alto saxophone in the ensemble passages of *Uptown Lullaby.* In the concluding chorus, Ben plays the B-part on tenor as beautifully as one might expect.

A weekly radio show called *Flow Gently, Sweet Rhythm* was transmitted from the Aquarium Restaurant, where Ben played with John Kirby's band during the summer, and transcriptions of many of these shows are preserved. Ben seems comfortable, as does trumpeter Dizzy Gillespie, who is sensational on several of the recordings. During the short time Gillespie was in the band, the two of them seem to have inspired each other, which is clearly illustrated in *Rose Room* from May 24, 1944, on which both play extremely well. The ballads create a platform for Ben to impress with his lovely sound and ability to play emotional and personal interpretations of tunes like *Yesterdays,* from May 19 and 22, and *No Love, No Nothing,* from May 10. At the time, his tendency was to adorn medium-tempo tunes with shakes, trills, and descending glissandi, usually keeping things clean and without growl, as in the versions of *Andiology* from June 21 and July 16 and *K.C. Caboose* (*caboose* is slang for jail) from June 14. He shows his more expressive side on *Passepied* from June 14, *Honeysuckle Rose* from July 12, and *Oh, What a Beautiful Morning* from May 22, introduced with a lovely paraphrase of the theme.

At the end of July 1944, Ben left John Kirby's orchestra for a booking in Chicago starting August 1 at the Garrick Lounge[21] next to the Garrick Theatre. The Garrick Lounge housed two music venues, the Garrick Stage upstairs and the Downbeat Room downstairs. Ben's quartet alternated with trumpeter Jesse Miller's band upstairs, while bands led by trumpeter Henry "Red" Allen and clarinetist Fess Williams alternated in the Downbeat Room. It has not been possible to determine the personnel in Ben's rhythm section during this booking, which lasted well in to January 1945, but Ben also played with Allen's band.

Alto saxophonist Johnny Board, who was a member of Miller's band, remembers that Ben spent many of his evenings off sitting in with Miller. "He was an absolute gas," said Board. "He had been influenced by Hawk, as many great tenor players were then. But while Hawk's lyrics [lyrical melody lines] were a bit punchy, Ben Webster played in a smooth, silky way. Some nights there would be three of us on the saxophone— Eddie Johnson, Ben Webster and me—and we would have a ball. Playing with Webster would make you want to go to the woodshed—that is, he made you want to practice."[22]

Ben liked Miller's rhythm section. Pianist Argonne Dense Thornton—he took the Muslim name Sadik Hakim a couple of years later— bassist Rail Wilson, and drummer Hillard Brown were more modern than Allen's rhythm section. When Ben's booking ended in mid-January, he offered Miller's rhythm section a job at the Onyx Club, his next booking. "We thought he was kidding," Hakim says. "But in about a month he sent us first-class sleeping train tickets."[23]

There are no recordings from Ben's six-month stay in Chicago, but on January 24, 1945, shortly after his return to New York, he was called in for a V-disk session. Records from V-disk sessions were distributed to American military personnel around the world, and in the United States as well, for use on public address systems. Most of the other musicians at this session were recruited from Woody Herman's orchestra, among them Herman himself, trombonist Bill Harris, and the young tenor saxophonist Flip Phillips. Surprisingly, *Somebody Loves Me* is performed as a ballad, with Harris soloing for a chorus after Herman's vocal. This is followed by Flip Phillips, playing nicely, and demonstrating how closely he has modeled his sound after Ben's. However, in an emotional and beautifully structured solo over the following, final chorus, Ben reveals who the true master is. Ben and Harris are the only horns on *John Hardy's Wife*, and Ben plays with inspiration, egging the rhythm section on in the final chorus, which swings irrepressibly. Unfortunately, he has technical problems with his saxophone in the middle of the chorus, making him unable to play, and he is forced to let the rhythm section finish the tune without him. Phillips joins them again for a real jam version of *Just You, Just Me,* soloing once again right before Ben, who by now has got his saxophone fixed. Both play good solos: Phillips flows more easily, but Ben is more emotional.

A week later, Ben recorded with trombonist Benny Morton and was reunited with Barney Bigard. Ben's finest contributions are in the ballad *My Old Flame* and the slow blues *Conversing in Blue,* on which he plays extremely emotionally without becoming rough. He almost tiptoes through the first chorus, and opens the second with a couple of shakes much more powerful than we have heard from him before. The fast-paced *Sheik of Araby* and *Limehouse Blues* show him playing inspired saxophone, articulating with ease and delivering fine runs and accents in the most surprising places.

Ben opened at the Onyx Club on January 30, 1945, alternating with Stuff Smith's quartet, replaced a week later by pianist and vocalist Una Mae Carlisle.[24] Ben's quartet at the Onyx Club was occasionally augmented with other horns, and after a while, some changes were made in the rhythm section. "I was with Ben for 15 months on 52nd Street," Hakim recalls.

> Brown and Wilson went back to Chicago when the brownouts came in 1945. New York was it for me. The rhythm section at the Onyx Club became Eddie Nicholson (drums), Gene Ramey (bass) and myself. Many times Roy Eldridge would play with us, or Stuff Smith, or Bob Dorsey, a great tenor player. Then it was Bird—always late. Mike Weston [*sic,* Westerman], the Onyx Club owner, would be frowning as Bird came in late, but after a couple of Bird's choruses, he'd be smiling. One night Bird was very, very late. Bird came in while Ben Webster was drinking at the bar; the rest of us were trioing. Bird picked up Ben's tenor and said *Cherokee.* He played that tenor like he owned it, and Ben was shook. He just kept saying "Give me another double." The thing about this was that nobody could get a sound out of Ben's tenor but Ben himself, due to the thickness of the reed, etc. I saw many

great tenor players try—Prez, Buddy Tate, Ike Quebec, no good![25]

Ben also clearly remembered the weeks Charlie Parker played for him starting in February 1945, and that he behaved in the band much like Billy Taylor the previous year. Parker had arrived in New York toward the end of August 1944 with Billy Eckstine, but left the band because he preferred staying in the city. "I worked at the Onyx Club which was almost directly across the street from the Three Deuces," Ben recalled.

> Dizzy was playing at the Three Deuces, and Charlie Parker was supposed to be playing with me at the Onyx. Just as soon as we finished our set, Charlie Parker would take his alto and go straight across the street to Dizzy's set. Mike Westerman was a real, real nice little guy—he had the place—and when it was time for Charlie to come back, he said, "Where is the fellow—Charlie Parker?" I looked around and asked somebody else in the band, "Where is Bird?" "Oh, with Dizzy!" So every time it was time to go on the bandstand I had to go across the street and get Charlie Parker and tell him, "You work in my band!" He said, "Oh, I'm sorry, Ben," and then he would take his horn. So he worked a full night, thirty minutes with me and thirty minutes with Dizzy, so he just blew the whole night![26]

The situation culminated in March when Charlie Parker left Ben's quintet to become a full-fledged member of Dizzy Gillespie's band.

The same month, Ben saw his friend Clyde Hart succumb to tuberculosis. Hart, who was Ben's age, had been ill for some time and was finally hospitalized. However, he would not stay at the hospital and despite his wife's loving care at home, "Buzzard" died March 19. He was one of the few swing pianists to adjust to the new sounds.

On three recordings under the auspices of Walter "Foots" Thomas on March 8, 1945, Ben is in fine form. On the up-tempo *The Bottle's Empty*, he plays with the same ease, elegance, and lack of growl as on *Limehouse Blues* from the previous session, and he provides a tough swing throughout *Save It Pretty Mama*, while his eight bars on the slow *Peach Tree Street Blues* are among his most lovely and serene from this session.

Between sets at the Onyx Club, Ben would occasionally visit the other clubs to listen. He was always eager to hear anything new, a curiosity that never left him. One time when he had gone over to the Three Deuces to listen to Don Byas, he met a young guitarist named Bill De Arango, just out of Cleveland. "I was introduced to some people down there and I sat in with Byas," Arango recalled.

> He had that speed then. We played something like *Sweet Georgia Brown* at a real crazy tempo. Ben Webster was in the room and when we finished the set he asked me if I'd like to go to work with him; he was across the street at the Onyx.
>
> It really was great working with him because Ben was receptive so far as the new sounds. In fact the first job that Charlie Parker had on the Street was with Ben—the same group that I'm talking about. Many of the older musicians were rejecting the sound at that time but not Ben. It was pretty exciting working there because Ben would allow people to come and sit in. Miles, who was just starting out, would come in and Dizzy, who I guess was the most influential trumpet man among the young musicians. Roy was still the popular big name trumpet player.[27]

In June Ben moved from the Onyx to the Spotlite Club. He alternated sets with pianist and blues vocalist Gladys Bentley, while a twenty-one-year old Sarah Vaughan played piano and sang during intermission.[28]

Aside from his regular jobs, Ben joined in at other musical events as well. Sunday afternoon there were usually jam sessions at Lincoln Square Center on 66th Street between Broadway and Central Park West, and the Audubon Ballroom in Harlem on Broadway and 166th Street. At Lincoln Square Center the band would play dance music.

A young Jackie McLean was present at several of these Lincoln Square Center sessions and remembers one that made an especially deep impression on him.

> I'll tell you who were on the bill that day. Art Blakey, Kenny Clarke, Max Roach, Ben Webster, Dexter Gordon, Sonny Stitt, Red Rodney, Charlie Parker, and Miles Davis. But Miles didn't

even play with Bird on that set. Bird was playing with Ben Webster and Dexter Gordon and Freddie Webster on trumpet. . . .

I heard Sonny Stitt, and then I heard Freddie Webster, and then I heard tenor saxophonist Skippy Williams. Then Bird came in, and they played *Cotton Tail*. I'll never forget that, man, like they played as soon as he came in. I think that's the first time I ever felt the true influence of Charlie Parker. Charlie Parker overwhelmed me. And I sat with my mouth open listening to Dexter Gordon, too. Ben Webster was on the set, and that was his famous solo on Duke's version of *Cotton Tail*, which he played with Bird, and it was beautiful. Kenny Clarke was the drummer and Klook [Clarke] was as hip then as he is now.[29]

In the middle of the summer Ben spent a short vacation in Kansas City. He had not seen his family for quite a while. He had "Ol' Betsy" with him, and a photograph dated July 31, 1945, shows him on stage at the Flamingo Club.[30] Whether he was sitting in, or the club had offered him a job, is not clear.

It may have been during this visit home that he sat in with Lionel Hampton's orchestra. Pianist Milt Buckner, a member of the orchestra recalled that

Lionel Hampton's band and Louis Jordan's band had a battle of music at the Municipal Auditorium in Kansas City. The hall was jammed and packed. Real late at night here comes Ben drunk with his horn. The policemen tried to stop him from coming up on the bandstand. They grabbed him, but Hamp said, "Tut, tut, don't hurt him, don't hurt him. That's the great Ben Webster." So he pulled out his horn and he was putting his neck-sling of his horn on and he leaned over to me and said, "Hey, Buck, play some *Swanee River* in A natural." I thought he couldn't play it, he finally got his mouthpiece on the horn. It took him about 10–15 minutes to get it on. But he played one of the most beautiful solos I've ever heard. In A natural [a difficult key]. And when he put down the horn, he staggered around, drunk. Next morning we had to catch a train from Kansas City to Los Angeles. It took us about two days. When we got there, Ben was already there. He

had flown in. He met us down at the station and he was apologiz-
ing, "No, fellows, I didn't mean that, getting drunk like that."
Because, he's a beautiful guy when he is sober.[31]

After his vacation, Ben returned to New York, where he was
reunited with Teddy Wilson for a session on August 14, 1945. A powerful
shake pops up on *Blues Too,* but the rest of his solo consists of fairly stilted
phrases, whereas his very personal interpretation of *I Can't Get Started* is
far more memorable. On the other tunes, *If Dreams Come True* and
Stompin' at the Savoy, he plays up to his usual standard but without particularly noteworthy details.

Ben plays extremely well at a session on September 1945, as part
of a large orchestra led by Hot Lips Page. He contributes a couple of emotional and well-structured solos on *Corsicana* and *Sunset Blues,* with his
solo on the latter ranking as one of this session's overall best, and on *The
Lady in Debt,* he leads the saxophone group backing Page's vocal, and
plays an exceptionally lovely and well-articulated obbligato during his
second chorus. The exact recording date is unknown—the recordings
probably spanned two days—just as the lineup of the big band is not
entirely identified. Consequently, a tenor saxophonist, often mistaken for
Ben, performs on *Florida Blues;* he may be Dave Matthews, who recorded
with Page during the same period.

On the next to the last day of 1945, Ben performed at New York's
Town Hall with Mary Lou Williams in a concert program including a presentation of her *Zodiac Suite,* a work in twelve movements, inspired by
musician friends born in various signs. Thus *Aries* was dedicated to Ben
and Billie Holiday, while *Taurus* portrayed Duke Ellington and herself.
The work is written for a symphonic orchestra, and Ben performs in one
movement, *Cancer,* dedicated to alto saxophonist Lem Davis. The piece is
played in a slow tempo, and Ben invests all his emotional powers and his
loveliest tone in the ten bars in which he interprets a theme. Following a
middle part for woodwinds, he solos for sixteen bars, playing equally
beautifully, building excellently to a climax before concluding with a well-
structured coda. He also played in the final part of the concert, *Gjon Mili
Jam Session,* in which classical and jazz musicians were united. Due to various misunderstandings along the way, it became quite chaotic. After a

drum solo, Ben was called out to solo. He does his best to salvage the situation, swinging through ten choruses, but losing intensity during the last five. Finally he gives the sign, and the rest of the musicians fall in on the last note.

During these years Ben was affiliated with Joe Glaser's agency, ABC (Associated Booking Corporation) along with several of the most popular acts of the day: Lionel Hampton, Louis Armstrong, Andy Kirk, Stuff Smith, Henry "Red" Allen, Billie Holiday, Ethel Waters, and Helen Humes among others. Glaser had booked him back at the Onyx Club for the last week of October, once again sharing the stage with Sarah Vaughan.

At the Onyx Club Ben still had Thornton, Gene Ramey, and Bill De Arango with him. Roy Eldridge had joined on trumpet and Kelly Martin was on drums. Musicians were still welcome to sit in with the quintet, and one of the very young players who did was Stan Getz, who visited the club in December 1945. "I was with Benny Goodman's band at that time," he remembered,

> and I wanted to get in with this exciting music on 52nd Street. But no one would let me sit in. No one except Ben that is, a beautiful guy.
>
> He knew I was keen and some nights he'd say: "All right, kid, get your horn." And I would blow with the quartet and enjoy that.[32]

Ben also enjoyed having young musicians in his rhythm section, because they generated the energy he liked, and, with his perfect pitch, he had no problem following the new stuff harmonically. However, drummers could be a problem, because he liked them to keep in the background and be timekeepers unless they were soloing or playing a break. "Prez, Ben Webster, and Roy Eldridge were the only people who were really vocal about the new rhythm sections," says Gene Ramey. "The other guys would say, 'Well, man, there's something new. I ain't going to put it down. I might have to go with it.' But Prez, Roy, and Ben played their solo in phrases, and when a guy dropped a bomb in the middle it killed the phrase."[33] Considering how much Ben played and fraternized with young musicians, it's remarkable that he was not influenced by bop music. In that respect, he was conservative and remained true to his own music all his life.

Milt Hinton was sure that the young, eager but inexperienced musicians in Ben's quartet had their share in his excessive drinking at that time. With the high wages Ben was demanding, the clubs could not afford good sidemen. "He got $315 a week," Hinton explained. "But he had to get a $60-a-week bass player, and of course, a $60-a-week bass player in those days was not a top bass player. And he got a $50-a-week drummer. And the things got real bad because those guys didn't know how to play well with Ben. He had to sit down at the piano and show the pianist the chords, he had to show the bass player what notes to play. And this is where his drinking really got the best of him, because he was so destroyed by what was happening to him. So he would go to the bar and sometimes overdo it."[34] Hinton's theory does not fit the evidence available for Ben's first years on Fifty-second Street, when, as we have seen, he was mainly in the company of established musicians. However, during 1947–48 his activities are not as well documented, and there may be some truth to Hinton's claim.

Ben still enjoyed playing pool in his leisure time, and he had become an avid boxing fan. The idol of the day, especially among blacks, was the heavyweight champion, Joe Louis, who held the title from 1938 to 1951. He was a jazz aficionado, a great admirer of Duke Ellington, and attended many of his concerts. Louis and Ben became friends, something Ben remained proud of for the rest of his life. Later Ben befriended the five-time Middleweight champion, Sugar Ray Robinson, and Archie Moore, a great fan of tenor saxophonists like Ben and Lucky Thompson.

There are various versions of the story of how Ben once knocked out Joe Louis. The real version, as told by Ben himself, is as follows: They were riding an elevator alone at the Theresa Hotel in New York, and Louis said to Ben, "Give me a punch!" Ben feigned, pretending to go for Louis's jaw, but instead hitting him in the solar plexus. Louis went down just as the elevator stopped and the door opened. The people waiting in front of the elevator saw him, and soon it was all over town that Ben had knocked out Joe Louis. Ben probably bragged a little about it himself. A few days later, Ben was sitting at the bar in a place called the Copper Rail, across the street from the Metropole. In the mirror he saw Joe Louis walk in. He strolled right over to Ben and hit him with a hard, short punch in the back—and that was the end of it.[35] "Boo-o-om!" Ben recalled later. "Joe hit me in the back, and this was the only time I thought I would really die. And he *laughed!*"[36]

At this time, Ben helped yet another young musician, clarinetist Tony Scott. In a way, Ben became his musical father figure, and he also introduced him to Charlie Parker. "The older men were interested in young musicians in those days," says Scott. "Ben Webster took me under his wing; he watched over me and became my teacher. At his suggestion, I moved from club to club each night, picking up much that I could use in my own playing. Just being around provided the sort of experience that young players can't find today. Whenever I could get to The Street, I'd sit in on all I could. When a half hour was over at one club, I'd go on to the next."[37]

The Onyx Club booking continued into February 1946, and Ben also took part in a couple of Sunday afternoon matinee jam sessions at Club 845 in the new Prospect Café in the Bronx.

On January 31, 1946, Ben joined his old neighbor from Kansas City, pianist Pete Johnson, for a session. Ben plays on two tracks, and his contributions are of varying quality. There are two takes of *Ben Rides Out* in two different tempi. The tune is a blues, and Ben solos all the way through with the exception of the third chorus in each take, where clarinetist Albert Nicholas takes over. The official take is a medium tempo, and Ben builds the first two choruses excellently, but after Nicholas's solo, he plays five choruses without overview or structure, until Nicholas comes in to support him in the last two, which are riff choruses. The alternative take is a little slower, and without question the better of the two in content as well as structure. Ben's first two choruses are quite good, with rising intensity, and after the clarinet solo he starts out playing expressive lines, slacking the dynamics in the following final chorus, creating a symmetrical structure around the clarinet solo. *Pete's Housewarming* is a fast tune, but unfortunately drummer J. C. Heard is somewhat rigid and inflexible, so although Ben builds his solo dynamically as usual, it falls short of full success.

On the afternoon of Saturday, February 9, 1946, a concert was held at New York's Town Hall with the far-from-heartening title "Exit

Singing—90 Minutes of What's Left of Jazz." The concert, which intended to show that not all "good" jazz was destroyed by bebop, presented the vocalists Red McKenzie and Stella Brooks in a series of Dixieland tunes and a number of new compositions by Willard Robison. Aside from Ben the performers included pianists Ram Ramirez and Joe Sullivan, drummers Cozy Cole and Danny Alvin, tenor saxophonist Bud Freeman, cornetist Bobby Hacket, and trombonist George Brunies.[38]

For a couple of weeks from the end of February, Ben and his trio were booked at the Bengazi Club in Washington, D.C. De Arango had left the group to play with Ray Nance.[39] One evening Art Tatum came in, and an enthusiastic Ben invited his idol to sit in. Although Tatum declined, Ben kept pressing him until Tatum aired his irritation by setting an impossible tempo for Webster to play with, so fast that Webster had to drop out after less than two choruses.[40]

Ben's young friend from Fifty-second Street, clarinetist Tony Scott, arranged a session for Gotham on March 6, 1946, and he sent for Ben to come to New York to record with him. The first tune recorded was *All Too Soon,* performed in two choruses. The almost-twenty-two-year-old Sarah Vaughan does a fine job on the first chorus, and Ben takes the tune out. His solo is very successful; combining paraphrase and freely articulated lines, it is played with a wonderful sense of structure and presented with an emotional and warm sound. The romantic and rarely heard *You're Only Happy When I'm Blue* is set in the same slow pace, and Ben solos for sixteen bars, sticking close to the melody line throughout, concentrating instead on imbuing his presentation with emotion. The final track from this session is the up-tempo *Ten Lessons with Timothy.* Ben plays well throughout his chorus, although without noteworthy details.

After the job in Washington, Ben returned to the Three Deuces on Fifty-second Street, and in May the whole rhythm section had been replaced by pianist Al Haig, bassist John Simmons, and—once again—Catlett on drums and De Arango on guitar. Seventeen-year-old drummer Ed Shaughnessy came by one evening to hear Catlett:

He was the one who approached me because I was certainly too shy to approach him. He asked if I was a drummer. I told him I was trying to be and Sidney said, "Well, I'll tell you what—you're going to play part of the next set." I almost flipped because the group included Ben Webster and John Simmons, one of Sid's favourite bassists.

I was too scared to say no and too scared to play! When it was time for the next set, Sidney came over and said, "Let's go." And I said, "I couldn't do that—I'm not good enough." And he replied, "You'll never get good unless you play with better players." And with that he just picked me up and scooted me along to the stand. All the sidemen were friendly and I played two or three tunes. I'm sure I was anything but good but they were gracious.[41]

Ben recorded twice for Haven in May 1946. On May 3, Bill De Arango was the bandleader. He took Ben's regular quintet, of which he was a member, with him, as well as trumpeter Leonard Graham, who later took the Muslim name Idrees Sulieman, and Tony Scott. Like De Arango, he was already based in bop, and plays with conviction within that new style. The rhythm section consisted of Argonne Thornton, John Simmons, and Sidney Catlett, whose insisting drive pushes the music on. Despite De Arango's leadership, Ben is featured most, and two of the four recorded tunes are his compositions. He is inspired on *The Jeep Is Jumpin'*. A general characteristic on this session are his lines of varying length, which break with the common two- or four-bar phrases. Played over one and a half choruses, *I Got It Bad and That Ain't Good* is a feature for Ben with the exception of a guitar solo over the B-part after the first chorus. The track is one of the best to come out of this session due to Ben's vivid and extremely sensitive interpretation. *Dark Corners* begins with breaks by Catlett, Simmons, Scott, Graham, Ben, and Thornton, followed by one-chorus solos from De Arango, Graham, Scott, and Ben. Ben plays a well-built solo, contrasting with *The Jeep Is Jumpin'* in that it is not filled with growled phrases. *Blues, Mr. Brim*—"Brim" is possibly a nickname for Ben, who used to wear a hat—is a slow-tempo tune, introduced over four bars by Ben, before De Arango plays a chorus, followed by two from Ben, and concluded with yet another chorus by De Arango. Ben builds his solo from soft-spoken and supple phrases in the first chorus to dynamic outbursts in the beginning of the second before finishing off with airy, descending figures of trills. This method of concluding a tune was to become one of his trademarks; in his last years, there was sometimes more air than tone.

The second session for Haven took place on May 15, 1946, and this time the group was Ben's regular quintet. Argonne Thornton had been replaced by Al Haig, but the rest of the band remained the same. Ben wrote all the music for this session, but later there has been some confusion as to which titles go with which tunes, because RCA jumbled some of them when reissuing the music on LP, and subsequently the mistakes have been repeated on several CD releases. The discographer Heinz Baumeister has studied this matter, and by comparing the original 78s with various releases on LP and CD he has surmised that *Frog and Mule* is a variation on *I Got Rhythm, Spang* is based on *These Foolish Things, Doctor Keets* builds on the harmonic structure of *Johnny Come Lately,* while *Park & Tilford Blues* is, as the title suggests, a blues.

The title *Frog and Mule* refers to the nicknames of Ben and his girlfriend, and in the beginning of his interpretation, Ben almost caresses the lovely melody. The tempo is medium, and Ben plays but one chorus after his theme presentation, telling a nice little story with few detours. The next chorus is shared between Haig and De Arango, after which Ben turns up the heat with an expressive concluding chorus. Apparently *These Foolish Things* was popular among jazz musicians at the time. Lester Young had already recorded it twice, and given it an especially masterful interpretation in January 1946, when he began improvising from the very start without prior theme presentation. Undoubtedly, Ben had heard this recording, and he gives the tune his own treatment in *Spang,* playing it over one and a half choruses, as did Lester Young. Ben starts out with a paraphrase on the theme, gradually building intensity and dynamics, and in the third A-part he plays a phrase containing catchy, large intervals. He fails to achieve Young's serenity and clarity until the final A-part; other than that, he is too busy, and his sound is a little rough. In contrast, he has a soft and lovely theme presentation on *Doctor Keets,* followed by solos from Haig and De Arango, who displays exquisite technique. Ben solos on the two last choruses. He strolls the first, meaning that the pianist takes a break, leaving the soloist alone with bass and drums. Ben plays gentle and sometimes stilted phrases. Haig reenters in the final chorus, and Ben takes off on a dynamic flight into altissimo notes, after which he swings for the rest of the tune, in regular phrases, and masterfully assisted by Catlett, who is a true pleasure throughout the session. De Arango commences *Park & Tilford Blues*—dedicated to a whiskey—with two choruses, and is followed by Haig and Simmons, Ben, Catlett, and Ben again, taking two choruses each. The tempo is medium, and Ben's first contribution is made up of excellent lines, building only slightly dynamically in the second chorus. Following the drum solo, he tiptoes in again on cat's-paws with a fine riff chorus; then, as in *Doctor Keets,* he introduces the final chorus with a slightly unmotivated expressive outburst in altissimo notes before concluding the tune somewhat abruptly.

During the summer Al Haig was replaced first by Billy Taylor and later by Sonny White[42] in an otherwise stable rhythm section.

By this time, Benny Carter had settled in Los Angeles. In August 1946, he visited New York briefly and put together a group consisting of Ben and his rhythm section, the young trombonist from Carter's own band, Al Grey, and trumpeter Buck Clayton. The band recorded four tunes on August 23, and, as usual, Catlett is a superb driving force. The first tune recorded was *Sweet Georgia Brown* with Carter playing the first solo on clarinet, while Ben is featured last. Ben builds an excellent solo in his customary pattern, going from restrained phrases to expressive, growled lines, and is lyrical in his sixteen bars on *Out Of My Way. Cadillac Slim,* composed by Ben, is dedicated to a friend with that nickname. The tune is an ill-disguised variation of Strayhorn's *Rain Check.* All four horns are featured in the up-tempo tune, with Ben dealing with the B-part of the theme, and subsequently taking the first solo. He delivers a fine solo, elaborating on a figure introduced in the second A-part, and beginning the B-part with a descending glide. Carter and Ben chase through the next chorus in four-bar exchanges. Carter takes the lead, and it is interesting that Ben attempts to pick up on Carter, imitating his figures and elegant phrasing, but as he has not developed Carter's fluid technique, he never quite succeeds.

By April 1947 Ben's daily alcohol intake was large enough for him to be diagnosed as an alcoholic, and in July he had a nervous breakdown and was admitted to Bellevue Hospital. His girlfriend at the time, Mule, took care of him after he came home, and had him admitted to a clinic in the country. He was detoxicated and put on an alcohol program, although without any long-lasting effect. However, his mind and body were given a temporary rest.[43]

September 1947 saw him back on Fifty-second Street, at the Famous Door, with a swing band with Buck Clayton, Eddie Barefield, and Benny Morton in front. At this time jazz business on the Street was low and declining, and this booking represented the last spasm from the Famous Door, before the club replaced jazz with striptease.

On New Year's Eve 1947, Dick Katz substituted for the regular pianist, Joe Springer. "I was just getting started," Katz says,

> and Ben Webster was one of my heroes, so I was very nervous. He was very kind, and he encouraged me.
>
> I never worked extensively with him. I knew him and played with him here and there, but I was never associated with him like I was with Roy Eldridge, who I spent years with. Ben's personality was overwhelming. He had a great charisma, a great magnetism. If he was coming around the corner, you would know it before he even got there. You could feel him—he had that electric energy. He belonged to one of the greatest. I would say that in his period the three greatest were Coleman Hawkins, Ben Webster, and Lester Young, and not far behind was Don Byas. In fact, Don Byas had more facility than any of those three.
>
> Ben was different from Coleman Hawkins, because he was a much more abstract improviser. He played like a singer. If you were a singer I would advise you to listen to him phrase. Rhythmically he was very sophisticated, much more sophisticated than Coleman Hawkins, much more complex. I'm sure he had a big influence on Charlie Parker, although people don't talk about that. I don't know of any other musician during the swing era that had this quality that Charlie Parker had where he could start a phrase in any part of the bar. Ben had that mastery of the meter. He could turn the time around, so you had to listen carefully to where he was in the piece. He never got credited for how sophisticated he was with the rhythm. You really had to pay attention or he could lose you, especially in medium tempos.

He also was a great blues artist. He obviously absorbed the blues he heard in the Kansas City and the Southwest, and he found his own way. And nobody had made that sound before. Ben was one of the true originals. He was also a terrific composer, and he had a style that fit in anywhere. It was no problem, because he rhythmically was so flexible.

He sacrificed speed. He never could play fast and long lines like Don Byas or Coleman Hawkins did. But it didn't matter. He played the fast tempos in his own way. Ben had a great sense of humor. He was so imaginative in his playing, but he was not an intellectual player like Benny Carter. Sometimes he could sound like a cello. There is something in his sound that reaches out and grabs you, actually more than any other player.

The entrance, the first few bars of a solo, tells you if you want to hear more or not, and Ben Webster made the greatest entrances to solos than anybody. Ben was very dramatic.

Ben made some recordings while he was on Fifty-second Street that really captures the sound of what a quartet sounded like in those days. The record with Al Haig, Sid Catlett, and John Simmons with *Spang* and *Frog and Mule* is beautiful. On one of the titles he strolls, which means that he would tell the piano player to lay out, to stop playing, and then he would build a whole dramatic solo, starting very soft just with the bass. He was very wonderful at that.

At a job he would go in with the rhythm section with a list of tunes, and maybe bring a lead sheet for some original pieces, but they had no arrangements. But Ben could spontaneously make an arrangement on the spot. By using dynamics, and by strolling he could shape a piece right there, just by playing the head, a solo, and take it out. I wish more young people could do this.

Ben had very good taste. He knew what he was doing. He didn't play long solos, but only a few did in those days. Even Charlie Parker didn't play long solos; that started with the advent of tape and innovations of John Coltrane. All during the swing era jazz had to function as entertainment. Improvised solos in public wasn't the main attraction. You had to have arrangements.

Even the small groups on Fifty-second Street had arrangements they would do, and it was all based on the idea to play a lot of material, but not real long performances. Ben Webster was aware of all that. He would never play long. He had a keen sense of structure when he played. He was also great at playing melodic variations rather than play on the changes.[44]

It is hard to trace Ben's activities—where he played, whom he played with—through all of 1948, possibly because he worked as a sideman in various groups. It was as a sideman that Charlie Shavers asked him to join a new band in September. Shavers, clarinetist Buddy DeFranco, and drummer Louie Bellson had left Tommy Dorsey's big band to start their own sextet, and they needed Ben to complete the band with pianist Hank Jones and bassist John Simmons. Ben accepted the offer, and they agreed that he would meet up with the rest of the group for their first booking, at Al Barnes' Horseshoe Club, Rock Island, Illinois, in the beginning of October.

However, Ben never showed up, the reason being that he had received an offer in Washington, D.C., to front a local rhythm section at a club for a substantially larger wage, a job that also began in October 1948. In Washington he ran into Duke Ellington, who was in town for the opening of Club Ellington, a tribute to him as a Washingtonian. The opening night was October 22, and the orchestra was booked for two weeks. Ben sat in a few times, and it went so well that his old employer gave him an offer. "We met," Ben recalled, "and I think Duke asked me how I was doing, you know. We talked a little, and he said, 'Why don't you come home?' So I said, 'You're crazy!' But he offered me more bread than I had with my own band, so I went back in the band. I won't say I fit right in the hole, because when you've been out of the band for awhile it takes time to fit back in. It was a sweet feeling to sit and play with guys like Johnny Hodges, Harry Carney, the brass section, and all the guys again."[45]

Ben started immediately and was already in the saxophone group at the orchestra's next booking on November 6 at Union College in Schenectady, New York. In a radio transcription from the date he is heard with Al Sears—who takes the first tenor solo—in *You Oughta*, playing with much expression but with poor overview. He is not sure how long his solo is, because he stops shortly midway, turning away from the microphone for a sign to either continue or stop.

The next booking, the orchestra's traditional annual Carnegie Hall concert on November 13, was a great success. "As befits a gentleman bearing a royal title, Duke Ellington, on the occasion of his sixth annual visit to Carnegie Hall, presented a performance that was superb," wrote *Down Beat,*[46] and Ben's contribution was highly praised. "Outstanding show stopper from the reed section, however, was Ben Webster, performing one of the two non-Ellington compositions on the program, *How High the Moon.* Obliging with three choruses, he displayed wonderful virtuosity, and the Ellington fans-of-long-standing gave Ben a welcome home he long should remember."

At the concert, Ellington featured Ben in three tunes, *How High the Moon, Cotton Tail,* and *Just a-Settin' and a-Rockin'.* The arrangement of the first tune was a stroke of genius from Ellington's hand, and the review of Ben's performance is quite right. Initially Ben interprets the tune at a slow pace. Following a short orchestral interlude, the tempo is doubled in the next chorus. This same procedure is repeated twice, each time after an interlude. This affords Ben the opportunity to show several sides of his personality in the same tune. His masterful interpretation in the slow tempo is performed in his most sensitive, intense fashion, and he starts improvising after only sixteen bars. He swings his way through the next chorus in medium tempo, and goes into high gear for the final two choruses, although slightly hampered now by Greer's drumming, which is somewhat heavy-handed. In the coda, Ben follows the same procedure as the arrangement of the tune; following a few quiet lines, he winds up on the root note of the song in fortissimo, growling in altissimo notes. *Cotton Tail* adds nothing new; the tune, as well as Ben's solo, follow the same structure as earlier Ellington versions. His beautiful and soft conclusion to the coda is noteworthy, although it clashes somewhat with the violent final big-band chord that follows. He interprets the theme of *Just a-Settin' and a-Rockin'* without frills—there are no surprises here either.

Aside from few exceptions, an Ellington concert at Cornell University in Ithaca, New York, on December 10, 1948, was a repetition of the repertoire from the Carnegie Hall concert. Ben's best contribution is on *How High the Moon.* The up-tempo passages in his solo are propelled by a fantastic drive and are far more aggressive and extroverted than earlier versions.

In January 1949 the Ellington orchestra traveled to the West Coast for five weeks of which the middle three, February 1–20, were booked at the Hollywood Empire Hotel. The booking was followed by a week at the Million Dollar Ballroom in Los Angeles.

In Los Angeles, Ben had the opportunity to get together with Benny Carter again. Carter had settled permanently in the city in 1942, working as a composer and arranger for movies and television. In early 1949, Carter and Ben organized a recording for the small label, Modern, using trombonist Vic Dickenson, pianist Dodo Marmarosa, and drummer Jackie Mills. Ben is the only soloist on the four sides recorded, and he plays with far greater enthusiasm, presence, and inspiration than on what is preserved from Ellington's booking at the Hollywood Empire Hotel. The records were released as performed by "Benny Carter and His All Stars," but should have been called Ben Webster and His All Stars, as Carter later recalled this session as Ben's.[47] The first tune is *Cotton Tail*. After the introductory chorus, Ben repeats his routine solo followed by an inspired chorus, in which the most interesting part is the B-part, where figures are played freely on the rhythm. Marmarosa solos for sixteen bars, after which Ben improvises over yet another B-part before the entire band brings the tune to conclusion. The next tune is the medium tempo *Time Out for the Blues,* with Ben doing all the soloing in two choruses between theme presentations. He begins with a couple of soft figures followed by a powerful shake, continuing with forceful and solid playing, demonstrating how a blues should be treated to be most convincing. Before release, applause and exclamations were added to both tracks to create the illusion of a live atmosphere, and the matrix numbers indicate that the two subsequent tracks were recorded a few days later. *Surf Board* is a Benny Carter composition in medium tempo, and once again Ben is the only soloist. He plays two choruses following the theme, going into overdrive in the second. Here, the two first A-parts begin with an outburst in altissimo notes, and he finishes the chorus with peculiar wavelike figures. He improvises the B-part of the final chorus, painting with a broad and soft brush with dynamics brought all the way down to piano. The pearl of the session is an extremely beautiful and romantic version of *You Are Too Beautiful*. His sound is full, rich, and dark in the middle register, and when going into the high register, he holds back slightly, thereby giving the sound a softer, lighter tone and creating an intimate atmosphere. Ben's phrasing is superb and his interpretation extremely emotional, creating a master-piece, and without question one of his very best recordings from the 1940s. Along with the live recording of *Danny Boy* from 1947, *You Are Too Beautiful* is the first example of the fully matured Webster's ballad treatment.

In July, the orchestra was booked at the Regal Theatre in Chicago. Bassist Richard Davis recalls that it was the first time he'd seen Ben play.

> I had been writing with Jimmie Blanton's mother for many years, and she told me they would be in town, because her nephew Wendell Marshall, Jimmie Blanton's cousin, was playing with the band. So I went to the Regal Theatre in Chicago to see the band, and I met Wendell Marshall, who told me to come back the next morning to the hotel they were staying in, before they had to leave on the bus. When I got there, all the band members were saying, "Who is going to wake up Ben?" And they talked about it for about five minutes. One guy said, "I woke him up the other night. It's your turn!" I didn't understand why there was so much conversation going on about who was going to wake up Ben Webster. Well, I found out that when you wake him up, he starts fighting. You had to touch him with a broomstick and jump back! That's the funniest thing I had heard in my life.[48]

In January Al Sears had left the band, and he was replaced by young Charlie Rouse. Ben and Rouse knew each other from Rouse's school days in Washington, D.C. "I liked Ben Webster an awful lot," Rouse recalled.

> We became very good friends. Ben was actually the first one who told me about Charlie Parker. At that time musicians would do that if they heard a musician who could play.
>
> But I was really close friends with Ben. In fact when he came to town, right after school I used to go up to the Howard Theatre and wait at the stage door. When he saw me he'd smile and say, "C'mon kid."[49]

Ben became an important person in Rouse's life, and it must have been like a dream come true to be part of the same saxophone group. "Somebody's always saying that I was influenced by this or that guy," he continues, "but never mention the guy who really influenced me—Ben Webster. I dug his sound so, the warm sound he got on ballads."[50]

Ben had played his last job with the Ellington orchestra that summer. Exactly when he left the band is not known, but his replacement, Jimmy Forrest, has a solo on *St Louis Blues* on a radio transcription from the Click Restaurant in Philadelphia from the week of August 26–September 3. The orchestra was not booked for more than two weeks following the Regal Theatre in Chicago, so it is most probable that Ben rode the band bus back to New York on July 8, leaving the band upon his arrival, with Jimmy Forrest taking his place at the next concert, on July 25 at Robin Hood Dell in Philadelphia.

The reasons for leaving this time could be that Ben, Ellington, and the orchestra could not fulfill each other's long-term expectations. Much had changed in the five-year interim since Ben's first departure from the group. Although Ben may have felt that he warranted star status, the band included many other musicians who deserved the same treatment. Ben was not featured as much as he may have hoped; one reason being that, except for a few months, the band included another tenor saxophone player to share solo space, first Al Sears, and from May 1949, Charlie Rouse. Finally, Ellington had disappointed Ben gravely by dissuading him from enrolling at Juilliard School of Music. Ben had asked for his advice, because he had wanted to study more advanced music theory, and Ellington had wisely answered, "You'll only learn what you already know, and it will mess you up." Ben had been furious, thinking that Ellington wanted to keep him from learning. He had complained to pianist Jimmy Jones, but had found no consolation there. After a short time in New York, he packed his car, said goodbye to his friends, and drove home to Mayme and Mom in Kansas City.

7. From Kansas City to Monterey
(1949–1959)

Ben was now forty years old, and it may seem strange that he returned to his childhood home at such a mature age, but the employment situation for jazz musicians in New York had been worsening for some time. By 1950, the only jazz club left on Fifty-second Street was Jimmy Ryan's, and it featured mainly traditional jazz. Birdland had opened on December 15, 1949, and along with Bop City and Jimmy Ryan's, they were the only venues in midcity presenting jazz. Greenwich Village boasted several spots with programs much like Jimmy Ryan's, for example, Eddie Condon's, Nick's, and the Riviera Lounge. Café Society had a broader program policy, but even the Village Vanguard had not been booking jazz for a while.[1] Venues were few, and even the small clubs in Harlem, previously Ben's safety net, were probably booking less.

His personal life was in crisis as well. While in New York, Mule had told him that she had done some thinking while he was touring with Ellington. She had decided not to marry him, but rather another beau, Bob, who was an airport porter and a friend of Ben's and, like him a Freemason. The news was a blow to Ben, but as was the case with Eudora, they separated as friends and remained in contact. Mule and Bob visited Ben together in Amsterdam and Copenhagen, and Mule even attended Ben's funeral.[2] However, at the time, the feeling of being rejected as a man, as well as professionally, apparently overpowered Ben. He left New York and went home to Kansas City, where he would be able to take some care of Mayme and Mom, respectively seventy-seven and eighty-five. They would help him regain his self-confidence, and he hoped that the musical situation in Kansas City would be less tight than in New York.

Kansas City had changed a lot since Ben left eighteen years ago.

The Pendergast regime had fallen in 1938, but the nightlife continued, although things changed here as well. Clubs closed, new ones opened, and others continued under new names. The city no longer housed big bands, but several small jazz and blues bands remained: the Five Aces and the Four Tons of Rhythm, as well as groups led by saxophonist Tommy Douglas, pianist Jay McShann, alto saxophonist Herman Walder, pianist and vocalist Julia Lee, pianist and vocalist Buster "Bus" Moten (brother of Bennie Moten), vibraphonist Bob Wilson, trumpeter Oliver Todd, vocalist Walter Brown, and many others.[3]

The consensus is that Ben culminated artistically during the 1950s and early 1960s, and though it is true that his best-selling albums were released during these years (*King of the Tenors* in 1957 and *See You at the Fair* from 1964), Ben developed his craft all through his life. His playing reached a great depth in expression, and during his last years, his ballad interpretations crystallized in sublimely touching statements. From 1952, when he became affiliated with Norman Granz, he toured with Jazz at the Philharmonic and recorded a long list of Granz-supervised albums in his own name and as a sideman, but took part in sessions for other labels as well. Ben felt at home in diverse musical settings, not least accompanying vocalists, and Granz often used him in situations where Ben's ability to immerse himself in a song lent extra dimensions to a session. His playing had always been complex, but these years saw it unfold in a richness of nuance matched by few other saxophonists. In fact, he was more versatile than two fellow stylistic giants and instrumental associates, Coleman Hawkins and Lester Young, in that he adjusted better to diversified musical demands, from jazz through R&B, even including a 1972 recording with the rock band Savage Rose.

Ben's sound reached new heights of richness and beauty, and over the years his ballads became subtle and delicate, radiating warmth, romance, and lyrical emotions without ever crossing the fine line to sentimentality. One often senses a smoldering intensity under the surface, a suppressed passion waiting to burst forth. His register of expression was overwhelming, and his drive in fast tempi was forceful, for presence and potency were still an important part of his style. His ability to swing and lead a rhythm section was great, particularly in medium tempi, and he remained a master of dynamics and phrasing. He always had a story to tell; while his ballads spanned a large range of expression from subtle and suggestive to profoundly stirring, his blues interpretations were usually much more direct, at times even sermonizing. His phrases and lines can be perceived as wordless speech, by which we surmise what is on his mind.

At forty, Ben had a certain amount of influence on many young saxophonists, despite the fact that he was not as original as his contemporary, Lester Young. Many young saxophonists admired Ben's ability to create a mood, his ballad playing, and his impressive sound. "Ben Webster was my first hero," Johnny Griffin recalled. "Ben Webster to me was a 'sound man.' When I say 'sound man,' I mean when he played the saxophone. Most times when he played a ballad he could make you cry. Then he could get rough and gruff; that's why I called him El Brutus. He was like someone out of *Jurassic Park,* or something, a dinosaur coming over the hill. But he would never bite, you know."[4] "Ben's sound was so warm and enveloping," said Griffin on another occasion. "Ben could play one note and you could play one hundred notes, and he'd get more effect out of one note than you'd get out of one hundred."[5] Archie Shepp was influenced by Ben's sound as well.

> My sound has been compared with Webster and I feel more and more humble every day about that because I think he was one of the most sophisticated and perfected voices on the instrument that I've heard. And then Webster seems to have added a dimension. Prez is very important from the point of view of sound, but his emphasis wasn't sound. Even Hawkins, who was gifted with perhaps the generic saxophone sound, it wasn't something he concentrated on so much as something he had. But Ben seems to have understood, the way Coltrane did later, the implications of what the saxophone could do. That these trick notes, as they call them, really weren't trick notes but were, in fact, another way of vocalizing sound. That was where I took off from. From Ben and Coltrane. They were my two biggest influences.[6]

Eddie "Lockjaw" Davis credits Ben as the greatest influence on his development, clearly heard in his ballad interpretations and his use of growl. In April 1953 they were both playing in Basie's orchestra, and Ben would call him "Little Ben," because Davis sounded so much like him.[7] Frank Foster was another tenor saxophonist who tried to copy Ben's sound. "I really did want to sound *something* like Ben Webster," he said, "but I still wanted to be myself! I liked the way he played, I liked the sound, I liked his way of getting over the instrument, and his tone was just beautiful. I've been striving for a beautiful tone for years and years, and it seems as though I'm only now on the threshold of acquiring a tone."[8] Ben's rich and translucent ballad interpretations influenced many saxophonists, among them Dexter Gordon, Sonny Rollins, Flip Phillips, John Hardee, Jimmy Giuffre, Harold Land, Ike Quebec, Georgie Auld, John Coltrane, and much younger musicians such as Scott Hamilton and Branford Marsalis. Charlie Ventura—and later David Murray—emulated his use of growl. This rough style also inspired R&B and rock saxophonists, who often combined the use of growl with altissimo notes.

Ben arrived in Kansas City during the fall of 1949. He moved in with his mother and grand-aunt at 1222 Woodland Avenue, and began going around to the clubs, sitting in and looking for a job. The rumor of his arrival traveled quickly, and he soon landed a gig at the Parkview Hotel, as well as two recording sessions for Capitol. On October 31, he recorded as a member of Bus Moten and His Men. Ben plays on four sides, and performs straightforwardly and well on *Turn It Over* and the moderately fast-paced blues, *Baby You Messed Up,* whereas his two blues choruses on the slow *Best Friend Blues* are given far more weight and emotion.

The following day, November 1, 1949, he recorded four excellent sides with Jay McShann's Kaycee Stompers and blues vocalist Walter Brown. He is far more inspired than at the previous day's session, which seems pale and superfluous in comparison. *New Style Baby* swings very well in a medium tempo, particularly in Ben's solo, which follows the same pattern in both takes, with more intensity in the second chorus, in which his figures are slightly more laid-back. *Let's Love Awhile* offers the same tempo and swing, with Ben even better, supporting Brown with one delicious obbligato after another after two outstanding solo choruses. In *Nasty Attitude,* he delivers an obbligato behind Brown's vocal, telling just as much of a story as the vocalist; then he plays an extremely heartfelt solo that develops into an obbligato behind Brown in the last chorus. On *Slow Down Baby,* Ben's solo is first-rate, as is his obbligato in the concluding chorus. Unfortunately, Ben did no more recording during his stay in

Kansas City until two years later, but this session is a fine conclusion to a chapter in his career, and proves that despite his personal crisis at the time, he was able to achieve superb results when in the right company.

At the latter of the two sessions with Moten, the young tenor saxophonist Harold Ashby dropped by to listen to his hero. "I liked Ben's sound," he says, "the sound of his instrument. I liked his playing, too, but nobody can play like Ben. It was his sound that influenced me."[9] "I was trying to play like Ben," he remembers. "You have to be inspired by someone. I heard all of them play, and I liked Ben. When I heard him—that was it."[10] "I was playing with a little group, and Ben used to come around and sit in with us," Ashby goes on. "We was young kids then, we was like 24. And Ben wanted to be around the young cats then, so he'd come around and sit in with us. That's the way we began to know each other." Ben liked Ashby and took him under his wings, a little like he had with Jimmie Blanton. When he discovered that Ashby's saxophone needed work, they drove in Ben's coupe to the best repairman they could find. "Ben drove me up to like Elkhart, Indiana [home of the Selmer saxophone factory], one time, to take my horn up there. And the man fixed my horn and gave me a *cut rate*," Ashby recalls. "You know, because I was with *Ben Webster*. The man overhauled the horn. Then Ben drove me back up there to get it. Yeah, Ben was a good friend, man."[11]

Often Ben would sit in with Ashby's group, and other times Ashby would go by the nightclub at the Parkview Hotel, which was a hangout for Kansas City's lowlife. One night was engraved in his memory as a picture of how Ben's music could affect an audience. "Everything he would play was very emotional and reached people's hearts, everybody. It told a story, man," he recalled.

> I was standing at the bar one time when Ben was playing a solo, you know, one of the ballads. And there was this girl, you know, one of the top-notch girls. There was a fellow there who bought her drinks, and he offered her about a hundred dollars while Ben was playing the solo. And she said, "No, no, not right now, I want to listen to Ben." And he said, "Look here, baby, a hundred dollars!"—a hundred dollars to turn the trick. At that particular time, in 1949, that was a whole lot of money. But she refused it.

She just stood there and listened to Ben play. I'll remember that. The cash register didn't ring, nothing, everybody stopped. That's how Ben played.[12]

Whom Ben played with at the Parkview Hotel is uncertain, but some time later he was performing with vibraphonist Bob Wilson's orchestra at the Jockey Club, and in 1951 he played an extended booking with Jay McShann's band at the Flamingo Club. The repertoire was mainly blues, as can be heard on the recordings the band made with Ben on October 27, 1951. There had been no stylistic development in the band in the two years since Ben's earlier recordings with McShann. The repertoire still consists of solid, swinging blues, and Ben's playing is rock steady. The most remarkable tune is his own *The Duke and the Brute,* a blues in minor, featuring Ben as the only soloist in an emotional rendition with beautiful, singable lines in the first couple of choruses. Several very distinctive intervals in the second chorus of *You Didn't Tell Me* are interesting, while *Reach* is given a more outspoken treatment concluding with a typical run of growled trills.

In autumn 1951, Mayme and Mom sold the house in Kansas City and moved to Los Angeles, where they had found a nice white house with a garden on Wilton Place, but Ben stayed on briefly. In early December vibraphonist, drummer, and vocalist Johnny Otis played a concert with his band in Kansas City, and Ben met him backstage. Ben must have run into serious financial problems at the time, because Otis remembered, "I asked him if he was still playing. He told me his horn was in hock and I said I'd love to have him in the band if he'd promise to stay sober onstage. He agreed, I got his saxophone out of pawn and he came on the road with us [back to Los Angeles] and we made some wonderful records together."[13]

Ben was most probably overjoyed by Otis's offer. Although the jazz situation in Kansas City was not bad, there was no future in it. The musicians were not of the stature Ben had been accustomed to in New York, and development was stagnant. Ben knew many first-rate musicians in Los Angeles, with whom he was most surely looking forward to playing, among them his old friends Benny Carter and Jimmy Rowles.

The recording sessions with Otis were scheduled for December 19 and 26. The orchestra was a big band consisting of fourteen musicians; the music was early R&B, not unlike McShann's, although the rhythm section was heavier. Ben was in great form at these sessions, playing magnificent, forceful, and emotional music on every take, showing many aspects of his masterful blues interpretations. Three takes of *One O'Clock Jump* and the boogie *Goomp Blues* are unsophisticated, but energetic. His subdued side is highlighted in the slow *One Nighter Blues,* but still an underlying presence of vigor peeks forth in the beginning of his second chorus, while *Untitled Piece*—a medium tempo blues in E-flat minor—is a showcase for Ben, who plays six choruses during which almost every facet of his temperament comes to the surface. Shake, growl, increasing dynamics, and a fine, extremely swinging riff are heard before he finishes the tune with caressing, subdued phrases with his beautiful sound in focus.

The masterpieces of the Otis sessions, though, are three very different and extremely inspired takes of *Stardust,* which give a fascinating impression of Ben's artistry. "Each take is a gem," writes Dan Morgenstern.

> The first begins with Ben a cappella, way up high, answered by Otis' vibes. Then Ben moves gently into the chorus, backed by soft organ chords from the band. He doesn't state the theme, improvising from the start and making wonderful use of dynamics as he builds his solo. A brief Otis interlude sets up Ben's return, the band fuller behind him. He shares the complex cadenza with Otis and concludes with a cascading chromatic run. Take two is introduced by Otis alone. Ben sticks closer to the theme this time, and has only rhythm behind him. This is the big man at his most romantic. Otis' interlude is longer now, and then Ben opens up his sound, takes the cadenza by himself, and gives the band the final chord. Take three (the issued one) follows the routine of take two, but Ben stays even closer to the melody, though he devises a new and lovely ending for the chorus, Otis, obviously inspired by Lionel Hampton's famous record of this tune, takes a few bars, and then Ben re-enters softly, then opens up into the most elaborate of the three cadenzas (with a slight reed squeak that doesn't matter at all). The tempo here is the slowest of the three takes, each of which, in varying degrees,

demonstrates Ben's unique use of the air escaping from his mouthpiece as part of his total sound.[14]

The following day, December 27, found him in the studio again, also for Mercury, this time to record in his own name for the first time in almost five years, and Benny Carter might have helped organize the session. Carter performed with a trio at Astor's, and one evening Ben came by with his old employer, John Kirby. Kirby had moved to California for health reasons, and Carter helped him out when he could, and on this particular evening both Ben and Kirby sat in.[15] Two tunes from this session stayed in Ben's repertoire for the rest of his life, *Randle's Island,* a medium tempo blues, which during his years in Europe more or less became his signature tune (though usually played faster and called *Blues in B Flat*), and the ballad *Old Folks. Randle's Island* is named after the Detroit and Cleveland disc jockey Bill Randle; the title is a pun utilizing Randle's name and Randall's Island, New York. Ben performs with great charisma on all three takes, but opens softest and builds his two solos better on the last. The first take of the up-tempo *King's Riff,* a blues in F, was to everyone's satisfaction. Ben plays forcefully, and his last effort is particularly overwhelming in its explosive energy. There are also three takes of *Old Folks* with Ben soloing over one and a half choruses. The differences between the three takes aren't as great as in *Stardust* from the previous session. He is in a more gentle, lyrical mood on the first take, keeping close to the theme, while expressing himself more freely and confidently after the first chorus on the following takes, which are set at a slightly higher pace. The third take is the best, with Ben turning the B-part into a pearl of beautiful phrases, utilizing dynamics optimally for emotional impact. The second ballad is *You're My Thrill,* likewise performed over one and a half choruses. The mood in the first take is pensive, just slightly hesitant; in the second chorus there is a small misunderstanding between Ben and the rhythm section. This is corrected in the slightly better and more relaxed second take, however never reaching the emotional heights of *Old Folks.*

The jazz community in Los Angeles was different. Most clubs presented Dixieland, while modern jazz was played at the Haig on Wilshire Boulevard and in Hermosa Beach at the Lighthouse. However, jam sessions were beginning to pop up around town, thanks to a liberal policy accepted by the local musician's union. The Royal Room, the Hangover, Sardi's, the Haig, and the Lighthouse all hosted jam sessions, and they were soon followed by others.[16] Among these places, Ben probably preferred mingling at the Haig. First of all, the music played was modern jazz, and second, Jimmy Rowles was often in the rhythm section.

In Los Angeles he moved into the house on Wilton Place, and before the new year, he had found a job in a hotel. It is not known whom Ben played with here, but at some point a young drummer named Ed Thigpen showed up, and later he and Ben would see a lot more of each other. Ed's father was Ben Thigpen, who had played drums with Andy Kirk's band when Ben played with them in Kansas City. "I first met Ben Webster after I got out of high school, but I'd heard about him," says Thigpen.

> When I was nineteen my mother died, so I moved to St. Louis, where my dad lived, and I stayed with him for about a year and a half until I got in the army. I was playing then, and my dad got me into a couple of bands. My dad had a band, too, and we sometimes talked about his approach to big bands and accompanying. Specifically he said about Ben Webster, that he sometimes laid back on medium to slow tempos. He said that to play with Ben you still kept the time on the bottom with your feet—the pulse is the same—but when you play with him or someone influenced by him, you could sometimes flex or even flow on top. This means physically that you keep the time, the pulse, with your feet, but you are able to support the phrasing of the soloist with your hands.
>
> This came in handy, because a few years after that, in 1951–52 I got in the army, stationed in California in Fort Ord, and we'd go out to Los Angeles for jam sessions on weekend gigs. I met Ben Webster there playing at a hotel, and I played with him there for the first time. He liked the way I played, and I remember that I applied what my dad had told me so I was more prepared, so to say. The hotel was in the Fillmore district of Los Angeles.
>
> He was beautiful on the jobs I played with him. I called him "The Gentle Giant." There are stories about his roughness, but

with me he was always beautiful. I think that because of my dad and their relationship and because all these guys knew me when I was a baby, they were my uncles in a way, so they were never hard on me. I think that if you respect people and treat them with respect, they'll take care of you in a way.

When you play with people like Ben Webster and you just lay back with restraint and discipline and do what is required, then they will entertain you. They will entertain you till no end, because they are so creative people, the way they express music. When you are accompanying these people while you are young, some of their foundation will be embedded in you. I think that's one of the things that you gain without even knowing it. You realize it as you grow older. If you are able to make them happy, then you know what is required of a whole bunch of people, because you know where they are coming from. Jo Jones told me, and my dad also told me, "Please the man you are working for. Make the man sound good, make him feel good. Then you'll realize that you have the best seat in the house, because he will entertain you the whole night long." And that is true.[17]

All through January 1952 Ben worked on several recording sessions, among them with vocalists Little Esther, Dorothy Ellis, and Dinah Washington. He recorded twice with Little Esther; the second time with alto saxophonist Preston Love, who perceived Ben as almost unbearable at the session. "He was a pure despotic asshole on the session," he remembered. "Ben took charge as though it was *his* session or *his* recording company. Although he had no official status, he growled angrily at other musicians, giving them orders. He acted pugnacious and superior to them, especially the other saxophone players, while giving us orders."[18]

Ben's best contribution with Little Esther is heard in two blues choruses on *Better Beware* from January 4, in which he as usual holds back in the first chorus, followed by a scorching, driving second chorus. He generates less energy on January 16 at a session involving both Little Esther and Ellis. His solos on *Ramblin' Blues* with Little Esther and *Drill, Daddy, Drill* with Ellis are both excellent but ordinary. However, two days later he is once again in great form with Dinah Washington. On the four tunes recorded here, Ben plays but one eight-bar solo on the slow *Trouble in Mind,* but it is extremely eloquent, utilizing glissandi and dynamics superbly to express soulful emotion.

Summer saw Ben working often with Benny Carter. Carter's quintet shared the billing on Sundays at Sardi's with a Dixieland band led by clarinetist Joe Darensbourg, who had an unpleasant experience when Ben turned sour without reason. Darensbourg remembers that "he used to drink quite a bit and sometimes he'd be half-drunk sitting there playing the piano. Freddie Slack, the piano player that made *Cow Cow Boogie* famous, came by one time to sit in with my band. For no reason Ben said to Freddie, 'Go up there, let me show you how to play.' Freddie didn't want to get up so they got in an argument. Ben pulled out a knife and cut Freddie on the arm right there on the stand; if it wasn't for Benny Carter, who pulled Ben away, he might have cut Freddie more than that. There's never a dull moment in music with all these little entertaining things!"[19]

When Ben was out of line, Carter was the only person who could get him under control. Ben had enormous respect for Carter and admired him as a person and musician. Jimmy Rowles, who worked with both of them, had experiences similar to Darensbourg's. "He was the only guy I knew in my whole life who could tell Ben Webster to go to the corner and sit down and stay there until he told him to get out," he recalls. "Ben Webster would act up something terrible; Ben was like a bull in a China shop. Benny Carter would just point his finger and say, 'Go sit down.' And Ben would sit down like a little kid in school."[20]

In autumn, Ben moved back to New York and put together a quintet with trumpeter Harold Baker, pianist Cyril Haynes, bassist Bill Pemberton, and drummer Joe Marshall. Saxophonist Walter "Foots" Thomas had stopped playing professionally and was now working as an agent. He took over Ben's booking affairs and got the band a job at Snookie's Café.[21] Ben opened in September and was so successful that the booking was extended into December.

The arranger Johnny Richards began collaborating with Ben on his last Mercury session, January 23, 1953. For this recording Ben was backed by a splendid rhythm section with Billy Taylor, Milt Hinton, and Jo Jones, and Richards wrote a score for an unusual horn section consisting of Don Elliott on trumpet and mellophone; Eddie Bert, trombone;

Sam Rubinowitch, alto sax and piccolo flute; and Sidney Brown on baritone sax, the idea being that the deep range of the backing horns allowed more room for the soloist in the middle and high registers. Three tunes were recorded; two by Richards, *Hoot* in medium tempo and the fast *Iron Hat*. Ben brought along a medium slow tempo blues in B minor called *Pouting*. Richards's compositions have a certain West Coast flavor, and although the introductions, interludes, and concluding choruses all function well and sound good with Ben, the backing under his solos is too busy; more passages with extended notes would have suited Ben's style better. Ben builds a great solo in *Hoot*, culminating in intensity right after the B-part. Elliot solos on the next sixteen bars and Ben wraps it up in good form.

He sounds a little more inspired in *Pouting*—in later versions called *Poutin'*—playing a four-chorus solo with authority and masterful variation of dynamics and phrasing. There are two takes of *The Iron Hat*, both revealing a light-footed, elegant, and hard-swinging Ben. He has more control of his solo in the alternative take, builds up more logically and seems more inspired; however the first take was probably chosen for its greater precision in the ensemble parts.

Following a few studio sessions in December 1952, Ben had a week at Minton's Playhouse, but at the end of the booking his rhythm section decided to stay on at Minton's backing Tony Scott, rather than move on to Birdland with Ben.[22] With a two-week booking starting February 19, 1953, Ben found himself without a rhythm section, but was helped out of the spot when Birdland hired the Modern Jazz Quartet to back him.

After the Birdland booking, Ben found himself without a band, but once again received unexpected help, this time from Count Basie. Paul Quinichette was leaving the orchestra in the end of March and left an open solo chair. Ben accepted a job filling in for him until Frank Wess was scheduled to join up a month later. Ben's first job with Basie was a week at the Apollo Theatre starting March 27, followed by two weeks at the Bandbox, a cellar nightclub next to Birdland. Subsequently the orchestra was booked for yet another week at the Apollo until April 23, at which time Ben left Basie.

A number of radio transcriptions from the Bandbox show a tightly swinging Basie band with Eddie "Lockjaw" Davis and Ben as two well-functioning tenor saxophone soloists. However, there was not as much contrast between the two as there had been between Lester Young and Buddy Tate earlier or between Davis and Quinichette, because Ben was one of "Lockjaw's" biggest idols. This becomes very obvious in a blues, *Smooth Sailing*, in which the two of them plus Ernie Wilkins solo successively over two choruses, first Davis, then Ben, and finally Wilkins. Ben comes out on top due to his greater intensity and emotional involvement. Other than this, Ben's best contribution is an inspired and disciplined solo over six choruses of *Perdido*, swinging excellently, but occasionally running out of ideas before routinely rounding off with a trill. Following half a chorus of full ensemble, he finishes the tune nicely over the next sixteen bars with a very energetic B-part and a short coda. He is equally inspired on *Sure Thing*, playing nine choruses of effectively swinging blues, well structured and full of vitality and drive. Ben and Basie was an effective and mutually inspiring combination.

Ben was booked with a trio at the Flame Melody Room in Harlem all through May,[23] perhaps longer, but at this time, Ben went more or less unnoticed by the press and the public, and his manager, Walter "Foots" Thomas, had not been able to do much about it. Ben was not the only one of the great swing musicians to be ignored; trombonist Vic Dickenson, Roy Eldridge, and Benny Carter suffered the same fate. In an article on this subject, Nat Hentoff pointed out, "When the Hawkins influence was paramount, Ben was accoladed. But since the Pres school justifiedly came into power, Ben has been largely overlooked and yet, aside from Hawk's historical importance, it was Ben who was the greatest musical development of that school. And as some of his recent Mercury records demonstrate, he still blows with that amazing blend of surcharged power and acute sensitivity."[24]

Ben's great musical maturity is obvious in the recordings Ben now made exclusively for Norman Granz. Granz had started recording him in his own name in May 1953. Combined with recordings from December the same year, the results were reissued in 1957 on the LP *King of the Tenors*, but initially released under the equally suiting title, *Consummate Artistry*, a classic in Ben's production.

These recordings show a broad spectrum of Ben's craft and can be heard as a summary of his artistic level at the time. The outstanding accompaniment is supplied by Oscar Peterson's Trio with Herb Ellis on guitar and Ray Brown on bass; in New York the drummer was J. C. Heard, in Los Angeles, Alvin Stoller. The Los Angeles sessions include Harry Edison and Benny Carter in supporting roles. On the blues tunes *Jive at Six* and *Bounce Blues*—included on the CD with alternative takes—he plays with gusto and drive, and *Cotton Tail* is exceptional, built up over six choruses, inspired and full of direction all the way, on a backdrop of the likewise fit-for-fight rhythm section. The B-part of the fourth chorus is particularly remarkable with its long, descending chromatic line, as is the last B-part with its elegant conclusion upon the restatement of the theme. *Pennies from Heaven,* and the CD reissue's bonus track, *Poutin',* are treated with equal skill, but other than that, it is the ballads that stand out, beginning with a one-and-a-half-chorus version of *Tenderly,* in a rendition perfectly reflecting the title. Ellington's *Don't Get Around Much Anymore* is played at a medium slow pace, almost as a ballad, with Ben at his most lyrical, presenting the theme almost seductively. In *That's All* he keeps close to the melody throughout the two choruses, lifting it an octave in the second chorus, imbuing the tune with his most beautiful tone, followed by a lovely, controlled vibrato. The CD includes a shorter, one-and-a-half-chorus version that doesn't pale in comparison with the original release. The most heartrending track is *Danny Boy,* an identical twin to the Irish folk tune *Londonderry Air.* Small melodic variations combined with magnificent composure, sublime phrasing, small modifications in accentuation and deep emotionality make this rendition of the tune one of his finest ever. The following episode illustrates just how deeply Ben's interpretation of *Danny Boy* touched audiences. "We were playing in New York City at the Metropole one night when visitors from Ireland requested that song three or four times," J. C. Heard recalled. "One party came up to the bandstand, brought drinks for everybody, explained how special the song was to them at home and said, 'We know you've already played it, but can you play it just one more time?' Another party asked Ben over to their table, told him how much they liked his playing, hugged him and had tears in their eyes as they told him how special it was to them. It was like a national anthem or something."[25] Naturally, such reactions must have made a deep impression on Ben and helped influence him to record the tune in order to please an even larger audience.

The high quality of the material, Ben's timeless, authoritative, and powerful performance, and a sparkling accompaniment made *King of the Tenors* Ben's best-selling album, as well as serving to consolidate his status as an unsurpassed ballad interpreter, not least among his European fans.

Bassist Niels-Henning Ørsted Pedersen often played with Ben in Denmark, and he noticed that Ben was especially selective with his tone on ballads such as *Danny Boy.* "Some musicians just play whatever they play on a ballad," he explains.

No matter what solution is played behind them, it has no effect on them. This is particularly common with young soloists intent on playing everything they know. But it was exactly the opposite with Ben, because he responded to everything. It was really a pleasure playing ballads with him, because it was fun finding the notes that created a good sound. He was also one of the few to play in keys with sharps. He often played in D major and E major and A major, and that's because he was incredibly sound-conscious. Almost all saxophonists play the same tunes in the same keys: wherever they're easy to play. But Ben found the keys where the tunes sounded best, which is why he played *Danny Boy* in D major.

He was a violinist first, and he actually played as if the saxophone was a violin, so it really isn't strange that he had that sound. He tried to make the sax sound like a violin, as regards the vibrato and the perfect intonation. Listen to *Danny Boy,* the place where he goes up to the high F-sharp. It's out of this world.

Many soloists are virtuosos; they are extroverted and can tear off a lot of runs, but musicians like Ben Webster, Stan Getz, Phil Woods, and Chet Baker relied heavily on the sound. The story they tell relates to the sound, develops in context with the sound and whatever virtuosity belongs there, but never in the opposite order. This is something you realize over the years. If you don't know that sound is the essential thing, perhaps you concentrate more on rounding all the corners in the runs. I'm not saying that this is wrong, but they are different approaches. The audience reacts to the sound as well, because it is the voice of the man. When the voice is clear, you can use everything else you have to tell your story. If the voice doesn't carry, it's hard to tell your story.[26]

September 2, 1953, shortly before the fall's Jazz at the Philharmonic tour, Norman Granz called some of his musicians together for a recorded jam session. Ben performs on four of the six tracks, playing competently although not extracting anything spectacular from *Jam Blues* and the up-tempo *Blue Lou*. He fares far better on *Just You, Just Me,* apparently finding extra inspiration during his third and final chorus, finishing off with a beautiful and lyrical phrase, a perfect prelude to his contribution to a medley of ballads, a wonderful, lyrical rendition of *Someone to Watch Over Me,* offering an appetizer of what audiences could expect on the forthcoming tour. September 10, found Ben in a studio once again, this time as part of the Gene Krupa Sextet. On a whole, the session is somewhat rocky, but Ben is in impressive and inspired form, contributing gems in the ballad *Don't Take Your Love from Me* and *I'm Coming, Virginia,* surprisingly played at a slow pace.

Granz gave Ben's career a much needed lift by booking him for his concert tours with Jazz at the Philharmonic in autumn 1953. This time they not only toured the continental United States and Canada as usual, but continued to Honolulu and Japan. Among others, the troupe included trumpeters Roy Eldridge and Charlie Shavers, trombonist Bill Harris, saxophonists Benny Carter, Lester Young, and Flip Philips, vocalist Ella Fitzgerald, and the Oscar Peterson Trio.

The Jazz at the Philharmonic tour opened in Hartford, Connecticut. On *Concert Blues* Ben plays six excellent choruses, swinging and building his solo without too much growl. The same concert offers a version of *Cotton Tail* with Ben and Flip Phillips chasing through five spellbinding choruses before finishing with the theme in unison. There is even more music from the Carnegie Hall concert eight days later. The jam session set starts off with *Cool Blues*. Ben's eleven choruses swing wonderfully, but in the last half of his solo, in which the other horns back him up with riffs, he relies on too much growl and too little music. *One O'Clock Jump* comes off better; he plays nine well-articulated choruses. He is the first soloist on *Flyin' Home,* playing four captivating choruses, whereas this evening's version of *Cotton Tail* is not played as a chase. Ben takes all of six choruses, performed with great energy and intensity, but the gem from this concert is *Someone to Watch Over Me,* in which he keeps close to the theme throughout his solitary chorus, enhancing it with all his emotional powers and playing the high notes *piano* for even greater beauty.

The two concerts in Carnegie Hall on September 19 were favorably reviewed. "In both shows, particularly the second, Ben Webster and Roy Eldridge were outstanding," wrote *Down Beat.* "Crowd-wise, the favourites are Krupa, Ella, Peterson, and Flip. I'd list Carter, Ella, the Peterson trio, Roy, and Ben Webster. In any case, this is a stimulating JATP that manages to bridge the difficult problem of satisfying a hyperthyroid audience in need of intense emotional purgation while retaining long sections of first-rate improvised jazz."[27]

True to tradition, the musicians were presented with large flower garlands upon their arrival in Honolulu, and in Tokyo, they were received as heroes with a grand ticker-tape parade through the city in open limousines. This was the first concert in the country by American jazz musicians that was open to the public. Previously, jazz musicians had visited the American army bases. Gene Krupa had been there the year before and had told Granz of the enormous interest in jazz on the other side of the Pacific. Granz was convinced by Krupa's enthusiasm, and the Japanese lap of the tour proved an immense success with twenty-four sold-out concerts in ten days.

The music from the concerts in Japan in early November shows Ben in great form, playing some of his longest recorded solos. He builds his seventeen choruses on *Tokyo Blues* with an almost raw savagery, never falling back on a routine performance, and plays with delightful drive and swing. The same goes for *Cotton Tail.* Following two run-of-the-mill choruses, he lets go in the subsequent four. *Someone to Watch Over Me* is in the same class as the Carnegie Hall version; the tranquillity and sensitive interpretation are sheer pleasure, whereas his solo in *Perdido,* played with Ella Fitzgerald, is too rough to impress.

Ben enjoyed spending time with Eldridge and Shavers on these tours, having fun and partying. On one occasion, however, Ben had too much to drink, and he and Shavers got in a fight in the dressing room. Ben took a punch at Shavers, barely missing his mouth. Eldridge knew this side of Ben's personality, and he was furious that Ben had risked hurting Shavers. "When Ben Webster was sober he was the nicest cat you ever met," Eldridge remembered. "But when he was drinking he'd turn rough. Sometimes he'd slap me or something like that, and I'd end up chasing him down the street, big as he was."[28]

On November 15, the JATP tour left Japan, and on November 19 Ben opened a booking in Chicago in a club called Nob-Hill. In the spring of 1954, he and Eldridge played the Café Bohemia in New York. Eldridge wanted to avoid a repetition of the Shavers episode, which he made perfectly clear to Ben on the first evening of the booking by putting a pistol on the dressing room table and in no uncertain terms telling him that he would not hesitate to use it. Ben took the threat seriously, and never again picked a fight with Eldridge.

In autumn 1954, Ben played a two-week booking starting August 31 at Chicago's Bee Hive Lounge. Immediately after Chicago, he went on tour with that year's Jazz at the Philharmonic troupe, this time including Ella Fitzgerald, Roy Eldridge, Dizzy Gillespie, Bill Harris, clarinetist Buddy DeFranco, Flip Phillips, the Oscar Peterson Trio, and drummers Louie Bellson and Buddy Rich, among others. Recordings from the opening night in Hartford, Connecticut, on September 17, 1954, find Ben virtually caressing *Tenderly,* and although his contributions in the jam session set are not sensational, they are performed with vitality, energy, and drive. Today his six tearing choruses in *Challenges* may not seem particularly exciting, and later a few critics have expressed the opinion that Ben was misplaced in the JATP troupe. What these critics forget is the experience Ben gave the audiences. Not only was he unique in the ballad medley, but his other contributions radiated a presence, an involvement, and a devil-may-care attitude that was compelling in a concert setting.

Granz always booked first-class transportation and accommodation for the musicians; however, the plane ride to Norman, Oklahoma, took an unexpected turn when one of the motors caught fire. "Ray Brown and Whitey Mitchell came running down the aisle with their basses," recalled Eldridge. "They wanted them in the back of the plane in case we crashed. Flip Phillips or Bill Harris—one of the two—started whistling *The High And The Mighty.* Buddy Rich got salty. Then we gathered together, shook hands and said it had been nice doing the tour and all that. We really didn't think we were going to make it. But obviously we did. We landed in Garden City, Kansas, with just one engine."²⁹ Ben remembers the situation just as vividly. He once told Harvey Sand, the waiter at Jazzhus Montmartre, Copenhagen, that the pilot's voice came over the speaker system, saying they had to turn around and land, because there was a problem with one of the motors. Ben looked out of the window, "And I tell you, Harvey, that motherfucker was burning!"³⁰ The experience scared Ben so much that after the tour was over, he never boarded a plane if he could avoid it. Consequently, this was Ben's last tour for Norman Granz. Even the temptation of high wages could not persuade him to join JATP again.

After the JATP tour, Ben, Eldridge, and Harris decided to form a horn trio to tour clubs playing with local rhythm sections. The first job was a two-week run at Cleveland's Loop Lounge starting November 2, 1954, after which they continued to Boston, Chicago, Philadelphia, and Detroit. The last job before Eldridge joined the JATP tour going to Europe was a week's revisit to Cleveland starting January 3, 1955.

In 1954 and 1955 Ben recorded little, but the quality is superb. There were several ballad sessions in his own name and a number of recordings with groups led by Johnny Hodges, Illinois Jacquet, and Buddy Rich. Hodges invited Ben to a session on April 9, 1954, where Ben is heard swinging in one chorus of *In a Mellotone,* and although he has but eight bars on *Don't Get Around Much Anymore,* he confirms that Hodges's influence still can be heard in his sound and phrasing. The Jacquet session was not planned. Ben knew that "The Kid," as he called him, had a recording date scheduled for December 13, 1954, and decided to go over and listen, but when Jacquet saw that Ben had brought his horn along, he invited him to join in. Together they recorded two tracks, *I Wrote This for the Kid,* a slow blues, and *The Kid and the Brute,* an up-tempo blues where the lack of precision in the ensemble parts confirms that this is indeed a jam. Ben shows plenty of commitment in both tunes, and his solos, especially in the slow blues, are far more intense, and consequently more interesting, than Jacquet's. The recipe is the same for both tunes; following solos, the two combatants play a chase, and particularly *The Kid and the Brute* offers extremely inspired performances from them both. Quotations fly through the air during the chase choruses, and it takes your full attention to discern the soloist, as the two saxophonists show many similarities when growling.

On February 23, 1955, Ben performed in a sextet with Roy Eldridge and trombonist Kai Winding on Steve Allen's TV show, *The Tonight Show.* Shortly after, on March 12, Charlie Parker died suddenly, and Ben played at a benefit concert for Parker's children at the Blue Note in Philadelphia, where Parker was to have started a booking the same day. The concert was a twelve-hour marathon show starting at 2:00 P.M., and it drew such large crowds that police were called in to keep things under control. Aside from Ben, a few of the other big names were Dizzy Gillespie, pianists Ray Bryant and Bud Powell, and drummer Philly Joe Jones. Parker's death affected Ben deeply. "I got to love the way Bird played, and to become a good friend of his," he said later. "You know, he always sounded like a tenor to me. He blew so heavy with a lot of power. Bird was a very likeable and a very intelligent man. He had a lot of friends."[31] Ben saw Parker's influence, but also the insecurity and confusion in his own generation of musicians caused by the first years of bop. "With Bird and some of the men who came after, things worked out well from the start. Bird started off playing like that and he devoted all of his time to that style. So he was at home in it. But there were men who came before him who had been playing in quite another style for 10 years or more. Some of them—and they were good musicians—tried to turn all the way around and play the new style that Bird introduced. It created a lot of confusion. It's one thing to keep up with modern trends, but to go all out for it body and soul when your own background is different is something else again."[32]

On May 16, 1955, Buddy Rich recorded a session for Norman Granz. The setup was a typical JATP jam session featuring a fast blues, *The Monster,* followed by a standard—on this session it was *Sunday*—and a ballad medley opened by Ben in *Over the Rainbow.* The rhythm section swings excellently in *Sunday,* and Ben cooks up steam in his three energetic choruses. On top of this storm of vitality, *Over the Rainbow* feels like an oasis, tenderly interpreted as only Ben could do, with the magnificent serenity and nuances in melody, dynamics, and phrasing that lend the statement life, presence, and expression.

The tracks in Ben's name are all ballad treatments recorded on March 30, May 28, and December 15, 1954, and February 3 and September 9, 1955. With the exception of *Almost Like Being in Love* from the May 28 session, on which Ben fronts a trio with Billy Strayhorn at the piano, the last four of these sessions find him backed by strings. *Love's Away, You're Mine, You!, My Funny Valentine,* and *Sophisticated Lady* from March 30 still stand as majestic masterpieces. Here, Ben's musicianship is no less than sublime. One example is *You're Mine, You!,* which he closes in the most delicate and controlled manner, hitting the tenor's E above the high C. The string arrangements are not always successful—although Strayhorn's versions of *Chelsea Bridge, Our Love Is Here to Stay, It Happens to Be Me,* and *All Too Soon* are brilliant. Rather than just floating behind or under Ben, the voicings surround him, inspiring him with melodic and harmonic movement that seems natural and logical. Hiring Strayhorn was Granz's idea: "I knew Billy wanted to write for strings, and he could do it, unlike most straight jazz guys," he recalled. "Since he never got the chance to write for strings with Duke, he jumped at it."[33] Ralph Burns did a fine job as well, whereas the anonymous arranger who contributed to the session on February 3, 1955, deserves no compliments for his saccharine and uninteresting work. Other than that, Ben's renditions are highlighted on all takes, never straying far from the theme, but set forth with tenderness, and at times deeply stirring, as in *Prelude to a Kiss, All Too Soon, Chelsea Bridge, Willow Weep for Me, We'll Be Together Again,* and *Early Autumn.* His improvisations are imaginative, resisting the prevailing tendency of playing in double time, as many other saxophonists would have done. He plays with great sensitivity and often surprising lines, as exemplified in the exuberant phrases beginning his solo in *There Is No Greater Love.* The recordings show that Ben enjoyed playing with strings. "I feel definitely at home recording with strings," he said.

> When I was very young I had to study violin and I hated it then, but strings create such a beautiful background, especially, I think, when written correctly. It will take a musician that will know how to write for strings, and it will take a musician that will know the saxophonist, the trumpet player, or any other instrument, to know exactly what kind of background to lay for him with these

strings. Yes, it is very beautiful, especially for ballads. When you play a ballad you try to tell a story, or at least try to treat the man's tune right.[34]

On another occasion he said, "It just relaxes you. You just automatically lay on that blanket that they lay out for you. You just lay there. The main thing is, have your horn playing, you don't have to think. They put it down."[35] His perfect pitch and developed sense of harmony were great assets when following the string arrangements.

Although Ben's affiliation with Norman Granz during these years was good for his career, club jobs were growing scarce, and although his records received favorable reviews, they did not sell particularly well; audiences were buying modern jazz. One night, Nat Hentoff dropped by Minton's Playhouse in New York and heard Ben sitting in with Tony Scott's quartet. "Ben blew with a power, passion, and imagination that gave me the most thrilling listening experience I've had all season," he wrote afterward. "Yet Ben is no longer a headliner at the jazz clubs and hasn't been for several years."[36] Just how difficult Ben's career was at this time is illustrated by the fact that Roy Eldridge and Ben were forced to disband a quintet including such outstanding musicians as pianist Ray Bryant and drummer Jo Jones. "It was a crime to break that group up," Eldridge reminisced, "but the agency couldn't find any jobs for us. Can you imagine?"[37]

In July 1955, Ben played at the Newport Jazz Festival. The previous year, George Wein had arranged a summer jazz festival in Freebody Park in Newport, Rhode Island, which proved such a success that it developed into an annual event. That year's festival fell on July 15–17, and Ben performed in the concluding set Sunday evening, which turned into the highlight of the festival. Ben, cornetist Bobby Hackett, Kai Winding, clarinetist Peanuts Hucko, and a rhythm section consisting of Billy Taylor, bassist Wyatt "Bull" Ruther, and Jo Jones played *Royal Garden Blues*. This was followed by a group led by Winding and J. J. Johnson, after which Ben once again entered the stage for a ballad set. *Down Beat* wrote,

> Hackett played just one chorus of *My One And Only Love,* and though it consisted of straight melody, Hackett was hauntingly eloquent on it. He is a marvel.

Bud Shank was next with *Lover Man,* and it was a shame it was to be his only contribution to the concert, so well did he play. Webster, who many consider the ballad daddy of 'em all, wrapped it all up with *Someone To Watch Over Me,* and people by this time were realizing this was to be a helluva night of music.

Taylor, Jones, and Reuther [sic] then whistled through *Sweet Georgia Brown,* on which Billy and Jo scintillated. The entire group then reassembled for *Fine And Dandy* and made way for the Count Basie band, which capped the evening with a shouting performance. This was the night everyone had hoped all three would be.[38]

Following the festival, Ben left for a booking at the Cadillac Lounge in Chicago. Ben discovered that jobs were more plentiful in Chicago than back in New York, so after completing a recording session in New York in early September, he moved to the Windy City. During the next half year he played with local rhythm sections in clubs such as the Stage Lounge, where he was accompanied by pianist Norman Simmons trio, and at Budland. At Budland, Ben shared the bill with Billie Holiday in March, and they both performed at one of the dances arranged at the Trianon Ballroom every Friday evening. The two old sweethearts enjoyed each other's company, and as they both had the ability to give themselves 100 percent, audiences had a fine time, even on those evenings when the club was not full. "Billie, in revealing her own vulnerability, made you, the listener aware of your vulnerability," said Studs Terkel. "So when Billie sang *Willow Weep For Me,* before those ten or twelve people, at 2:00 in the morning, at Budland, in this basement (and Ben Webster, the tenor saxophonist was there) it was not just her mortality she was singing about it was ours too . . . willow weep for me . . . and we wept."[39]

In the summer of 1956, the situation in Chicago began looking like the previous year in New York, as jobs were becoming scarce, but this time Ben moved in with Mayme and Mom in Los Angeles and stayed there for the next year. In the eighteen-month interim before returning to New York, he contributed to no less than thirty recording sessions, twenty-three under the auspices of Norman Granz. Only one of these sessions was solely in his own name; among the musicians involved in the other sessions were Billie Holiday, Harry Edison, Art Tatum, Woody Herman, Red Norvo, Buddy Rich, Benny Carter, Ella Fitzgerald, Barney Kessel, Bill Harris, and Coleman Hawkins.

Ben was soon busy in the studios, whereas the clubs did not present many possibilities. He was reunited with Jimmy Rowles at a few Billie Holiday sessions, and the two of them spent some time on the golf course as well. Ben's golf was not as good as his pool, according to Rowles: "We'd tee up, and all these fancy types would be waiting their turn, mumbling under their breath about that big black guy who was holding them up. Ben would have one of those little hats on the back of his head, and he'd stand there before the ball, his big front sticking out, and talk to himself: 'Now, Ben, do it just like when you were in the Masters. Keep your head down, and not too many Wheaties.' And he'd take a terrific swing— pouf!—and the ball would dribble 10 feet up the fairway. We only saw each other on the tees and greens, but we laughed our way around the whole course."[40]

However, they did not always get to play golf when they had planned. Often, when Rowles came by to pick up Ben, an unexpected hurdle would pop up in the shape of Mom. "She was the one who gave the orders," recalled Rowles.

> And he was very well behaved at that house. He did not fool around like a bad boy there. When I was there and we'd be ready to go, all of a sudden his grandmother [sic] would say, "Benjamin Francis! You have to take care of the garbage and make sure that lawn is together before you go out to play golf. Jimmy, you just gonna have to wait!" Art Tatum would be playing on the [phonograph] machine and I'd sit and listen to Art while Ben took care of his charge before we could go. And that was it.[41]

Oscar Peterson said that Ben would occasionally take tenor saxophonist Illinois Jacquet with him to play golf. On one occasion, "as Ben prepares to tee off on the first hole (some 240 yards away)," Jacquet said, "'Go on, Frog, go ahead and lay it up there on the green.' Ben pauses in his stance and glares at Jacquet, 'What in the hell do you mean, lay it up there on the green? Shit! There ain't nothing up there but green!'"[42]

Rowles and Billie Holiday had been good friends since 1942 when

they both were in Lee and Lester Young's group. They were on the same
wavelength musically, and Holiday often asked Granz to hire Rowles on
piano rather than Oscar Peterson. "Get all of us in a studio with Billie
Holiday," Rowles recalled.

> Some fun. Billie was very thin, very bony, very drawn. She was
> there though. The Verve sessions usually started around 2:30 in
> the afternoon. There was always enough to drink and Norman
> sent out for sandwiches if anyone were hungry. Her voice was a
> little weak. Billie and I would be working out keys and a basic set
> of chords so we would have an idea of what was going on. That
> way we had an idea of what people would be doing. The key we
> recorded in depended by and large on what she had been up to
> the night before. If she been celebrating, you know, her voice
> might be rougher than normal. We got into some pretty weird
> keys that way trying to smooth over the ups and downs of her
> voice.[43]

Ben remembered well these recording sessions in August 1956
with Holiday.

> She was like you would say, one of the fellows. Beautiful person.
> All she wanted was friendship. I remember the last thing I did
> with her and with Harry "Sweets" Edison, we did it in California
> about three, maybe four days to do it. But she knew Sweets well,
> she knew me a long time, and every day she came you could see
> she was more relaxed, because she could make jokes with Sweets
> and myself. And every day she came I think she sang better. She
> just wanted friends, and she just looked better to me and was
> more and more happy every day.[44]

"If Billie Holiday sounded unhappy and full of despair in her later days, I
really think you can attribute that to loneliness," he continued. "I think
she was a lonely person, but she was a swinger. She just loved to be among
friends."[45]

The Billie Holiday recordings spanned two sessions in August
1956 and five in January 1957, and all sessions featured Ben, Harry Edison,

Jimmy Rowles, Barney Kessel, and drummer Alvin Stoller, while Joe Mondragon and Red Mitchell alternated on bass. At this time, the range of Holiday's voice was somewhat limited, and in the two 1957 sessions, she was fairly rusty, but the listener catches the feeling that all the musicians are devoted to Holiday, and committed to reaching the best possible result. No one seeks exposure at the expense of others; all function as a homogenous group rather than as a pickup band for the occasion. The transitions from vocals to instrumental solos are gentle, and with the exception of Edison, whose contribution is somewhat routine, all solos are kept in the spirit and feeling set by Holiday's vocal. Ben is particularly considerate in his obbligatos, never getting in the way, but always keeping his velvet tone under her voice and thus helping to carry her forth. He is equally considerate in his solos, never using growl in fast tempi, probably instinctively feeling that it would be overpowering in comparison to Holiday's fragile voice. Ben's contributions are all at a very high standard. From the August 1956 session, his playing is beautiful in *Ill Wind,* inspired and romantic in *We'll Be Together Again,* handsome and swinging in *Do Nothing Till You Hear from Me.* His *Sophisticated Lady* has a lovely singing quality. The January 1957 recordings reveal him in a lovely melodic mood on *I Wished on the Moon* and with a buttery, melting sound on *Darn Dat Dream.* He contributes solid and excellent playing to *Just One of Those Things, But Not for Me,* and *They Can't Take That Away from Me,* while he is lyrical and empathetic on *Moonlight in Vermont* and *Stars Fell on Alabama,* heartfelt and tender on *I Didn't Know What Time It Was* and *Embraceable You,* and warm and inspired on *Body and Soul,* the masterpiece from these sessions, which are Holiday's best as well as last for Norman Granz.

When listening to these recordings, one sees why Holiday felt at home in this company and appeared happier at each session. Edison and especially Ben challenge her wonderfully and congenially. Some reviewers have claimed that Ben's remarkable ballad interpretations and outstanding work with vocalists was due to the fact that he—like Lester Young and Dexter Gordon—knew the lyrics to the songs he played, but he rejected that explanation vehemently. "I don't know the lyrics to any ballad or any tune," he says. "I get the feeling from the tune sometimes. But it all depends on who is in the rhythm section, who's in the band. Every day is a different day, and it is hard to explain, you know, when you talk about feeling, yourself, and a tune."[46]

The two sessions with Ella Fitzgerald for *Ella Fitzgerald Sings the Duke Ellington Songbook* show none of the empathetic atmosphere of the Holiday recordings. Fifteen tracks were recorded at a marathon session on September 4, 1956, with Ben performing on eleven of them with Stuff Smith, Joe Mondragon, Alvin Stoller, and pianist Paul Smith. Although the end product didn't reach the same high artistic level as the Holiday sessions, there is a lot of good music, and Ben and Stuff Smith are both in a generous and inspired mood, assisted by a likewise excellent rhythm section. Once again Ben's obbligatos are lovely and heartfelt, as can be heard in *Just a-Settin' and a-Rockin', I Let a Song Go Out Of My Heart* and *Prelude to a Kiss*. On *Rocks in My Bed* and *It Don't Mean a Thing* his solos are powerful, and he dishes up a few rhythmically exiting phrases, while showing a much more subdued and sentimental side on *Do Nothing Till You Hear from Me, Sophisticated Lady,* and *Prelude to a Kiss.* The next session was recorded on October 17, 1957, with Oscar Peterson's Trio and Alvin Stoller, with Ben participating on three tunes. He swings well on all three, but doesn't sound particularly inspired on *Love You Madly* and *Squatty Roo,* and his phrases end more or less predictably on *In a Mellotone.*

A classic recording from this period is the album Ben made with Art Tatum, barely two months prior to Tatum's death. The music is permeated with a relaxed and mutual, almost telepathic, empathy; Ben and Tatum almost outdo themselves. The recording took place on September 11, 1956, as the eighth and last album in Granz's series of Tatum with guest soloists. Assisted by bassist Red Callender and drummer Bill Douglas, they produced a perfect and timeless masterpiece, in which Ben's carefully articulated and simple lines fit hand in glove with Tatum's sparkling and highly ornamented style. There is a pleasant, relaxed atmosphere throughout the entire session. It is obvious that Ben doesn't feel inclined to challenge Tatum, while for his part, Tatum refrains from bulldozing Ben; he is supportive and often follows up on Ben's phrases, as if completing his train of thought. "Sometimes Tatum and me would go to somebody's house and have a little jam, you know," Ben recalled. "The album I made with Tatum was made in first takes during two and a half to three hours. We just talked and I said, 'I take the first chorus, you take the second one, and I'll come in after the piano and take it off,' you know. But it was not that easy for me, because to play with Art Tatum, the first thing that pops up in your mind is, 'What in the world can you play?' So that's why I more or less stuck to the melody."[47] Perhaps the greatest contributing factor to the integrated atmosphere of the album is that Tatum gave Ben room to express himself. "Art played for *me*," Ben continued. "And I haven't heard Art play for anybody like he played for me on that date. I've never heard that. And I won't call a name, but I've heard him play with other people, and he just played through them, but he played for *me*. Yeah, he did that. I'm so glad I knew the man, I'm so glad that I knew him."[48] All the tunes are played in medium tempo or slower, which serves to accentuate the composed atmosphere as well as reduce the risk of Tatum intimidating Ben with his florid technique. Ben always admired Tatum, in fact ranking him as the greatest of all jazz musicians, and finally having the opportunity to record with him must have been the fulfillment of a dream.

Each track follows more or less the same strategy. With the exception of *My One and Only Love,* Tatum begins with his interpretation of the theme, before letting Ben take over for one or two choruses. Then it is Tatum's turn to improvise, followed by a joint conclusion of the tune. In *All the Things You Are,* played in a medium slow tempo, far slower than the usual tempo set for Kern's lovely tune, Tatum weaves a spell through the first chorus, utilizing just about every harmonic alteration he can think of, after which Ben plays two choruses, keeping very close to the theme with very few ornamentations in the first one, improvising the second chorus in deliberate and calm phrases with a big, rich, and warm tone. Following a short piano introduction, Ben interprets *My One and Only Love* with incredible beauty and tenderness, turning the song into a declaration of love, stated in the high register with a sound enhanced with all the singing quality he can muster. The same goes for *My Ideal.* Here, his use of dynamics also lends warmth to the interpretation. Although Ben remembered differently, first takes were not enough for every tune. Three takes were recorded of *Gone with the Wind;* they don't differ much. Tatum plays the first two choruses, using the same transition between

choruses on all three takes. Ben takes the following chorus, playing similarly on takes one and three in a light paraphrase of the theme, whereas he
improvises more on take two. However he seems slightly unsure of the
conclusion, entering four bars late. *Have You Met Miss Jones* once again
finds Ben close to the theme in his chorus, and the two takes are very similar with the exception of a slightly slower pace in the first—alternative—
take. *Night and Day* is a solid swinger. Ben plays competently and
confidently, although never quite rising above a routine performance.
The last track is *Where or When* with Ben again presenting small variations on the theme. Tatum plays the first sixteen bars of the last chorus
and Ben joins him for the remainder of the tune, nicely tying up a lovely
session with a concluding phrase moving upward step by step toward the
root note of the scale in the top register, warm, full, and in perfect pitch.
Although Tatum had achieved greater results previously and seems to
play slightly routinely on this session, the overall impression is of such
perfection and mutual stimulation and inspiration, that it is easy to
understand Ben's pride and pleasure in this recording.

When Tatum died on November 4, 1956, Ben attended the
funeral on November 10 at the North Neighborhood Community
Church. After the ceremony he and a few other musicians, among them
Harold Land, stayed behind to pay their last respects to Tatum, playing
for him without an audience.

In April–May 1957, Ben and Rowles played at Zucca's Cottage in
Pasadena. The booking was so successful that it was prolonged.[49] Rowles
picked Ben up every evening, because he had been forced to let go of his
little car. "One time he woke up, and he was sitting in his car in a ditch,"
says Birgit Nordtorp. "He drove off the road, but luckily nothing happened. That was when he decided to give up his car, because naturally he
had been drinking and fell asleep at the wheel."[50] It was not the first time.
Another time, he was lucky not to be charged with attacking a policeman.
"He was driving one day, in Kansas City, and fell asleep at a stoplight,"
says Clark Terry. "A police officer walked over and shook him and woke
him up, and when Frog woke up he knocked the cop right out. He used to
say, 'I don't want no surprises!'"[51]

Off work, Ben would spend a lot of time with other musicians,
and one of his friends, saxophonist Bill Green, invited a number of saxo-

phonists to his wedding in 1957. Among them were Ben, Bumps Myers, and Buddy Collette. After the ceremony Green put all of his saxophones on a table, because he wanted everybody to play a little tune for him. Ben was the last one to pay his tribute.

> He got the horn, put it in his mouth, and . . . nothing, just a burst of air came out of that horn. "What the . . . ," and he tried again. Still just air.
>
> Then Bill leaned over and said, "Ben, take in a little more mouthpiece."
>
> We screamed, everyone together, because you don't tell Ben Webster anything!
>
> He looked at Bill and said, "Bill, you tell that to your students!"
>
> Everybody just hollered again. Ben didn't appreciate that at all. Bill could get away with it, because they liked each other so much, but even then, that was dangerous. Ben was noted for hitting people for less.[52]

Over the following months, Ben found himself working in the studios quite a lot. In June, July, and October 1957, he participated in a number of sessions for Contemporary with bandleader Benny Carter, and on May 2 and June 12 he participated in sessions with popular singers Dave Howard and Billy Daniels in bands likewise conducted by Carter. The ten recorded sides with Howard and Daniels offer only short glimpses of Ben on four of them, the longest and most interesting being one fine blues chorus on *Fickle Hearted Blues* with Howard. The recordings for Contemporary worked extremely well due to Carter's arrangements and a star-studded band. Ben isn't equally inspired throughout, and his best contribution is in *Old Fashioned Love,* with a deeply swinging and well-structured, wonderfully logical solo, utilizing glissandi and a couple of shakes as a means of emotional expression. *I'm Coming Virginia* is played as a ballad, and Ben's sixteen bars are low key but expressive, and dynamically subdued. When the musicians arrived at the Contemporary studios on August 16 for the final recording sessions, Benny Carter was absent, prey to a sudden bout of illness. Rather than cancel the session, they made use of the studio time and recorded two extended takes, *Tiger Rag* and *Jersey Bounce,* with Barney Kessel acting as bandleader. The theme of *Tiger*

Rag is played in a Latin rhythm in medium tempo, after which Ben falls in, leading the band with a good swinging feel for his three choruses. His two choruses in *Jersey Bounce* are just as well structured, with no less swing in lines usually accenting the offbeat.

However, the music recorded at a relaxed session under the leadership of trombonist Bill Harris with Ben, Jimmy Rowles, bassist Red Mitchell, and drummer Stan Levey on September 23, 1957, was more original. There is a striking contrast between Ben and Harris. While Ben always made his phrases and riffs fit together logically, Harris plays in a percussive style with each note seeming to puncture the melody rather than bring it together. Ben plays on five of the seven tracks. He is featured on the ballad *Where Are You?,* transforming it into a tonal poem through his rendition in the high register. He produces a likewise unforgettable solo in *I Surrender Dear,* and his three inspired choruses in *In a Mellotone* are refreshingly free of clichés and growl, and offer many lyrical moments, particularly in the beginning of the second and third choruses. The most problematic take from this session is Ben's and Harris' failed attempt to make fun of *Just One More Chance,* turning it into a slapstick comedy.

Ben recorded in his own name on October 15, 1957, accompanied by Oscar Peterson's Trio with the addition of Stan Levey. The seven tracks from this session were released as *Soulville,* and the CD edition includes three bonus tracks with Ben playing piano. Although these tracks disrupt the pensive mood of the album, they serve to show how accomplished a pianist Ben was at the time. The title track, *Soulville,* is a slow blues in which Ben plays four masterful, emotional choruses, concluding the third with several figures played freely on top of the rhythmical structure. The fourth is a stop chorus in which Ben is more dynamic than in the previous choruses, concluding with a descending line of trills. Following solos by Peterson and Ray Brown, Ben finishes off the tune with another two choruses, building the last up to a climax and a majestic, authoritative conclusion. *Late Date* is a blues in medium tempo. Ben plays the theme twice before soloing for three swinging choruses. The middle chorus is the most subdued; the last features a couple of growling phrases and several quite original lines. After piano and guitar solos, Ben takes four more choruses before restating the theme, once again performed with a fine swing and many uniquely shaped phrases. The theme of *Lover Come Back to Me* is played with inventive accents, the last A-part stated almost as a prayer to the loved one before Ben swings through the next two choruses, filling the second chorus mainly with short lines, but always with inspiration, creativity, and a fine sense of continuity. The concluding chorus begins with a lyrical line followed by a couple of runs, after which he takes the theme home in a relaxed and singable rendition. *Makin' Whoopee* is performed at a slightly slower pace than *Lover Come Back to Me,* with Ben playing loosely but still with great inventiveness. *Time on My Hands* and *Ill Wind,* both ballads, are played romantically, but the most beautiful track is *Where Are You?,* given the same singing, tender treatment as on the Bill Harris session; but here the improvised chorus descends perfectly from the high register to easygoing lines in the middle register, followed by an ascension before restating the theme. On the three piano tunes, Ben is accompanied by Stan Levey's brushes, and Brown (and sporadically Herb Ellis) appears on *Boogie Woogie.* Ben's stride technique is shown off in *Who* and *Roses of Picardy,* but an uninventive right hand makes *Boogie Woogie* monotonous. Other than that, this is one of Ben's most homogenous and poetic albums.

The very next day brought yet another Norman Granz session with an almost identical rhythm section—Alvin Stoller replaced Levey—and the addition of Coleman Hawkins. And like the day before, this session also produced outstanding music. The atmosphere is not competitive. The two old friends obviously enjoy each other's company, finding stimulation in the other's performance, never letting it deteriorate into a cutting session. Hawkins takes the first solo in *Blues for Yolande,* building intensity to a climax in his third chorus, which begins with altissimo notes that almost sound like bird cries. Ben's following three choruses contrast Hawkins's statement, as they are shaped in melodic lines with a soft sound up to the third chorus, where he adds a little growl. Ben interprets the ballad *It Never Entered My Mind* wonderfully; he is at his most emotional, caressing the theme with a tone that almost sounds like a cello. Hawkins doesn't say as much in his chorus, after which Ben brings the tune home with sixteen romantic bars and a coda that is just as emotional as his introduction. *La Rosita,* originally a popular tango from the 1920s, is played with a Latin feeling in the theme presentations and as swing during Ben's improvisations. Initially Hawkins states the theme with the rhythm section and Ben adds a second harmony before soloing. The tune is in E major, not a very comfortable key for a saxophonist, and Hawkins wasn't very enthusiastic about playing a solo. Ben was willing to take up the challenge: "I had been down to the studio with Oscar Peterson and Ray Brown to play *La Rosita*," he explained, "and this particular tune was still fresh in my mind, I should say. So Hawk played a chorus first, and then he said to me, 'Now you take it. You don't leave me in E natural!' He cracked up, and so did Oscar and Ray, they just fell to pieces, and they more or less said, 'Play a joke on him!' So I said, 'OK let's go ahead, I'll try.' Hawk was a great kidder."[53] Ben's solo starts with a translucent phrase, followed by some very original lyrical lines in the high register, unlike anything he had ever played before, then finishing up with a few natural lines, inviting Hawkins to join him in the concluding chorus. *You'd Be So Nice to Come Home To,* the lovely *Prisoner of Love,* and *Shine On Harvest Moon* are played in medium tempo, and Ben uses the same approach on all three solos, introducing all of them with lyrical, romantic lines in a lovely, rich tone in the upper register. The latter track features a chase in one chorus with Hawkins starting it off and Ben answering well. Apparently Ben is not as inspired by *Tangerine,* because the first sixteen bars of his solo are relaxed, while the second half of the chorus is formed as a paraphrase on the theme. All in all, it is a fine and inspiring encounter featuring two of the greatest tenors of the swing period.

Ben had come to appreciate the Peterson trio immensely. "Oscar Peterson and Ray Brown had played together so long and knew that the one can anticipate what the other will do," said Ben. "And it was such a pleasure, I mean they laid such a nice, feathered bed out for you. If you'd ever be fortunate enough to play with Oscar, your horn should be in good shape, because they'll really put you in a groove."[54] The admiration was mutual. Oscar Peterson recalls that

> to play for Ben Webster was a unique and joyful experience. Belonging to that school of the big tenor sound, he would walk to the mike and, if we were playing a ballad at the time, his sound was so huge that it really necessitated a very sparse harmonic approach behind him. On the other hand, when he played on the up tempos, I once again would resort to the sharp staccato-like

fills at various times so that the piano would not mush into his mellow tenor sound, remaining a distinct voice in the background. Ben Webster was also quite a pianist and would forever be challenging the various horn players about playing in some of the very rough keys. He seemed to get a kick out of this, although occasionally he'd call for a tune in one of these rough keys and get himself smothered with its difficulty in turn! He was a very fine stride piano player, and I can still see that huge frame swinging from left to right as he fairgrounded and exaggerated the difficulty of the stride he was playing.[55]

Ben had been without an agent for quite some time, and consequently jobs were scarce. In late October 1957, the situation once again looked hopeless, and he packed his bags and headed for New York. Contrary to his usual preference, Ben did not move to Manhattan. This time he rented a room in Miss Sutton's boarding house in Queens, where vocalist Clarence "Big" Miller also lived. They each had a big room in the cellar, and before long, they were joined by Harold Ashby. Ashby and Ben had kept in touch since Kansas City, and when Ben found out that Ashby was in New York and in need of a place to stay, he arranged with Miss Sutton that he could rent a third room in the basement. When Ellington played the Apollo Theatre in New York, Ben took Ashby backstage to say hello to his friends and introduce him to Johnny Hodges and "The Guv'nor." Ashby wound up with a replacement job in the Apollo house band, and later, in 1968, he was hired for the Ellington orchestra.

Once Ben had moved in, he contacted Roy Eldridge, who was playing at the Café Bohemia in Greenwich Village. Eldridge ensured Ben's first rent by bringing him into the group. Ben joined in late October, and stayed until the job ended on November 10. A radio transcription shows Ben and Roy Eldridge from their fiery side on *Riff Tide* in front of an excellent, lightly swinging rhythm section. They are more contemplative on *Bohemia*, whereas *In a Mellotone* does not seem to inspire any of the musicians particularly.

Ben and Hawkins met again in late November for a recording session arranged by Rex Stewart with an orchestra he called the Henderson Reunion Band, because all the involved musicians had played with

Fletcher Henderson. Saxophonist Garvin Bushell felt a tension between Hawkins and Ben. "There was a lot of jealousy between them," he recalls, "more so on the part of Ben, who was fearful of Hawk. They played back to back and wouldn't look at each other. Hawk didn't bother anybody, because he knew he could blow. He also knew how limited Ben was—how little harmony and theory he knew. Still, when Ben matured, he became one of the greatest ballad players there ever was."[56] Ben and Hawkins were probably pulling a practical joke, teasing the other musicians. There was no tension between them. Ben solos on four of the nine tracks. On *Sugar Foot Stomp* he and Hawkins alternate through four steaming choruses that send sparks flying through the air, but aside from this tune, Ben seems more or less uninspired on *Honeysuckle Rose, Wrapping It Up,* and *King Porter Stomp.*

In early December, 1957, Ben played on *The Sound of Jazz,* a television show on CBS, legendary for several reasons: It was the most star-studded jazz show ever, the atmosphere was kept informal and relaxed like a jam session, and it featured an extremely touching performance by Billie Holiday. Originally, Ben had been called in to perform with Holiday, but as Lester Young was extremely weak, and unable to complete the Basie session, Ben was asked to take his place in the orchestra as well. He plays the quick-paced *Dickie's Dream* very energetically, and supplies a lovely obbligato to Jimmy Rushing on *I Left My Baby.* On Billie Holiday's performance of *Fine and Mellow,* he opens the solos, and his intense and emotional solo suits Holiday's vocal well. Neither had any idea that this would be their last performance together.

Often Ben went to Harlem to join in on jam sessions, which is where a young pianist from Pittsburgh, Horace Parlan, met him. "I came to New York in October 1957 and went right away to play with Charles Mingus," Parlan explains.

> It took a little while before I got acquainted with the local scene. Slowly but surely I began meeting younger musicians, and also some of the older ones. It was around this time, late '57 or early '58 that I met Ben for the first time.
>
> He used to come around to a club in Harlem called Branker's where they had Monday night jam sessions. Branker's might not

be well known, but it was one of the many places in Harlem that was known inside the circle. It was always funny, because all the other young cats who were sitting in wanted to play real up-tunes, fast things, you know, but Ben always ended up playing a couple of ballads. I enjoyed that, because it gave me a chance to play with him and to learn some of that material from the American songbook.[57]

Ben checked out the jazz clubs on Long Island as well, and not far from where he lived in Queens, he ran into tenor saxophonist Willene Barton, an acquaintance from Chicago. She remembered that "he came into a club I was working and used to sit in with us. One time a young horn player came to cut Ben, you know. And even though Ben was a lit-tle—under the weather, you might say—he proceeded to straighten that guy *out*. Later on, when we were packing up, I said to him, 'Ben, I sure hope you never do that to me.' He looked at me and said, 'I wouldn't do that to you, sugar.'"[58]

Ben spent most of his free time at places his musician friends frequented, either Beefsteak Charlie's on Fiftieth Street between Broadway and Eighth Avenue, or, if he felt like playing pool, a place next to the Metropole on Seventh Avenue between Forty-seventh and Forty-eighth streets. Musicians also used to hang out at the Metropole or a bar called the Copper Rail, right across the street. The Metropole presented jazz, at this time usually Dixieland.

During the spring of 1958, Ben did not have many jobs, but on April 6, he performed at a concert in Carnegie Hall arranged by Norman Granz, presenting a concert version of the recently released album *Ella Fitzgerald Sings the Duke Ellington Songbook.* "It was not one of Ella's best nights," wrote *Billboard,* "possibly due to the fact that neither her session with the Ellington ork nor her songs with the Ben Webster quartet was rehearsed. Ella sounded good with the Webster combo but missed with the ork, and the concert ended on a note of chaos. Not that the sellout audience cared; they loved it."[59]

In late April Ben was booked for two weeks at the Village Vanguard. Dan Morgenstern heard the group one evening and wrote, "It is an occasion as rare as it is welcome when a group formed on a casual basis, such as a two-week club engagement, performs as if it were a permanent unit, and a choice one at that. Hearing Ben Webster's Quartet at the Village Vanguard was to bear witness to such an occasion. There was almost perfect rapport between Webster, Jimmy Jones on piano, Joe Benjamin on bass and Dave Bailey at the drums." The reviewer continued, "That Ben Webster is one of the masters of the tenor sax is of course not news. Not a past master, by any means. The tone is as beautiful as ever, whether soft and breathy in the upper register or fat and burry further down, albeit not as voluptuous as in the past. This tonal development goes hand in hand with a passion tempered but not diminished, and perfect coordination of intent and execution. These are characteristics of maturity. When Ben Webster plays, he is telling a story, and it doesn't take twenty choruses to tell it. The average length of a number was six to seven minutes—a welcome relief from the two-number sets so often the rule these days."[60]

Despite Ben's fine playing, he did not draw very many people at the Village Vanguard, nor did he pack the bar on Second Avenue a little later in May. He played for four people apart from himself on the night Whitney Balliett visited the place. Balliett described Ben's style as

> easy, magisterial, and enveloping. It *embraces* the listener. Many jazz musicians, through timidity, lack of technique, or plain blurriness, make the listener do much of the work; Webster, an old family retainer, meets his audience three-quarters of the way. After a time, the remarkably sustained assurance and invention of his work paralyse one's critical instinct, for they slip past objectivity and into the subconscious. Webster's tone, a wonder of music, has a good deal to do with this. It is probably the broadest ever achieved on the instrument. The magic and delicate combination of embouchure, lung power, choice of reed, and manner of tonguing out of which jazz saxophonists fashion their extraordinary variety of tones is one of the conundrums of jazz. But ultimately, perhaps, tone is a direct extension of personality, an unwitting mirror of soul.[61]

In April and May 1958, Ben played on two more television shows, the first of which was produced by pianist Billy Taylor. "In 1958, I had the opportunity to hire him once for the first educational series that was carried on television here in New York," Taylor recalls. "Actually, it was coast to coast. It was called *The Subject Is Jazz*. We did a history of jazz and I put together a band where he was the featured tenor player in things from the swing repertoire."[62] The band offered little solo space, but on *Flyin' Home* Ben was featured in a small group, the only other horns being Buck Clayton and Benny Morton. His playing is nice, but without soul, as he stays on sure ground.

The other television show was Art Ford's *Jazz Party,* shown on Thursday, May 15, but probably recorded a few days earlier. At this time, Art Ford produced a series of jazz programs for WNTA, in which a regular studio band played with invited soloists. The music was an informal jam session with no rehearsals. The programs were recorded in a studio in Newark, NJ, and Ben received $59.50 for his work. Judging from Ford's remarks, this program was one of the first in the series. Among the other musicians were Rex Stewart, Buster Bailey, Johnny Guarnieri, and "Big" Miller. Much of the music is Dixieland, but Ben plays a solo version of *You Are Too Beautiful* that is by far the most beautiful take in the program. Performed with a wonderful tranquillity contrasting sharply with the somewhat hectic Dixieland tunes, Ben plays with a lovely, singing sound, especially in the conclusion, raised an octave.

In addition to a scarcity of jobs, Ben was plagued at the end of the 1950s by an inability to hold together a regular rhythm section. Whenever a job turned up, he had to find whoever was open for the date, as when he landed a couple of days at the Metropole in June and played with pianist Earl Knight, bassist Carl Pruitt, and drummer Denzil Best.

"I have seen Ben Webster several times, but the first time I really met Ben was at the Copper Rail, a bar across the street from the Metropole where they had wonderful soul food," Dan Morgenstern recalls.

> He was with Oscar Pettiford, and it was a little before Oscar left for Europe in 1958. They came in together, and Oscar was a bad drunk, really. Ben was trying to take care of him, calm him down and trying to get him to sit down in a booth. It was difficult, but Ben was big and strong and I guess it worked out all right. Of course, I didn't intervene, but it was at the Copper Rail that Ben and I eventually became friendly. There was so much fun there at

the Copper Rail. I remember one time when Coleman Hawkins
and Ben got into these "age" things. They would tease each other
[about] age. Ben would say to Coleman that "the first time I saw
you I was still in short pants." And Coleman would say, "That
wasn't me, that was my father!" They would go on like this.[63]

Summer brought a rare busy period for Ben. He performed at
three jazz festivals and recorded in his own name as well as in orchestras
under the leadership of Michel Legrand, Mercer Ellington, Mundell
Lowe, Carmen McRae, and Johnny Hodges, with whom he recorded three
times during 1958. The first session took place on April 5 and included
Ben, Roy Eldridge, Vic Dickenson, Billy Strayhorn, bassist Jimmy Woode,
and drummer Sam Woodyard. Ben was featured on four tracks, all blues
and three of them in slow tempi. As can be expected, Ben puts on a solid
and genuine blues performance, warm, but with a touch of routine. The
next session, which was more varied as well as more successful, took place
on August 14 with Eldridge, Lawrence Brown, Strayhorn, Wendell Marshall on bass, and Jo Jones on drums. Ben is more inspired throughout,
and his three choruses in the moderately up-tempo blues shuffle *You
Need to Rock* are logically structured, beginning with a long, soft line of
ingenious figures, and building to a climax in the last chorus. He expresses
himself in subdued, romantic lines while still keeping a strong, swinging
drive going in *Let's Fall in Love,* but his most beautiful contribution is an
extraordinary rendition of *Just a Memory,* in which he gives his story an
extra tender twist by playing his melody line slightly behind the beat. The
recordings from the next session, on September 10, became the album *Not
So Dukish.* Ben's performance was not extraordinary, and his best contribution is in the title track with three blues choruses shaping a fine solo,
balanced in dynamics and intensity, with his most original lines falling in
the middle chorus.

At the Newport Jazz Festival Ben performed with Rex Stewart
and His Ellington Alumni All Stars, consisting of Cootie Williams, trombonist Tyree Glenn, Hilton Jefferson, Billy Strayhorn, Oscar Pettiford,
Sonny Greer, and naturally, the bandleader himself. The evening of July 3
was devoted to Ellington and his music, and the first band on stage was
the Alumni All Stars, receiving, however, a somewhat cool review:

"Despite Pettiford's strong hand in the rhythm section, the group reflected the wages of years and economic pressures, Stewart's unfortunate valve-flicking, Williams' now-mild growl, Glenn's often tasteless gyrations, and Greer's inconsistency marred the group's performance."[64] To someone listening to the recording today, the review seems unjustified. Glenn is not nearly so bad as the review makes him, and there are good things to be said about the performance. Everyone swings well on *C Jam Blues* and *Rockin' in Rhythm,* and Ben's feature, *Chelsea Bridge,* is played excellently, although with less depth than he was able to produce.

On Sunday, July 13, there was a star-studded festival in Stony Brook, New York, where Ben was in the company of Hawkins, Shavers, Rex Stewart, J. C. Higginbotham, Rushing, and many others. Two weeks later, Stewart invited Ben to join a band opening the Great South Bay Jazz Festival, stretched over two weekends in East Islip, Long Island.

Although Ben's first job at the Village Vanguard did not bust the box office, he was rebooked for a couple of weeks over the summer, this time with pianist Ray Bryant and drummer Roy Haynes in the rhythm section. Trumpeter Bill Coleman, who had moved to Europe, was visiting New York and heard him one evening in good form. "My wife had never heard him in person, and it was a most thrilling night for her. And it was just as thrilling for me, because Ben told so many stories in so many moods that I had never heard him do. There is always a surprise for you when you listen to him, regardless if it's in person or on record."[65]

The summer of 1958 offered recording sessions other than those with Hodges. The French composer and arranger Michel Legrand spent the month of July in New York, recording a number of arrangements with three different groups of musicians. Ben participated with an unusual instrumentation, four trombones, a flute, and a rhythm section, and is heard in an advantageous setting on *Blue and Sentimental,* a solo feature in two and a half choruses. Following a careful and translucent statement of the theme, he becomes more active during his improvisation, stating his lines in the A-part more busily than usual, perhaps inspired by the modern musicians surrounding him. A month later he recorded *The Soul of Ben Webster* with trumpeter Art Farmer, Ben's protégé Harold Ashby— it was his first recording session—and a rhythm section consisting of

Jimmy Jones, guitarist Mundell Lowe, Milt Hinton, and drummer Dave Bailey. Ben arrived at the studio with five themes, four of them blues, and all of them highly original and modern, reminiscent of Horace Silver's method of composition, giving the album a consistent mood. "I never saw anybody write tunes that way before," says Ashby. "I thought you could only do that at the piano. But Ben had perfect pitch, and everything was in B-flat anyway, so he only had to write out one line for the three horns."[66] Ashby's memory is only partially correct concerning the keys, because *Fajista* and *Ash* are in D major and E-flat major. Although the choice of material is fine, the arrangements leave a lot to be desired, giving the impression of a jam session. This feeling is especially strong in the fifteen-minute-long *Charlotte's Piccolo*—dedicated to Hinton's daughter—which gets downright boring with six successive soloists. However, Farmer and Ben play well through the whole album, and Ben's solos are well proportioned, building nicely throughout, as can be heard in *Coal Train, Ev's Mad,* and *Ash.* He demonstrates great sensitivity in *Charlotte's Piccolo,* as in the ballads, *Chelsea Bridge* and *When I Fall In Love,* the latter highlighting his dreamy, romantic side.

In July he participated in three sessions with Duke Ellington's orchestra, conducted by Mercer Ellington and recording his compositions and arrangements. The orchestra, including Ben, seems heavy-handed and uncommitted. The one exception is Ben's solo feature, a ballad called *Be Patient,* which he performs fervently in subdued lines. He recorded George Gershwin's *Porgy and Bess* as a member of Mundell Lowe and His All Stars over a couple of sessions in the same period. The arrangements were by Lowe, and Ben does a particularly fine job on *My Man's Gone,* capturing the desperation and hopelessness of the song in his solo, and on *Summertime,* reflecting the mood with warmth and soul.

In August, Ben worked three sessions recording Carmen McRae's album *Birds of a Feather* with Ralph Burns's excellent arrangements. The tunes are kept short with very few solos, most of which were given to Ben, whose performances alternate between routine and inspired. Among the latter are *Bye, Bye Blackbird* and *Chicken Today, Feathers Tomorrow,* which show him idly swinging and bouncing along. Other details worthy of mention are his stepwise ascent to altissimo notes in the conclusion of his solo in *Bob White,* and several phrases in *Flamingo,* shaped in a befitting descending movement like the beating wings of a landing bird.

At this time, Ben had bought a Wollensack reel-to-reel tape recorder. Like Louis Armstrong, he was fascinated by hi-fi equipment, and he often took his tape recorder along to the clubs on Long Island, recording himself on whatever jobs he had. One of the clubs, called the NuWay in Hempstead, held jazz concerts on Sunday afternoons. A recording from one of these afternoons reveals Ben in fine, though not outstanding, form, fronting a somewhat ordinary rhythm section. Ben tears off on *Indiana* and plays his most compelling contribution on *Ad-Lib Blues,* a medium tempo tune. Surprisingly, there are no ballads.

He is in more competent company, and consequently more inspired, on October 23, once again performing on Art Ford's *Jazz Party,* this time with Shavers and Vic Dickenson. Ben swings wonderfully on *Please Don't Talk about Me When I'm Gone,* drives impressively on a very fast *I Got Rhythm,* and injects all the soul he can muster into *Stardust.*

Ben was featured in Leonard Feather's blindfold test in *Down Beat* on November 27, 1958. "As one of those musicians inclined to be kindly disposed to fellow jazzmen, Webster was a little reluctant to take a *Blindfold Test,*" says Feather. "Once involved, however, he evinced a great interest in the proceedings. A couple of the items played were stereo records, and he was full of inquiries about the nature and quality of the hi-fi rig. During several of the numbers, he was jumping up and down, checking on the keys of the performances (and revealing that he has absolute pitch)."[67] Ben proved extremely knowledgeable about the various musicians, and guessed correctly most of the time. He liked the younger saxophonists like Harold Land, Bud Shank, Bob Cooper, and Sonny Rollins, who received these comments: "I always did dig Sonny because when he was coming on in the mid-40s, most of the kids had a small sound, and Sonny always tried to have a bigger sound."[68]

In early December he went to Chicago for a two-week booking at the Sutherland Lounge following Sonny Stitt, but in the beginning of 1959, he was back in New York. Jobs were still scarce and finances low, and there were a few serious personal bumps as well; first upon receiving news of Lester Young's death on March 15, barely two weeks before Ben's fiftieth birthday, and again three months later, on July 17, when Billie Holiday died. Both were among Ben's closest friends, and he was disconsolate for months.

Spring brought a slight financial improvement when he played on a CBS television program and shortly after worked for three consecutive days on Norman Granz recording sessions, first with Johnny Hodges and then in his own name. On April 2, 1959, the television show *Jazz from Studio 61* presented Ben leading an excellent sextet including Buck Clayton and Vic Dickenson, pianist Hank Jones, bassist George Duvivier. and drummer Jo Jones. The sextet played *Mop Mop* and *C Jam Blues* with fine contributions from all, and Ben interpreted *Chelsea Bridge* as beautifully as possible by almost exclusively keeping to the theme.

The top-notch rhythm section assembled for the Hodges sessions swings a lot better than the previous Hodges sessions. There is not much to say about Ben's solos on these recordings. He performs as expected with no surprises of any kind, with the possible exception of his solo on *Free for All,* a blues in medium fast tempo, in which his four choruses are logically structured. In the third chorus he plays a couple of seldom heard runs before going into high gear with added growl, giving his conclusion extra drive before restating the theme in the final choruses.

On April 9, 1959, the day after the last Hodges session, Ben returned to record *Ben Webster and Associates.* Ben wasn't the only horn player present: Roy Eldridge was there, and so was the man who first taught him to get a sound out of the saxophone, Budd Johnson. As often occurred, there were some guests as well, among them pianist Billy Taylor, who recalls,

> Jo Jones, who was a big influence on me and sort of adopted me, would take me around and introduce me to people at different times, and he was on the date and brought me with him. I hadn't seen Ben in quite a long time, and I just went in to say hello and listen to him for a while. Norman Granz was producing the record, and Budd Johnson was on the date. Jimmy Jones was playing the piano, Ray Brown was playing the bass, and it was quite a session. As a matter of fact, Ben was feeling so good he went into the control room after one take and said to Norman,

"Bean ought to be here today. I'm ready for him!" Norman got on the phone immediately and called up Coleman Hawkins and invited him, and he came in. I waited around because I wanted to see this, and the record they made at that time was one of the swingingest records that I think Ben made at that particular time. *In a Mellotone* was about twenty minutes long, which was very long in those days. It was brilliant. I especially like the groove that they got, because Jimmy Jones was really playing, and everybody in the rhythm section was up for it.[69]

Ben had brought three blues along. Two of them, *De-Dar* and *Young Bean,* were based on short riffs that sound so much alike that they could have been alternate takes of the same tune, especially since the tempi and keys (B-flat) are the same. The third, *Budd Johnson,* played at a medium slow pace, is in A major.

As Taylor recalls, it was a fine session resulting in a lot of good music. Budd Johnson plays with an easy flow, occasionally reminiscent of Sonny Stitt in the blues tunes, although his solos are somewhat lacking in depth. The most routine performance comes from Hawkins, whereas Eldridge does a fine job, building his solos well. The rhythm section swings excellently, and Ben is in control throughout. As bandleader, he solos last, and has reserved a little more solo time for himself, but his performance is more pensive than usual and less direct, coarse, and aggressive. Of everyone, his playing is the most dramatic, utilizing the most effects. He holds back at the onset of each solo, using plenty of air in his sound; in the blues tunes working his way up in intensity—in *Young Bean* combined with riffs and growl—whereas *Budd Johnson* is given a more varied treatment. Following a short piano introduction, *Time after Time* is a ballad feature for Ben in two choruses, interpreted with exceptional sensitivity and feeling; here too, the highest harmonic notes are played pianissimo. On *In a Mellotone,* laid-back melodic lines alternate with short outbursts or phrases consisting of single notes moving up or down on the offbeat during a three-chorus solo that swings elegantly in a well-rounded statement, culminating right before his last chorus.

In the middle of May, Ben took part in a Leonard Feather project called *One World Jazz.* The basic music was recorded in New York after which the tapes were flown to London, Stockholm, and Paris, where new solos were dubbed in by local musicians in the three other capitals. There was a fine rhythm section consisting of Hank Jones on piano, George Duvivier on bass, Kenny Burrell on guitar, and Jo Jones. The other American horn players were Clark Terry and trombonist J. J. Johnson. The European musicians were saxophonists Roy East and Ronnie Ross and trombonist George Chisholm from Britain, trombonist Åke Persson from Sweden, and violinist Stephane Grappelli, trumpeter Roger Guerin, saxophonist Bob Garcia, and pianist Martial Solal from France. Ben plays excellently, with lovely performances on *Misty* and *Nuages,* and a nicely swinging solo in *Big Ben's Blues.* On *Cotton Tail* he and Garcia each play a chorus, followed by a chase chorus in which Ben plays with great drive and energy. In comparison, his performance in *In a Mellotone* is more abrupt; his focus seems to shift several times during his solo.

Ben couldn't rely on recording sessions for an income, and as prospects for club jobs were still very bad, he decided to leave New York sometime during the summer of 1959. Disillusioned and hurt that no one seemed to need him or his music any more, he once again headed for Los Angeles and Mom and Mayme's hospitality. Over the autumn, new possibilities opened up, and his performance at Monterey Jazz Festival was especially important, as it became the starting point for two years of fruitful collaboration with vocalist Jimmy Witherspoon.

Jap Allen and His Orchestra, Kansas City, Mo., 1930. *Left to right:* Joe Keyes, Booker Pitman, Clyde Hart *(seated)*, Ben Webster, Alton "Slim" Moore, O. C. Wynn, Jap Allen, Alfred Denny, James "Jim Daddy" Walker, Raymond Howell, Dee "Prince" Stewart, Eddie "Orange" White.   W. Bert, Kansas City. Courtesy mr.jazz Photo Files, Theo Zwicky, Zurich, Switzerland

Blanche Calloway and Her Joy Boys, Kansas City, Mo., October 1931. *Pictured:* Blanche Calloway, Leroy Hardy, Clyde Hart, Herb Alvis, Booker Pitman, Cozy Cole, Ben Webster, Joe Keyes, Clarence Smith, Joe Durham, Andy Jackson, Alton "Slim" Moore, Edgar "Puddinghead" Battle.   Stiger Photo, Kansas City. Courtesy mr.jazz Photo Files, Theo Zwicky, Zurich, Switzerland

Andy Kirk's Twelve Clouds of Joy, Denver, Colo., February 1934. *Left to right:* Mary Lou Williams, John Harrington, Ben Webster, Pha Terrell, John Williams, Ben Thigpen, Harry "Big Jim" Lawson, Ted Brinson, Irving "Mouse" Randolph, Andy Kirk, Ted Donnelly, Earl Thompson.   Courtesy mr.jazz Photo Files, Theo Zwicky, Zurich, Switzerland

Willie Bryant and His Orchestra, New York, Roseland Ballroom, spring 1935. *Left to right:* Edgar "Puddinghead" Battle, Robert "Mack" Horton, Benny Carter, Bobby Cheeks, Cozy Cole, Arnold Adams, Louis Thompson, Glyn Paque, Stanley Payne, Teddy Wilson, Ben Webster, Johnny Russell. Shorty Haughton and Willie Bryant in front of the band.   Courtesy mr.jazz Photo Files, Theo Zwicky, Zurich, Switzerland

Teddy Wilson's Big Band, New York, Golden Gate Ballroom, December 1939. *Front row:* George Irish, Pete Clark, Rudy Powell, Ben Webster. *Middle row:* Buster Harding (piano), Al Hall (bass), Al Casey, Jake Wiley, Floyd "Stumpy" Brady. *Back row:* J. C. Heard (drums), Harold Baker, Karl George, Doc Cheatham.   Courtesy mr.jazz Photo Files, Theo Zwicky, Zurich, Switzerland

Duke Ellington and His Orchestra, Chicago, ca. December 1941. *Left to right:* Juan Tizol, "Tricky Sam" Nanton, Lawrence Brown (trombones), Fred Guy (guitar), Johnny Hodges, Barney Bigard (reeds), Duke Ellington (standing), Ben Webster (tenor saxophone), Sonny Greer (drums), Otto Hardwick (alto saxophone), Jimmie Blanton (bass), Harry Carney (baritone saxophone), Wallace Jones, Rex Stewart, Ray Nance (trumpets).   Timme Rosenkrantz Collection, University Library of Southern Denmark, Odense

Ben Webster Quartet, Washington, D.C., Bengazi Club, February or March 1946. *Left to right:* Argonne "Dense" Thornton, Ben Webster, Gene Ramey, Eddie Nichols.   Courtesy mr.jazz Photo Files, Theo Zwicky, Zurich, Switzerland

Al Hall Quintet, New York, Wax Recording Studio, January 24, 1947. *Left to right:* Dick Vance, Denzil Best, Ben Webster, Al Hall, Jimmy Jones.   Courtesy mr.jazz Photo Files, Theo Zwicky, Zurich, Switzerland

Part of Count Basie All Stars, CBS television show "The Sound of Jazz," New York City, December 8, 1957. *Front row, left to right:* Ben Webster, Earle Warren, Coleman Hawkins, and Gerry Mulligan (saxophones). *Back row, left to right:* Count Basie, Ed Jones, Freddie Green, and Jo Jones.   Courtesy mr.jazz Photo Files, Theo Zwicky, Zurich, Switzerland

Ben Webster, Alan Dawson, Larry Richardson, Horace Parlan, Boston, Mass., Connolly's Star Dust Room, early June 1963   Ben Webster Collection, University Library of Southern Denmark, Odense

Ben Webster skiing outside Oslo, Norway,
February 1965   Ben Webster Collection, University
Library of Southern Denmark, Odense

Ben Webster Quartet, Copenhagen, Danish TV Studio, March 9, 1965. *Left to right:* Alex Riel, Kenny Drew,
Ben Webster, Niels-Henning Ørsted Pedersen.   Jan Persson, www.janpersson.dk

The front line of Arnvid Meyer's Orchestra, Copenhagen, Jazzhus Montmartre, 1965. *Left to right:*
Ole Kongsted, Arnvid Meyer, John Darville, Ben Webster. Drummer Hans Nymand in the background.
Jan Persson, www.janpersson.dk

Ronnie Scott at Chelsea Bridge, London, spring 1965   Ben Webster. Ben Webster Collection, University Library of
Southern Denmark, Odense

Grethe Kemp in her apartment, Copenhagen, 1965   Ben Webster. Ben Webster
Collection, University Library of Southern Denmark, Odense

Jimmy Witherspoon, Albert Nicholas, Ben Webster in Jazzhus Montmartre, Copenhagen, December
1965   Courtesy mr.jazz Photo Files, Theo Zwicky, Zurich, Switzerland

At Pori Jazz Festival, Finland, July 14, 1967, with Niels-Henning Ørsted Pedersen on bass and Al Heath on drums   Ben Webster Collection, University Library of Southern Denmark, Odense

With the Danish Radio Big Band, Danish TV Studio, April 18, 1968. *Back row, left to right:* Trumpets: Allan Botchinsky, Palle Mikkelborg, Palle Bolvig, Perry Knudsen (almost hidden). *Middle row, left to right:* Trombones: Ole Kurt Jensen, Torolf Mølgaard, Per Espersen, Axel Windfeldt. *Front row, left to right:* Saxophones: Dexter Gordon (almost hidden), Bent Nielsen, Sahib Shihab, Jesper Thilo.   Jan Persson, www.janpersson.dk

Right: In Dum-Dum Jazzklub, Düsseldorf, Germany, July 11, 1968   Heinz Baumeister, Ingå, Finland

Below: In the studio of Steven Kwint, Amsterdam, December 1968   Ben Webster Collection, University Library of Southern Denmark, Odense

With friends in his apartment, Copenhagen, ca. 1970   Ben Webster Collection, University Library of Southern Denmark, Odense

Ben feeding the male giraffe "Lucky" in Circus Knie, Aarau, Switzerland, June 21, 1971   Chris Krenger, Jona, Switzerland

Tivoli Gardens, Copenhagen, July 12, 1970, with Birgit Nordtorp *(left)* and unknown female companion *(right)*   Courtesy Birgit Nordtorp

Ben with *(from left to right):* Russell Procope and Paul Gonsalves. Cootie Williams is seated in front in Ben'
apartment, July 12, 1970   Courtesy Birgit Nordtorp

Ben demonstrating stride piano
for Russell Procope in his apartment, July 12, 1970   Courtesy
Birgit Nordtorp

In Jazzhus Mont-
martre, Copenhagen,
with Charlie Shav-
ers, February 28,
1971   Jan Persson,
www.janpersson.dk

Meeting Benny Carter in Copenhagen Airport, May 30, 1971   Jan Persson, www.janpersson.dk

In Downtown Jazzkeller, Germany, May 6, 1972   Heinz Baumeister, Ingå, Finland

In Danish TV Studio with Savage Rose, February 27, 1973. Anisette Koppel, Thomas Koppel, Anders Koppel.
Jan Persson, www.janpersson.dk

In the Danish Radio building with Eubie Blake, July 1973.   Jan Persson, www.janpersson.dk

At the last gig, Café Sociëteit De Twee Spieghels, Leiden, Holland, September 6, 1973, with Irv Rochlin (with back turned) and Henk Haverhoek   Maria Wierdsma. Courtesy John Jeremy Productions

8. Last Years in the United States
(1959–1964)

At fifty Ben had become very compact. He was thickset and broad-shouldered, his bearing erect, and although he had gained weight over the years, he was not really overweight. He was of medium height with thin legs that didn't fit in with the rest of his body. He still had immensely strong arms, and enjoyed showing off his strength. "Ben Webster was one of the strongest musicians I ever knew," recalls record producer and critic George Avakian,

> and that includes Zutty Singleton. Sid Catlett was even bigger than Zutty, but he didn't have muscles like Ben or Zutty.
>
> Ben and I were listening to somebody at the old Birdland bar, and for the third time since midnight I said, "Ben, I really have to get home." Ben looked at me in the eye, said, "Uh, uh!" and picked me up, turned me sideways and held me over his head. But he was always a gentleman through and through—the moment I said, "I'll stay!" he set me down gently and picked up all the change that had fallen out of my pocket.[1]

When Ben played, he stood erect, was well-dressed, and held his horn straight in front of him, almost like a soldier presenting arms. His face, with its eagle-beaked nose, was expressionless, and he stood completely still, totally concentrated with closed eyes, as if listening to something inside his head. Only when playing an altissimo note, would he open his upturned eyes, as if in need of extra space or of help from above. Once in a while, he would remove the saxophone from his mouth after a phrase, ever so slightly shake his head—on which he always wore a hat that seemed too small—and continue with the next phrase.

When Ben arrived in Los Angeles late in the summer of 1959, the only fixed point in his life was the house in which he lived with his aging mother and grand-aunt, who were eighty-seven and ninety-five years old, but still able to take care of themselves. He had no bookings, but calmly awaited a change of events. He did not wait long. The first days of October were hectic, with bookings at two simultaneous festivals in Monterey and Los Angeles.

In 1958 Jimmy Lyons had arranged the first jazz festival in Monterey, the small California town where writer John Steinbeck had settled in the early 1930s and which had inspired him to write *Tortilla Flats* and *Of Mice and Men.* Lyons's jazz festival was so successful that he continued in the years to come, and in 1959, the festival had grown to three days over the weekend of October 2–4. Ben performed Friday evening and Saturday afternoon, the first evening with blues singer Jimmy Witherspoon and the Monterey All Stars with, among others, Eldridge, Hawkins, Earl Hines, and Mel Lewis. Recordings from the concert reveal an attentive and interested audience of six thousand, and an equally inspired band driven forward by drummer Mel Lewis's effective and swinging drumming. Ben is featured quite a lot, and in the rocking *Big Fine Girl* he starts up a series of backing riffs that lift the music an extra notch, and in the slow *Ain't Nobody's Business* he plays two lyrical and sensitive choruses that fit Witherspoon's vocal like hand in glove.

The day after, he played with a combination of musicians quite different from anything he had been accustomed to. He had always followed new directions in jazz, and often listened to young musicians at their gigs or hired them in his groups, but he had never played with avant-garde jazz musician Ornette Coleman before. Following a set alone with a rhythm section, he concluded the afternoon's program with Hawkins and Coleman in a group announced as The Three Saxes. "One of the most stimulating performances came from Ben Webster, Coleman Hawkins, and Ornette Coleman," one reviewer wrote. "This was a study in contrasts, with Webster and Hawkins embodying the virile tradition of jazz and Coleman hinting at another and esoteric direction that may be in its future."[2] Alas, this group is not documented on record.

The same evening, Ben and Hawkins drove back to Los Angeles to perform at the first Los Angeles Jazz Festival at the Hollywood Bowl.

The festival was an enormous musical and financial success. The crowd of eighteen thousand would not let go of the swing group Ben played with. "Coleman Hawkins, Ben Webster and Roy Eldridge, backed by Pete Jolly's piano, Curtis Counce's bass and Frank Butler's drums, provided the spark," *Down Beat* wrote.

> They did only two numbers, a fast riff tune and a medium tempo blues, but the audience was yelling for more when they got off.
>
> Hawkins played bitingly on the first number, inspiring Eldridge to follow him and build logically to a series of stratospheric blasts before Webster entered, calm, collected, and dynamically effective. Drummer Butler, who certainly is not from the swing era but fit in well with his own distinctive modern style, was a dynamo of support. Jolly soloed briefly and made his point. Counce provided the base for blowing.
>
> The second number was testimony indeed to Webster's jazz immortality. His long solo moved thousands to quick applause, applause that was still crashing down upon the stage after the number ended and the Basie band swung out onstage.[3]

These concerts not only gave Ben's self-confidence a much-needed boost, but the success of the Witherspoon concert enticed the blues singer to invite Ben to join his band at the Renaissance Club in Los Angeles, which consisted of Jimmy Rowles and Leroy Vinnegar with either Mel Lewis or Frank Butler at the drums. "And *that's* a boss rhythm section," Ben recalled. "They lay it down for you."[4]

Witherspoon and Ben hit it off immediately. They also shared mutual musical experiences, because "Spoon" and he had both worked with Jay McShann in the late 1940s. Playing with Spoon ensured Ben a good steady job, and the blues repertoire played by Witherspoon was much more varied than Ben had experienced with Jay McShann or Walter Brown. "Ben Webster—he was my number one. We didn't take no job without each other," Witherspoon remembered.[5] "I was shocked that he would work with me at that time," he said at a later occasion.

> A lot of entertainers said, "Oh, they can't work it, they can't make it. Spoon is crazy, and Ben is crazy!" But we never had an argument.

Even today I benefit from his knowledge. He could come up with the most beautiful lines. One night the joint was packed, but nobody applauded when we came through. We went into the dressing room, and Ben put his horn away. I said, "Ben, what happened out there? No one applauded." He said, 'Well, Spoon, we'll get them next time. There are only three tempos, slow, medium, and fast. If you get in between the crevices, ain't nothing happening." He never did say, "Spoon, you kicked them off all wrong." But I knew what he meant. I'm one of the few entertainers that you ever hear who can open in a tempo like that (snaps a slow tempo with his fingers). And it works, and all of it is Ben Webster. He was a great blues player. This man could bend a note on a blues like nobody.[6]

"You can sing or play all night and not get it," he said in another interview. "Ben Webster taught me that. And he taught me this also: that *time* is the greatest thing in the world."[7]

During the last few months of 1959, there were a few musically rewarding Verve sessions. *Gerry Mulligan Meets Ben Webster* was recorded in two sessions, November 3 and December 2, with Ben's regular rhythm section, Jimmy Rowles, Leroy Vinnegar, and Mel Lewis. Mulligan and his wife stayed in a rented house, which became the site of many small musical gatherings. "The date grew out of sessions we would have, little things I would have at my place," Mulligan recalled. "Ben and I were friends, we went back together a little bit. We were both out in L.A. and did musical sessions—for ourselves—frequently on Sundays. I even went to his place many times and met his mother. They were very nice to me. I enjoyed those visits and, of course, I enjoyed the blowin' with Ben as we did—for ourselves—at these little jams I would set up for us. We'd even try out some of our new tunes at these little pick-up sessions. This grew into a desire to do something together in public, which we did. The rhythm section players on the Verve recording with Norman were the same we had on our thing and also for many of our little or even some big gigs we did."[8]

Photographer William Claxton was present at the sessions at the Radio Recorders Studio and remembered that "Gerry knew that Ben liked booze around when he recorded, and he very much wanted to please him, to make him comfortable. But Ben got so caught up in the spirit of what was happening that the bottle just sat there. He had maybe one shot; ordinarily he would have drunk the whole bottle. Gerry told me, 'I'm finally with one of my childhood heroes.' He was thrilled. He was pretty much in awe of Ben and very much trying to please him with solos and arranging ideas. Gerry was one of the smartest people I knew, and he could be delightful to be around. But he also had a boundless ego, and he could be insufferable at times. So to see him so boyish and bowing down to Ben was kind of nice. It made me like Gerry even more."[9] It was a nice, relaxed encounter with both horn players in fine form, and as in Ben's session with Hawkins, this is not a cutting session; the recordings are permeated with a sense of mutual respect, friendship, and warmth. Ben's good mood that day was instrumental in creating the relaxed atmosphere. Rowles recalls that "Mulligan was married to Sandy Dennis, the actress, and they were doing a picture at MGM together, and Mulligan was doing some acting. I never saw the picture, but Ben was in a kind of frisky frame of mind that day and he was funny, and he was kidding Mulligan for being a movie star and all that. He looked at him and said, 'Hmm, movie star! Did you get your bread yet?' You know, putting him on, kidding with him. But everything went fine and we had a good time laughing at Ben."[10] The rhythm section plays extremely well, and deserves their share of credit for the fine outcome. The ballads *Chelsea Bridge* and *Tell Me When*—written especially for Ben and fitting his style like a glove—are fine examples of the lovely, mellow chemistry working between the two horns in the theme presentations, with Ben playing lead as Mulligan weaves long notes and contrapuntal lines. Ben's performance is unusually beautiful and mature; he never plays a superfluous note. His *Blues for Bessie* is a lovely melodic statement, and in the final chorus's joint improvisation they build and ease tension uniformly. The whole recording is saturated with Rowles's sense of humor, and on *Sunday* he plays an introduction clearly addressed to Willie "The Lion" Smith.

Another classic recording, from November 6, 1959, has Ben playing with Oscar Peterson's Trio with Ray Brown and drummer Ed Thigpen. The rhythm section plays brilliantly, and Peterson's accompaniment is at its very best, attentive and supportive. Ben himself is in great form, swinging magnificently in *Sunday,* one of his favorites throughout his career, and *The Touch of Your Lips, This Can't Be Love,* and *Bye, Bye Black-bird* are likewise full of drive, even though his phrases are generally short. Ben's translucent, beautiful sound, diversified phrasing, and dynamic variations all contribute to a very expressive performance, particularly in the slow tempi. *In the Wee Small Hours of the Morning* is dreamy, and the melancholy mood of *When Your Lover Has Gone* is interpreted with emotion. Here, as on the Mulligan sessions, Ben doesn't play an unnecessary note.

On December 2, Gerry Mulligan was invited to sit in at the Renaissance with Ben and Witherspoon. The evening was recorded and shows an effectively swinging rhythm section and inspiring contributions from Spoon, Ben, and Mulligan. Mulligan falls right in to the routine built up by the band, and occasionally, as in *St. Louis Blues,* the interplay with Ben behind Spoon is telepathic; other times the two of them initiate effective riffs. A week later, the group performed on vocalist Dinah Shore's television show without Spoon, first playing *Go Home* and *Who's Got Rhythm?* followed by *Lazy River* with Shore. Humor bubbles through the fast *Who's Got Rhythm?* in the chase choruses with Lewis, with Ben quoting from his own solo in *Cotton Tail* in the B-part and Mulligan picking it up and quoting from the same solo in the following A-part. The show was never aired as originally planned but first broadcast during Shore's next television series some two years later.

Ben and Spoon performed at the Renaissance continuously until early March 1960, when they were booked by Omega Enterprises for a short package tour of San Jose, San Francisco, and Oakland with the Miles Davis Quintet with John Coltrane, the Jazztet, a dynamic, newly formed sextet under the leadership of trumpeter Art Farmer and tenor saxophonist Benny Golson, and vocalist Nina Simone. Despite the great acts, the tour was a financial disaster, attracting fewer than five hundred people at the concerts in San Jose and Oakland.

During the summer of 1960, Ben performed on several sessions with vocalist Jo Stafford along with Rowles and Mel Lewis. The big-band arrangements were written by Johnny Mandel, and although Stafford's reputation was made in popular music, *Jo + Jazz* turned out very well. Ben's big, warm sound and sensitive playing can be heard in several obbligatos and in solos in *For You, You'd Be So Nice to Come Home To, I Didn't*

Know about You, Dream of You, S'posin', and *I've Got the World on a String*. He is inspired in general and comes up with quite a few original phrases and lines, making for interesting listening, for his sake alone, throughout the album.

Late on the afternoon of October 14, 1960, Ben called Lester Koenig at Contemporary Records to persuade him to record that evening's show during a new booking at the Renaissance. Koenig consented, all the last-minute arrangements were made, and the recordings were issued as an instrumental album without Witherspoon. The rhythm section plays excellently—one understands Ben's enthusiasm. Rowles bends his playing exceptionally well to Ben's, and guitarist Jim Hall's and bassist Red Mitchell's solos are all first rate. Ben has an inspired evening, and all tracks are concluded dynamically and energetically. His muscular traits dominate *Caravan* and *Mop Mop*, his interpretations of *Stardust* and *Georgia on My Mind* are sensitive and lovely, and *Ole Miss Blues* and *What Is This Thing Called Love* are given a relaxed, after-hours treatment. The concluding blues in B minor, called *Renaissance Blues* on the CD, is in reality *Poutin'*. It was not Ben's style to spice his solos with quotations, but following fine solos from Rowles and Hall, he enters with a quotation from *Summertime*.

That autumn, Ben's days were spent playing at the Renaissance, and with jobs at The Digger Club to break the monotony. The rhythm section now consisted of Rowles, guitarist Jim Hall, bassist Red Mitchell, and Frank Butler. In November he and Witherspoon performed at the Jazz Cellar in San Francisco with a local rhythm section. During this booking, Ellington came to town with his orchestra, and Norman Granz eyed the chance to get Johnny Hodges and Ben together to record an album. Ella Fitzgerald was likewise in the Bay City, and Granz suggested using her excellent rhythm section with pianist Lou Levy, guitarist Herb Ellis, bassist Wilfred Middlebrooks, and drummer Gus Johnson. The musical outcome was very nice, the two old friends obviously enjoying the easy swinging rhythm section immensely. However, there are no magical moments, although we hear many fine solos from members of the rhythm section as well. But there is great joy to be derived from the horns in the ensemble choruses. Certain places reveal themselves as studies in perfectly adjusted phrasing and dynamics. *Ben's Web, Dual Highway,* and *Blues'll*

Blow Your Fuse are excellent examples. Ben is not unaffected by Hodges's presence; on *Big Ears,* which features one of his most inspired moments, he begins his solo with a perfect imitation of his idol's sound, so much so that for a split second it sounds as if Hodges is starting up a new chorus. Another remarkable solo is in *Side Door,* in which Ben opens his second chorus with a few excellent unorthodox figures.

Outside of the aforementioned recordings, 1960 found Ben participating in a few sessions where his contributions were less prominent. Among these were albums with vocalists Nancy Wilson, Helen Humes, and Big Miller, with whom he and Witherspoon also worked on *Evolution of the Blues Song* with singer Jon Hendricks.

It was not the South, but California was not free from racial prejudice, although this did not influence Spoon's and Ben's desire to play with white musicians such as Rowles, Red Mitchell, or Jim Hall. Ben just wanted to play the best possible music. Privately, however, there were restrictions. He never visited with Rowles. "We were living in Culver City, before we moved to Burbank around 1960," Rowles recalled. "There was so much prejudice among the neighbours that I never brought Ben to the house. I was afraid because Ben was so imposing and so black and so strong looking. This was terrible. I had to worry about my daughters. I couldn't do something that would interfere with their happiness or daily life. There were three little girls right next door my girls played with. I was afraid that people would tell their children, 'Don't hang out with those little girls.'"[11] But Rowles visited Ben in Wilton Place whenever he pleased.

Ben was kept busy on January 18 and 19, 1961, first recording his own album, *The Warm Moods,* then continuing with vocalist Anita O'Day's Billie Holiday tribute, *Trav'lin' Light.* Here his solo on *The Moon Looks Down and Laughs* is lovely and melodic, and *Miss Brown to You* features a spirited chase with O'Day.

The Warm Moods is one of Ben's best recordings with strings. Johnny Richards wrote the arrangements, and it was the first album recorded and released for Frank Sinatra's new label, Reprise. The lineup consisted of a rhythm section with strings, and Richards's arrangements are melodious, varied, and intelligent, never getting in Ben's way, but supporting and working with him, at times creating a dialogue with him, as in *Accent on Youth* and *I'm Beginning to See the Light.* The tempi never surpass medium, which contributes to the sensation that this album is saturated with Ben's big, rich sound. The tracks are short, two choruses at the most, so the improvisations are not long, which doesn't matter because it is a pleasure just listening to Ben play melody with a sound perfectly suiting the strings. From a stirring session, *But Beautiful* is perhaps the most lyrical and beautiful track.

Less than two weeks later, on the last day of January, Ben recorded with Hodges again, in what turned out to be Ben's last session for Norman Granz. The session was somewhat anemic. Ben has but two real solos, on two medium tempo blues, *Tipsy Joe* and *Waiting on the Champagne,* playing two choruses in both. With the exception of the powerful and aggressive opening phrase on *Tipsy Joe,* his performance is disappointing and uninspired.

In March 1961, Ben recorded a session with organ player Richard "Groove" Holmes. It was a jam session; almost nothing was prepared. The only other horn was trombonist Lawrence "Tricky" Lofton, and the swinging rhythm section included pianist Les McCann and drummer Ron Jefferson. Ben is in great form, contributing intense, powerful, and exciting playing in *Licks a Plenty, That Healin' Feelin',* and *Seven Come Eleven.* However, the loveliest track of all is *Deep Purple,* interpreted beautifully, with a very moving solo that never becomes sentimental.

The booking at the Renaissance continued into 1961, broken by a trip to San Francisco in July–August to play at the Jazz Workshop. The job was very successful, and Ben and Spoon were rebooked several times. During the summer and autumn of 1961, Ben recorded a Witherspoon album called *Hey, Mrs. Jones* for Reprise, which was disappointing in that Ben played but one solo. He also worked on sessions with vocalists Wynona Carr and Kay Starr where his performances were sporadic and mostly limited to obbligatos that he duly filled with all the emotion he could.

The 1961 Monterey Jazz Festival was planned as a showcase for Duke Ellington and Dizzy Gillespie, and Ben was part of a set called the Modern Mainstream Set.[12] Ben had his camera with him, and took many pictures during the various concerts, including the opening concert with the Terry Gibbs Big Band. The orchestra played a version of *Cotton Tail* featuring Ben's famous solo in a five-part saxophone arrangement, which took Ben completely by surprise. "You should have seen his face!" said Ralph Gleason. "He could not believe his ears. It was a beautiful moment."[13]

That fall, Witherspoon went on tour in Europe, and at the Renaissance, Ben Shapiro put Ben together with valve trombonist Bob Brookmeyer as his substitute. Things began to get interesting when the quintet started alternating sets with stand-up comedian Lenny Bruce. Bruce (1925–1966) was a controversial entertainer who shocked audiences with his outspoken and lewd humor on touchy subjects such as blacks, Jews, religion, politics, drugs, and sex, and his frank performances paved the way for later comedians like Richard Pryor and Eddie Murphy. Many people of Ben's generation did not condone swearing in public, and there is no doubt that he also shocked Ben more than once. They shared the stage not only in Los Angeles, but also at the Jazz Workshop toward the end of the year. Ralph Gleason was in the audience one evening at the Jazz Workshop, and remembered that Bruce in his performance

> divided the world into "goyishe" and "yiddish." That is to say, into Jews and non-Jews and in Lenny's book, all the best jokes were Jewish. Eddie Cantor was goyishe. People like Billy Graham and things like TV dinners were scary goyishe.
>
> But Benjamin Francis Webster was Jewish.
>
> I will never forget Ben when he heard that. Lenny shot off the remark in that clipped delivery he had, looked quickly over at Ben who was standing against the wall and smiled. Ben just collapsed. Simply went to pieces. It was one of the funniest things I ever saw.
>
> But it was also a beautiful tribute to a great man, because Ben Webster was Jewish in the sense that Lenny meant it and that sense was a supreme compliment to Ben's warmth, humanity and artistry.[14]

After Witherspoon had returned from Europe, he and Ben were booked at the Jazz Workshop during December 1961–January 1962 with an excellent, hard-swinging local rhythm section with pianist Vince Guaraldi, bassist Monty Budwig, and drummer Colin Bailey. A series of recordings from this job have been issued with various dates. However, all of them feature the Vince Guaraldi trio, which was working there during December 1961 through January 1962, so most probably, they all come from this time period. Many tunes are repeated, but the recordings show that each tune has a regular routine, with rare deviations. They also document that Witherspoon has thoroughly accepted Ben's claim that there are only three existing tempi: slow, medium, and fast. They play nothing in between. The recordings also illustrate that Ben's solos have their regular routine. He never plays the same solo in, for example, *'Tain't Nobody's Business If I Do*. Still, his solo follows the same pattern each time, the first chorus in lyrical, subdued lines and moving to the high register in the second chorus while continuing to play lovely, lyrical phrases. In the slow *Please Send Me Someone to Love,* he demonstrates his ability to swing effectively and with great drive even in a slow tempo. There is quite a lot of inspiring music from the various nights, including all the versions of *Every Day I Have the Blues, St. Louis Blues, Roll'em Pete, Hello Little Girl,* and *Time's Getting Tougher Than Tough,* in which Ben somehow fits one original idea after the other into his solo.

The year 1962 was as meager in recording as the previous one, although it began well with a fine Benny Carter session with Shorty Sherock on trumpet, Barney Bigard, and a rhythm section consisting of Jimmy Rowles, Dave Barbour on guitar, Leroy Vinnegar, and Mel Lewis. Carter brought two tunes, *Lula* and *When Lights Are Low.* Leonard Feather, who had set up the sessions, contributed *Opening Blues* and the slow *You Can't Tell the Difference When the Sun Goes Down Blues,* which also went by the shorter title, *Heavy Hearted Blues.* The latter had a somewhat original if slightly forced structure built on an eighteen-bar chorus, which doesn't seem to have inspired any of the soloists, including Ben, although he does manage to put warmth into his chorus. He plays with much more intensity and presence in *Opening Blues,* and adorns his solo in *Lula* with his most beautiful and lyrical tone. *When Lights Are Low* is mainly a showcase for Carter, but Barney and Ben share a chorus where Ben swings along nicely with pretty lines. The session doesn't produce monumental solos, but the atmosphere is relaxed, and Rowles delivers small humorous surprise licks here and there in his solos and accompaniments.

The rest of that afternoon—April 10—and the next day, Ben was part of a large orchestra backing Frank Sinatra. He solos only once, on *I'm*

Beginning to See the Light. A month later, Ben and Spoon filled a studio vacancy arising when Sinatra canceled a session—a stroke of good luck, because *Roots* is the best album the two recorded together. Everything comes together on this recording where blues and jazz merge wonderfully and naturally. Witherspoon's vocal and Ben's playing are equally author- itative. Witherspoon's laid-back phrasing and exceptionally emotional and moving interpretations bring the two of them closer musically than ever, occasionally verging on the symbiotic, as in the slow *Did You Ever, Please, Mr. Webster, Nobody Knows You When You're Down and Out,* and *Just a Dream,* where Ben's sensitive and touching obbligatos follow Spoon's vocal. Ben is the featured soloist, and here too, he complements Witherspoon perfectly. In *Key to the Highway* he follows Spoon with two lyrical choruses, and in *Your Red Wagon* he comments on the preceding vocal with notes—and glissandi leading up and down to them—that say more than words. The rhythm section with Ernie Freeman on piano plays excellently, and Gerald Wilson's pensive trumpet fits in well.

With the exception of their bookings in San Francisco, Ben and Spoon did not tour very much together, but in late April 1962, they were booked for three weeks at the Archway Supper Club in Chicago, accom- panied by pianist John Young's trio.

In late May, Ben visited the East Coast for a short while. First he played at the First International Jazz Festival in Washington, D.C., on the weekend of May 29–31. Ben was reunited once again with Roy Eldridge in a short set with Oscar Peterson's Trio "for four delightful, singing perfor- mances."[15] He then left for New York and a recording session with Harry Edison in early June, taking the opportunity to visit Birdland to hear John Coltrane, whose music he enjoyed.[16] "One guy I thought was really trying was John Coltrane," Ben once said. "He had a method, a real system, y'know. I liked to hear Coltrane. He was searching all the time, but he died. In jazz like in life, you need a little luck to get along."[17] Ben and Coltrane were close friends. In 1960, photographer Roy DeCarava por- trayed the warm sentiments between the two when he shot a picture of them in warm embrace, probably while on tour together for Omega Enterprises. Ben, with his small hat on, is hugging Coltrane with his right arm around his neck; Coltrane's face rests on Ben's neck. The touching image appeared in a retrospective collection of DeCarava's work published by the Museum of Modern Art in New York in 1996.

With Harry Edison, Ben recorded for Columbia the fine album *Ben and Sweets,* on June 6 and 7. Both are in good form, accompanied by an all-star rhythm section consisting of pianist Hank Jones, bassist George Duvivier, and drummer Clarence Johnson. Ben blossoms on this session—it is clear that he enjoys the rhythm section and playing with Edison again. He contributes two compositions, *Better Go,* a medium tempo blues, and *Did You Call Her Today?* which—as *In a Mellotone*—is structured on *Rose Room.* A shorter version of *Better Go* would have been more interesting, as Edison's solo slips into neutral toward its conclusion, but Ben's swinging eight choruses are built up gradually from easygoing phrases to intense lines without relying on clichés other than a few repeated descending triplets in the sixth chorus. *Did You Call Her Today?* is a hard-swinging, rocking tune with a lively solo by Ben, bursting with good ideas and intensity. As in *Cotton Tail,* he has written a chorus for the horns played in unison—almost, for Edison fluffs in the B-part. In *Kitty,* written by Edison with a Horace Silver–type theme, the rhythm section swings perfectly from the very start. Ben's solo is shaped of short phrases, as if intent on keeping the strong swing going, but still full of original, ingenious ideas. *How Long Has This Been Going On?* and *My Romance* are features for Ben; both ballads remained in his repertoire for the rest of his life. The former is introduced with a seldom-played verse. The exceptionally warm and tender renditions lift these two tunes up among the highlights of the album. Once again Ben astounds us with his phrasing and his ability to shape his sound to express as much as possible. By omitting a note here or adding a couple there, or taking a breath unexpectedly, he changes the tune enough to make it his own while still fully respecting the original version.

While in New York, Ben was booked for a week in Harlem at the Shalimar later in June, but the booking went more or less unnoticed by the public, although Ben was in fine form here, too. Meanwhile in Los Angeles, the health of both Mayme and Mom was deteriorating, so Ben decided to go back after his engagement in order to spend time with them. Their ill health apparently also caused him to cancel a booking at the

Newport Jazz Festival, where he was scheduled to appear on the opening night, July 6, with Roy Eldridge.

In California his collaboration with Witherspoon was reestablished with jobs in Los Angeles and at the Jazz Workshop in July–August and again in December 1962. They also both performed at that year's Monterey Jazz Festival, once again a personal triumph for Ben despite a partially chaotic program. Ben performed in several sets, including the opening concert on Friday, September 21 with a band called The Swingers with Rex Stewart, trumpeter Conte Candoli, Bill Harris, Benny Carter, Stuff Smith, Earl Hines, bassist Buddy Clark, and Mel Lewis. According to *Down Beat,* Ben "was astounding in several long, flowing tenor solos."[18] This was followed by a blues program in which The Swingers accompanied Helen Humes, Jimmy Rushing, and Witherspoon. The first tune was catastrophic; the rhythm section was unaware that Witherspoon's opening song was not a straight blues. "Jimmy Witherspoon tried to sing eight-bar blues while Hines, bassist Buddy Clark, and drummer Mel Lewis attempted 12-bar blues, which, according to Clark, they had been told to play. The tune ended with Witherspoon visibly shaken, Webster calling the chords, and Hines hunting for the proper place to play them but never letting a smile leave his face."[19] At the rehearsal that afternoon, when Ben sat in for Hines, who had not yet arrived, everything had gone smoothly. "All us jazz fans are so ignorant, really, of the depth of talent of the artists we love that almost no one was aware that Ben was a fine stride pianist," reminisced Ralph Gleason. "There was a rehearsal one afternoon, and Ben dropped onto the bench and started playing the piano for Jimmy Rushing and for an hour the swingiest place in the world was that rehearsal shed at Monterey."[20]

Saturday afternoon, the program was dedicated to the inventor of the saxophone, Adolphe Sax, and Ben performed in two sets. In the first, he played with Benny Carter, alto saxophonist Phil Woods, tenor saxophonist Bill Perkins, and a rhythm section of Vince Guaraldi, Buddy Clark, and Mel Lewis. The repertoire played by this septet consisted of Benny Carter's compositions and arrangements and was received favorably by the critics. "As a section, the men blended better than one might normally expect in such a short time of working together; and in this day of five-man sax sections, it was enlightening to hear the brightness of the four-man unit," wrote Don DeMicheal in *Down Beat*.

> Carter's arrangements are of the sorts that allow light and shade full play.
>
> Webster was the outstanding soloist. Never have I heard him in better form—chorus after chorus of undiluted inspiration that had me jumping up and down inside with a combination of joy and sadness. And on *Cotton Tail* Lewis was particularly sympathetic behind Webster's solos, using for the most part a sizzle cymbal that sounded like a crowd roaring behind the tenorist, and crowds *should* roar when Webster is as inspired as he was that afternoon.[21]

Toward the end of the afternoon's program, Ben played a set with eight other saxophonists, but unfortunately the pleasure provided was smaller than one might anticipate despite other fine names such as Carter, Phil Woods, Paul Desmond, James Moody, Mulligan, and Bill Perkins.

Duke Ellington visited Los Angeles on November 15, 1962, to perform in the Embassy Auditorium in sharp competition with the heavyweight championship fight a few blocks away between twenty-year-old Cassius Clay (now Muhammad Ali) and Ben's friend Archie Moore. Ben had no intention of missing out on anything that evening, so after the fight—lost by Moore in the fourth round—he went on to Ellington's concert, where the audience was in for a few late, but pleasant surprises, as both Rex Stewart, Gerry Mulligan, and Ben sat in on the concluding *C Jam Blues*. This was not the only time Ben sat in with the Ellington orchestra. He sought them out whenever the opportunity arrived, and played with them later in New York and several times in Europe at planned concerts as well as spontaneous occasions.

Mayme's and Mom's health had deteriorated so much by now that they were unable to take care of themselves. Much as he would have liked to, his bookings made it impossible for him to take care of them, and they were admitted to an old-age home. Ben visited them as often as he could, but his drinking—under control for a while—worsened as his fear of losing them grew. Following their traditional two-week New Year's booking at the Jazz Workshop in 1963, Ben's collaboration with Spoon stopped, and he found himself without steady bookings and alone in the big, empty house on Wilton Place. There was no one to talk to or keep him in line, and his spirits sagged as his drinking increased.

The monotony of this daily futility in which he hardly touched his saxophone was broken by the offer of jobs in Chicago in early March. Once again, Ben played with Eldridge, accompanied by Bill Doggett's Trio at McKie's Disc Jockey Lounge. On March 13, the same evening Cassius Clay beat Douglas Jones in New York's Madison Square Garden, a reporter from the *Chicago Defender* showed up to interview Ben and review the evening's concert. Ben and Eldridge had watched the fight on television and showed up at McKie's shortly before their first set. "My chops don't feel too good," admitted Ben, "but I'm going on."[22] The reviewer then asked him if he thought that any of the young jazz musicians could replace Charlie Parker, to which Ben answered prophetically, "I don't know. I do feel that John Coltrane has more to say than most of the youngsters currently on the scene. If anyone brings about a change, as 'Bird,' he'll do it."

Despite Ben's reservations, the evening went very well. "Over the years, Webster has matured a bit, but his tone and sound still is as big as it was 15 years ago," remarked the reporter from the *Chicago Defender*.

> Like Gene Ammons, he blows with force on up-tempo tunes, and with the softness of silk on slow melodic ballads . . .
>
> Roy Eldridge and Webster traded fours on a great many numbers, and when the first set was over, fans left with the feeling that even though Ben has developed a bay window [gained some weight], he still knew his horn. And he always will.

Mayme and Mom died in the old-age home within a few months of each other in the first half of 1963, ninety-one and ninety-nine years old. Mom's death notice tells us that Ben participated in her funeral at Utter McKinley Chapel, after which she was buried in Lincoln Memorial Park. Since Mayme and Mom both lived in the same old-age home, it is reasonable to surmise that Mayme's ceremony was at the same chapel and that she too was buried in Lincoln Memorial Park. Jobs in Los Angeles were few, and Ben had no desire to stay on in the house, so he asked Joyce

Cockrell and his cousin Harley W. Robinson, Jr., to sell it, and, depressed at the loss of his dear ones, he once again traveled cross-country to New York.

He arrived in the city around the end of May and was working in the first week of July—not in New York, however, but at Connolly's Star Dust Room in Roxbury on the outskirts of Boston. He was accompanied by a fine trio with Horace Parlan at the piano, Alan Dawson on drums, and Larry Richardson on bass.[23]

A reporter caught Ben between sets one evening in the middle of the week, and once again Ben enthused about John Coltrane and expressed his joy in working with musicians playing within different styles. "As much a gentleman as he is an artist, Webster declined to 'put anyone down,'" the reporter wrote. "His only comment about the current crop of musicians was a glowing one for tenor John Coltrane. 'He's striving, searching for a way to express himself. Man, you've got to be an individual in jazz. You have to search and find out what it is you're going to say. 'Trane has found it, and that's why he's one of the best around today.'"[24]

A few weeks after his return to New York in the summer of 1963, Ben was once again back recording, this time with trumpeter Clark Terry. Terry had signed with Cameo to record an album titled *More*. Terry and Ben had become close friends and often worked together in later years, especially in Europe. "We loved to play together," says Terry. "I enjoyed very much working with Frog. In his playing he sometimes would get rough, but other times he was smooth, very melodic, and a very tasteful player and a very honest player. Frog was my favorite ballad player on the tenor saxophone, and I loved it when he played. I can see him now with his beautifully blocked hat, shoes shined, trousers creased, necktie, and yelling 'Fav'rin!,' which is what we called each other. One of the things I can say about Frog is that he was one of the most beautiful people in the world."[25]

For the recording date, Terry had booked a rhythm section consisting of pianist Roger Kellaway, guitarist Gene Bertoncini, bassist Bill Crow, and drummer Dave Bailey, but before the studio date on June 17, they decided to have a short rehearsal. "The date was called at a large recording studio in Bayside, Long Island," Bill Crow remembers.

Clark lived near the studio at the time, so we met at his house on the morning of the date for a rehearsal, and Clark's first wife, Pauline, made breakfast for us. Ben tucked away a large portion of scrambled eggs with hamburgers, downed a few cups of coffee, and then leaned back in his chair, put his feet up on a coffee table, and fell asleep. We had heard stories about the danger of waking Ben, so we ran through the tunes that Clark had picked out. Roger Kellaway had worked out some sketches on a few of them. Ben slept through the hour and a half rehearsal, but as soon as Clark said, "Well, we'd better head over to the studio," Ben woke right up. We were relieved not to have to wake him.

At the studio, a large room with a very high ceiling, Ben set up his reed and walked across the room to the far wall where he warmed up, playing directly at the wall. To me it sounded as if he was painting the whole wall a rich, golden brown. When he walked back to where the rhythm section was setting up, I said to him, "I love to hear the beautiful sound you make." He scowled and said, "Can't get no damn reeds anymore."

Either Ben was sleeping lightly at the rehearsal, or his instincts were finely tuned. He played everything just right, and we didn't do any retakes.[26]

Terry, Kellaway, and Ben play very well in an enjoyable session. Even in a fast blues, *Blues Fr' Ell,* Ben plays with ease, and in *Sid's Mark,* he jumps into a succession of runs, something he rarely did. He plays but one chorus in a slow blues, *Hobo Flats,* but that is all he needs, for it is an exceptionally expressive chorus, especially the concluding phrase, ending in notes played with alternative fingering. A ballad, *This Is All I Ask,* is a feature for Ben; he plays the tune once through, beautifully, simply, and with a rich singing sound. That's all it takes.

Shortly after, from June 18, Ben was booked at the Shalimar in Harlem, a booking to be extended from one to six weeks. Ben was in fine form, and his alcohol intake was the lowest in years. It was as if he had started a new life, for the first time dependent only on himself, without a family to support him. Indeed, during the next year things seemed to work out well for him, and he had quite a few bookings and concerts. At the Shalimar, his rhythm section varied during the first couple of weeks until he found the lineup of his choice. With pianist Dave Frishberg, bassist Richard Davis, and Mel Lewis, Ben had a regular group for the first time in years.

Frishberg recalls the following from his time with Ben,

> Soon after I joined the band at the Shalimar, Ben was at the microphone introducing the next song, *Danny Boy,* and he turned to me at the piano and said, "Reminisce."
>
> I said, "What?" He said, "Reminisce."
>
> I said, "What are you talking about?"
>
> He said, "When I'm talking to the people, you reminisce behind me."
>
> Then I understood and began to play soft chords as he spoke to the audience.
>
> Ben was very emotional and his feelings were close to the surface. I knew that Ben was famous for unpredictable outbursts of anger and violence, but I never saw him pull any of those stunts, perhaps because he was trying to abstain from hard liquor at that time. He did drink beer—Rheingold. When he drank he was quick to weep. He would ask Richard to play solos with the bow, and then he would stand listening with tears rolling down his cheeks. He would get tearful when he spoke of his mother. Once he told me that he missed Jimmy Rowles, who was back in California, and as he told me about his friendship with Rowles he began to cry. One night at the Half Note we heard radio reports of rioting in Harlem, and Ben wept openly as he listened.
>
> I think Ben got some heat from black musicians because he included me and Mel Lewis in his band. Ben was protective of both of us. During the Shalimar engagement Ben took me and Mel next door to the little grocery store where he knew the proprietor. He introduced us to the man, who assured us that we could take refuge in his store if it ever became necessary. I didn't know what he was talking about.
>
> Many great musicians came into the Shalimar to see Ben, and I got a chance to play with Johnny Hodges, Paul Gonsalves, Ray

Nance and others. Billy Strayhorn came in one night and asked me, "Would it be all right If I played a tune or two?" I stood by and watched him play with the band. It was one of those moments. I was happy to be in New York, and privileged to be a musician, consorting with these giants.[27]

Richard Davis also has fond memories of the year he spent with Ben.

My good friend, the drummer Mel Lewis, worked with Ben Webster over many years, and when Ben asked for a bass player to join, Mel recommended me, as we at that time worked together on many different jobs. So there I was, working with one of my idols. I remember we worked at the Shalimar, a beautiful jazz club uptown, in Harlem. I learned a lot from Ben Webster up there, because many of his longtime friends would come to see him. I mentioned to him once, "You have so many old friends who come to see you up here," and he said, "Keep the old ones, because new ones are hard to find." I will never forget that. It was words of wisdom coming from a guy who had been around and was of age.[28]

One of the first of his old friends to come listen to Ben in Harlem was Hilton Jefferson who said that "he still sounds great and he still has that big fine sound. Ben is one of those kind of musicians who, when he plays a tune, spoils it for anyone else. You just don't want to hear anyone else play it. Tunes like *Cotton Tail, All Too Soon, Chelsea Bridge* and my favourite—*Just A-Settin' And A-Rockin'*."[29]

Ben and his quartet received great reviews from the booking. Dan Morgenstern wrote,

On opening night, Ben sounded marvellous. Relaxed and in full command of himself and the situation, he charged into *Cotton Tail* with all the old fire—and then some. He brought stars into the eyes of the pretty girls at the bar with *My Romance,* and silenced all idle chatter with his inimitable rendition of *Danny Boy.* He was the gruff and growling Ben on the up-tempos, and the ever so tender and lyrical Ben on the ballads—and sometimes a combination of both. His tone is surely one of the marvels of jazz saxophone playing: rich, full and velvety, yet never for even a moment cloying or sentimental. His approach to a song distils the essence of the melody in a manner matched only by such supreme solo architects as Louis Armstrong or Johnny Hodges. His superb sense of time enables him to swing even at the slowest of tempos, and his phrases—so distinctly his own that he is among the handful of instantly recognisable players in jazz—constitute separate, almost sculptured entities, which nonetheless merge into a structured whole as they unfold, one by one, in majestic, floating cadences. Even the non-jazz minded people in the audience seemed to sense that Ben's music was something special. . . .

After a few weeks, during which a steady stream of musicians visited the Shalimar. . . . the quartet had grown as tight as a brand new snare. It has been a long time since I've witnessed such open and unabashed empathy between jazz players, and, needless to say, it was a joy to behold. Everybody was working for the *group,* and Ben's pride in his band matched the pride in the young men in working for and with someone they admired whole-heart-edly.[30]

In August, Ben's quartet played two equally successful weeks at the Half Note, returning in late September and again in January 1964. Morgenstern caught Ben here a couple of times as well. He wrote, "He did very well indeed (on his closing night I counted sixteen musicians in the audience) and was asked to return a month later. It now appears that Ben can be added to the team of regulars at the Half Note, and this is good news indeed—regular bookings are a rare plum in New York jazz today."[31]

The fact that Ben had hit a high point is documented by yet another review from the two bookings. "Go hear Ben Webster as soon as you get the chance. Ben is really proving himself a great artist these days."[32]

Unfortunately, no recordings were made of this quartet; the reviews show that the musicians had already developed a close musical empathy. Considering what a formidable team Richard Davis and Mel Lewis were only a couple of years later in the rhythm section of the Thad Jones/Mel Lewis Jazz Orchestra, it is no wonder that Ben was proud of this group. In between the two bookings, Ben performed at a couple of concerts. On June 15 he played at New York's Town Hall, and on August 8, his quartet and Budd Johnson's band played at the Philharmonic Hall in Lincoln Center. The concert was reviewed in two newspapers. One reviewer preferred Budd Johnson's set,[33] while the other was of the opposite opinion, stating that Ben's set

> opened with an easy, pulsating treatment of Monk's *Straight No Chaser.* Webster's firm, clear tenor sax blown with a minimum of vibrato, proved to be a refreshing contrast to the sweet style of Johnson and he propelled the music with tidy upward phrases.
>
> Next was beautifully lyrical, behind-the-beat version of *Our Love Is Here To Stay,* and to add to the effect there were color effects from the side spotlights in the darkened hall. Then came a rousing *The Jeep Is Jumpin'. Cotton Tail,* which Webster blew in the famous old Duke Ellington recording, was another item on the program.[34]

When Ben arrived in New York, he booked into a hotel as usual; but in late June he ran into pianist Joe Zawinul at Birdland. Zawinul and Ben had met in San Francisco, where they played next door to each other, Ben with Witherspoon and Zawinul with Cannonball Adderley. They began talking; Zawinul was leaving July 4 for a tour of Japan with Adderley. As he was not scheduled to return till late August, he suggested that Ben move in and take care of his apartment at 372 Central Park West while he was gone. Ben accepted with pleasure. "I came back after a month or so and he had bought a tape recorder, a two-track tape recorder, and I had a little piano in there, and he used to practice a lot, you know," Zawinul recalled.

> When I came back, he said if it was all right if he could hang around? For me it was OK because I was traveling quite a bit, and we shared the rent money. He was helpful, you know. I got a lot of practice with him. Coleman Hawkins was our neighbor. He

came over every day, almost, during the time I was in New York. We played, Coleman, Ben, and me, a trio. They always had this competition, even though they shared the greatest among friendship and respect. Ben was a great ballad player, the best, and we played Duke Ellington's *Come Sunday* with difficult changes, you know. For instance, I would go down in the elevator with Coleman and he said, "Listen, man, write down the changes for me. I'll come up some time when Ben isn't there so I can check some of the changes out because I will burn on him on that ballad."[35]

A private recording from Ben's collection, with Ben, Zawinul, Milt Hinton, and drummer Louis Hayes may very well have been taped in Zawinul's apartment, as they can be heard practicing two takes of *Come Sunday*, preceded by a nice, swinging, and inspired version of *Sometimes I'm Happy*, and followed by an equally inspired unidentified tune, probably written by Zawinul, because it is he who takes the lead in the theme presentation, while Ben follows as best he can.

Not only Hawkins dropped by the apartment; many of Ben's other friends came by: Dizzy Gillespie, Eldridge, and some of the musicians from Ellington's orchestra. Zawinul, an Austrian, immigrated to the United States in 1959, but was still not quite used to the habits of older jazz musicians. "These guys used to hang out like I never seen!" he once said. "They'd hang out for three days in a row, come back once, take a shower, change their clothes, then go to some more parties."[36] They would also give him advice on anything from clothes to revitalizing and keeping the freshness in his music. "Don't ever buy anything inexpensive," Ben told him. "How can you be a great musician if you don't buy great things?" And Hawkins told him, "When you learn a lick every day, you're gonna be a rich man."[37]

During the summer of 1963, Ben began to wonder if there might be jobs for him in Europe. The Swedish bassist Simon Brehm had met him in New York and discussed the possibility, and Ben had been interested. Back in Sweden, Brehm had contacted Anders Stefansen's agency in Copenhagen, and on October 14, 1963, Stefansen wrote Lester Koenig at Contemporary Records inquiring how to get in touch with Ben. In his reply, November 11, Koenig wrote,

I spoke to Ben Webster on the phone and am sending him a copy of your letter of October 14.

Ben can be addressed care of [the bar] Jim and Andy's, 116 West 48th Street, New York, N.Y. This is where he gets his mail. I suggest that you get in touch with him directly.

Stefansen did get in touch with Ben, but plans of a European trip did not materialize at this time, because Ben's demands were too high.[38] But a seed had been sown, and Ben did a lot of thinking about his options as a soloist in Europe. At one of the many parties in Zawinul's apartment, Dan Morgenstern was present, and he remembers that Ben pulled him aside to discuss the subject.

Ben who knew, of course, that I was originally from Europe, said, "I want to talk to you." Ben was asking me questions about Europe, and he was really like a child. He asked me questions like, "What if I get lost and nobody speaks English and I can't tell them where I want to go?" I said, "Ben, in Europe, unless you go to a place like Turkey, everybody speaks English, and if they don't understand you they'll quickly find someone who will. It's not so different from being here." And he said, "What about food?" This was about the time that McDonald's went overseas, so I told him that. "Fine!" This was the kind of questions he asked. I was trying to tell him that he would be very welcome over there and that he would be treated wonderful and that everybody over there would know who he was, and all that.[39]

In the long run, Ben's living situation became unbearable. He had begun drinking again, and often treated Zawinul badly. "At the time he got obnoxious," Zawinul recounted. "I said, 'Listen, Ben, it's been a while now and I have met this lady that I'll marry, so you gonna have to move.' He didn't want to move. He said, 'Man, I'm so used to this. It's nice and we play together and all that.' I said he could take over the apartment and that I could get another apartment. He didn't want that either, so the only thing I could do was to let him go. He got drunk and got wasted, and he really took it to his heart."[40]

Ben played on a few tracks on two Joe Williams albums recorded in July and November 1963, but the only interesting take is on the second album with an outstanding, lyrical, and moving solo in *Rocks in My Bed*. Between these two Joe Williams sessions, he recorded his own album, *Soulmates*, over two dates, one with a quartet on September 20, and one with a quintet, with the addition of Thad Jones on October 14. The pianist was Joe Zawinul; Philly Joe Jones played drums; Richard Davis played bass on the quartet recordings and Sam Jones with the quintet. Unfortunately the two lovely ballads, *Too Late Now* and *Come Sunday*, are marred by the addition of echo. Adding synthetic effects to any of Ben's recordings is vandalism and sacrilege; his sound has its own natural, tender beauty. It is heard most advantageously without any synthetic effects. Other than that, his simple and lucid interpretation of *Too Late Now* is brilliant, and *Trav'lin' Light*, a ballad, is one of the highlights of the album, with lovely, sensitive playing from Ben and excellent accompaniment from Zawinul. Two of Ben's compositions were recorded with Thad Jones, *Soulmates*, a minor blues, and *The Governor*, an Ellington tribute with an inventive theme. Ben plays well on these tracks, and likewise on the tight *Like Someone in Love* and Thad Jones's *Evol Deklaw Ni* (which is *Love Walked In*, backwards), but he is more inspired in a Zawinul blues, *Frog Legs*, structuring his solo with ever-building intensity finally released in a chorus of call-and-response with himself.

Between two bookings at the Half Note, Ben and pianist Dave Frishberg were invited to participate in a private jazz party held by Jim Dunn in his house in Darien, Connecticut, on September 2. Frishberg recalled the occasion and remembers that "Ben was the nominal leader, and the band was Vic Dickenson, Buck Clayton, Al Lucas, Jackie Williams and myself."[41] A private recording from the party shows Ben in fine form and playing with great drive on *Just You, Just Me*. He performs the slow blues that follows with exceptional sensitivity and inspiration; his feature in the ballad medley *That's All* is also played beautifully. During this period, his tone is more velvety and supple than before without losing any of the beauty or richness, as can be heard to fine effect in *We're in the Money*.

At the end of 1963, Ben still had a lot of work. A week at the Five Spot was followed by a long booking at Birdland through the month of November. Ben also participated in two benefit concerts. On the afternoon of Sunday, October 20, the Five Spot held a Sit-In for Freedom Jazz Concert featuring Ben's quartet together with, among others, Don Friedman, Sonny Rollins, John Coltrane, Kenny Burrell, and Billy Taylor. The following Sunday, Birdland held a benefit concert for Bud Powell, who was hospitalized in Paris with tuberculosis. The past half year had been productive in recording as well. Ben had worked as a sideman on records by Clark Terry and Joe Williams, and recorded an excellent album of his own.

December was meager as far as work was concerned, but Ben did have three successive evenings at the Kings and Queens in Pawtucket, Rhode Island. Actually he was only booked for two evenings, but he showed up a day early to check out the local rhythm section, who were accompanying twenty-six-year-old vocalist Carol Sloane. "We were in the club for the date and Ben wasn't due until the following night," remembered Sloane. "He just asked me if he could sit in. Imagine. HE asked ME!"[42]

The recordings reveal Sloane as a fine singer, influenced by Ella Fitzgerald. Later she said of playing with Ben, "Standing next to that man was like being inside his bell. You know how it is when a musician feels his instrument, the vibrations from his bass, trumpet, or the reed moving inside his mouth? Well, that's how I felt being on that stage with Ben; it was as if I were playing that thing. The vibrations were going right through me, but passing through him. More like a vicarious experience than a real one. But it was very real for me. When someone like Ben is out there in all his awe-inspiring elegance, you just do things you never thought were possible. The musicians were smiling and you know that's a good sign."[43] However, Ben was not particularly inspired that evening; the exceptions are *Honeysuckle Rose* and *When Your Lover Has Gone*, showing him swinging intensely and generating great drive.

Ben is in much better form the following two evenings without Sloane. The rhythm section plays excellently. Highlights are *On Green Dolphin Street, Bye, Bye Blackbird*, and *Sometimes I'm Happy* for their sure swing, *Go Home* for Ben's superbly structured and intensely executed solo, an extremely inspired *Lover Come Back to Me*, and an immensely romantic *Embraceable You*.

Ben spent the Christmas holidays in Detroit, performing in a holiday show, and January 9, 1964, he went to hear Duke Ellington's orchestra on their opening night at New York's Basin Street East. Trombonist

Chuck Connors was late, and Ben was invited to sit in for him. Ellington featured Ben in *Cotton Tail* and Paul Gonsalves came down to play a chase with him at the end of the tune, much to Ben's pleasure. Ben said later about this evening, "If Duke likes you, you're home free."[44]

In January 1964, jobs were as few as they had been in December. In February, the quartet was working again. A week at the Village Vanguard was followed by a week at the Café Au Go Go in Greenwich Village. Then came a job at Pio's Lodge in Providence, Rhode Island, on February 18, where Ben played with vocalist Joe Williams and an all-star rhythm section with pianist Junior Mance, bassist Bob Cranshaw, and drummer Mickey Roker. Once again the tapes show him in fiery form. Some of the tracks with Joe Williams are absolutely amazing—among them a rarely spirited version of *Honeysuckle Rose* . Among Ben's most beautiful solos are *A Hundred Years from Today* and *How Long Has This Been Going On?*

A few days later, Ben and Coleman Hawkins initiated a new series of jazz concerts at New York's Little Theatre. Both saxophonists were accompanied by Paul Neves on piano, Major Holley on bass, and Eddie Locke on drums. Ben opened the show. According to a reviewer who attended the first concert Friday, the room's acoustics were an asset for Ben.

> For those who relish Mr. Webster's rich, sinuous lines, this was a real treat, for he has suffered more than most of his colleagues at the hands of amplification systems. He was in excellent form, playing lyrical ballads and surgingly rhythmic pieces with calm, unruffled authority.
>
> There were depth, variety and economy in his playing, qualities that were not always evident in Mr. Hawkins's performances.[45]

During this period, Ellington's son, Mercer, arranged a series of monthly jam sessions at various venues around New York. He called Ben a few times, among these in February, using Ben's quartet as a basis group at Count Basie's Club in Harlem. This date was to be Ben's last job with his own quartet.

On an undated session with vocalist Sylvia Sims, recorded in 1964, Ben can be heard on three tracks: sympathetic and sensitive obbligatos in *You've Changed* and *Goodnight My Love,* and a short but good solo on *It's Funny to Everyone but Me.* There where three Impulse sessions in March 1964; two of his own, released as *See You at the Fair,* and a recording date with Clark Terry, which produced *The Happy Horns of Clark Terry,* on which they were joined by Phil Woods, Roger Kellaway, Milt Hinton, and drummer Walter Perkins. It is a lovely, varied album full of contrasts, and with fine contributions by all three horns, backed by an inspired rhythm section. Ben's best offering is *Do Nothin' Till You Hear From Me,* a pensive and tender rendition. *Rockin' in Rhythm* and *Perdido* show him swinging hard and steady, *Impulsive* brings forth his soft, dreamy side, and *Jazz Conversation* is played with vitality and feeling.

See *You at the Fair* was Ben's last album recorded in United States, but it is an outstanding exit, on a par with *King of the Tenors.* Richard Davis and Osie Johnson played on both dates; Hank Jones played piano on March 11 and was replaced by Roger Kellaway on March 25. It is no surprise that the ballads stand out as the loveliest tracks, and, unlike *King of the Tenors,* no tunes are set faster than medium. Each ballad is a perfect example of Ben's artistry; using the exact right, tiny shifts in phrasing, he makes you feel as if you are hearing old favorites like *Someone to Watch Over Me, Over the Rainbow* and *Stardust* for the first time. And his sound is lovelier than ever. The romantic, caressing version of *The Single Petal of a Rose* and the melancholic, poetic *Fall of Love* are just as outstanding. In a virile, steaming *In a Mellotone,* he plays a string of repeated triplets in the break leading into the first chorus of solos, which he duplicated in virtually every following version of the tune. His solos in *Lullaby of Jazzland* and his own blues, *See You at the Fair,* are likewise heavy swingers, the latter featuring several excellent, logical phrases.

In the same month Ben was involved in an embarrassing scene at the Five Spot. Charles Mingus was playing with his Workshop, which was going through a number of changes from tentet to quintet, and occasionally he would use guest soloists for an evening, among them Coleman Hawkins, Sonny Rollins, and Ben. Ben and Mingus were both known for their fiery tempers, and at one point the sparks between the two of them were so violent that Mingus felt compelled to run out to the street and jump into a cab with Ben running after it down the street as fast as his heavy body and thin legs would carry him.

Unfortunately, jobs were swiftly getting harder to find despite all the good reviews. It was as if the clubs didn't have any use for Ben's music anymore. He had a little studio work, and he played on a television show for WNDT in April as a guest with the Clark Terry/Bob Brookmeyer quintet with pianist Derek Smith, bassist Bill Crow, and drummer Dave Bailey. In the studio, the recording went well, but Crow recalls that this was one occasion when Clark Terry's wild sense of humor went too far. "When the taping began," says Crow,

> we played a couple of tunes with the full ensemble, and then Bob and Clark left the stage in opposite directions while Ben played a ballad alone with the rhythm section.
>
> During Ben's first chorus, I glanced over at Dave Bailey and saw that he was laughing. He nodded in the direction Clark had exited. I looked over and saw Clark crouched down behind some scenery, only visible to Dave and me, with his trousers down around his knees. He was mooning us on television.[46]

After his falling out with Zawinul, Ben had moved into the Hotel Forrest at 234 West Forty-ninth Street close to Broadway, and in his collection, photographs from the time bear witness of visits by, among others, Harold Ashby in the modestly furnished room with a small refrigerator, bed, and armchair. Ben had decorated the naked wall over the bed with photographs of jazz musicians, Ellington being one of the most prominent. When jobs were coming in a steady flow, he had no problems paying his bills, but during 1964, as his income dwindled, Ben was often forced to borrow money. His regular hangout was the bar Jim & Andy's on Forty-eighth Street west of Sixth Avenue, the new popular meeting place for musicians. The proprietor, Jim Koulouvaris, was an unusually generous person who often extended credit and cash loans to needy musicians, and he never turned Ben down when he was in need of cash. Milt Hinton, like Ben a regular, says, "He paid Jim every dime he owed him. He must have left here for Europe owing Jim at least two or three thousand dollars. But I do know before Jim died, he would tell me every time, well, 'Ben sent me three hundred dollars,' and maybe a month later he said, 'Ben sent me five hundred dollars.' So every time Ben would make a good deal over in Europe, he never forgot to return it. I'm sure he died not owing Jim one nickel."[47] Other of Ben's snapshots from this period were taken on the sidewalk in front of either Beefsteak Charlie's or Jim & Andy's, revealing that Art Farmer, Gerry Mulligan, Harry Edison, Archie Shepp, Mel Lewis, Ruby Braff, Jo Jones, Doc Cheatham, Sonny Greer, Tommy Flanagan, and Milt Hinton were among the regulars.

He often visited Hinton in his house in St. Albans, Queens at 173–05 113th Avenue, and once he arrived while the priest was visiting. The priest was a jazz enthusiast and had heard Ben before, so Ben agreed to visit his church, too. "The very next Sunday morning he got up and came out here to come to church," Hinton recalls.

> He loved Charlotte, my daughter, very much. Charlotte must have been twelve to thirteen years old, and she had some speech to make in the service. I was sitting up front with Mona [Hinton's wife].
>
> Charlotte made this speech and it was most inspiring, and she always had good diction, and she sounded so lovely, we were so proud of her. After the service the minister always goes to the front of the church to shake hands with everybody as they come out of the church. So when I'm coming out of church, I stopped to shake hands with the minister, and I said, "You know, Ben promised me faithfully that he was coming to church this Sunday." And Reverend Johnson said, "He was here, Milt. He sat in the back. When Charlotte got up and made that speech, he just filled up and tears were in his eyes and he started crying. And he took out a handkerchief and he got up and walked out."
>
> The church is right across the street from our house, and he didn't even come over here. He went back into town. But that's what a warm, beautiful, sensitive guy he was. He loved us so, he was so proud seeing this child making this speech. He hadn't been in church so long, and I guess it was too much for him.[48]

At one point, Ben's financial situation became so tense that he could no longer afford his hotel room, and Hinton invited him to stay with him and Mona. They offered him a small room in the basement with a sofa bed and a small piano. The two of them spent much time down there, drinking beer and jamming, like back in the old days, sometimes with Ben on the piano. They recorded quite a few of these informal sessions, and they show that Ben's piano playing is no longer as fluid, and has become somewhat heavy-handed.

And still jobs were few. Ben received a tepid response from the critics to his performance at that year's Newport Jazz Festival. He performed with a version of the Newport Jazz Festival All Stars also including Al Grey, Buck Clayton, and pianist Sir Charles Thompson. "Thompson was most impressive," wrote *Down Beat*, "throwing off several crisp, to-the-point solos during the course of the performance. Webster was very good on *Stardust*, Clayton on *Take The A Train*, and trombonist Grey on a plungered *Perdido*, but there was no one tune in which all played at the height of their ability."[49] Voice of America taped the concert for their *Jazz Hour*, and they show that the review is right and that Ben's contributions were uneven. His best solo is on *Stardust*, whereas he has a hard time in a fast *Take the A Train*, understandably playing but one chorus. *Perdido* is performed emotionally and energetically with building intensity and dynamics. Shortly after the festival, Ben played a week at the Metropole in New York, but after this, the only known job is on September 21 in Stony Brook, New York, where he played with pianist Mose Allison.

When out of work, Ben spent his afternoons and evenings in the company of other musicians at Jim & Andy's, the Copper Rail, and Beefsteak Charlie's, or sitting by himself in his basement room in Queens, listening to some of his numerous tape-recordings. Hinton had plenty of work, but to his great disappointment, his attempts at bringing Ben in on a job always failed. "At the time, Barry Galbraith, Hank Jones and Osie Johnson and I were known as 'the New York rhythm section,'" Hinton said, "and we'd make as many as three recording sessions a day, at forty-one dollars and twenty-five cents per—which wasn't bad, because a hundred dollars went a long way then. Ben would get calls to make some of these sessions, but he'd ask for triple scale, and the producers always turned him down."[50]

Finally Mona Hinton intervened. It made her sad to see Ben sitting around with nothing to do. "My wife said to Ben," recalls Hinton, "very kindly, because she loved him, 'Ben, how can you sit here all day? You are a star and Milt is just a bass player. How can you sit here and eat and drink, and people can offer you a job and you won't take it? Milt worked nine hours for the same amount of money you didn't make. We want to help you, so how can you do that?' I think that really broke his heart and made him feel bad."[51]

We can only speculate on what made Ben demand triple pay for a recording session. One explanation may be the almost instant success he experienced upon arriving in New York, the many offers and constantly enthusiastic reviews. It must have been extremely hard to accept the fact that he was no longer in demand, especially since his playing was as good as ever. Another obvious explanation is that he wanted to make as much as possible in order to pay off his large debt to Jim Koulouvaris, which troubled him a lot. In any case, Ben had great respect for the opinion of women. He took Mona's criticism to heart and accepted the next offers that came his way, both for Impulse, a Lionel Hampton session in October, in which Hinton also played, and an Oliver Nelson session in early November.

The recordings with Hampton on October 28 and 29 produced a lot of joy-filled music. Most tracks are moderately paced with the exception of *A Taste of Honey,* played as a ballad and including a short but lovely solo by Ben. The tune fades out to a beautiful, singable riff played by Ben behind Hampton. All three blues tunes, *Vibraphone Blues, Pick-a-Rib,* and *Trick a Treat,* follow the same recipe: Ben plays two solo choruses, shifting to a more aggressive and extroverted approach in the second. Ben is in fine form throughout, and *Tempo's Birthday* and *Cute* also feature dedicated and authoritative performances.

Ben can be heard on two tracks from the session with Oliver Nelson from November 10, playing particularly well on *Midnight Blue,* especially in a call-and-response part with the orchestra.

In Ben's collection of reel-to-reel tapes, there is one called *Faberge;* the box reveals no titles nor names of musicians. In 1999 these tunes were issued as bonus tracks on the CD *No Fool, No Fun: The Rehearsal Sessions* (Storyville STCD 8304), featuring Ben with the Danish Radio Jazz Orchestra. In the CD notes, the *Faberge* sessions are considered mystifying; the author guesses that they might stem from Ben's first years in Europe. The music is simply numbered as takes 1–12, and consists of two complete takes of a minor blues in medium slow tempo, six short takes of rehearsals of the concluding chorus of the same tune, one short and two complete takes of an up-tempo blues, and one complete take of the same blues, this time at a moderate pace. However, the titles are not as mysterious as the CD notes indicate; the slow blues is *Poutin'* with a tiny alteration of the theme, and the up-tempo blues is *Randle's Island,* likewise with the smallest variation in the first few bars. There may also be a simple explanation for the "Faberge" written on the tape box. "Faberge," of course, is the name of the famous jeweled eggs, but it is also a perfume and one of the world's finest vodkas. Most likely, Ben named the box after the liquor.

We can deduce that the recordings were made in the United States because the technician calling each new take is obviously American. It is a little more difficult to pinpoint the period and the rhythm section, but my guess is that the sessions were recorded at some point between 1959 and 1962. The interaction between Ben and the rhythm section indicates that they know each other well. The pianist's subtlety, the trills he uses to adorn the final chorus of the minor blues, and the humor with which he begins his solo in the slowest version of *Randle's Island,* mimicking Ben's concluding descending trill, points toward Jimmy Rowles. The drummer's easy swing suggests Mel Lewis, and the bassist sounds a lot like Leroy Vinnegar; in other words the exact rhythm section Ben played with most frequently at that time.

Ben plays excellently throughout the *Faberge* sessions, and his solos are energetic and intense. In the second, complete take of *Poutin'* his solo is inspired from the very start, and after the piano solo he plays a chorus of very pretty, singable phrases before the concluding choruses. The best version of *Randle's Island* is the last and longest take, showing Ben playing imaginatively and swinging exceptionally well.

When taking all these sessions from Ben's last years in America into consideration, the conclusion is that his performances were very steady. He never plays poorly, and although his form fluctuated, he was never less than good and often outstanding. He was always inventive, often surprisingly so, and, at the time of his departure for Europe, he had achieved a mature artistry, with his joy in playing still prevalent.

That fall, Ben received another European offer, this time from

Ronnie Scott's Club in London, and he did not hesitate to accept, making no extravagant financial demands, but accepting the pay offered by the club. Ben was booked for four weeks from December 8, 1964, till January 3, 1965. In the end of November he said goodbye to his hosts and other friends, unaware that he would never see many of them again. Promising to hurry home after his British booking, he boarded the S.S. *France* to Europe.

9. First Years in Europe
(1964–1966)

Ben stepped ashore in Southampton on Monday, November 30, 1964. He was welcomed by tenor saxophonist Ronnie Scott and the manager of the club, Pete King. The two men had established the club in 1959, and within a few years it had become London's most important jazz venue. Ronnie Scott's Club, the Blue Note in Paris, and the Jazzhus Montmartre in Copenhagen were the three European clubs offering most American musicians to the public. Situated at 39 Gerard Street in London's Soho, the club featured a house rhythm section to accompany visiting soloists. In 1964 it consisted of the pianist Stan Tracey, who had created his own original style influenced by Ellington and Monk, bassist Rick Laird, and drummer Jackie Dougan. The bill was often shared with Ronnie Scott's own quartet or—as was the case during Ben's first booking—tenor saxophonist Tubby Hayes's quartet.

Scott and King drove King's Morris Mini car to meet Ben, who had arrived in England in good time before his opening night on December 8. "We'd had a somewhat garbled telephone call from him in Cherbourg," says Scott,

> which apprised us of nothing except that he'd spent a considerable amount of time in the bar—but when he came off the boat at Southampton he seemed quite straight and steady, if a little subdued. We helped squeeze his sixteen stones [in weight] into the back seat of the Mini and set off back for London. Within minutes Ben had dozed off and was snoring vigorously. Then suddenly, after we'd been travelling for half an hour, he woke up and roared: "Well, give them what they want—as long as they don't

want too much!" Then he lapsed immediately back into a sound sleep. Pete and I exchanged glances, shrugged, and wondered what we were getting ourselves into.[1]

In London, Ben was accommodated at the White House in Albany Street, a hotel with small apartments. The following days Ben wandered about town, visiting a few of its attractions, such as Piccadilly Circus, and he found Dobell's Jazz Record Shop at 77 Charing Cross Road, soon befriending the employees there. The shop was to become one of his regular hangouts during later engagements at Ronnie Scott's. Ben became especially close with the doorman at Ronnie Scott's, Henry Cohen, who was built a little like Ben, and also made a habit of frequenting Dobell's during the day to pass the time with Ben before they both went to work.

Ben enjoyed London, and—just as Dan Morgenstern had said—his anxiety at being alone in a foreign country was unfounded. Ben said later,

> I've always wanted to come to Europe, but it's been a case of here one day and there the next. I preferred to wait until I could do it like this—take my time and see the country.
>
> And from what I've seen already, I'm going to like it. People have been wonderful, you know, sincere. I've found that people go out of their way to do things for me.[2]

Subsequently, the discussion touched on music, and Ben said, "I'm tone conscious. I like the big sound. There used to be a lot of jazz players with big sounds. All of a sudden they changed, sacrificing sound for speed." Ben liked to listen to whatever was happening, but urged that one should not be tempted to join in on new fads. "Now I think it's better to play what you can play," he said. "Otherwise you're liable to wind up playing nothing."[3]

Reviews from Ronnie Scott document that Ben was in fine form. As an American writer once put it: "If it's possible, Ben plays words," a review stated.

> At Ronnie Scott's club in London last week, Webster came close to playing words—verse as well as chorus, sometimes—as he

worked warmly and limpidly through such worthy material as
Chelsea Bridge and *Tenderly* and, in the second show, *I Got It Bad,*
Stardust and *My Romance.*

In between the slows, played with an airy vibrancy and
unwasteful phraseology which remind the listener keenly of
Johnny Hodges, Webster treated us to medium-tempo pieces
(*Gone With The Wind* or the militantly swinging blues, *Poutin'*)
and surging up-tempo numbers on which his singing tone took
on added harshness.[4]

A book about Ronnie Scott's Club tells about Ben's performance
of *Our Love Is Here to Stay* that "he would blow smoke rings of sound that
both maximised the effect of his rich, shimmering tone and simultaneously highlighted the ingenuity of the composer. Roland Kirk, in the audience during Webster's season, remarked that such a sound ought to be
impossible to produce on a saxophone."[5]

All taped performances from the club, radio, and television prove
that the reviews are right. On all the private recordings from Ronnie
Scott's Club Ben performs with great warmth and exceptional presence,
making versions of *Pennies from Heaven, In a Mellotone, How High the*
Moon, and *Gone with the Wind* far more pleasurable to the listener than
other versions from the same period. *Confirmation* and *Night in Tunisia,*
which he rarely played, are extremely spirited and inspired. The ballads
are superb, with *Danny Boy, Chelsea Bridge, Stardust,* and *How Long Has*
This Been Going On? as grand highlights. Ben found a kindred spirit in
pianist Stan Tracey, whose sense of harmony was very much to Ben's liking. Before leaving London, Ben had him write down the chords he played
on tunes like *My Romance* and *How Long Has This Been Going On?* He
kept them in his horn case for later use on the continent. It always surprised house pianists when Ben produced the chord sheets. They had
never experienced this with other visiting American jazz musicians.

Ronnie Scott, a saxophonist himself, had noticed one particular
aspect of Ben's playing. "Ben is one of the master technicians of the saxophone," he said.

But his technique is not one of the obvious kind. What I mean is,
he doesn't play cascades of notes at ultra fast tempos. I think

Ben's technique is a much more basic and important kind of thing. He has this ability to convene himself emotionally through his instrument with great mastery. I know from experience, and any saxophone player will tell you, that one of the most difficult things to do on the instrument is to play the notes in the lower register of the instrument with a full sound and good tone and complete control. Ben is such a master of this facet of technique that he seems to have added an extra dimension to the range of tone colours of the instrument.[6]

On a television show, part of the BBC series *Jazz 625,* telecast on February 28, 1965, Ben plays outstandingly from the very first tune, a fast-paced version of *Sunday.* The rhythm section is no less excellent, with the driving powers of Jackie Dougan adding extra force to the performance. The quartet seems closely knit, and Ben is remarkably inspired throughout the entire half hour, not least in *Poutin', A Night in Tunisia,* in which they were joined by Ronnie Scott, and *Perdido,* all played with a driving, straightforward swing, whereas *Over the Rainbow* and *Chelsea Bridge* are interpreted in the most beautiful and tender fashion, focusing on his full and lovely tone.

Ben's presence in London brought him the attention that he had missed during his last months in New York. He often received visitors to his small apartment and was interviewed several times, by photographer and writer Valerie Wilmer, among others, who visited him after hearing him at the club. "When the solid, well-groomed, slightly mean-looking Webster walks on to the stand," she wrote,

it's hard to tell whether he has rehearsed the music that follows. He uses few "head" arrangements, just picks up his horn and blows. "I don't think too far in front because the piano player may make a thing that inspires you just like that!" he said. "If you think too far out you'd get confused. I never did go for that too much because it can turn into a fight. You have to try to play something that would fit, otherwise it might not gell.

I don't go in for too intricate things. We only have a couple of rehearsals. You can make it hard for the other guys and for yourself, too, if you get too involved. I can become very unrelaxed and I like it relaxed."

Ben usually plays numbers the same way, but varies the feeling a trifle each time so that you never get bored with hearing *Cotton Tail* or *Mellotone* again after all these years. "I just try to swing and play with feeling," he declares. "A lot depends on the rhythm section of the group. I'm really lucky to run into a group like Ronnie's. These are three guys that feel like playing every night. It seems to me they're getting better as we go along, too. . . .

When I have the chance I go to hear everybody. You just have to listen, you know. I like Coltrane, Yusef Lateef, Tubbs [Tubby Hayes], Freddie Hubbard, Wayne Shorter and so on. I like Benny Golson very much. He always sounds full with a big, round tone. He never gets too far out, I'd say he sticks to the pattern. And I dig Zoot Sims a whole lot, too, he's a steady swinger."[7]

Rumors of Ben's success in London quickly reached other European venues, and soon clubs were fighting to book the celebrated visitor before he returned home. The Danish agent, Anders Stefansen, founder of SBA (Scandinavian Booking Agency), contacted Ben in mid-December with engagements in Sweden, Denmark, and Norway. The first was at the Gyllene Cirkeln in the Swedish capital, Stockholm. Ben was on their program January 4–16, immediately after the conclusion of his run at Ronnie Scott's Club. Much to Ben's regret, he was forced to fly to Stockholm.

At Gyllene Cirkeln, Ben was accompanied by pianist Gunnar Svensson, bassist Roman Dylag, and drummer Bosse Skoglund. Before the opening night, they had time for a short afternoon rehearsal. Dylag recalls, "In one of the tunes we played, he gave me a solo chorus and of course I started to play as I used to, more or less in the manner of a horn. After a few bars Ben moved closer to me and in a low voice said to me, 'Walk, bassman, walk!' I never forgot that lesson. On another occasion Ben stood in front of my bass and turned to me between two numbers saying, 'I love to feel your big sound right in my back.'"[8]

The reviews in Stockholm were excellent, too. "Over the past years, he has blossomed into a completely unique and majestic ballad interpreter," wrote a paper,[9] while another reviewer noticed, that "the excitement he creates and the freshness he lends to even the most well-worn sweet tune is astounding. The sound of his tenor is large and rich, and intimately human like a cello."[10]

Swedish Public Radio recorded two shows with Ben on January 8, 1965, one in a studio, the other live from the Gyllene Cirkeln. The stage recording reveals Ben playing almost as magnificently as in London. However, the rhythm section has a hard time keeping up with him; the drummer does not have much drive, particularly in medium tempi. He is replaced by the slightly more gutsy and aggressive Leif Wennerström on the studio recordings, and consequently Ben feels compelled to shift to a higher gear in *Randle's Island, In a Mellotone,* and *The Theme.*

On January 10—his day off—Ben flew to Copenhagen to perform at a radio concert. Ben was accompanied by the American pianist Kenny Drew—now a resident of Copenhagen—the eighteen-year-old bassist Niels-Henning Ørsted Pedersen, and twenty-four-year-old drummer Alex Riel. The trio was the house rhythm section in the Jazzhus Montmartre and a tight unit. The concert went well and Ben was in fine form. He felt comfortable with the rhythm section, and young Ørsted Pedersen's authority and impressive technique especially made a deep impression on him. Ben perceived in him a successor and heir to Milt Hinton, Jimmie Blanton, and Richard Davis, and he looked forward to his coming booking at the Jazzhus Montmartre.[11]

Ben finished at the Gyllene Cirkeln on January 16. As his booking at the Jazzhus Montmartre started on January 19, he had plenty of time for the trip, and chose the safe route: a train to Malmö in Sweden and a ferry over the sound to Copenhagen.

After Herluf Kamp-Larsen took over the establishment at Store Regnegade 19, he changed the name to Jazzhus Montmartre, and built a dressing room and a recording control room on the second floor, enabling stage recordings for radio transmissions or albums.

During Kamp-Larsen's ownership, the Jazzhus Montmartre developed into one of Europe's most important jazz venues, and many black American musicians settled in Copenhagen over the decade spanning 1963–72, including Kenny Drew, Dexter Gordon, Stuff Smith, Sahib Shihab, Idrees Sulieman, Ray Pitts, Horace Parlan, and Ed Thigpen. There was hardly any racial discrimination in Denmark; in Copenhagen the musicians were treated as equals, and they soon felt at home. Another attraction was the easy access from the Danish capital to other venues on the continent.

Ben's first evenings in Copenhagen were not as fiery as his other recent bookings. He had warned people not to expect too much of him, as he probably would be tired at the beginning of his booking. He was right. "Webster's performance was marred by weariness on the opening night," wrote one daily paper. "The almost fifty-six-year-old saxophonist seemed to be holding back. The sets were short, the breaks long; the rhythm section carried the major burden of soloing in fast tempi, and for the fourth set they took the stage alone."[12]

Trumpeter Arnvid Meyer, also the jazz writer for another daily, *Aktuelt*, listened to several of Ben's performances and wrote,

> The opening night featured quite a few fine moments, even though Webster seemed somewhat weary and the interplay with the otherwise very accomplished house rhythm section . . . revealed many disagreements: the chords played by Drew apparently often deviated from what the soloist would have preferred, and Riel's complex patterns often seemed to get in the way.
>
> The problems did not disappear completely during the first week; the rhythm section never quite reached the rich, driving elasticity that suits a musician of Webster's school best.[13]

A radio transmission recorded on January 21 does not reveal disagreements between the soloist and rhythm section, though. Ben plays with bite, edge, and sharpness on the up-tempo numbers, whereas the ballads contain great warmth. Alex Riel still remembers how the soloist wanted him to play.

> He wanted the drummer to play two-beat on the high hat in the A-parts of the theme presentations, changing to the cymbal in the B-parts and then back to the high hat for the last A-part. That was very common in that style back then. But the special thing about him was that he wanted you to keep the high hat open so the cymbals made that pss, pss sound, cooking, like in rock. This was

unheard of in jazz at the time, it just wasn't done. I said to Ben, "What?!" But that's what he wanted, and he could sing it with a very loud, high sound—"bee, bee, bee." Other than that, he wouldn't ask for anything. I still use that trick occasionally, in jazz too. It's come to stay.

When we played ballads, he didn't want you to play in double time. He wanted the tempo to stay down, and he was a world champion ballad player. The singer Sting once said in an interview that ballads were difficult, but there was one person he knew of that played them in a way that you could understand the melody; that was Ben. Ben could play a ballad and almost make you cry, it was so good. When I was playing with Ben, I never listened to music during the day. I wanted to arrive empty and ready to get the full benefit of playing with a great artist. Niels-Henning and I have often talked about how we miss Ben.[14]

Niels-Henning Ørsted Pedersen also has many memories from the first period with Ben.

I was very young then, and his size and demeanor could be scary; you would really take care not to make mistakes. Dexter Gordon probably would have said that he taught us a lot, because he told us what he wanted. But Ben wasn't very educationally minded. Actually, he didn't say anything at all. He had a lot of ballads; I remember that they were harmonized extremely well by the British pianist Stan Tracey, and if we followed them—he was very sensitive as to which chords you played to a melody—there were no problems. He had a very good ear and noticed what went on behind him. So we learned a lot of discipline from him, even though he never really demanded it.

One thing that reveals a lot about a musician is the manner in which he plays, and the reaction caused from playing with someone who plays in a way that captures you. The following emotional development is deeper than if you drank beer together. Ben would sometimes phone Milt Hinton when he got back home from the Montmartre, and after the first time we played with him, he called him to tell him about this young bassist. He told me the next day, which is typical of him and other shy people. It's true that he bellows, but at the same time he reveals that he had to tell Milt Hinton about "this goddam kid!" The communication he and I have had like this, and we were equally shy, was very deep. There is no doubt about it. Because if you played the right bass note behind him, and usually I did, then you would get a lot in return because it made him happy. I remember a place toward the end of *Autumn Leaves* where you can go in two different directions, either descend chromatically from Gm to F#m to Fm to Bb7 and then on to Eb, or you can play the changes that Kenny Drew and I figured out, going from Gm to C7 and then from F7 and Bb7 to Eb, which concludes the song in a lighter fashion.

When we did things like that, things that sounded good, Ben would stop playing and light up in a smile. And he discovered that he didn't have to keep strictly to Stan Tracey's arrangements; we could do it on our own. It always made him happy to hear something that sounded good.

In the making of yourself, all the impressions made on you are utilized, the negative and the positive. It's in the ballads that I really use what I learned from Ben. In the beginning, I could hardly keep my fingers still when I played a ballad, because there seemed to be so much space between the beats. A big, empty hole. Your excuse is to tell yourself that a bass doesn't have the resonance of a saxophone, so you have to play more notes. In reality, it is a matter of personal maturity. Do you dare leave that pause alone?

When I think of Ben, I often think of vocalists. They are dependent on whether or not you can hold your breath a certain amount of time. They can't, as some horn players can, use what is called circular breathing. And thank God for that, because that means they have to think about how to phrase the song, how to tell the story, what to add, what to subtract. And in situations like that, you use the inspiration someone like Ben has given you. Why was it so difficult to play a solo after him? Because he cut to the bone. He said everything that was relevant in that song. Whenever Ben played *Danny Boy,* Kenny Drew and I would always glance at each other, because one of us had to play a solo while Ben rested, but neither of us wanted to, because what in the world was left to say? He had just told the story. The knowledge of what the story means to you, is something I trace back to people like Ben. He didn't try to sound like Hawkins. He aspired to get the violin into jazz, and he succeeded.[15]

Three sets, from the next to the last evening in the Jazzhus Montmartre, Copenhagen, January 30–31, 1965, were recorded for later release. *Blues for Herluf*—actually identical with *Randle's Island* performed at a hectic pace—reveals a very inspired Ben, aggressive and virile in the chase choruses with drummer Alex Riel. In *Blues for Herluf,* the rhythm section plays with wonderful ease and irresistible swing, not least due to bassist Ørsted Pedersen's drive. Kenny Drew's accompaniment is attentive throughout, and on *I Can't Get Started* his piano merges beautifully with Ben's sensitive interpretation, and Ørsted Pedersen answers Ben's phrases congenially and humorously in the theme chorus of *I'm Gonna Sit Right Down and Write Myself a Letter. Teach Me Tonight* and *Misty,* each performed over but one chorus, are good examples of how simple, short, and expressive Ben's ballads could be. The rhythm section's natural and extroverted swing from the first bar, regardless of tempo, enables Ben to relax, giving his interpretations serenity and tranquillity, as in *Yesterdays, Gone with the Wind,* and *Over the Rainbow*—a true gem.

During his booking at the Jazzhus Montmartre, Ben became romantically involved with the thirty-three-year-old vocalist and author of children's books, Grethe Kemp, and Ben moved in with her. Her stepfather was the well-known architect and lyricist Poul Henningsen, also called "PH." He lived north of Copenhagen with his wife—Grethe's mother—and Ben and Grethe often visited them. "Seeing Ben and PH together was definitely entertaining," says Henrik Wolsgaard-Iversen, a mutual friend of Grethe Kemp and PH.

Someone should have taken pictures of the two of them together. I remember him in a teasing mood, serving a very strong type of Norwegian Potkäse to Ben, a cigarette dangling from his mouth, "This a good cheese. Tastes good!" He spoke Danish very slowly to Ben. "Okay!" Ben answered, and wanted to try it. Everybody knew that it was like putting a bomb in your mouth, and then you died. But Ben didn't move a muscle. He finished it up and said, "That's very good. I could eat a little more, please!" He never let on, but he knew his leg was being pulled and played along all the way. Afterwards, he admitted that the cheese had been hard to eat. But he had a second helping just to get back at PH![16]

For the next year, Ben and Grethe Kemp were almost inseparable, and she went with him to London, Paris, and Stockholm, and that summer, she and her eleven-year-old son Farah took Ben with them for a few days' vacation in PH's summer house by the North Sea coast in Skagen.

Knowing Grethe Kemp was the perfect introduction for Ben to the jazz scene in Copenhagen. A singer herself, she knew the scene from the inside. Her home was always open to friends, and there were many parties when Albert Nicholas, Stuff Smith, or Yusef Lateef made their way up the many steps to the third floor.

After the last night at Jazzhus Montmartre, January 31, Ben set off for Stockholm on a tour that would take him through most of Sweden from north to south. Grethe Kemp traveled with him for most of the tour, and following a short television show in Stockholm with Gunnar Svensson at the piano, they continued north. He was accompanied by a different rhythm section than during his first visit, and pianist Lars Sjösten tells the following of his first experiences with Webster, "The first time Webster visited Stockholm to play at the Gyllene Cirkeln, I went to hear the concert. Webster was standing outside when I arrived, and at the time I didn't know him at all. But he called me over and said, 'Hello, young man, how are you?' as if we'd known each other for years, and then we walked into the restaurant together. It occurred to me that he was shy. He wanted company when he walked in, when people were sitting in there. He was a little afraid of going in there on his own. It felt a little weird, because you usually tend to think that your idols don't have any weaknesses."[17]

The critics in Sundsvall were enthusiastic about Ben and his rhythm section, with Sjösten receiving the most praise among the Swedish musicians. "The most memorable pieces were the wonderful, lovely *Chelsea Bridge,* but even tunes like *Pennies from Heaven, My Romance,* and *The Theme* made this writer roll off his chair, not to forget Webster's showcase tunes *In a Mellotone* and *Perdido,* played, as always, with the same feeling," wrote *Sundsvall Tidning.*[18]

Another newspaper commented that "Webster's solos were characterized by exceptional class, authority, routine, and feeling, and combined with a wonderful tone on his tenor saxophone, the result is no less than music on the highest level."[19]

A private recording from the first set of the concert shows that the rhythm section lacked the elasticity to which Ben had become accustomed in the Jazzhus Montmartre, but Sjösten is an excellent accompanist as well as soloist.

The last concert was in Lund on February 9, and two days later, Ben was booked for a short tour of Denmark with trumpeter Arnvid Meyer's orchestra, one of the few Danish jazz groups playing solid swing music at a time when traditional or modern jazz was most popular in the many jazz clubs spread across the country.

"Ben was really pissed off to begin with," Meyer recalls. "He had expected to play with Kenny Drew, and all he saw was this group of bearded monkeys, and the guy who sometimes brought him beer in the Montmartre was the bandleader! We went in a huddle and said, 'What can we do with this old guy? Well, we can think of all the Ellington tunes we know, and play a kind of Ellington concert before calling him up for the next set.' And Ben turned completely, typical of him. When he heard us playing *What Am I Here For?, Just Squeeze Me, Blue Light,* and a lot of other Ellington tunes that most audiences, or even musicians, usually didn't know at all back then, we became the best of friends."[20]

The band's drummer, Hans Nymand, also recalls that Ben melted when they started playing Ellington in the second set. "The clouds disappeared and he became friendlier, and suddenly we were his band," he recalls. "When we got back to the hotel, he insisted on calling up Duke Ellington to tell him about us, and I guess he did, because he had a huge telephone bill the next morning. But Ben didn't think about things like that."[21]

After this tour, Stefansen had booked Ben at the Metropol in Oslo for the week of February 15–21. Ben and Grethe Kemp sailed from Copenhagen to Oslo in Norway. Perhaps Ben had too many strong beers on the way over; at any rate he was unable to go through with the first evening's concert. "He tried, but soon discovered he was suffering from 'sea legs,'" says journalist Randi Hultin. "'I still have these sea legs,' he explained a couple of days later. When he eventually did get back into shape and played at the Metropol, we were treated to a glorious musical feast. No tenor player since has been able to match his tone. When he played, it was as if the notes remained suspended in the room long afterwards—like musical smoke rings."[22]

At the Metropol, Ben played with the young pianist Tore Sandnæs's trio. Sandnæs and Ben became close friends, and one sunny afternoon, he took Grethe and Ben skiing. Several snapshots were taken. While Grethe looks totally relaxed in skis, it's obvious that Ben, fully equipped and with woolen cap and mittens, felt uneasy and not quite sure how to make the skis work. "When we went skiing, Ben Webster had more fresh air than ever before in his life," Sandnæs recounts. "That same evening he ate well, settled in a soft chair, had a cognac, and then he was well on his way to dreamland. We were watching television, the ski-jumpers on their way down the hill, and suddenly one of them fell. Ben was almost asleep, but when he saw the man fall, he sat up straight in his chair and yelled, 'My friend!' He had fallen a few times himself, and now he saw a fellow sufferer. I remember it very clearly because he mobilized his last strength before slumping down and falling asleep."[23]

Ben played a couple of jobs with Arnvid Meyer in March, including a television show on March 9, where he is at least as enthusiastic as the band, swinging with wonderful elasticity behind him. On *Duke's in Bed* and *Stompy Jones* he performs with drive and imagination, while he is more subdued but no less focused on *What's I'm Gotchere?* Although interpreted in a lovely fashion, *Over the Rainbow* has a routine feel. Immediately afterwards he was filmed for television with the rhythm section from the Montmartre, opening with an uninspired *In a Mellotone*, followed by an exceptionally beautiful and sensitively interpreted *Danny Boy*, while *Mack the Knife* swings irresistibly from the very start, inspiring Ben as well. Unfortunately the film stops just as Ben and Alex Riel engage in chase choruses.

Later that month, Ben and Grethe took a short well-deserved vacation in London, before continuing to Paris. Ben was booked to play the famous Blue Note in the French capital for four weeks, starting March

27. The club was owned by the expatriate American Ben Benjamin. On paper, the lineup looked impressive: Ben was to be backed exclusively by other expatriate Americans, pianist Mal Waldron, bassist Jimmy Woode, and drummer Kenny Clarke. But nothing euphoric resulted, because Ben disliked the rhythm section. "He became angry at Mal Waldron on the very first evening, because he didn't like his playing," wrote *Jazz Magazine*. "The following evening, Mal Waldron was replaced by René Urtreger, but soon an unbearable tension developed on stage between Webster and Kenny Clarke. Jimmy Woode, whose friendliness is legendary, tried reconciling the two men, but to no avail. Finally, on Saturday, April 10, Ben Webster and Ben Benjamin agreed to discontinue the contract."[24]

We can only guess at what caused such disagreement, but as far as Mal Waldron is concerned, it is possible that Webster found Waldron's playing too original for his taste. As for Kenny Clarke, perhaps disagreements arose concerning the manner in which Ben wished to be accompanied. Clarke's style was polyrhythmic, but he was open to lesser demands from soloists, as documented by his sensitive accompaniment behind Lester Young on his visit to Paris in 1959. The recordings from Birdland in 1953, when Ben played with the Modern Jazz Quartet, show that Clarke's busy drumming is far from what Ben wanted, and it is very possible that Ben remembered, and tried to get him to subdue his style a bit.

Originally, Ben was to have returned to London after the planned monthlong booking in Paris, but with Ben returning to Copenhagen before scheduled, Stefansen was lucky to get him another job at the Gyllene Cirkeln in Stockholm. The last-minute booking was made possible by a cancellation from Stuff Smith and Kenny Drew, due to Smith's hospitalization in Oslo. Sjösten also remembers this job with Ben, and that it coincided with a concert with another American jazz legend. "Earl Hines came to Stockholm at the same time," he recalls,

> performing with drummer Nils-Bertil Dahlander, who had played a lot with Teddy Wilson in the U.S. under the name Bert Dale. Their concert was in the same building as the Gyllene Cirkeln, in a room right next door. After their concert, the two of them came in where we were playing, and Webster was really

happy to see them. "Hey, Lars, you gotta meet these people. They are my old drinking buddies!" And a little later he walked over to me and said, "Hey, Lars, do you think maybe Earl could play a couple of tunes?" And of course Hines played with Webster for the rest of the night. Later, when I was on my way home, they were drinking and having fun, and Webster was laughing so hard, the roof almost lifted.[25]

Bassist Roman Dylag recalls that Ben called a rehearsal before their first evening. "We tried a couple of tunes, and suddenly Ben quit playing, went to the piano, and asked Lasse to stand up, sat down at the piano, put his hands over the keys very close together, and said, 'Not so!'; then moved his hands apart and started to play a real stride piano. After a chorus or so he stopped playing and said, 'That's what it should look and sound like.' Poor Lasse, so young, so talented, but playing stride certainly wasn't his thing. Anyway, we all had a real good time. Ben was a very nice, soft, and soulful person."[26] Apparently Ben was overly sensitive about pianists at the time.

A live recording from April 23, aired on *Jazz vid Midnatt*, adds little to the perception of Ben or the rhythm section from the January recordings—even the repertoire is more or less the same—but it confirms that Ben had begun to put some of his solos in a fairly set framework. For years, *Cotton Tail* and *Danny Boy* had been well-known examples of this, just as various interpretations of ballads such as *My Romance, How Long Has This Been Going On?* and *That's All* can only be distinguished by small nuances and variations in melody and phrasing. The past few months had seen him also starting his improvisations on *Pennies from Heaven* with identical phrases throughout the first half chorus, which is heard on all recorded versions from Ronnie Scott's Club and subsequently.

After Stockholm, Ben set out for England, where he started a two-month visit with a concert at the Royal Festival Hall on May 8 called "Jazz from Kansas City." The lineup was strong: aside from Ben, the band included Buck Clayton, Vic Dickenson, Ruby Braff, and blues vocalist Joe Turner, accompanied by Stan Tracey's trio. Also on the bill was Humphrey Lyttelton's orchestra with alto saxophonist Bruce Turner as featured guest. The evening offered two almost identical concerts, and the critics were a little disappointed, especially with the jam session set, placed in the second half of both concerts.[27]

On May 10, Ben opened the first of four weeks at Ronnie Scott's Club, backed by Alan Branscombe's trio during the first three weeks and by Stan Tracey's for the last week. Judging from a review of one of the first evenings of the booking, Branscombe's trio was not particularly stimulating to Ben: "what existed at Ronnie Scott's was a brilliant musician, playing for and with people who had no idea of the context in which his playing must be understood at all deeply. His playing was inevitably half-hearted, since nobody could tell the difference anyway between the genuine act of creation, with its risk of self-exposure and total involvement, and merely going through the motions. 'The motions' in Webster's case, happen to be very enjoyable ones, but they are not any substitute for what he is really capable of."[28]

Recordings from May 14 and 15 document the reviewer's comments concerning the rhythm section, but Ben does not play on half-power all the time, at least not on these two evenings. Although his solos are short, the up-tempo tunes are aggressive and virile; but the ballads are all uninspired and seem played out of duty alone.

Things changed for the better when Stan Tracey took over the piano. One evening halfway through the run proved exceptional when Ben had unexpected visitors on stage. "Webster had hardly begun to play when he was joined by a blues singer, Joe Turner, and by Memphis Slim, whose old-time boogie piano accompaniment would have scandalised modern audiences 10 years ago but today just make them tap their feet," Benny Green wrote. "Later that same night Webster played chaotic but inspired duets with another old partner, baritone saxophonist Gerry Mulligan, and it was in these duets that the secret of Webster's appeal was fully revealed. Mulligan contorted himself in his attempts to execute his own complex thoughts. It was excellent playing, demonstrating his happy knack of giving the baritone the buoyancy of a tenor. But when Webster followed, there were fewer notes, longer gaps, no semi-quavers and yet the result was richer in texture than anything that had gone before."[29]

Immediately after this booking, Ben engaged in his first tour of Britain with the accompaniment supplied by Bruce Turner's Jump Band. The tour lasted for fifteen days. A private recording from Grimsby reveals an average swing band with a somewhat heavy rhythm section. Ben is uninspired and seems tired even in the tunes played alone with the rhythm section.

After the concert in Grimsby, the musicians returned to their hotel, where they were treated to a lesson on Ben's ability with a billiard cue. "We had a billiards table in our private rooms," recalls Fred Everett, "and after the session Ben saw this, and gave us a wonderful display of the trick shots that he had learned on the pool tables back home. He told us that he had never been able to make a good living playing jazz, but that he had often had to keep himself by hustling at pool, and that he thought that he played pool better than he played the tenor sax!"[30]

Later on the tour, Ben expressed his satisfaction with the band, and invited everybody to have dinner with him on the last evening—spare ribs and black-eyed peas—which he would prepare himself. As a vegetarian, Turner protested, but to no avail. "When the time came," Turner recalls, "we all sat around a big table and feasted on this stuff, under Ben's watchful eye. Every time he looked at my direction I had to shovel another mouthful down, somehow managing to force a smile. I don't think I would have done it for anyone else but Ben Webster. He was the greatest jazz musician I ever worked with, the gentlest and sweetest of men, and one who holds a special place in my memory."[31]

Ben returned to Denmark from England, but during autumn, he moved out of Grethe's apartment and into a rented room at Aurikelvej 7 in a part of Copenhagen called Frederiksberg. The two of them were unable to work things out in the long run, and it had become increasingly difficult for Ben to climb the stairs to the third floor. Anders Stefansen found the room for Ben, and he recounts that "it was in the distinguished home of an old lady, with very delicate armchairs. When Ben got home and settled heavily in an armchair, both it and the porcelain would crash down. But she liked him. She spoke no English and he didn't speak Danish, but they did all right. When he sat around drinking, and feeling comfortable, she was a little fascinated, so she never threw him out."[32]

Although Aurikelvej was farther from the center of Copenhagen, Ben did not mind, because it was very close to Copenhagen's Zoo. Ben loved animals and often visited zoos when he had the opportunity. Ben preferred having company whenever he went anywhere, and occasionally the waiter from the Jazzhus Montmartre, Harvey Sand, would go with him. Ben had established just as warm a friendship with him as he had with Henry Cohen in London, and they often spent time together. "He would walk around talking to all the animals," Sand recalls, "except the birds. He didn't want to see the birds. But he talked to the lions and monkeys, all kinds of large animals, the tigers too. He loved the tigers. It was as if they understood what he said to them. Not one of them made a fuss or screeched or bellowed. They all sat quietly, listening to him. And then he would go around giving out ice cream cones to small children—and their mothers! He liked to act the rich uncle. He made a lot of money, but he used it just as fast."[33]

The summer of 1965 was somewhat quieter for Ben than his first half year in Europe, but in September, jobs began picking up again, and that month Ben recorded with Kenny Drew's trio and Arnvid Meyer's orchestra. John Darville, the band's trombonist, and Ben developed a close friendship, beginning one of the first evenings Ben spent in Denmark. "The first time I met him, was at the home of Henrik Wolsgaard-Iversen and Rosita Thomas," Darville recalls.

> She was a world-champion spareribs cook, and I was seated next to him. We talked about this and that, and naturally we talked about Duke Ellington. I said that the orchestra changed completely when Sonny Greer quit. And Ben turned toward me and yelled, "What did you say? What did you say?" I thought my final hour had arrived, because he sounded pretty violent. As gently as possible, I repeated what I had said, and he hammered his big fist down on the table and turned toward me again and said, "What's your name?" And I thought, what now? And told him my name very quietly. And he hugged me, that big man, and said it was the pure truth, and that he was happy to hear that somebody realized how much Sonny Greer had meant to Ellington's orchestra.[34]

The pianist in Arnvid Meyer's orchestra, Niels Jørgen Steen, also has many fond memories of Ben, even though their first encounter proved a demonstration of power on Ben's part.

> The first time we played together was on a tour of Jutland, and before the gig, he invited me into his hotel room and said, 'I

wanna show you something!' Then he took out a knife. It was apparently some kind of threat, and I recalled the rumor about him beating up pianists. I didn't know what to say, so I just said, "Very nice, very nice!" After he heard me play, everything was all right. I was a modern pianist, but when I played with Arnvid's orchestra, I changed my style to fit the band. I've always loved swing style, so it wasn't difficult. But Ben could play with all kinds of musicians. He had a fantastic ear. You just had to play one chord, and he'd play something incredibly beautiful on top of it.[35]

During the first couple of years when Ben played with Arnvid Meyer's orchestra, Ole Kongsted was the band's tenor saxophonist, replacing Jesper Thilo, who had been drafted. "Jesper Thilo knew all Ben's solos from the records by heart," Niels Jørgen Steen says. "We were playing at the Montmartre with my own band, and when Ben Webster came in with Stuff Smith I said to Jesper, 'Let's play *Cotton Tail.*' 'I'm scared,' Jesper answered. 'C'mon, just for the hell of it,' I said, and so we played it and Jesper started out with Ben's solo. To start with, I could see Ben was furious. He didn't like it, but then he looked over at Stuff Smith, who thought it was hilarious, and then Ben gave in, too. Ben and Jesper wound up the best of friends. They would share experiences about reeds and mouthpieces like saxophonists do."

Ben recorded at Metronome's studios in Copenhagen on September 5, 1965, with the same rhythm section that had accompanied him at the Jazzhus Montmartre. The mainstay of the repertoire was ballads with a few medium-tempo tunes thrown in for variation. With the exception of *Stardust,* played only once through verse and chorus, the other ballads follow a set pattern, as they are performed over two choruses, with Kenny Drew soloing over half of a chorus after Ben's interpretation of the melody and Ben bringing the tune to conclusion.

On the recordings, Ben's wonderful tone is captivating and placed perfectly in the overall sound. No nuance in his phrasing or dynamics is lost. The accompaniment is very attentive, exemplified in the majestic version of *Stardust.* It, along with *What's New, I Got It Bad (and That Ain't Good), Yesterdays,* and *There Is No Greater Love,* is among his very best interpretations from these years, beautifully structured, and expressed with plenty of romance and longing. In this context, *There Is No*

Greater Love is a surprise, as it is rarely played as a ballad, but Ben's interpretation brings the best out in the tune, adding a lovely dimension to an otherwise stale theme. The three medium-tempo tunes swing well at a pace perfectly set for the themes, and *Close Your Eyes* and *Autumn Leaves,* both in minor keys, are especially enriched by Ben's powerful drive and storytelling abilities, and his inspired phrases in the final choruses.

Later the same month, Ben recorded at the Metronome studios again, this time on three sessions with Arnvid Meyer's orchestra. Four of the nine tunes came from the Duke Ellington songbook, and indeed, the band sounds like a small Ellington group, because they copied riffs and arrangements from their idol.

On these recordings, Ben's performance is of the same standard as at the previous sessions, perhaps even more facetted. His superb timing is demonstrated very well in the blues *What's I'm Gotchere,* in which he plays a two-bar break in his first chorus, a study in the art of utilizing pauses, followed by a solo with lots of original figures and phrases. On *Stompy Jones,* he begins with relaxed, soft-spoken phrases, after which the dynamics become more aggressive. However, the balance on the final choruses, when the ensemble enters with riffs, is bad; unfortunately, Ben is relegated to the remotest corner of the overall sound. It must be noted that Ole Kongsted, the other tenor saxophonist on the session, was very influenced by Ben, and it is he who plays the first solo on *Stompy Jones, Brother John's Blues,* and *The Jeep Is Jumpin'*—a fact that has escaped some reviewers.

Following a trip to Oslo in September for the opening of a new jazz club, another series of jobs in Denmark was lined up with Arnvid Meyer's orchestra, and this time, J. C. Higginbotham joined them. Darville had persuaded the proprietor at the restaurant Westfalia in Copenhagen to book jazz, and Meyer's orchestra with Ben and Higginbotham played there on October 13 and 14. "It wasn't a big success as far as the audience went," recalls Hans Nymand.

> At one point Higgy had played a feature tune—probably *Confessin',* which was his big number—and Ben didn't feel that the audience had responded well, so he went over to the microphone and said, "It seems to me that the applause was a little meager. But I'd like to call to your attention that even though we are a

couple of elderly gentlemen, this man has made jazz history. You may hear this and that around town that seems more fantastic, but you should know that you will never hear this again!" And then people woke up, and started clapping at Higgy all the time. It was typical of Ben. He could be jealous of Higgy, but he could be generous too.[36]

On October 29, Ben performed at Berliner Jazztage, the second year of an annual jazz festival in the German capital organized by Joachim-Ernst Berendt. Ben was on the program with Don Byas and Brew Moore, but unfortunately, he arrived inebriated and created a minor scandal. Ben had celebrated the reunion with his American friends a little too heavily, and had fallen asleep in the dressing room. Berendt knew nothing of the risk in waking Ben, and started to shake him when the time came for him to go on stage. Half asleep, Ben took a punch at him and hit Berendt smack on the chin. However, he apologized many times before going on stage.

The concert was transmitted live on German radio, and the first tune played by the three tenors was *Perdido*. Despite excellent support from the rhythm section of Kenny Drew, Niels-Henning Ørsted Pedersen, and Alan Dawson, none of them offered anything beyond clichés, and the ending was chaotic because apparently no one remembered what they had agreed on. After this, each of them was to be featured in a solo tune, and Ben was the first of the three. However, when Drew began the introduction to *How Long Has This Been Going On?* Ben waved him off and began speaking to the audience instead, only to be distracted a moment later. The emcee took the opportunity to regain control of the microphone and said,

> Ladies and Gentlemen, perhaps some among you do not understand English. I can only say shortly that Ben Webster would like to express his pleasure at being reunited with a couple of his old colleagues, with whom he has played for many years, and I think I should tell our audience at this time that Ben Webster is very happy tonight and in an extremely good mood. (Applause.) We are pleased to have him, because he is a fine representative of the swing tenors, and I also think that it is obvious that jazz musicians aren't pompous, but can be gay as well, and have fun, as

now when Ben Webster is strumming the piano. But now to his feature, *How Long Has This Been Going On?*

Kenny Drew began his introduction again, but Ben was far from ready and yelled over to him, "One more time!" This repeated itself several times while Ben continued talking, until he finally started up the tune. He played one tender chorus, but was forced to leave the rest of the tune to the rhythm section. Joachim-Ernst Berendt, intent on avoiding new scandalous scenes from Ben, persuaded him to leave the stage during Drew's solo.

Back in Copenhagen, Ben was busy for the rest of the year playing with Arnvid Meyer's orchestra, and with a booking at the Jazzhus Montmartre for the first two weeks of December with Don Byas and Brew Moore. The combination of Ben, Don Byas, and Brew Moore, two African Americans and a white musician, was a study in different styles. They offered a varied program of music, but none of them seemed able to stimulate the others. I heard them on one of the first evenings in the Jazzhus Montmartre, and I remember that Ben and Byas seemed wary of each other, while Moore came out solidly on top, playing in his lovely Lester Young–influenced style. One evening, Hugo Rasmussen filled in for Ørsted Pedersen and, of the many foreign saxophonists he has accompanied over the years,

> Ben, Dexter Gordon, and Brew Moore were the best. They were the stars. Perhaps Brew wasn't a star in the eyes of the public, but he was to me. He was one of the most amazing saxophonists. And as far as I'm concerned, he came out on top when he was on stage with Ben and Don Byas. Those two black guys were always watching each other. Don set the tempi as fast as possible, and Ben set them as slow as possible. Brew just accepted whatever they came up with. It was interesting to hear the differences in their styles, but on this occasion, Brew was best. It was always Ben or Don who suggested what to play. There was a battle of power going on between them [Ben and Don], about who took the lead, who was the biggest star. They never did find out.[37]

Ben had trouble in the up-tempo tunes, but treated us to his all-encompassing serenity and rich sound in a few wonderful ballads. Byas's performance was a mite more controlled and without the technical exaggerations often causing his music to become superficial; he seemed to administer his inventiveness better than usual. A radio transcription of the three tenors from Jazzhus Montmartre on December 9 shows a somewhat chaotic theme presentation and a set solo order with Moore first and Ben last. Byas and Moore had not yet coordinated their phrasing on *In a Mellotone,* much less their tuning. Ben plays fills. Byas plays the theme to *Sunday* while the other two accompany him with long notes that are supposed to be in two-part harmony, but occasionally more or less collide. Ben's solo is potent, extroverted, and forceful, contrasting with his following solo tune, *Danny Boy,* as usual a classic example of tenderness and the art of dynamics and instrumental control. *Perdido* is performed in a moderate medium tempo, and they seem to have a small disagreement as to who leads the B-part in the first chorus, whereas the traditional riff in the concluding chorus is delivered perfectly in three-part harmony, far from the embarrassing Berlin version.

When he played with Arnvid Meyer at a jazz festival in Elsinore, Ben was in for a surprise. "Steen Vig played as well," Arnvid Meyer remembers,

> and his playing affected Ben deeply, because Steen Vig was a Hawkins tenor a la 1928–29, the same style Ben began with and grew up with when he was very young. And here was this young Dane, playing almost just the same way, and with a whole lot of talent. After that, Ben had a reserve orchestra—when we couldn't take a job, he took Steen Vig's band along. Once Steen Vig told me that they were returning from Jutland with Ben and on their way off the ferry to Zealand, Ben said, "Call the captain! Let's go directly to Copenhagen. I'll pay!" He was drunk and thought he could get the captain to sail all the way around Zealand for a couple of hundred kroner![38]

Ben's enthusiasm for Steen Vig was such that when he heard that Vig was playing for a few evenings in Vingården, Copenhagen, he persuaded Byas and Moore to time their own breaks to enable the three of them to grab a cab to Vingården and catch a few of his tunes before returning to Montmartre.

Ben continued touring in Denmark and Sweden during the first months of 1966. A couple of times, Ben guested with Danish saxophonist Steen Vig's orchestra, which played traditional jazz as well as more swing-orientated music. A job in Padborg Jazzklub on March 19, 1966, was taped, and Ben was given a copy of the amateur recording. He fits in well, although it is strange hearing him backed by a banjo in tunes like *Ain't Misbehavin'*, *Perdido*, *If I Could Be with You One Hour* and *Exactly Like You*. The rhythm section is tight, even slightly hectic. In the tunes where the banjo is replaced with a guitar, Ben adjusts by playing more directly on the beat. Throughout the evening he is the first soloist, playing well; he is quite inspired on *Lady Be Good* and *Exactly Like You,* but *Danny Boy* sees him waging a heroic but losing battle with a very noisy audience in his attempts to get his message across. When Ben was a guest soloist with an established band, he had the opportunity to play a somewhat different repertoire than usual—a welcome variation from a daily routine in which he tended to play the same tunes again and again.

Throughout the month of May, Ben was once again booked at the Jazzhus Montmartre, this time with trumpeter Carmell Jones. A recording from that evening offers music with a relaxed and easy swing. *Cotton Tail* is a ball, featuring an excellent chase with drummer Rune Carlsson, and the interpretation of *My Romance* is among his most beautiful versions of the ballad, with pianist Atli Bjørn's solo performed in an empathetic spirit.

Ben spent some of his free time visiting Stuff Smith at his apartment. They would talk, drink beer, and occasionally jam with Smith on violin and Ben on piano. Ben recorded one of these sessions. Some of the tunes were played without Smith, who did not seem to be in a very affable playing mood that day anyway, perhaps because Ben's piano playing is somewhat heavy-handed, and consequently not particularly inspiring.

In late May, Ben had stayed in Denmark for such a long time that his work permit could not be renewed. Anders Stefansen explains that Ben "had to leave the country for three months before he could get in again. When the day arrived for him to move, he asked me what to do, and I answered that if he went to Amsterdam, I'd call up Don Byas, and he could pick him up when he arrived. I put Ben on a train to Amsterdam and called Don Byas to tell him that Ben was on his way."[39]

10. The Dutch Years
(1966–1969)

Ben's last evening in the Jazzhus Montmartre, Sunday, May 29, was also his last legal working day in Denmark. The following day, Stefansen accompanied him to Copenhagen's Central Station, as they had agreed, and Ben boarded the train to Amsterdam. When he arrived, Don Byas was there to meet him. Byas had come to Europe in 1946 with Don Redman's Big Band and had lived there ever since, first in France for many years, later in Holland. Since Stefansen had asked him to take care of Ben, Byas had arranged for him to rent a room with Mrs. Hartlooper at Waalstraat 77 in the Rivierenbuurt district of southern Amsterdam. Upon entering the building, a narrow and steep stairway led up to the second floor, where Mrs. Hartlooper—a lively seventy-two-year-old Jewish war-widow—lived in a three-room utility. She supplemented her modest pension by renting a room for what amounted to twenty dollars a week. The thirteen-foot by thirteen-foot room had a closet and was furnished with a bed, a desk, a small table, and two chairs. Although Mrs. Hartlooper knew very little English and Ben spoke no Dutch whatsoever, they liked each other from the very start. Johan van der Keuken remembers that she "was a very simple person, but she had a fantastic communication with Ben, and also a fantastic authority."[1] Ben would buy the food he wanted, and Mrs. Hartlooper would prepare and serve it for him at a prearranged time. On a whole, she took care of him as best she could, washing and ironing his clothes, and Ben enjoyed having the substitute mother he had missed for so long. "She treats me like her own son," he said.[2]

Pianist Cees Slinger played with Ben on many occasions, and he remembers that "Mrs. Hartlooper was a very nice old lady. She was great, and I loved her very much. I picked Ben up at her place always when we had a gig, and when I picked him up, she always said, 'Ben, don't forget this,' and 'Ben, be careful.' She was really mothering him."[3] On another occasion, Slinger said, "he must have really loved her, because it was like they were married, almost. He would say, 'Well, she is scolding me again because I did something wrong!' but it was always with a smile. And she must have loved him, that's for absolutely sure, because of the way she was talking about him was beautiful. She would come to gigs and listen to him, an elderly lady of whom you would never believe that she would like that kind of music."[4]

Ben's first weeks in Amsterdam were pure relaxation and vacation. He divided his time between golf, billiards, canal tours, and visits to the city's zoo. However, the rumors of his arrival reached jazz critic and radio host Michiel de Ruyter, who hired him for a television show on June 30. He was accompanied by Slinger, bassist Jacques Schols, and drummer John Engels, a trio that had played together often. In the studio, Slinger remembers, "Ben was straddling a chair with his sax case in his lap, and started testing a reed, 'wooh-wooh.' Two deep sighs. I heard that sound for the first time, and I'll never forget it. What was so special about it? First of all: it was Ben. There he was, the legendary Ben Webster. That was quite impressive in itself, for a couple of simple Dutch boys. That afternoon, we all listened to him with utter adoration."[5]

After a short visit to Brussels, Ben was booked as a soloist with Boy Edgar's Big Band in Amsterdam. The occasion was the annual music and theater festival, the Holland Festival, a big media event, and the concert was broadcast directly by the radio on the evening of July 13. Unfortunately, Ben's performance here was just as unsuccessful as at the Berliner Jazztage, beginning with the afternoon rehearsals. A few days before the concert Jacques Schols's wife had been killed in a traffic accident, and naturally he was not himself. "Ben, in his own way, joined him in his grief," explained Michiel de Ruyter.

> We soon decided that it would be too dangerous to let him descend the stairs at the back of the stage that night, so Ben spent the concert in the front row. Boy pretended not to see him—he sensed the impending disaster—but when the piece was over, Ben unsteadily got to his feet and shouted, "Now it's my turn."

Boy had an orchestra with six trumpets, ten saxophones, trombones and rhythm—altogether about thirty people. Ben started by greeting every single one of them. He slowly moved through the entire group—"Hi, how are you doing?"—until Boy finally got him to the microphone. But now—still during a live broadcast—he started telling the audience all kinds of funny, but disjointed stories.

The music was nothing special, a little buzzing, some ballad-type things, but Ben just wouldn't stop. In the background, you could suddenly see Boy walking through his orchestra. He gave everyone a note, and created a chord that way—something we always called "Boy's swimming." . . .

Ben was really too out of it to carry on. Just when he was about to launch into a new chorus, Boy got up, waved to the orchestra, and [called for the concluding chord]. Ben whirled around as though he'd been bitten, suddenly unsure of what was going on. Boy grabbed the microphone: "Ben Webster, ladies and gentlemen, Ben Webster!"[6]

Ben's unfortunate behavior was once again blown up in the press, and he began to get a reputation as an undependable, alcoholic musician. The true state of things was in no way that bad. Earlier, particularly in the 1940s, Ben might easily have been diagnosed an alcoholic; now, however, that diagnosis would have been an exaggeration, at least in the sense that he was not compelled to consume alcohol every day. Many a day would pass without Ben drinking, especially before a tour, or if he was booked as a soloist with musicians he respected greatly, such as Duke Ellington or Benny Carter; and in his daily routine his intake was moderate. He never drank before or during a recording session. Whenever he went over the limit, there was always a reason, often a reunion with American musicians, when his pleasure led him to excessive celebration. Rehearsals for television and radio shows with long hours of waiting were often problematic as well, as were extended train trips on his way to jobs around Europe. Tours were beginning to tire him. There were no problems if they lasted no more than two weeks, but on longer tours he would occasionally show up late at the last jobs, drunk, tie loosened, hair uncombed, and jacket open.

The first time Ben played with Duke Ellington in Europe was at the jazz festival in Antibes on the French Mediterranean coast on July 29, 1966. By last-minute arrangement, he took part in the last of Ellington's four concerts. "I was in Juan-les-Pins," Anders Stefansen remembers.

> While I was there, Norman Granz called because he was arranging recording sessions and radio and television shows. He asked me which American jazz musicians were in Denmark at the time, and if I would send them down. There was Ray Nance, Don Byas, and Ben Webster, but I had Don Byas booked in Århus at the time, and he couldn't cancel. Ray Nance was open and he wasn't afraid of flying, so we sent him a plane ticket. Ben was open as well, but he took the train. The day arrived for me to pick the two gentlemen up, and Ben Webster rolled into the station in Nice right on time, an hour before Nance's flight from Copenhagen. We drove out to the airport and took a seat on the top floor where we could see the planes. Sure enough, a Scandinavian Airlines plane landed on schedule and we watched everybody leave, but there was no Ray Nance; we even saw the crew leave the plane. Five or ten minutes went by and finally Nance stumbled out, drunk out of his mind. We managed to get him in the car and drove to Antibes/Juan-les-Pins.
>
> I didn't see Ray Nance until he was scheduled to play that evening with Ella Fitzgerald. Norman Granz was angry because he was drunk, and they got in a fight, and there was a lot of hassle. Ray Nance said he wasn't satisfied with his fee, which was around one hundred dollars plus travel expenses. That was the going rate back then. "Well, how much do you think you're worth then?" Granz asked him. He answered, "Five hundred dollars." So Granz said to me, "Go over to Mercer [Ellington] and get a thousand dollars." All this was going on in the dressing room before the band went on. Another band was playing on stage, and the room was full of Ellington musicians, and naturally Ben Webster was there too. I got the thousand dollars from Mercer and gave them to Granz, and he said to Ray Nance, "Here's your five hundred dollars, and don't expect ever to play with this

orchestra again." And to me he said, "Here is five hundred dollars for Ben. I can't pay one more than the other." I gave Ben the money, but he didn't say a word. I've never seen him that pale and quiet.[7]

Ben was in fine shape for the concert with "The Guv'nor," playing with persuasion and concentration throughout the seven tunes in which he was featured. A wonderful paraphrase of *All Too Soon* was the melodic high point. There were no rehearsals, and Ellington did not tell Ben beforehand what tunes would be played, a pattern that was repeated each time Ben played with him later as well. Ben swings forcefully on *In a Mellotone;* he is accompanied by encouraging shouts from the band and keeps up the momentum in the conclusive chase chorus with Nance. Billy Strayhorn's waltz, *Martell,* a variation on *Take the "A" Train,* inspires him to play unusual lines in the beginning of his solo, although the last half cruises along in neutral, and at the end of *The Old Circus Train* he and Hodges have fun with a few spontaneous riffs on top of the shuffle rhythm. Another new tune was the moderate up-tempo *Jive,* which turned out to be built on *I Got Rhythm,* and Ben plays four red-hot choruses climaxing in the last with a finely shaped ascending phrase. He performs *It Don't Mean a Thing* with Ella Fitzgerald, and a wonderful, easygoing *Just Squeeze Me.* His solos in both of them are short but all the more inspired.

From the warm south of France, Ben traveled to the cooler climate of the Norwegian summer. In the week of August 10–14, he played at Oslo's Club Manhattan, accompanied by the same trio that backed him at the Metropol the previous year. Ben had arrived in Oslo a few days early to record with the trio; a composition he had written for the movie *Liv,* directed by Pål Løkkeberg and produced by his wife, Vibeke Løkkeberg, who also played the leading role. In his first attempt at writing music for a movie, Ben's music was structured on Ellington's *Satin Doll.*[8]

The autumn saw Ben touring in Belgium and Denmark. In Copenhagen, he performed on a television show on November 25, with some of the musicians from the previous evening's Jazz at the Philharmonic concert: Coleman Hawkins, Clark Terry, Dizzy Gillespie, Teddy Wilson, Bob Cranshaw, and Louie Bellson. Hawkins, Wilson, and Ben played a practical joke on producer Sten Bramsen. Ben and Hawkins had each played a solo tune with the rhythm section, and the plan was for them to play a tune together. Bramsen suggested *Honeysuckle Rose*. Hawkins grunted, "Don't know it," and Ben added, "Could you please whistle the tune?" Wilson said, "I'm not familiar with the changes!"[9]

Two days later, Ben, saxophonist Sahib Shihab, and trumpeter Idrees Sulieman were guest soloists at a radio concert in Copenhagen with the New Radio Dance Orchestra—the forerunner of the Danish Radio Big Band—and once again, Ben was in excellent form. The Ellington classics *Things Ain't What They Used to Be* and *Cotton Tail* were given superb treatment, and in the first tune his melodic phrases float on top of the rhythmical big-band riffs, creating a wonderful contrast. I was present at the concert, and in my diary I wrote that Ben had played excellently, particularly in a ballad. *That's All* bears witness to this statement. In the part of his solo, when he is alone with the rhythm section, he plays an exceptionally beautiful paraphrase, full of emotion and with as rich and expressive a sound as ever. The audience responds with extended, rhythmical applause.

Starting December 12, 1966, Ben played a week into the new year at Ronnie Scott's Club. The previous year, the club had moved to larger rooms at 47 Frith Street, some few hundred yards from the original premises on Gerrard Street. One of the reviews from the booking documents that Ben was in a good period: "In all his numbers, from the gentle *Danny Boy*, to the finger-popping *Mellow Tone*, Webster's command of tonal shading and his power to swing were exemplary."[10]

A few weeks later, Max Jones interviewed Ben. One of his questions pertained to whether he planned to return to the United States. Ben was not clear on the matter; he had no plans to return in the near future, but he did miss many of his old friends. He added, "I like it here and find it very relaxing, and there's a lot I want to see. It's always nice to visit strange places and I plan to go down around Spain and Italy when it can be arranged. Then the office has some things lined up for me in England during April, so I'll be around for most of 1967." When asked if he was happy in Europe he responded, "I should say so. I've met so many nice people over here. You know, they read so much about the jazz musicians here in Europe that they really want to go out and see them."[11]

Following his booking at Ronnie Scott's Club, Ben recorded an album for Philips on January 11 and 12, 1967, in a quartet with the British pianist Dick Katz—not to be confused with his American namesake—and the following day, he recorded in a trio with organist Alan Haven. The rhythm section with Katz plays excellently and swings with a nice drive on *The Jeep Is Jumpin'*, where Ben's phrasing is exceptionally supple, but especially on *Wrap Your Troubles in Dreams*, on which the soloist is inspired to play a fine, personal interpretation of the theme. Otherwise, Ben is a little restrained, refraining from committing himself fully, although he gives the ballads *How Deep Is the Ocean?* and *Solitude* a warm and dedicated treatment. Haven's somewhat impersonal organ fails to entice Ben's emotions to the surface. *My One and Only Love* and *Where or When* are interpreted in a disinterested manner, whereas his playing is more deeply felt on *You Forgot to Remember,* although still not bursting with presence.

After this sessions, he went on a tour of Britain and Wales until January 22, 1967, accompanied by Ronnie Scott, Stan Tracey, bassist Rick Laird, and Jackie Dougan. Jimmy Parsons arranged the tour and traveled with them, taking care of Ben, who was pleased with the opportunity to sightsee outside London. "Ben, an enthusiastic photographer, went with Jimmy the morning after the gig to Coventry Cathedral, intent on taking pictures of the interior," Ronnie Scott recalls.

As soon as they arrived Jimmy spotted a very emphatic sign forbidding the use of cameras in the cathedral without written permission. Ben was unimpressed. He went in, checking his lenses, winding on film and consulting his light meter—and immediately caught the beady eye of a tiny friar who could not have been more than four feet seven inches tall. The friar waved an admonishing finger and whispered, "No photos." Ben and Jimmy moved slowly up the aisle amid a crowd of visitors, Ben continuing fiddling with his cameras and the friar hard behind, now jumping up and down to catch the first sign of an attempt by Ben to take a photograph. Ben saw this movement out of the corner of his eye, turned round and glared at the friar, and then announced to Jimmy, with a roar that reverberated throughout that hallowed house of God: "Hey Jim, that evil mother-f . . . er is looking at me!"[12]

From London, Ben traveled directly to Switzerland, where agent Arild Wideröe had booked a few jobs with pianist Henri Chaix's orchestra in Geneva, Baden, and Solothurn. To Ben's great satisfaction, Chaix was an excellent swing pianist with a strong left hand. His band had four horns in front, and was modeled on Ellington's small groups.

Ben and Chaix's band received excellent reviews on their tour. *Badener Tagblatt* wrote that Ben's "power of expression is so great that even a ballad—his first selection—immediately enchanted an audience usually accustomed to responding to fast tunes. It was wonderful to hear a famous musician of Ben Webster's stature in a good musical setting and in good form." After the concert in Solothum a critic wrote, "Perhaps it was Ben Webster's imaginative ballad interpretations that made the deepest impression on the audience. He played his instrument with sonorous force, often soft and supple, indeed almost whispering, soon to return to sharpened, quick runs. The fast tunes, with their soaring rhythm, were convincing as well, despite unmistakable associations with the late swing period."[13]

In March, film producer Johan van der Keuken contacted Ben about making a short documentary on his European residency. At their first meeting in Hartlooper's apartment, van der Keuken had planned to tape their conversation, but this resulted in uncertainty and suspicion on Ben's part. "He retreated into his room," says van der Keuken, "and made me wait in the living room. After a while, he came back to tell me he was willing to continue working together. He later told me that he had thought I wanted to 'steal' his stories. That maybe I wanted to show off with his anecdotes. Out in his room, he began to think that I might be sincere after all. At which he became so touched he started crying. And by the time he came out, I could do no wrong in his eyes."[14]

The black-and-white movie was shot over March–June 1967, and lasts approximately thirty minutes. The first pictures of Ben show him in his room in Amsterdam, playing along with a Fats Waller record, and talking briefly about his childhood and of how his mother spoiled him, buying him anything he wanted. This is followed by an excerpt from a television show from May 5, in which Ben and Mrs. Hartlooper participate. Then Ben is seen playing a bit of stride piano, followed by a little talk about his days in Fletcher Henderson's orchestra. A sequence from a rehearsal with Slinger's trio and with Don Byas offers short excerpts from *My Romance, Perdido,* and *You'd Be So Nice to Come Home To,* before Ben talks about his years with Ellington. He is shown spending his free time playing billiards and visiting the zoo before we see him playing part of *Chelsea Bridge* and *Perdido* during a London concert, probably Ronnie Scott's Club in late May. The movie closes with pictures of Ben traveling by train and car while we hear the last bars of *My Romance* played by Ben and Slinger's trio.

The documentary depicts the conditions under which a touring musician works, with travel and rehearsals, and opens a small door to Ben's personality and musical ability. From the viewpoint of a jazz aficionado, however, the short musical sequences are frustrating, and the movie would have done better to conclude with the full-length version of *My Romance,* giving Ben's sublime ballad interpretation the attention it deserves. Nevertheless, according to van der Keuken, Ben was satisfied with the end result.[15]

It is strange that Amsterdam of the mid-1960s, with a population exceeding one million, did not house a permanent jazz club. Finally, in the spring of 1967, a jazz venue opened in rooms at Arti et Amicitiae, a club for artists and authors. The club was private, but an artist, jazz aficionado, and big Ben Webster fan, Steven Kwint, persuaded the proprietors to have weekly concerts on Thursdays in one of the rooms, in which there was a bar, a couple of billiard tables, and a stage with a grand piano.

The club, called Jazzart, opened on Saturday, April 8, 1967, to the sound of Ben Webster and Don Byas, among others, dueling in front of a rhythm section. "There was, of course, some rivalry between the two of them," recalls Bert Vuijsje. "Don Byas played rather flamboyantly, and then Ben, after a few bars of silence, with his tone and expression specifically, he really put him in his place. So there was no doubt that he was the greater of the two."[16]

Ben alternated between tours and one-nighters in England and the Netherlands over April and May. After the opening of Jazzart, he spent the rest of April in England, starting his visit with a series of concerts titled "The Tenors of Jazz" in London, Manchester, and Bristol. He played in different combinations with Eddie "Lockjaw" Davis, Bud Freeman, and Eddie Miller. The backing was supplied by either Lennie Felix's trio or the rhythm section from the Alex Welsh Band. All four tenors were in fine form at every concert, which always ended with a joint version of a blues by Davis. "It was the kind of improvisation you can expect will delight a middle of the road jazz audience," wrote *Melody Maker* of the London concert, "and it didn't disappoint. The question it raised in my mind was why more multi-horn parleying had not been indulged in earlier."[17]

In *Jazz Journal* the review included these thoughts on Ben's playing in Manchester: "Once again we saw from Ben the micro-second timing which only the greatest jazz men have. Each note was of perfect duration and intonation."[18] The concluding tune was apparently a little chaotic, for "at the end of the first chorus, all four stepped up simultaneously to take the first solo. The result was a quite remarkable and unintentional improvised ensemble which lasted for four bars before Jaws won and took the solo."

His British visit resulted in two recording sessions, both times with a rhythm section with pianist Fred Hunt. The recordings from April 16 are historical for Ben, because he had composed and arranged four themes for four tenor saxophones, and he was joined by Eddie "Lockjaw" Davis, Eddie Miller, and Bud Freeman. *Jaws Is Bookin' Now, Lamb, Bud,* and *Hi Eddie* are all thirty-two-bar themes, arranged in four-part harmony by Ben with parallel lines in the voices. All themes are distinctly Ben, as they are fairly stilted with many accents on the offbeat, and all performed in a tempo close to medium.

There is a story attached to *Jaws Is Bookin' Now,* mistakenly called *Jaws Bookin' Now* on the album cover. Naturally, the tune is dedicated to Lockjaw Davis, and the title refers to the period in 1963–64 when Davis had retired from the life of a professional musician to become a booking agent in New York. "Some of the older musicians thought I had made a good decision, but they felt I should not have discontinued playing," says Davis. "They held that I should have tried to arrange my affairs so that I could still play saxophone as well as conduct business. But generally the comedy bit prevailed and Ben Webster even composed a poem for me called *Jaws the Booker,* which went like this":[19]

> Jaws is booking now,
> Jaws is booking now,
> Don't offer him a gig
> Or he'll blow his wig,
> 'Cause Jaws is booking now.

One can easily sing Ben's lyric to the melody of the tune's A-part, which is based on the harmonic structure of *Honeysuckle Rose.* The rhythm drives nicely, and Davis and Ben play one chorus each before the final chorus, in which the two soloists share the B-part. As throughout the entire session, Davis is in very lively form, whereas Ben holds back a little.

Lamb is Ben's tribute to his friend, stride pianist Donald Lambert. The tune, based on the harmonic structure of *If Dreams Come True,* builds nicely with rising intensity. Freeman solos first, followed by Ben, after which a sixteen-bar interlude is played in—almost—unison; then comes a fine piano solo and the concluding chorus. Ben is a little livelier here, performing a fine, well-structured solo. The rhythm section is somewhat heavy-handed on *Bud,* based on *Stop, Look and Listen* and dedicated to Freeman. He solos with Miller. The rhythm section is slightly lighter on *Hi Eddie,* dedicated to Miller and based on the harmonic structure of *California Here I Come.* All four saxes solo on the tune, first Miller, then Davis, Freeman, and Ben, and once again, the composer is more restrained than usual.

Generally, the ensemble parts would have been more fruitful had there been more time to run through the material, which Ben admitted on a later occasion. "I tried to write the changes down," he explains, "and I think that we really should have had a little more time to run down that, because I wrote four tunes on that [album]."[20]

More good music was played at the session, because Ben performed a hard-swinging *Rosita* and *You'd Be So Nice to Come Home To* alone with the rhythm section; the latter interpreted with an underlying current of longing, and a crisper and tighter rhythm. His duet with Davis, the moderately up-tempo blues *Griff and Lock,* shows how Davis blows

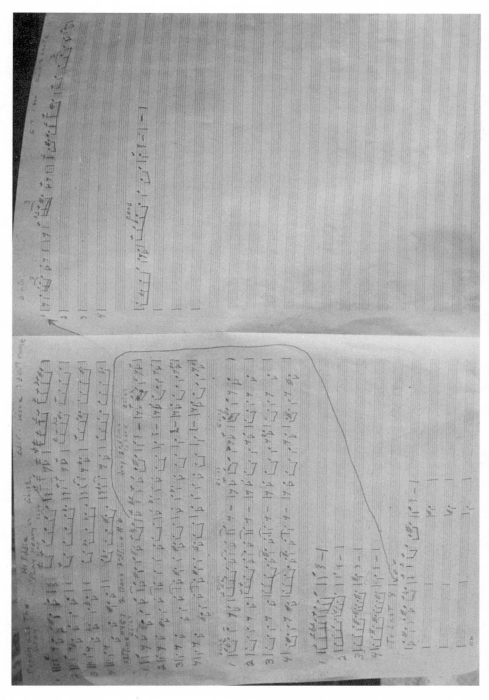

Ben's score to "Hi, Eddie," Ben Webster. Ben Webster Collection, University Library of Southern Denmark, Odense

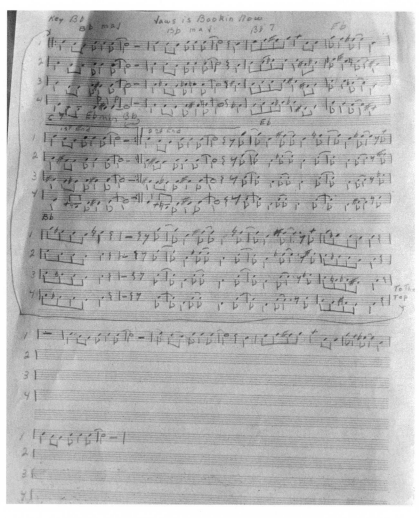

Ben's score to "Jaws is Bookin' Now," Ben Webster. Ben Webster Collection, University Library of Southern Denmark, Odense

away from the very start, whereas Ben is far better at structuring a solo with building intensity, while the concluding chase choruses reveal just how close they really are stylistically.

The next session, on April 27, did not work out quite as planned. Ben was scheduled to record with Buck Clayton, who had prepared arrangements, and Bill Coleman, but Clayton had been hospitalized the previous evening. When Ben arrived, the others had recorded three tunes without him, and the two old friends, who had not played together for twenty years, were reunited in three tunes, *Pound Horn, For Max,* and *Bill Coleman,* while Ben played two ballads alone with the rhythm section, *Moonglow* and *For All We Know.*

Pound Horn is a medium-tempo blues with a simple riff. In his four choruses, Ben articulates melodic, but routine, phrases. His imagination is better on the solid swinger *For Max,* on which the two lyrical horns exchange a series of beautifully connected chases before the final chorus. *Bill Coleman* is yet another a medium-paced blues, and although it is credited to both horn players, it bears more of Ben's fingerprints. He is far more aggressive and expressive in this solo than in the two other tunes, contrasting with Coleman's contribution nicely. However, Ben's best playing is done on the ballads. *Moonglow* is given a slightly dreamy and languishing interpretation, with a somewhat restrained approach but with his sound in the focus, a characteristic of *For All We Know* as well, on which his sound is even softer. His rendition is freer than before, and the concluding chorus is masterful in its moving and faceted expression.

Ben was back in London for the last two weeks of May to play a week at Ronnie Scott's Club, followed by a couple of festivals with Bill Coleman in Birmingham and London. He continued his European tour in early June, traveling to Switzerland with Buck Clayton for jobs in Geneva and Baden with Henri Chaix and his orchestra.

Once again the Swiss reviews were positive. One critic wrote of the concert in Baden that Ben "produces rhythmical tension and dynamic explosions with the same ease as which he improvises poetic phrases of great length."[21] Another paper wrote about Ben that he "houses two souls in his breast. One reveals a remarkable sensibility as heard in ballads such as *My Romance* and *Our Love Is Here To Stay,* moving in their lyricism; the other finds its expression in wild exalted escapades, at times bordering on the orgiastic."[22]

The collaboration with Clayton went smoothly, as documented by a fine recording from the concert in Baden. Despite an occasionally rigid rhythm section, both soloists play at their best. Ben swings powerfully on the five tracks with Clayton, avoiding clichés and seemingly at ease with Clayton taking the lead. The collaboration with Clayton continued in Belgium two weeks later when they played a concert on June 16 in Antwerpse Jazz Club. As in Baden, both soloists were in excellent form, and Ben is in an extremely good mood, which can be heard in his small comments to Clayton.

Ben was pleased with his affiliation with Wideröe, who made sure that Ben caught the right trains back and forth as well. Very few letters from Ben's hand are preserved, but the following is one he wrote after the concert in Antwerp.

Friday

Hi Arild—

Thanks so much for fixing the trains for me, I had no trouble at all. Also, thanks again for the write ups of the concert & the tape, which I got from Buck in Antwerp. I met some wonderful people there, the concert was a success, & Buck & I had a ball. (Smile)

The tape is so much better than I expected, & I'm having a grand time playing it. Henri, sure knocks me out playing piano.

I certainly appreciate your trying to fix some dates for me.

So, take care, & I'll write more next time. Give my best to all of the gang.

Sincerely,

Ben

In July, Ben left for Finland and the Pori Jazz Festival over the weekend of June 14–16. Ben was booked for the first two days with Kenny Drew, Niels-Henning Ørsted Pedersen, and Al Heath at the Pori Teatri and the outdoor stage Kirjurinluoto. "Ben was the official Guest of Honour of the festival and treated accordingly," recalls Seppo Lemponen.

The official festival photographer Mr. Matti Juutilainen took Ben around before the festival so he could pursue his hobby and showed him interesting places to shoot. Matti didn't realize how strong Ben's phobia for heights was until he took Ben up to Pori's water tower to take pictures. When they came back, Ben went to his hotel and stayed there the rest of the day to recover.

After the festival Matti transported Ben to Helsinki in his car. Ben stayed in Helsinki about ten days at Merihotelli (Sea Hotel) and played both the Down Beat Club and Poli (the student union club room of the technical university) which presented jazz on Monday nights. YLE (the Finnish Broadcasting Company) also took advantage of Webster's stay in Helsinki and took him to the studio with a Finnish trio. Ben's jam sessions were eagerly attended by many Finnish top musicians, and he was much appreciated. A funny and true story is about his visit to the Helsinki Zoo on an island just off the city. There was (and still is) a boat service, and you have to know its timetable. Poor Ben! For some reason he missed the last boat of the day and got panicked. The staff of the Zoo eventually got him a police boat transportation back to Merihotelli.[23]

Ben does not play up to his best on recordings on July 14, 1967, from Pori. Only *Perdido* is truly inspired, although he evades the most obvious and cliché-ridden phrasing on *How Long Has This Been Going On?* On a radio recording a few days later, the local rhythm section is competent but anonymous, and the music is fairly uninspired. Ben seems tired, and the charisma that was his usual trademark is often absent. Perhaps he still suffered from the message he had just received, that John Coltrane had died.

After Helsinki, Ben was booked at the jazz festival in Molde in Norway. Ben was very comfortable in Helsinki and stayed on for so long that—much against his will—he was forced to fly to Molde, where he played exceptionally well. He performed on August 4 and 5 with the same rhythm section as in Pori, the only change being that Alex Riel replaced Al Heath. According to Joachim-Ernst Berendt, Ben's performance was one of the highlights of the festival. Another critic wrote, "His music is full of noble melancholy. He sings out the most beautiful musical content with the simplest means."²⁴ Norwegian television filmed *How Long Has This Been Going On?* on August 4, and the broadcast justifies Berendt's judgment. Ben delivers the tune with a soft and supple tone and a phrasing that can leave no doubt as to the authenticity of his message.

Ben traveled by train from Molde to Oslo, accompanied by Randi Hultin and Berendt, and he displays great enthusiasm for the Norwegian inlets and waterfalls on the movies he shot on the eight-hour trip. Ben and Berendt's relationship was unproblematic; they had become good friends once again after their unfortunate conflict at the Berliner Jazztage two years before. The atmosphere in the train was pleasant, conversation lively, and at one point, Ben started talking about Don Byas. Berendt suggested that Ben and Byas record an album together in Germany in the near future, as soon as practicalities could be worked out, and Ben agreed.

Ben went on to Denmark from Oslo to play a few jobs with Arnvid Meyer's orchestra in Copenhagen, before yet another trip across the channel for bookings in London, Manchester, Glasgow, and Hampstead. "He was as enjoyable as ever," wrote *Jazz Journal,* "but seems to be taking things a lot easier, relying more on the exploitation of his beautiful tone than on really rewarding improvisation. Highlight of his performance was a great attacking version of *Sunday* for which he will no doubt receive complaints from the Lord's Day Observance Society."²⁵

Ben had good reason to take pride in his sound, and when a record was released with Clark Terry playing electric trumpet, journalist Steve Voce felt compelled to ask him his views on such new experiments. Ben answered that he too had once been accosted by someone trying to sell something similar. "He said it would suit my sound and I'd be able to do a whole lot of things I can't do now, which was nice of him. I just said yeah, you think so? (Benny Carter always told me to tell an idiot just what he wants to hear). But hell, man! You spend forty years just getting your own sound and then some guy invents a way to take it away and expects you to jump at it."²⁶

On September 21, BBC filmed a fifteen-minute television show in London with Ben backed by pianist Pat Smythe, Dave Green, and Jackie Dougan. By this time, Green and Ben had become close friends, "and we used to go out to places together," Green recalls. "We went to London

Zoo. There was a huge gorilla named Guy, and he loved that gorilla. We also went to Wembley Arena to see the World Fighting Championship in September 1967."[27] After the television show, Ben went on another two-week tour of Britain. Rex Stewart had been booked for the tour as well, but he died on September 7 back in Los Angeles. Upon his return to London on October 4, Ben was in for yet another shock when he received the news that Stuff Smith had passed away on September 25 in Munich. Ben was disconsolate and looked up members of Chris McGregor's Blue Notes who were in town and most probably staying at the same hotel as Ben. The Blue Notes originally came from South Africa, but had moved to Europe in 1964 because the apartheid policy of their native country prevented the racially mixed band in finding work. Drummer Louis Moholo remembers that Ben "was crying and we looked after him for one day. We gave him respect, the respect that we came with from South Africa, he was our father, and he liked us for that, he liked us."[28]

Ben was back on the continent, playing one-nighters in Germany and the Netherlands for the next two weeks. The first booking was in Esslingen, Germany, with trumpeter Benny Bailey and Henri Chaix's band on October 8. The tapes from the concert show that his versions of *My Romance* and *Daddy Blues* are heartfelt, romantic, and sensitive, and he plays excellently on *Now's the Time,* building a lovely solo. On the tunes with Bailey, he gives the audience time to digest the trumpet solo, just as during the concerts with Clayton, by letting the applause die out before beginning his own solo, a fine move that allows the rhythm section time to fall back, as well as sharpening the audience's anticipation of what is to come.

By this time, he had put on a lot of weight, according to himself twenty-five pounds, since arriving in Amsterdam, partially due to his sweet tooth. "My landlady is a wonderful cook," he once told a journalist. "The apple tart Mrs. Hartlooper makes is the best I have tasted since I left home."[29] When Mrs. Hartlooper didn't have time to bake, Ben would buy something sweet at the nearest bakery.

On October 24, Ben was booked for the Newport Jazz Festival All Stars in London, called "Jazz Expo '67" in a package including Ruby Braff, Budd Johnson, Buddy Tate, and Bill Coleman. Ben was backed by the rhythm section from the Alex Welsh Band. Although they had played together previously and should have known each other, the performance was unsuccessful, most certainly due to lack of rehearsal time.[30]

This visit to London was a down trip in other ways as well. Ben's and Budd Johnson's hotel rooms were robbed. "The burglar came back a second time when Ben was still in bed," wrote *Jazz Journal,* "and was unsuccessfully pursued by a pyjama-clad Frog down the hotel corridors."[31]

The next day Ben was back in Amsterdam, where, to his great pleasure, he received a surprise visit from Phil Woods, in town performing with Thelonious Monk. "Phil had arrived in the afternoon and he wanted to go to Ben," recalls Hans Dulfer, who had met him. "I said, okay and took Phil in my car, and we drove to where Ben was living and went upstairs. They started talking together about what had happened to them all those times in the past, really awful and terrible stories. Phil told about a fight in the streets with sailors, and Ben stood in the middle and took two of those sailors and shook their heads against each other, 'Bam!' just like that. And believe it or not, but suddenly I got tears in my eyes and almost started crying. Then they both looked at me and said, 'Ah, what are you crying for? It wasn't that bad!' I got so upset about what had happened to them all the time with all the fighting and, for Ben, all the racism."[32]

Unfortunately, Jazzart was forced to close in November that year. As Vuijsje says, "The final concert in Jazzart was on November 16, 1967, when Tony Scott was playing there, and Ben Webster was in the audience, but did not play. It was a nice scene when, as soon as Ben Webster entered the hall, Tony Scott immediately started on his clarinet to imitate Webster's style with lots of air. Ben Webster seemed to enjoy this tribute to his playing."[33] From then on, and for the following year, Amsterdam again was without a regular jazz venue.

Ben had been a regular at the concerts at Jazzart, even when not on the bill himself. With it closed he played billiards and cultivated a growing friendship with Steven Kwint. Ben often visited Kwint at his home at Palmstraat 90 or in his atelier on the other side of town, where they would listen to records while Kwint painted. Kwint spoke very little English, but they both felt an instinctive affinity for the other, as they both lived for their art alone, while everything else was secondary. At one point, Kwint suggested that Ben pose for him, and Ben acquiesced. He brought along Ol' Betsy and some Ellington and Tatum records at each sitting. "While he painted I practiced along with the records," Ben said later. "This broke the monotony of just sitting and posing."[34] Kwint painted two large portraits of Ben entitled *Uncle Ben's Mood* and *Webster's Soulmates*. Kwint was an expressionist in the broadest sense; his large-stroked style could be difficult to interpret, and Ben was curious and intent on understanding his work. "After going to his studio quite a few times and after asking questions about what this or that meant, I rather became aware of what he was trying to do. Now I can understand things I didn't in the beginning. Steven believes in himself. This is a different style. It's the same in music; everyone wants to have his own style, you can only get so far emulating another person. You have your own style or try to create it."[35]

Ben was booked at Ronnie Scott's Club for four weeks from January 1, 1968, but he arrived in London quite a while before his job in order to hear Coleman Hawkins at the same club. A review offers an interesting comparison of the two saxophonists. "Hawk has lost a little in lyrical tone and in ability to sustain notes," Derek Jewell wrote, "but nothing in ideas, or daring, or big sound, or, above all, in his ability to swing. Webster, by contrast, has kept all of his tone, which was always rather silkier, dreamier, sexier than Hawkins's—pastoral rather than urban. He is as much the arch-romantic of the Thirties and Forties as Stan Getz has been of the Fifties and Sixties. But he does not now seem to push himself in search of new ideas as hard as Hawk; nor does he take so many chances. Hawk gambles furiously all the time—and it will be splendid if he becomes, as intended, as much of an annual fixture at Scott's as is rare Ben. Both are irreplaceable."[36]

Ben and Coleman Hawkins played a double billing on January 17, 1968, at Reading University in England. A private recording reveals an inspired Ben airing many new ideas without falling back on routine solutions. Even *Sunday* and *In a Mellotone* seem new and fresh here. The solo on *Johnny Come Lately* is given an extra expressive twist, and lovely lyrical phrases adorn the concluding chorus, while *That's All* and *How Long Has This Been Going On?* are small masterpieces, the first tune with an exceptionally expressive laid-back phrasing in the final chorus. Ben played first, and his set was given a roaring response, after which Hawkins went on stage to play four tunes in which he played constantly. He seems tired; *Body and Soul* and *Sweet Georgia Brown* are delivered without sparkle, the latter even with a slightly unsure rhythmical phrasing. The drummer kicks a little more life into the soloist on the concluding *Stuffy*, without changing, however, the impression of Hawkins as fragile on this date. Indeed, upon returning to London, he was diagnosed with pneumonia.

The encounter with Don Byas in the first days of February 1968, was—with the exception of a couple of musical highlights—a disappointment, as neither soloist played up to par, and the rhythm section consisting of pianist Tete Montoliu, bassist Peter Trunk, and drummer Al Heath never merge as hoped. However, the album demonstrates how differently the two saxophonists had developed from the same background, with Hawkins as the primary influence. Stylistically, Byas, four years Ben's junior, had traveled farthest from his starting point, utilizing influences from Sonny Stitt and John Coltrane in a highly personal manner. He was also more advanced harmonically than Ben, which is illustrated well in the slow *Blues for Dottie Mae*, dedicated to his oldest daughter, whereas Ben's two choruses are hushed and kept in lovely phrases. From Ben's viewpoint, the moderately fast *Sunday, Perdido,* and *Caravan* are not particularly interesting; he has trouble getting his playing under control. *Sunday* is marred by a solo that sounds as if Ben is drunk and having difficulties with a new reed, but he pulls himself together for the two chase choruses with Byas. The best music on the album is in the two ballads; Byas in *Lullaby for Dottie Mae,* and Ben in *When Ash Meets Henry.* The ballad consists of an improvisation over one chorus of *Stardust,* and Ben is accompanied by only Peter Trunk, but together they tell an extremely serene and beautiful story.

Apart from this session, that spring saw Ben in fine and steady form. His music rarely fell below a high standard, and he seems to have been feeling good. He was in Denmark for the first two weeks of March, beginning his visit with a short tour with an excellent amateur rhythm section under the leadership of guitarist Hans Jacob Sahlertz, followed by a booking with Kenny Drew, Niels-Henning Ørsted Pedersen, and Al Heath in the Jazzhus Montmartre, and a couple of concerts with the Danish Radio Big Band before finishing off with a job with Arnvid Meyer's orchestra.

"There were no preparations or rehearsals before we played with Ben Webster," Sahlertz recalls. "We drove our car to the venues, and Ben took the train and met us there. We played in a style that was a little more modern than swing but not really bop. I remember the three-day tour we had together. It was a lot of fun, because he was really lively on the last day in Hjørring. He was an extremely pleasant man to be with, and usually in a pretty good mood. Musically, there weren't any bad vibrations between us and Ben. Never any problems."[37]

Violinist Finn Ziegler played on the job in Hjørring as well, and he remembers that Ben "was in fine form. He was fantastic. I've never heard him play as well as he did then. During the intermission he stayed on stage playing his saxophone. At one point he asked me what I wanted to play, and I suggested *Sweet Georgia Brown*. I could see that he was a little wary, because you normally play it in a fast tempo—it's an up-tempo tune—but I didn't. I played it very slowly, and he lit up like a little sun. A few days later, after we got home from that little minitour, I dropped by the Montmartre when he was playing, and when he saw me, he lit up and said, 'Oh, ladies and gentlemen, now we're gonna play *Sweet Georgia Brown* in the Finn Ziegler tempo!' Well, I grew fifteen feet on the spot!"[38]

At the Jazzhus Montmartre Hawkins had played before Ben— just as in London—but this time, the reviews were not as favorable because Hawkins seemed tired. On the other hand, Ben's booking was given a glowing evaluation.

> While the encounter with Hawkins was not without its sad moments, Webster's latest visit was a pure triumph. . . . He appeared to be immensely focused and inspired—just about everything he played on his horn was no less than outstanding.
>
> It has been said of Webster that after years of being an important soloist, he did not become one of the greats before he accepted the limitations brought on by age, and developed his current simple and melodically so finely honed ballad style. But this time we were not only moved by the magical world of sound and balance in the slow tunes. At a faster pace, his playing gained enormous edge and force. Add to this those surprising, feverishly hot figures that sometimes make phrases halting and forced, but this time were right on target.[39]

A tape of almost three hours of music from the booking at the Jazzhus Montmartre on March 5–7 documents Ben's incredibly good form. Judging from the presentations, the tape contains the first set from two different evenings. Ben is playing longer sets and longer solos than usual, and even well-worn tunes like *In a Mellotone* and *Perdido* are inspired and full of new statements. Moreover, *Sunday, Indiana,* and *The Theme* are performed much faster than usual with great force and biting phrasing. *Autumn Leaves* is interpreted caressingly and delivered with enormous swing, due to a combination of Ben's forceful drive and drummer Al Heath's elastic playing. We find masterful, romantic interpretations of *Come Sunday, Old Folks,* and *Danny Boy* in which Ben's vibrato, his slightly delayed phrasing, melodically sensitive playing, and brilliant control of horn and tone all come together to form a synthesis. The surprise of the tape is *Mack the Knife* in which Ben, almost uncontrollable, performs with an amazing surplus of energy.

Ben plays just as well when featured as a soloist with the Danish Radio Big Band in front of an exceptionally enthusiastic audience at the Studenterforeningen in Copenhagen on March 9. Alone with the rhythm section, he gives *You'd Be So Nice to Come Home To* a contemplative and romantic interpretation, whereas *Come Sunday* is performed with the big band in an outstanding and beautiful Ray Pitts arrangement, tailor-made for Ben and one of the best recordings of him from these years, enhanced with an emotional and interpretive quality exceptional even for him. The concluding *Things Ain't What They Used to Be* swings and rocks brilliantly in an arrangement that stays close to Ellington's own, and if Ben refrains from adding new dimensions to his playing, he gives the tune all the more of that special lift that creates a unique experience.

On March 10, Ben was booked with Arnvid Meyer's orchestra at the Mad House Jazzklub in Vejen in Jutland, but Ben's behavior took events in a different direction than planned. "We had a few jobs without Ben before that gig, so we couldn't pick him up in Copenhagen and drive together as we usually did," Arnvid Meyer explains.

> So we told him which train to catch from Copenhagen. When we arrived in town, he was blown up as a "leading Ellington soloist on his first visit to Vejen." It was a big music event in town. The mayor went down to the station to meet him, and the Vejen Girl

Brass Band was there to play a tune for the visiting dignitary. But he wasn't on the train! Well, that can happen to anybody, and the good people of Vejen gave him another chance. But when he wasn't on the next train, everybody went home, and I guess the mayor was a little annoyed. But we could live with that, and we [Meyer's orchestra] began to play on time.

Then he suddenly showed up, dead drunk, reeling onto the stage, found a chair, and fell into a deep slumber. I think he just managed to unpack his saxophone, but he didn't play a note. He looked like a washed-up whale in his chair.

After we had played a few tunes, Ben suddenly woke up, and he discovered that he had put himself and us in a bad situation, and he began to play and it turned into one of the best evenings we ever had with him.[40]

A few days later, Ben took the train to Paris for a concert on March 29 with Johnny Griffin, pianist George Arvanitas, bassist Alby Cullaz, and drummer Art Taylor. It was another great success for him; after his set, the applause rose to the level of a storm.[41]

In the middle of April Ben performed with the Danish Radio Big Band on a television show. Four numbers are adorned with strings, but Ray Pitts's arrangements are a little too lush. The best music on the show is *Going Home,* in which Ben's brilliant interpretation—almost completely free of ornamentation in the theme—and Pitts's arrangement are a perfect match. Recordings from this spring of 1968 document that Ben now had fully developed the airy and whispering tone in the deep notes that many consider most typical of his sound.

Ben performed at a jazz quiz contest with Arnvid Meyer's orchestra on Danish Broadcasting Corporation on April 23. "We had a rehearsal for the show in the morning, and Ben was in a great mood," says Hugo Rasmussen, the bassist in the band.

There is a very, very long stairway leading down to the studio, and when he reached those stairs, Ben performed a big opera scene. It was great! He hit the right mood immediately, with stupid lyrics, and gesturing with his arms and legs.

For the contest, there was a blindfold test, and one of the things they played, was a tune with Bud Freeman. The panel consisted of five or six contestants, and they were supposed to guess who the soloist was. None of them could. They tried various names, and maybe some got a little closer than others. Then one of them suggested Ben Webster, and you could hear Ben say, "Shi-i-i-it!"[42]

A trip to Poland for four concerts, June 9–13, provided Ben with plenty of food for thought. In the capital, he played with the excellent pianist Adam Makowics, and on June 9 he performed at a concert at Warsaw Philharmonic Hall with the talented vocal quartet Novi and a rhythm section of pianist Witold Krotochvil's trio, which accompanied him in Kraków as well. At the time, Joachim-Ernst Berendt wrote of the vocal quartet, "Novi is—since the Double Six of Paris no longer exists—the freshest, most musical and most enjoyable vocal ensemble in jazz I know of in Europe."[43] The concert with Novi was reviewed as one of the best of the season.[44]

Ben was given a tape of the radio show in Kraków, and even through the poor sound quality Ben comes across with great sensitivity and a generally high standard with an incredibly intense *Our Love Is Here to Stay* as one of the high points.

Ben's visit to Poland made an indelible impression on him. Shortly after returning home one of his Dutch friends visited him. Ben

lay on his bed, completely worn out. Mrs. Hartlooper told me that the cab driver had dragged him up the stairs the night before. I sat down next to his bed, and he slowly reconstructed the experience.

He had seen the poverty, the oppression in Poland. All those poor, terrified people, who saw him as a representative of the free West. He had spent an eternity on the train at the borders between East and West Germany, and between East Germany and Poland.

Everything he earned there he gave back to his Polish accompanists, and he returned with his sax and a few bottles of Polish vodka. Over the course of that endless train trip he drank them all—there was just a splash left in one bottle. He was so shocked that it took months before he could talk about it all.[45]

On July 9, Ben performed in a Dutch television show with tenor saxophonists Piet Noordijk, Harry Verbeke, and Toon van Vliet, and Cees Slinger's Trio. They played three of the four tunes composed the previous year by Ben for four tenor saxophones. However, their interplay is better here, as they had more rehearsal time. Although Ben keeps his high standard on *Jaws Is Booking Now, Bud,* and *Lamb,* Noordijk comes across as the most interesting soloist with a soaring solo on *Lamb.*

Two days later, Ben was booked at the Dum-Dum Jazzklub in Düsseldorf, Germany. Heinz Baumeister recalls that when Ben began playing, "I felt a touch of paradise. The atmosphere was wonderful all through the evening, and his ability to communicate with an audience was remarkable. Everybody, standing or seated, had a smile on their lips, and everybody enjoyed his music. The lasting impression from the evening was his magnetic personality, and the fact that you never tired of listening to him. I could easily have listened all night."[46]

In August, Ben was booked for the third Hammerfeld Jazz Festival in Roermond in the farthest southeastern corner of the Netherlands. The weather was pleasant, and Ben shot some film from the festival, but was nearly prevented from entering the stage himself. He was the main attraction, and his characteristic image adorned the posters, but the large advertising campaign for the event caught the eye of a lawyer from the Ministry of Justice. In her professional eagerness, she discovered that Ben did not have a work permit and called the chairman of the festival board, Piet Trummers forbidding Ben to perform. Protestations and objections were to no avail: if Ben went on stage, he would be removed by force.

The chief of police in Roermond received a telex with orders, but as he held a positive view of the festival and its board, he found a suitable solution. When Ben started his set, an officer among the audience began looking for Trummers. When he finally found him, he escorted him to the castle where a report was taken to the effect that the chairman was to bring an end to Ben's performance. However, this took some time, because first names and surnames had to be checked for spelling mistakes. Finally, the officer wrote that Ben's performance was already over, and the organizers were fined one hundred guilder. Innocent of the commotion behind the stage, Ben played to the great pleasure of the audience and was so successful that he was brought out for several encores.[47]

On Friday, September 6, the Antwerpse Jazz Club organized a benefit concert, and Ben was invited to perform with Bill Coleman, Buddy Tate, Milt Buckner on Hammond organ, Joe Turner on piano, Jimmy Woode on bass, and drummer Wallace Bishop. "Ben played beautiful that night," said Milt Buckner.

> That night he was with Louis Vaes, from the Antwerp Jazz Club. Louis knew that Ben had to catch a train the next morning at ten o'clock to go back to Amsterdam. Ben wanted to play billiards first, but he was too drunk and Louis Vaes put him in a hotel room. On Sunday they finally got him to the train and Louis Vaes said, "Goodbye."
> On the train he saw a sign with something like "——dam" and he got off. It was Rotterdam. There he went looking for another billiard parlor, and he finally found his way home to Amsterdam. He didn't get there till Monday evening. From Friday night to Monday evening![48]

Around this time initiative was taken to open a new regular jazz venue in Amsterdam. Tenor saxophonist Hans Dulfer made a deal with the managers of Paradiso, originally housing a Protestant sect, but now reopened as a gathering spot for young people. "Every time Ben came to Paradiso he took a cab," Dulfer said.

> He said to the driver, "Wait in front of the door." And he let him wait for about four hours and paid for it!
> Paradiso at that time was a very strange place. There were hippies, and everybody smoked hash in pipes, you know, but Ben didn't complain about it. Sometimes I saw him talk to weird girls with green hair, or something like that, and he was standing in the middle with those people around him. And that was one of the things I wanted when I started jazz in Paradiso, that there should be a communication between the young people who were brought up on rock and musicians who really meant something out of the past, the men who made the music.[49]

Ben's first job at Paradiso was on October 16, 1968. He played with drummer Han Bennink, Slinger, and Rob Langereis. As Dulfer also remembers, he was in fine form that evening, certainly egged on by Ben-nink's elastic, swinging style, on this occasion somewhat reminiscent of Louis Hayes. Although many of Ben's favorite phrases pop up, he delivers them with extra warmth and bite, as in *Sunday* and *Cotton Tail,* where he tops off the final chorus.

December saw Ben at Ronnie Scott's Club once again, and he played well from the very first evening. "Ben makes no concessions to showmanship," *Melody Maker* wrote. "He does not announce his reper-toire; he just lets his playing speak for itself. And his musical voice has not diminished with the passing years."[50]

In January 1969, Ben was back in the Netherlands, performing in Amsterdam and recording an album with the young pianist Frans Wieringa's trio, all of whom were amateurs. The trio is no match for Ben. Among other things, the bassist continuously plays out of tune, which must have been quite a trial for Ben, with his perfect pitch. It is a general problem, but particularly disastrous in the passages played in unison with the piano on *Hymn to Freedom.* Ben builds his solos well on *Benny's Blues* and *Ben's Blues,* and on the former, he plays call-and-response with him-self in the fifth chorus, answering expressive phrases with dynamically hushed phrases. The ballads *Once in Awhile, Sweet Lorraine,* and *Hymn to Freedom* are interpreted beautifully, although no great inspiration is pres-ent. The final tune, *St. Louis Blues,* is marred by a rigid, unswinging, and bashing rhythm that even Ben finds impossible to loosen up, although he tries to put things in place by playing short phrases.

Ben should have been accompanied by people like Slinger's trio instead—professional musicians with whom he was at ease—as can be heard on recordings from the Gerrit Rietvald Academie and the Lurelei Theater in Amsterdam later the same month. The latter was organized by Egbert de Bloeme, who had held occasional jazz evenings there after Jaz-zart closed.

Ben and de Bloeme became friends, and de Bloeme often acted as chauffeur. "I usually met Ben at his place," de Bloeme recalls. "Ben usu-ally slept until eleven o'clock or noon. After his breakfast with three fried eggs on toast with bacon or ham and coffee, he maybe would play some piano, and go out in town in the afternoon. It was strange to see him play the piano, the way he moved his shoulders. The left hand was going up and down in stride, and he moved his shoulders with it, those big shoulders, massive shoulders. It was a funny style, and very swinging. But he didn't play very fast; he was out of practice."[51]

In March Ben was reunited with his old employer from Kansas City, Jay McShann, in Antwerp, with a quartet including alto saxophonist Eddie "Cleanhead" Vinson, bassist Gene Ramey, and drummer Paul Gunther. Ben was hired as guest soloist for their performance at the Café Samson on March 10, and judging from recordings, it was a fun if not particularly inspiring musical encounter. However, there was an abundance of good music and outstanding musicians at the party thrown by Hans Dulfer at the Paradiso to celebrate Ben's sixtieth birthday. His birthday was on a Thursday, but the party was held on March 26, a Wednesday, which was the regular jazz day at the Paradiso.

Dulfer sent out invitations, and Ben performed early in the evening with Slinger's trio and trumpeter Roy Kaart. Ben came in from Antwerp with the flu, and for a while it looked as if the party would have to be canceled, but luckily he recovered enough to participate. Paradiso had a license for one thousand people, and the fire department was called in to stop the inrush of guests when they had reached 50 percent over the limit. Ben was overwhelmed and visibly moved at the huge crowd that showed up to pay tribute to him.

"That night everybody was trying to take care of him, that he shouldn't drink too much," Dulfer recalls. "He said to me, 'Dulfer, this is my birthday and I'll stay sober.' And he really stayed sober all night. Every time I met him that evening, he asked, 'Are you sure I'll get my money?' And finally, of course, he got his money. A little later he took me apart and said, 'Dulfer, come here, come here!' I thought he would talk again about money, but he looked straight in my eyes as if he had something important to say, and said, 'Dulfer, you may call me your friend!' To be his friend seemed to be very special!"[52]

Ben had asked that vocalist Ann Burton, with whom he had performed at the jazz festival in Roermond, be invited. She sang a set before Ben came on again and stopped on the stroke of midnight when his real birthday began. "I brought Ben Webster a big birthday cake with sixty candles, which he blew out in one breath," Dulfer says. After that Burton sang *Happy Birthday to You.* The musical highpoint was the arrival after midnight of bassist Eddie Gomez and drummer Marty Morell from Hilversum, where they had recorded with pianist Bill Evans. They lent an extra memorable dimension to the night by sitting in with Ben and Burton in the last set.

A few days later, Steven Kwint opened an exhibition in the Gallery Felison in IJmuiden. His show included the portraits of Ben, and he had asked Ben to play at the opening, which Ben did with pleasure. "The four-square jazz musician felt completely at home among the mainly youthful audience, who followed everything he and his musicians did breathlessly," wrote a critic. "The audience enjoyed this jazz quartet to the fullest."[53]

This was to be Ben's last performance as a Dutch resident. A couple of days later, he was forced to leave his room in Mrs. Hartlooper's apartment. Although Ben most probably felt comfortable in Europe, deep inside he was lonely. He often phoned across the Atlantic to friends in the United States like Milt Hinton in New York and Benny Carter in Los Angeles. "As time went by, this essential loneliness which is there for many expatriate artists in a way became more heavy for him," Johan van der Keuken explained.

> I think it has a lot to do, also, with the racist society in which he was living [here in Amsterdam]. So he was inevitably someone living in between several frames of reference, and this must be a very hard thing to do. This is the same for probably all refugees and other people who for whatever reason are not living in their own country.
>
> So in the end he was making all these phone calls all over the globe to the West Coast of America, and I remember there was huge problems about telephone bills, which went up to over one thousand guilder. He was talking to the West Coast, and afterwards he didn't remember that it had been for so long, so there was an increasing fuss about these things, and it just got too much for the old lady. And as far as I know, she made him feel

that he should start looking for another place. That might have been the reason why he moved to Denmark, eventually.[54]

Ben tried to find another place to stay in Amsterdam, but as he was unable to document a steady, regular income, it became impossible—perhaps also due to racist undertones—and in early April, he moved back to Copenhagen, where a booking at Timme's Club waited.

11.

The Last Busy Years in Denmark
(1969–1973)

Ben arrived in Copenhagen shortly before April 9, the opening night of his booking at Timme's Club at Nørregade 41. The club had opened on the initiative of the Danish jazz journalist Timme Rosenkrantz in the fall of 1968 in premises formerly housing a nightclub called Adlon. Since 1934, Rosenkrantz had spent many years in New York, arranging recording sessions, concerts and jam sessions, and hosting jazz shows on the radio. Now he had settled in Denmark, and the opening of Timme's Club was the fulfillment of an old dream.

Originally, Ben had been booked for only two weeks, but his visit was such a success that it was extended till May 17. He played extremely well, even on the first night, although he made excuses for being tired. On the opening night, one critic wrote that Ben's performance was so relaxed and intimate that it was like being in his home.[1]

Ben had various accompanists during the six weeks. The only house musician was drummer Larry Reeves. The piano was played by Bent Schjærff, Niels Jørgen Steen, or Hans Fjeldsted, and the bass by either Erik Moseholm or Mogens "Gus" Jensen. Rosenkrantz's girlfriend, vocalist Inez Cavanaugh, worked as hostess, but she would occasionally perform with Ben.

During the booking at Timme's Club, Ben lived in the storage room at the home of journalist Henrik Wolsgaard-Iversen and his wife, vocalist Rosita Thomas, whom he knew from previous stays in Copenhagen. They lived on the fifth floor on Nørre Farimagsgade 39, and Henrik's father, Herman Wolsgaard-Iversen, lived just below with his wife, vocalist Matty Peters from the vocal trio the Peters Sisters. With Bamse Kragh-Jacobsen, Herman owned Vingården, a restaurant offering jazz, and he often invited Ben to jam with the musicians on the bill. "Ben and my father became buddies," Henrik Wolsgaard-Iversen recalls, "and they were just about the same age. My father lived precisely the life that Ben liked, full speed ahead. They would drive off in his open Porsche, Ben holding his hat, off to visit friends in the King's Garden."[2]

Ben did not want to return to Holland, so the search went in among his friends to find him a place to live. John Darville and Ben's ophthalmologist, Dr. Godtfredsen, succeeded in finding him an apartment in a newly built complex with elevators overlooking the lake, Peblingesøen, at Nørre Søgade 37B, fifth floor, apartment 53, not far from Wolsgaard-Iversen. The janitor was Mr. Olsen, and he and Ben became good friends, although Olsen had problems with Ben's last name; he always called him "Mr. Wesber."

"His apartment consisted of a large eat-in kitchen, also used as living room, and a large room which he made his bedroom," Wolsgaard-Iversen recalls.

> Most of the activity was in the big kitchen, sitting around the table. There was a bathroom with a tub "made for Japanese," as he said. I once saw Ben in that small sit-up tub, and it was a funny sight. But he couldn't get out of it. He had created a vacuum and was stuck, and called out, "Help, help!" And I had to go in and helped pull, and he came up with a big swuush!
>
> That apartment on Nørre Søgade was the first place Ben had of his own. That was the first time he had his name on a door. Earlier on he had lived in rented rooms and hotels, and in the Netherlands he had lived with Mrs. Hartlooper. But the apartment on Nørre Søgade was all his own. He had to unlock the door himself, and lock it when he left. Nobody went in there unless he let them in himself. Which meant that nobody cleaned either. He hadn't thought of that, because other people used to do that for him, and he didn't know how to wring a washrag or anything. So a while passed before he realized that he would need help. As far as I know, the janitor's wife, Mrs. Olsen, would come in once in a while and muck out with a vacuum cleaner and washrag.[3]

On May 19, 1969, Coleman Hawkins died. Ben took it very hard, and for a while he was depressed. A few days later, he went to the Netherlands, in part to move the last of his things to Denmark, partly to record an album dedicated to Duke Ellington and to play a couple of jobs. Despite the many friends Ben made in the Netherlands, an interview by Henry Whiston from 1971 reveals that he was relieved to be back in Denmark, with its absence of racism. "I stayed with a cold, like, down there," he explained. "But as soon I went back to Denmark the cold disappeared. But there are so many friends there, and there are so many friends here in London and in England, and I have so many friends in Copenhagen. It is so good to see the friends, and that's what I play for, to see my friends smile."4

On the session May 26, he recorded his tribute to Duke Ellington in celebration of his seventieth birthday, *For the Guv'nor*, this time with his faithful rhythm section, Cees Slinger, Jacques Schols, and John Engels. Unfortunately, the record is marred by a bad sound balance, placing Ben too far in the background, by which his usual presence and emotion is lost. Five Ellington tunes were recorded, while the title tune is Ben's with a concluding phrase highly reminiscent of *The Jeep Is Jumpin'*. For some reason, Ben is not in especially good form this day, playing mostly out of duty, correct but lacking commitment. There are some nice moments in his first solo chorus on *Drop Me Off in Harlem*, and likewise in the first rounds of his chase with Engels in the conclusion of *For the Guv'nor*. The energy soon evaporates in *Rockin' in Rhythm* as well, despite an excellent opening phrase. In general, Ben's contributions on the album are disappointing, even when disregarding the poor quality of sound in the recording.

He was back in Denmark in early June, and as jobs were scarce that month he had plenty of time to settle in his new apartment. In July, he played at a jam session at La Fontaine in Copenhagen, and a few days later he performed at a concert at Vallekilde Folk High School with Dexter Gordon, with a wonderful version of *How Long Has This Been Going On?* as the high point.

Gordon and Ben went back twenty-five years. At that time, Gordon had settled in Denmark and was living in Valby, a suburb of Copenhagen. In the United States, his skinny six-foot five frame earned him the nickname "Long Tall Dexter," but Ben never called him anything but

"Copenhagen Slim." Gordon's experiences living in Copenhagen had influenced Ben's decision to settle in the Danish capital for good. For the La Fontaine job, Ben had brought along his reel-to-reel and pianist Tommy Flanagan and Ed Thigpen, both in Copenhagen for a series of concerts in the Tivoli Gardens with Ella Fitzgerald. Ben had recently leased a completely new piano for his home. "It's a beautiful piano. But I got that piano so Teddy Wilson could have a piano to play on. Oh, and Tommy Flanagan, he came, and he came every day and played that piano. What I didn't really know was that Tommy was so advanced on the piano."[5] The recording is far from high fidelity, but tells its own story of an evening of memorable music, with an extremely inspired Ben in front.

Ben was invited to appear at that year's jazz festival in Molde, but his performance was not all pleasurable. On Saturday, August 2, he performed with Norwegian swing musicians, but Ben never really felt comfortable in this context, and surely he must have felt slighted at a festival presenting an abundance of other American musicians of a much higher standard than his accompanists. He plays reasonably well in *Perdido*, never gets control of his solo in *Sweet Georgia Brown,* and abstains from playing altogether on *Just One of Those Things*. Once again, the high point is an extremely beautiful *Stardust,* almost reaching the tender version of *How Long Has This Been Going On?* from his previous visit to Molde. However, that very same evening he was in much better company with Phil Woods and his rhythm section, and here he is in fine form. A reviewer wrote that "it all contributed to create one of those rare moments when everything comes together."[6]

And then it was on to Stockholm and a concert August 12 at the Solliden stage in the outdoor museum, Skansen, and a couple of days at a venue that had opened the previous year and, inspired by the pawnbroker's shop next door, taken the name Stampen—slang for pawnbroker.

Solliden hosted jazz concerts throughout the summer, and they were transmitted on the radio. Clarinettist Ove Lind's quintet was the house band, featuring a new soloist every week. Of Ben's performance, a reviewer wrote that "I prefer hearing him as a ballad interpreter where his exquisite tone is heard most favourably. In fast tempi his sound becomes a little rough, which naturally does not prevent him from swinging."[7]

Just how comfortable Ben felt in Stockholm is clearly documented by the recordings from Stampen. Even the fast tunes find him in fine form, greatly enjoying the rhythm section. Most remarkable, however, are several smoking chase choruses with drummer Fredrik Norén on *In a Mellotone,* and the fast-paced *Indiana* and *Sunday.* On the latter, he is more wildly inspired than ever before, bursting with energy and ideas.

Ben played at Stampen many times over the following years, and Sjösten, usually his pianist, recalls that "on one occasion he played *Danny Boy* so beautifully that the audience became silent. I'll never forget that. Another time, he arrived at Stampen in a really bad mood, angry and drunk. When we went on stage, he asked me, 'What do you want to play?' '*In a Mellotone,*' I answered, and then I played the introduction as quietly as possible. It made him forget his anger completely. He relaxed and concentrated on the music. It was very strange; he was really something else."[8]

After Sweden, he returned to Denmark and a booking from September 6–12 at Tagskægget in Århus. It was bassist Jens Jefsen's first professional job, and he recalls

> that Ben's mood would vary a lot from lighthearted to dark and sad. The first evening, we played a tune without him. He went downstairs, either to the dressing room or the bathroom, and then he came upstairs and said that we were playing "way too loud!" He was angry and really annoyed. We looked at each other and agreed that we hadn't played louder just because he wasn't there. But apparently he thought so. He was very sensitive about sound, very sensitive. During the next tune, he began correcting the drummer. He turned around and said, "Soft!" "I am playing soft," the drummer answered, but he wanted it softer, he hardly wanted him to touch the cymbal. When he was all the way down, barely touching the cymbal with a feather, Ben Webster said, "Keep it!" And then the drummer was supposed to continue like that, and it did sound good, but it wasn't a natural level. That was when I realized how sensitive Ben Webster was to sound.
>
> Ben Webster has influenced my views on what simplicity is. Dexter Gordon, with whom I've played more often, influenced my energy in the rhythm section, my ability to stay in the middle and let the soloist do what he wants while the bass takes the cen-

ter role against which the soloist can play ball along with the drummer. Dexter liked the rhythm section to cook, whereas Ben Webster wanted quiet water behind him, a completely tranquil accompaniment, as tranquil and attentive as possible.[9]

On September 16, 1969, Ben recorded two tunes for the movie *Quiet Days in Clichy,* with pianist Bent Schjaerff and bassist Hugo Rasmussen in Copenhagen. Only a little more than half of one tune was used in the finished movie. The trio played an improvised blues in a medium slow tempo, with Ben soloing over seven choruses, followed by Bent Schjaerff, before Ben closed with an additional three. Ben's solo progresses calmly, an epic story with few digressions or aggressive effects. He does not build to a climax, but keeps the same dynamic level throughout in a nice, relaxed structure. The unabridged recording is released as *Our Blues,* whereas the part of it used for the soundtrack—Ben's first seven choruses—was called *Blue Miller* on an album with music from the movie. The second tune is a long improvisation on *I Got It Bad,* in which Ben for once abstains from performing Ellington's theme, but starts improvising immediately after the piano introduction. Once again, he plays with a subdued sound, performing one chorus. After solos by Schjaerff and Rasmussen, Ben closes with an improvised chorus, kept in a quiet, heartfelt mood all the way. Ben also appears in a short scene in the movie, filmed at Timme's Club.

Around the same time, the Thad Jones–Mel Lewis Jazz Orchestra played a concert in Copenhagen, and Ben went to hear them and meet old friends. In a letter to Mary Lou Williams a few weeks after the concert he wrote, "Richard Davis, Thad Jones, Roland Hannah, Jerome Richardson, Snookie Young were up to my place about two weeks ago, and we really had fun."[10] Being in regular contact with his American friends meant a great deal to Ben, and the only thing that really upset him about living in Europe was that he never had the opportunity to visit his nonmusician friends. In an interview a couple of years later, he expressed the possibility of going over to visit with them some time. "I see my musician friends," he explained. "They all come over here now. But I have some friends there, some dear friends and old friends that can't come over here. So I must go back to see them."[11] This was one wish, however, that he never fulfilled.

In late September, Ben and Dexter Gordon traveled through a barren Sweden, suffering from the results of the worst hurricane ever a few days earlier. They were booked for a television show with, among others, clarinetist Gunnar "Siljabloo" Nilsson. After the show, Gordon, Nilsson, and the rhythm section were booked at Jazz Artdur, and it would have been very unlike Ben not to tag along and sit in.

A somewhat unusual session took place on October 19, 1969, when Ben recorded with two pianists, Kenny Drew and Frans Wieringa, bassist Niels-Henning Ørsted Pedersen, and drummer Makaya Ntshoko. The repertoire was far from Ben's usual. They recorded three bop and hard-bop standards and one traditional song, and considering the fact that the two pianists play the longest solos—and to a certain degree draw the most attention—it is strange that the record was released in Ben's name. However, Ben performs with presence and vigor, and although his solos are short, they provide good listening. He swings with fantastic drive on *The Preacher* and *John Brown's Body,* and his phrasing in the final chorus of the latter is on a level of its own. *Straight, No Chaser* is set at a medium slow pace, and his solo here, as well as on *Worksong,* is excellent, although they offer no surprises.

The same month, Ben had an unfortunate accident that would have consequences on his mobility ever after. "One day, I went up and rang his doorbell," says John Darville. "I knocked as well, and yelled, 'Brother Ben!' He called back from the apartment, 'Brother John!' and I heard him moving furniture aside to get to the door in a hurry. Suddenly there was a big crash, and I could hear him lying there, groaning, and he couldn't move or open the door. I got hold of the janitor, Olsen, and he unlocked the door, and it turned out that Ben had slipped on a loose carpet on the polished floor in the hall, and fallen and broken his ankle."[12]

Almost simultaneously, Bent Kauling, manager of the jazz LP department in Bristol Music Center in Copenhagen, dropped by. He and Ben met often and had become so close that Ben would refer to Kauling as his nephew. Kauling recalls that

> Ben was fascinated by the Danish welfare system. When he fell and broke his ankle, he paid two to three dollars a day for hospitalization. Back then, it wasn't totally free for foreigners like it is

today. At the hospital, they served a beer along with his food, and he was washed all over by sweet, young nurses. He liked the hospital so much that he would go over there every year on the day of his discharge with a bottle of whisky for the doctor and chocolate for the nurses. He told all his friends in America that if they ever got sick, they should do it over here because they would be treated well.

On a whole, he was very enthusiastic about Denmark, but he never figured out the tax system. I've talked taxes a lot with Ben, and he didn't like paying taxes, but he understood why, once he realized how much you got for your tax money.[13]

Darville became his helping hand concerning taxes. "One day Ben called me," Darville remembers.

He was all befuddled and he said, "You've got to come over, there's something wrong here. There's a man who says he's from the tax department." I asked to speak with him, and he said that Ben had to pay taxes. He had an income, because the clubs had reported it, but they hadn't heard from him. Well, that was a problem, but they had to tax him, and Ben was shaken, because he'd spent all his money. But I went over to the tax department and explained that he was a great artist from America, but that he hadn't the faintest knowledge of the Danish tax system, and when he left a venue, he didn't take anything at all with him. I explained that he had large expenditures on transportation and upkeep of his instruments, on clothes and rent, and when all that was deducted from his income from the clubs, there wasn't much left, because he had to live. I went to three or four meetings at the tax office, and at last they gave up. But I had to promise to tell Ben to save his vouchers in the future, and I promised to take over his books. In return, they promised to let bygones be bygones. A stone fell from Ben's heart, and I explained how he was supposed to save all his bills and write everything down, and once in a while, I would come by and go through his books and keep an eye on things.[14]

Ben and Kauling became very close. "Ben was interested in politics," says Kauling,

> and we talked a lot about Malcolm X and Martin Luther King. Ben knew Malcolm X, not as Malcolm X, but as "Little Red." His original name was Malcolm Little, and he was a redheaded pimp from New York, and he and Ben used to move in the same circles and frequent the same bars. So he knew Little Red—he wasn't called "Red Little" as you might expect—and Ben was fascinated by his oratorical abilities. A black American gave me the tapes of Malcolm X's speeches, which I copied for Ben.
>
> Martin Luther King held a speech a couple of days before he was murdered. He had just returned from Vietnam and said, "How can I tell the brothers back in the U.S. not to use violence, when the same brothers are forced to use violence in Vietnam?" He had begun to reevaluate the nonviolence doctrine, and he was shot. Ben and I often talked about how King wasn't dangerous until he came back from Vietnam and began talking about how he could no longer preach nonviolence. So Ben didn't believe that James Earl Ray, a fanatic, was behind King's murder. He was certain that larger powers were behind the murders of Robert Kennedy and Martin Luther King. The U.S.A. couldn't afford to lose a war, so President Johnson couldn't bear the idea of removing troops from Vietnam.
>
> Ben got much of his information on the U.S.A. from Swedish television. They were able to quote the American war opposition more freely than Danish television because Sweden wasn't a member of NATO. We were like a lapdog. American antiwar people were heard far more often on Swedish television. Ben wasn't very enthusiastic about Nixon, and he became more radical through his years in Europe, that's for sure. He used to talk to other blacks in Copenhagen, but Ben wasn't a Black Panther. He didn't understand what they were into, but he wasn't against them either.[15]

At the hospital with his broken ankle, the doctors discovered that Ben suffered from general edema. He was advised to take better care of himself and to keep off the liquor, and for quite a while he followed the advice. He was discharged in late October with a cast on his leg and a pair of crutches. Ben had put on even more weight, and he would always have trouble walking hereafter. His ankle continued to bother him, and he began using a cane and playing seated.

In August, Timme Rosenkrantz died in New York, and a memorial concert was held in Copenhagen on November 14. The participants included Ben, the Saints and Sinners, Charlie Shavers, Don Byas, Teddy Wilson, Papa Bue's Viking Jazzband, Kenny Drew, and many more. Eddie Barefield was a member of the Saints and Sinners, and he remembers the evening being very special. "We were only in Copenhagen one day," he says, "and one of the biggest thrills I had was when I walked into this hall that night. Ben Webster was standing there. And I hadn't seen Ben for maybe four or five years or five or six years. And we had such a good time talking to each other, because I'd been getting letters from him. And that wasn't enough. I went up on stage, went backstage, and who else do you think was there? Don Byas. I hadn't seen him for about twenty-five or twenty years. I had been to Europe several times looking for him, and he was always someplace else. This was really a great reunion to find Ben and Don there together. The only heartbreaking thing was that they weren't friendly with each other, but I made them get together."[16]

Ben played a set with Teddy Wilson, Niels-Henning Ørsted Pedersen, and Makaya Ntshoko, retaining his usual high standard on *Perdido* and *In a Mellotone,* and giving *Stardust* yet another fine interpretation that was followed by steadfast applause. Subsequently, Rosenkrantz's girlfriend, Inez Cavanaugh, joined the quartet for a moving version of *I'll Never Be the Same.* True to Rosenkrantz's spirit, the concert ended in a long jam session with all the famous foreigners on stage. "And so this concert was given a framework and content that Timme Rosenkrantz would have thought ideal, and the audience reception was more enthusiastic and spontaneous than at any other jazz concert in Copenhagen for a very long time," read one review.[17]

While Ben was living in Holland he had no steady girlfriend; so as far as women are concerned, he reverted back to his New York habits of visiting prostitutes. However, in 1969 he met a woman named Birgit Nordtorp who was to become very important to him. She worked at Frederiksberg Hospital in Copenhagen and lived in a small house in Hundige, south of Copenhagen by Køge Bay. "The first time I met Ben was in Timme's Club in Nørregade in 1969, when he was playing there," she says. "My first thought was that it was terrible that such an intelligent person was so self-destructive. I think that's why I became interested, because he was very drunk that evening. We talked a little, and then I didn't see him for half a year."[18]

At the time, Birgit Nordtorp was around thirty, half Ben's age, pretty and blonde, and they soon took a liking to each other. Ben's relationship with her was the longest he had with a woman since Mule. "My friendship with Ben lasted for four years," Nordtorp says, "but there were periods when we didn't see each other. Of course he was on tour often, but he wasn't easy to live with. Actually, he was pretty hard living with, and when he was drinking, it was easy to surmise that we were better off apart. In 1972 there were a lot of bad periods with a lot of drinking, and sometimes I thought we would never see each other again. Every time we separated I thought, now it's over, but then he called, or I called him after a month or so, and then we were together again."[19]

"Ben was a good cook," she continues.

> Occasionally I would go over to butcher Arildsen in Store Kongensgade and buy a couple of big T-bone steaks. Ben always wanted the best. It made no difference what it cost. I never did understand why we couldn't just eat a hamburger once in a while. But when he had money, it didn't matter, then he just wanted what he wanted. Could be he was broke the next day, but he didn't think that way. One time he was going to Århus. It was in 1972, and I was on the evening shift at Frederiksberg Hospital. When I got home, Ben called around 1:30 A.M. from the club. He was playing with Dexter Gordon, and he was annoyed because Gordon wouldn't get off the stage. I insisted that Ben should go back to his hotel and go to bed. He wasn't drunk yet, but I was a little afraid that he was going to [be]. Early the next morning I woke up to the sound of a cab outside. Ben had taken a cab all the way from Århus and home to me, and that's how he solved the situation. And that's the way Ben was with money. I think that his royalties from records and copyrights often saved the rent.

Ben liked children and was very understanding. I saw a lot of my sister and her children and wanted to be with them. Usually when Ben and I were together, it was on his conditions, and we spent a lot of time doing what he wanted. But when I wanted to be with my family, he was never angry. He was very understanding about that. Family was very important to him too.

He needed someone to take care of him. Shortly after I got to know Ben really well, he went to play at Tagskægget in Århus. He called from Århus to ask me to come over. That was exciting, and it was possible, because I only worked every other week. When I got there, his drinking was really bad, and I managed to get him home by ship and train.

Another time, he was in London playing at Ronnie Scott's, and I was on vacation in Tenerife at the same time. Once again, Ben called asking me to come over there. Naturally I did so, because he was getting in a bad way again. We spent a few wonderful days there, and he gave me a lovely red suit. They had thrown Ben out of the posh hotel he usually stayed at because he was so drunk, and he had moved into the Regent. I guess one of the reasons he stayed with me was that I never joined him on his drunken binges. Some of the other women he had probably drank along with him, but that was of no help to him.

But I can't drink. Once I had been working and went over to his place afterwards. We sat at his big rosewood table talking. He had his beer, and I had a beer as well. Suddenly I had to lie down on the couch. He was very sweet and said, "One drinker in the family is enough!" He made me some soup and nursed me. It was my turn to be taken care of.

He was really a very sweet and thoughtful man. In London I had a migraine headache one day and spent the day in bed at the hotel. Ben was washing my underwear, and said his friends should see him now, washing a woman's underwear! Actually, it was below his dignity, but he did it, and it was very touching. There were no limits to his good intentions.[20]

Ben's temper probably contributed to the fact that few people tried to control his drinking. But on the other hand, he was entertaining, and many people probably chose to ignore his drinking in order to continue visiting him and calling themselves his friend. "At one point, he had become fat, he was suddenly very big," Henrik Wolsgaard-Iversen recalls, "and unfortunately it was all the beer. Clark Terry once said—and I think we Danes must accept the truth of it—that we didn't take good enough care of Ben. We should have been stricter with him. But Birgit Nordtorp came along and lifted that burden. While the rest of us just wanted to party, she was more careful and she was good for him. Birgit was really his lifeline. She didn't compromise, not too much at any rate. The other women more or less scratched his back."[21]

In early 1970, Ben was in Sweden a couple of times, still with his foot in a cast.[22] In Uppsala he played sitting on a chair on stage, exhausted. "However, the vitality with which he played was remarkable," read one review.

> After but a couple of tunes, nothing suggested that the man on stage was a tired sixty-one-year old. Seldom, or never, have I heard Webster play so electrifyingly, so rhythmically alive.
>
> He delivered a totally outstanding concert of two hours, alternating lovely ballads with livelier songs. The full room at Måndagsklubben was highly appreciative of Webster's performance, and it is not strange that the old master looked happy when he left the stage way past midnight accompanied by the audience's glowing ovation.[23]

March brought more travel, when shortly after the removal of his cast, Ben visited Trondheim in Norway for six concerts in three days: two at the National Museum of Decorative Art, three at the Students' Society, and one at the Down Town Key Club. Once again, Ben was afforded the pleasure of Tore Sandnæs on piano.

"Ben was very comfortable up there," remembers Tore Sandnæs, who accompanied him on piano. "I lived on a big farm, and Ben was supposed to stay with me. When we got home after playing one night, the lights were on everywhere, in the barn and all the outhouses, and we wondered what was going on. It turned out that the sows were delivering a lot of pigs. There was Ben Webster with his saxophone over his shoulder, in his handsome blue overcoat and hat, but we went over and watched all the pigs coming out of that big sow for around an hour. He was very interested. He was moved by all those deliveries, so we took the time to watch."[24]

Private recordings from the concerts in Trondheim document that Ben was playing very well, clearly inspired by the excellent rhythm section, delivering a solid, elastically swinging foundation. The repertoire is well known, offering no surprises, but we find wonderful, powerful versions of *Sunday* and *Cotton Tail* featuring sparkling, bubbling chases with drummer Egil Johansen, slyly swinging standards like *Perdido* and *In a Mellotone,* and a version of *Satin Doll* in which Ben finds new phrases. There was also a series of beautiful ballads that, alhough they add nothing new, are blessed with serenity, awesome tone, and unique art of phrasing.

Artist and musician Ove Stokstad took care of Ben during his visit to Trondheim, and often took him on trips around town. They took an immediate liking to each other and wrote regularly later on. Stokstad says of the first concert,

> Ben arrived hobbling, with his little hat and a cane, somewhat overweight, to put it mildly. It was obvious that he had difficulty moving around. Somewhat worn-out from the trip, but charming. Slightly nervous atmosphere among the organizers, who had never met Ben and hadn't been expecting a semi-invalid and heavily breathing artist on stage.
>
> Horn up to his mouth, the room is silent—and then—his first attack leaves no doubt: The room fills with the wonderful sound that most of us had previously only heard on record.
>
> This was Ben Webster, no doubt about it—the tender, rough, powerful, whispering, unique and constructive improviser, the unsentimental and touching artist of sound, full of vitality and authority with his amazing tone. When playing, this 61-year old artist and musician needed no cane. The magic and power were still there.
>
> It was my job to take care of him around the clock and be his "My man!" Not just take care of most things, but everything. I had his nickname, "The Brute," in the back of my head, but the man I met was an extremely culturally curious, open-minded and

friendly gentleman, and the program I had planned for him got an overwhelmingly enthusiastic reception.

Ben felt at home at the Ringve Museum, the national museum of music and musical instruments. We were given a special tour by a charming female guide dressed in a folk costume, and Ben revealed the buttery side of his personality. He played several strange instruments including a violin built entirely out of wooden matches.[25]

When Ben returned from Norway, a couple of very different surprises awaited. He had a few bookings with Arnvid Meyer's orchestra, and at the first, J. C. Higginbotham was the second guest soloist. "When we put those two together, we thought they would throw their arms around each other for pure joy," Jesper Thilo says, "because we knew that they had played together in the Fletcher Henderson Reunion Band and with Henry 'Red' Allen. But as it turned out, they detested each other! The whole of Arnvid Meyer's horn section had to stand between them on stage to prevent them from killing each other, and they did whatever they could to annoy each other and ruin the other's playing."[26]

Jesper Thilo and Ben had much in common as saxophonists, and the young Thilo absorbed what he could from the old master. "Being with Ben gave me something," says Thilo, today considered one of Europe's best saxophonists.

It's not like I took lessons with him, you couldn't do that. What he taught me were all the things that came spontaneously in certain situations, when I was complaining about something. Then he would say, "Just do this or that." One of the things that fascinated him was that I played the clarinet, because he wasn't very good himself. He had a clarinet, and he had an alto sax as well. I bought his alto sax, and it turned out to be an excellent alto sax, a Selmer Mark VI, and I've played it ever since. Niels-Henning Ørsted Pedersen told me that Ben brought it into the Montmartre once. After he played it once, the others told him not to play it again because they had heard more than enough! Ben wasn't a multi-instrumentalist. The tenor saxophone was *his* instrument.

Ben discovered that I used a clarinet embouchure, and that I used it on the tenor saxophone as well. He had played enough clarinet to know that you have to change your embouchure when you change from clarinet to saxophone, and he also taught me something that is true of both instruments, and that is that you should not tense up too much, not chew the mouthpiece. You're supposed to drop your jaw and create a huge space in the back. The reed has to lie as loose as possible in order to vibrate as much as possible. You have to use all the muscles around your mouth except the ones you chew with, and that's hard to learn. When Ben called this to my attention, it actually took me several years to get used to not having the sensation of biting something, because I'd always felt that. But since then, I have derived great pleasure from doing as Ben taught me.

Ben called my attention to something else as well. When Benny Carter came, he went wild. Ben told me to keep an eye on the way Carter attacked the instrument with his fingers. And it was really true that Carter played the saxophone in a unique manner. I may not have noticed if Ben hadn't told me, but Carter's fingers never left the keys for a moment, no matter what he played. His fingers moved as little as possible, and he utilized a minimum of force and energy. It was impeccable, and this is what Ben had noticed.

Ben had a fantastic personality, like Louis Armstrong. As soon as he entered a room, everything naturally rotated around him. He took over everything immediately. He spoke the loudest, ordered everybody around, and told stories, and his stories were the funniest. It was hard to cut through when he was around, because he had this great charisma and filled out the room, as he did when he played as well. And people got their money's worth, because whether he was playing saxophone or ordering gin from the bartender, it was always a show. He was 100 percent honest. Everything came directly from the heart; there was no acting involved. He wasn't very good at sweeping things under the carpet.[27]

The Danish Radio Jazz Group visited southern Jutland several years in a row with a small detour to Flensburg, West Germany. In 1970 Ben was a guest soloist, and recordings of *Sunday* and *Old Folks* are preserved from the concert in Flensburg on April 28. The first tune is played somewhat too fast for Ben's taste, but he offers a fine, serene version of the latter.

From Flensburg, Ben continued to Switzerland and a reunion with Teddy Wilson. The concert in Bern on May 1 was very nice, resulting in a beautiful version of *Stardust,* an emotional *Ben's Blues*—the theme of which is identical to *Go Home*—and as the evening's surprise, *I Can't Give You Anything but Love,* normally not included in Ben's repertoire, but given a very poetic and warm interpretation.

To Ben's great sorrow, Johnny Hodges died on May 11. He received the news a day or two later, shortly before filming a television show in Copenhagen. *Old Folks* is particularly moving, with tears streaming down Ben's cheeks as he played. The following week, Ben was invited to participate in a memorial program for his great idol on the radio, and he decided on a rerun of the recordings he made two years earlier with the Danish Radio Big Band with strings. In an interview, Ben later said about Hodges death. "It was so sudden, like if you hit me in the head with a sledgehammer. It really knocked me down. I didn't know what to do."[28]

The following month, Ben was once again playing with Henri Chaix's orchestra, first in Lörrach in southern Germany, and the following day in Aarau, Switzerland, joined by Albert Nicholas. In Aarau Ben was treated to a special experience as Circus Knie, Switzerland's largest circus, was in town. Chris Krenger, Circus Knie's press agent, had met Ben in London, and upon meeting Ben again at the concert in Aarau, he invited him to the afternoon show on the following day. Before the show, he was given a tour of the animals. He fed the large male giraffe "Lucky," and he met the Polish circus musicians in the intermission. Krenger recalls that Ben "sat in the first row for the shows, and enjoyed the whole program despite the heavy summer heat, enthusiastically applauding the performers. Ben laughed heartily at the well-known Swiss clown, Dimitri, the main attraction at Knie that year."[29]

Albert Nicholas lived in France, but he often visited Denmark to play with Papa Bue's Viking Jazzband, and he always looked up Ben. "Ben treated Nick like a nice old gentleman," Bent Kauling recalls.

Once, the three of us were sitting at Ben's place talking, when somehow it came up that it was Armstrong's birthday that day. Ben said, "Huh! Armstrong, he just can't play anymore. He's just repeating himself!" And Nick gets up and walks over to Ben, pulls him up by his jacket—and he was just a small man—and hisses in Ben's face, "If it wasn't for Pops, you would still be a newspaper boy in Kansas City! Because Pops made the music, he made the audience, and he kept jazz alive to this very day!" Ben was scared. He went pale and sat down and apologized to Nick, and then Nick sat down too, shaking with rage. You didn't question Armstrong's role in jazz when he was around!

After Nick had left, Ben shrugged it off saying, "Oh, that old man!" Later he told me that he had been afraid that Nick was going to pull his knife, because he knew that Nick had a knife.[30]

In July, Ben played at Jazzhus Montmartre, and on July 12 Duke Ellington came to town to play an afternoon concert in the Tivoli Gardens. It was Paul Gonsalves's birthday, and he and a few other Ellington musicians went to visit Ben and celebrate before the show. "I really didn't know how to look at the guys, after Rab's passing, you know," he explained in an interview a month later. "Well, that really tore me to pieces, but you know how I felt about Hodges. Of course I enjoyed the band, though it was sad to see them without him."[31]

The orchestra wasn't scheduled to leave for Munich until the following day, and that evening Harold Ashby sat in at the Montmartre. "Herluf Kamp-Larsen had been farsighted enough to book Ben at the Montmartre when Ellington was in town, because then he knew Ellington's musicians would drop by," says Bent Kauling. "Gonsalves came running in and sat down right in front of Ben. He didn't play, he just sat and listened to him and watched him. They were very, very close friends, and he admired and respected Ben a lot."[32]

Three weeks later, on August 5, 1970, Ben was in the Netherlands recording an album called *Ben Op Zijn Best* with three other horns, and Cees Slinger's Trio as the rhythm section. Slinger and Ben had always been fond of each other, but unfortunately a later reissue of the album had a negative influence on their friendship. "There is one thing that I am very sorry about," reminisces Slinger.

> Ben and I had a very good acquaintance and relationship together. He trusted me completely, and if I picked him up from where he lived, he came off the stairs and gave me his little bottle that he always carried, a hip flask, and said, "Here, Cees, you keep that for me and don't give it to me if I ask for it." That's the way we worked together. And then something happened that I had nothing to do with. We made an album for Albert Heijn, a big supermarket chain, and it should be a very low-price product with tunes with no copyrights, old tunes and stuff like that. Then, all of a sudden, Ben was in Belgium somewhere, and he saw the same album in a completely different cover but with the same tunes and everything, and also with somebody else's name as an arranger on the cover. He was absolutely sure that that would be my doing, which it was not, because I was just as surprised about it as he was. He never understood that I had nothing to do with it. So we parted actually as no longer friends anymore, and I was very sorry.[33]

The album opens with Slinger's frisky *Ben's Little Scheme*. Langereis is a little heavy-handed, which makes it somewhat difficult for Ben to get started, but he succeeds in building his solo to a climax at the end of his second chorus. *Billy Boy* is played in up-tempo, and Ben is a little sloppy in his theme presentation, before diving into a dynamic solo of rising intensity. Toward the end, a few of his phrases are slightly sluggish, as if the tempo is a mite too fast, but he gets through, closing nicely. His solo on the moderately slow *Ida, Sweet as Apple Cider* is wonderfully relaxed and straightforward. Slinger's second contribution to this session is a medium-tempo tune dedicated to Steven Kwint, *Steff's Shoes*. Slinger delivers the theme in call-and-response with the ensemble, and Ben tells a little story without getting overly involved. *Greensleeves* has Ben carrying the tune. He is a little more committed here, though once again not overdoing it. Nor is he particularly enthused by the Dixieland version of *Carry Me Back to Old Virginia*, despite his sneaky phrases in the beginning, hinting at more. Ben's absolutely best contributions come in two spirituals played alone with the rhythm section, *Nobody Knows the Trouble I've Seen* and *Deep River*. Both are given ballad renditions, and his sensitivity and commitment are strong. It is hard to imagine more beautiful interpretations—the first tune especially highlights his exquisite sound and extremely personal, laid-back phrasing.

Three weeks later, Ben was once again in the Netherlands, this time to play for a radio show and a television show, and he was accompanied by Slinger's trio on both occasions. Ben appears somewhat uninspired on the radio show, playing carefully most of the time, and holding back. He is also slightly out of breath. The trio, as well as Ben, are in much higher spirits on the television show. Ben has more presence, varying his playing more, swinging better, especially on *Perdido, Johnny Come Lately,* and *Rain Check,* in which he is more aggressive, utilizing shakes and double-time runs, and dueling successfully in a few hot chases with the drummer. While interpretations of *Come Sunday* and *For Heaven's Sake* are tender and graceful, *Danny Boy* lacks conviction. Ben has problems producing altissimo notes on this track—indeed achieving them seems a battle—perhaps because his reed has become too soft.

Following his visit to the Netherlands, Ben played a few jobs in Denmark before returning to London for yet another two-week booking at Ronnie Scott's Club. While in London, he recorded *Webster's Dictionary* in two sessions, October 12 and 13. The album contains ballads arranged by Stan Tracey for strings, clarinet, vibraphone, and rhythm section. Generally, Ben plays well, but today the arrangements seem syrupy, and the saxophone would have gained more impact with a little more volume in the mix. However, there are certain fine details and magic moments. Among the gems are *Willow Weep for Me* and *That's All.* On the latter Ben leaps an octave upward after his theme presentation, interpreting the melody once again and with more emotion. *Someone to Watch Over Me* is another spellbinder, and on *Come Sunday* and *Old Folks,* Ben's playing is extremely sensitive and dedicated. On the latter, his phrasings and restrained approach in the B-parts is wonderful. In comparison, one senses little commitment on the remaining songs.

A few days later, he was back in Copenhagen, where he played at a jam session in the Jazzhus Montmartre with Dexter Gordon. Gordon had recently returned from Germany, where he had purchased a pink saxophone. Jesper Thilo was present in the Montmartre, and he recalls that "Dexter always claimed stubbornly that he bought it because it was a good instrument, not because it was pink. I don't remember how they played that particular evening, but I remember going into the kitchen where Ben was sitting on a chair taking a breather. I asked him, 'Did you see Dexter's saxophone?' And he answered, 'Yeah, but I'm not gonna say anything.' He knew that if he mentioned it to Dexter, he would probably tease him saying, 'Oh, so now you see pink saxophones?' "[34]

On October 27, Ben had a rehearsal with the Danish Radio Big Band that was being taped for later broadcast, and vocalists Matty Peters and Freddy Albeck were also among the soloists. Ben was not there when rehearsals started, and after a while, Herman Wolsgaard-Iversen picked him up at home. He was still sleeping after a wet party.[35] Indeed, he was still slightly drunk when he took his place in front of the orchestra, and more or less assumed Niels Jørgen Steen's conducting responsibilities. In one of the tunes, his own *Did You Call Her Today?*, Ben clowns around with the orchestra, but he's also firm about how he wants certain figures phrased, occasionally swearing to get his point across. They play eight takes before he is satisfied. While his obbligato to Peters's rendition of *Baby It's Cold Outside* is lovely, emotional, and extremely sensitive, with the exception of a couple of phrases, his contribution to this version of *Cotton Tail* is a little tired. On the other hand, Ray Pitts's beautiful arrangement of *Old Folks* is one of the musical high points of the session; Ben has a story to tell, and does so in his most sensitive mood.

Bent Kauling recalls,

A Friday evening a few days later, Ben called me up to tell me that Erik Moseholm had phoned saying that the show was going on the air that Sunday. "How about coming over," he said, "and we can listen to it together." I came over, and as we sat there listening, Ben's face got redder and redder, because they hadn't censored any of it. When Ben blushed, his face turned darker, a reddish black, and his face became so round that you could draw a circle around it. Right after the show, I remember the doorbell ringing, and Ben was certain that it was the police, come to throw him out of the country. "Don't open the door!" he said. I don't remember who it was, maybe it was janitor Olsen.

The radio gave him a tape of the session, and he copied it for several musicians. It's an "anatomy of a jazz session."[36]

Come late January 1971, Ben was in Stockholm at the Stampen. "Over the years, Webster has consolidated his interpretations of standards," a critic wrote.

> When he plays ballads like *For All We Know* or *Chelsea Bridge*, he does so with a minimum of divergence from the version he has made his own. And if he plays fast tunes like *Perdido*, the model is equally predefined.
>
> But the small, hardly noticeable variations have their own improvisational value. They are often simplifications. Gradually, the phrases become fragmentary—it is almost up to the listener to fill in the spaces.[37]

After yet another short tour to Switzerland, Ben played several jobs with Arnvid Meyer's orchestra. Much to his pleasure, they were joined in late February by yet another guest soloist, Charlie Shavers. Sunday, February 28, was a trying day for the two elderly men as they spent all day rehearsing in front of an audience for a television show at the Jazzhus Montmartre, and playing through the evening with Arnvid Meyer. The footage was joined with additional footage and interviews with producer Per Møller Hansen throughout the week, to produce a television portrait of Ben called *Big Ben*—not to be mistaken for Johan van der Keuken's portrait from 1966. The sequences from the Montmartre have a lovely, happy quality, and Ben and Shavers take great pleasure in each other's company. They play an improvised blues, *Stardust,* and *Perdido.* The gem is *Stardust.* Shavers takes the verse, followed by Ben on the chorus in an exceptionally beautiful and sensitive rendition enhanced with a supple, big tone and plenty of air on the low notes.

During the same week, recordings were made of Ben with strings and the rhythm section from the Danish Radio Big Band conducted by Ray Pitts, who also had written lovely arrangements of *Some Other Spring* and a very short version of *Danny Boy.* Ben invests all his emotional powers in his interpretation of *Some Other Spring*, by delaying his phrases slightly and enhancing the notes with an occasional glissando. After the show, Ben told a journalist, "Ray Pitts wrote a string arrangement for it, and oh, my, he can write. I could've played a little better myself. . . . but strings. . . . beautiful."[38]

Shavers was not in Denmark very long on this occasion. He had other bookings in Europe, before he and Ben were to play in Italy together. "Then one night he got in from somewhere in Germany and wanted to visit Ben," Bent Kauling recalls.

> His plan was to talk first, and then go out and jam all night.
>
> I was at Ben's place when he called to announce his arrival, and when he got there, we had a drink. Since it was already past midnight, Shavers asked about jamming, so we headed for La Fontaine, and Shavers brought his horn along, but Ben didn't feel like bringing his.
>
> When we got there, Shavers asked me to see if he could sit in with the band. It was Per Carsten and some of the young lions, but Per Carsten answered, "Well, it's not such a good idea, because we only play our own arrangements." So I had to explain that to Shavers. He didn't say a word, he just stood there staring, turned around, and went back to his seat. Ben just said "Huh!" and began laughing. But it was the first time Shavers was ever rejected at a jam session anywhere in the world. He was usually number one at any jam session.
>
> Ben would often show up unannounced to play with musicians he liked. He played with Papa Bue's band because he liked the rhythm section. He did that two or three times. One time Higginbotham was playing with Papa Bue at Vingården, and Ben went down and sat in. Ben and Higgy had a sort of love/hate relationship. When both of them were drunk, Ben called Higgy "Juice Bottom" and he called Ben "Frog Eye."[39]

While Shavers was in Germany, Ben had a couple of jobs in Sweden, after which he returned to Denmark to rest before his and Shavers's Italian tour, which would bring them to the Third International Jazz Parade in Bergamo on March 20, followed by concerts in Venice, Terni, and San Marco. The tour had been booked by Jenny Armstrong, and she and Birgit Nordtorp joined them for the tour.

Nordtorp recalls that she and Ben spent a few wonderful hours together in Venice before Ben's mood suddenly changed, and he and Shavers began drinking heavily. They also began arguing constantly, including on the train, and Ben and Nordtorp finally took a compartment of their own. For Ben, the musical outcome was mediocre. The idea was for the two of them to play together, accompanied by German pianist Joe Haider, Swedish bassist Palle Danielsson, and drummer Art Taylor, but at the last minute Ben puffed up and decided to play alone with the rhythm section, demanding that Shavers play before him.[40] At the concert at the Teatro Donizetti in Bergamo, Johnny Griffin and Shavers bested him musically,[41] and indeed, a radio recording of *Old Folks* reveals that Ben lacks the depth usually present in his ballads.

In Bergamo, one of the other acts was Lionel Hampton's orchestra, whose pianist was Milt Buckner. "We came in that night," Buckner recalls,

> and Ben and Charlie Shavers, Jimmy Woode, and Richard Boone, the trombone player, they'd just done their concert that night and they were in the bar. So I rush in and I see Ben, I grab him, you know, and he said, "Where is the Kid?" He always called Jacquet "the Kid." We came in, so when he saw Jacquet, he said, "Ki-i-i-d" and went [fell] back. We tried to catch him, Charlie Shavers was trying to catch him, but he was too heavy, you couldn't get him from the floor.
>
> Jacquet said, "Man, what are you doing, Frog?" "Hey, Kid, I was waiting for you," said Ben. They all got together in a big hug-up. They were lifting each other like a baby. We got him in the elevator, took him upstairs into his room, and laid him on the bed. And Ben on his bed was still saying, "Ah, the Kid, the Kid." Jacquet wanted to soothe him, you know, and he would get his horn, brought it back, and played real slow *All Too Soon* for him. And Ben said, "Ah, Kid, you never forget. And you still don't hold your bottom lip slack enough. All those young boys play too tight with that lower lip."

The next morning he was looking bright, he had his camera on. They had to take a bus; Johnny Griffin was also on that tour. He was in the back with Richard Boone. Charlie Shavers sat behind, and in the front was Ben sitting with the driver, and we were waving goodbye.[42]

Upon their arrival in Copenhagen, Ben and Shavers said good-bye, after which Shavers took a plane back to New York. They never met again, because Shavers died only four months later.

Following a couple of weeks of much needed rest in Copenhagen, Ben left for a two-week booking at Ronnie Scott's Club beginning April 19. Two reviews document that he was playing much better than in Italy.[43]

However, Dave Green is of the opinion that Ben was in less impressive form than on previous occasions. "The first few times he came over to England he was fine, and most of the time he was straight," he tells.

When he came over for the last time in 1971 he was drinking more, and he had to sit down to play. He was not in great form, and he talked a lot to the audience. I always knew when he had been drinking. I used to look over at the door at Ronnie's where he would come in for the gig, and if he had been drinking—he was so immaculate, normally—a little strand of hair just above his left ear would be raised up. If his hair was all flat he was cool, you know.

He was an incredible player, and his time was wonderful. I learned so much by playing with him. Just the time, that wonderful beat. There was only one place for the beat, you know, it was just like the bass was playing itself. That was the feeling I had. There was only one way to play with him, it came naturally. And his phrasing when playing ballads—it was an absolute lesson for me. In those years I played with many famous musicians, like Coleman Hawkins, Sonny Rollins, Zoot Sims, Roland Kirk, but I think I probably learned more from Ben because of his wonderful time and phrasing. There was space in his playing. With just one note he told you so much. I was absolutely thrilled to be chosen. Those years with Ben were a wonderful time for me. I will never forget it. He was wonderful to be with, and such a warm presence on the bandstand.[44]

This was to be Ben's last visit, and consequently the last time he had occasion to play with Stan Tracey, whom he appreciated greatly. "Ben loved Stan Tracey's playing, which was wonderful because Stan was not so popular with some other guys," Green goes on. "He was and still is a very unique player, very original and his own man. I think Ben liked the way he voiced the chords, especially in the ballads. Thelonious Monk and Duke Ellington were his biggest influences, and I think that what Ben heard in Stan was the Dukish thing, and that's why I think he loved him, you know."

In an interview a couple of days into the booking, Ben expressed his pleasure with the rhythm section. "I'm fortunate to be able to play with Stan Tracey, Dave Green, and Tony Crombie," he said. "They are old friends, and I think that when you play with friends it makes it so much easier. I try to be easy, because you don't get results when you drive. You don't drive anybody, you treat people nice. That's what I think. Treat people nice, and then they come to you."[45]

June brought heat and a joyful reunion with Benny Carter, who arrived in Denmark on May 30. Ben and Jesper Thilo met him at the airport, and for the next two weeks they played together. "Hearing Ben Webster and Benny Carter together in 1971 was of course a rather sensational experience, and it was obvious that the two musicians themselves were tense about this meeting," wrote *Jazz Forum* after a concert at Jazzhus Montmartre. "They almost tiptoed on the first tune, but when that and the applause was over, everybody relaxed and the two of them really played. On the third night Ben Webster was so strong that many of his fans claimed that they had never heard him play like that since he came to Europe."[46]

Ben and Carter traveled together to France, where they both were due to perform at Trois Nuits de Jazz in Joinville-le-Pont, a Parisian suburb on June 21, 22, and 24. The other musicians included the Golden Gate Quartet, the Delta Rhythm Boys, Johnny Griffin, Richard Boone, Memphis Slim, Claude Bolling, and Bill Coleman, who was to play with Ben and Carter with the festival rhythm section consisting of Kenny Drew, bassist Michel Gaudry, and Kenny Clarke.

Ben was again in fine form, and according to a critic he produced the most beautiful music of the evening.[47]

Shortly before the last concert, after the dinner, Ben felt the need to relieve himself. Instead of using the toilet, he went outside in the warm evening to urinate in the nearby Marne River, but slipping on the shore, he landed in the river with a splash. The cook heard his cries for help from the restaurant kitchen and ran to the rescue, but there was to be no concert that evening for Ben.

While in Paris, Ben visited the Selmer factory with Kenny Clarke to find a new saxophone. "He found two Mark VI models which he brought back to Denmark," says Jesper Thilo.

> He told me that he and Kenny Clarke had sat there all day without deciding which one was the best, so they let him take those two home with him on trial. I said that I was looking for a Selmer too, but they were hard to get a hold of at the moment. "Well," Ben said, "you can have one of them. I can't decide which is best, so you just pick one of them!" I tried both of them, and told him which one I liked the best. "Good," he said, "because actually I think the other is better!" Suddenly, he knew what he wanted, but I'm pretty sure that if I had chosen the other one, he would have said the same thing!
>
> Once, he came into the Radio Building with that new horn, and he swore and cussed over it. He was dissatisfied. The rest of us couldn't hear the difference, but that's the way it is! You want it to be easy. You go for the same result with less effort in order to focus on the emotional content. If your tools don't work right, it takes your attention, you can't abandon yourself to what it's all about. Ben got his emotions out, but it took more on the Mark VI.
>
> These days, when I play the Selmer Balanced Action that I bought later, I can feel the difference. I can hear what Ben was looking for, and couldn't find in the Mark VI. It has to do with the way the horn responds, how rapidly the note comes. Some

instruments take a long time to produce the note, when you blow, but on the Balanced Action it comes immediately, so if you've been accustomed to that all your life, I can understand why Ben never really felt comfortable with the other horn. The older you get, the harder it is to get used to something new.[48]

Ben never felt familiar with or enthusiastic about his new Mark VI, so after approximately a year, in November 1972, he sold it to Dexter Gordon.

Ben and Mary Lou Williams were still in contact, and in September he wrote this letter to her:[49]

> Hi Mary—
>
> How are you my love? I hope O.K.
>
> I've seen quite a few cats over here from the States and it sure was a real pleasure. However, some of my old buddies that I was raised up with can't come, and I would really like to see, and chew the fat with them.
>
> I had the chance to play with Benny "The King" Carter here in Copenhagen for three days, in the Montmartre, and two days in Paris. "What a thrill." He knows so much music, and he is the only person that I get the shakes trying to play my horn behind or with him (smile) however it was a ball.
>
> I lost my "medal" you had blessed for me somewhere between Paris and Copenhagen, and I'm afraid to be without it. So, if you can, please send me another one, soon I hope.
>
> So far I've heard nothing but sh-t, where in hell has swing gone to? So disgusting.
>
> Please say hello to Milt Hinton and the gang.
>
> Take care
>
> I'll always love you
>
>> Sincerely
>>
>> Ben
>
> P.S I've never forgotten what you showed me on the piano.

Ben's critical remark at the end of the letter refers to several experiences he had in the Jazzhus Montmartre with the new fusion of jazz and rock. On one occasion he had heard Weather Report, and had become so enraged at what he heard that he walked on stage in a fury and knocked over Zawinul's electric piano.

Later in the fall of 1971, Ben toured Norway for a week, beginning October 3 in Oslo. He then traveled north to Trondheim, south again to Molde, and finishing with two days in Oslo. The rhythm section for the tour consisted of the American pianist Jack Reilly, who was a music teacher in Molde at the time, bassist Sture Janson in Oslo and Bjørn Alterhaug in Trondheim and Molde, and drummer Trygve Windingstad, who had organized the tour.

Ben had mixed feelings about the rhythm section. Alterhaug says that Ben "didn't like Reilly and Windingstad. Ben wasn't particularly gentle when speaking about his drumming!"[50]

In Trondheim Ben met with Ove Stokstad, who remembers that

he did his best to be friendly towards me, and I was still his "My Man!," but he couldn't conceal that he was tired and worn-out.

It's remarkable, but over the years I have discovered that everyone that played or in some other way got close to the person and artist Ben Webster, feels that they have met someone they will never forget, a very special man, you can't help but like. He had a violent, in the most positive sense, spiritual aura. I hope that over the years, The Brute will be forgotten, and Ben's music, which radiates so much power, beauty and warmth, will be his final testimony as long as we listen to jazz music.[51]

The music recorded justifies to some degree Ben's criticism of the rhythm section.[52] Reilly is an original and moderately modern pianist, and actually does his job excellently, whereas one understands Ben's criticism of Windingstad much better. At times he is heavy-handed and lacks drive, and his work on the cymbals is often quite deafening. Ben does his best to compensate for these deficiencies by placing his phrases right on the beat. He plays with a rare passion, violence, swing, and force in all tunes with the exception of the ballads, which are performed with more warmth and pensiveness, although they are not quite as deep and touching as he can play them.

Over the last year, Ben had found a new friend, the very young and talented pianist Ben Besiakov, whose interest in jazz was developing. Besiakov recounts,

> I was around thirteen when I met Ben Webster in the Montmartre. I was there to hear Bill Evans with his trio with Eddie Gomez and Marty Morell in May 1970. When Ben discovered that my name was Ben, too, and that I played piano, he became interested in me and invited me to his apartment. I visited him a lot, in some periods once a week, and helped him with various things like his washing and fetching beer. Usually, his apartment was full of people, and I met a lot of musicians like Charlie Shavers, Richard Boone, Bent Jædig, and Jesper Thilo. When Ellington was in town, some of the guys from his band would visit Ben—I remember Ray Nance.
>
> He tried to help me with my piano playing. He would say, "Do like me," and then he would play something. I tried to play it, and when it sounded sort of the same, he would say, "Yeah, you got it!" But usually I couldn't really catch it.[53]

In Ben's tape collection there is a recording from his living room of him instructing Besiakov and bassist Mikker Lauridsen in *Autumn Leaves* and *Greensleeves*. At one point, he isn't satisfied, and starts instructing little Ben directly by making him practice certain rhythmical figures intensively, and by showing him the series of correct chords and listening afterwards as the pupil plays them—"No, no, no, that's a G7!" The most surprising part of the tape comes after almost an hour of practicing, when Besiakov, guitarist Mikkel Nordsø, Mikker Lauridsen, and Ben play a Miles Davis repertoire consisting of a blues, *So What,* and *All Blues.* It is a fine characteristic of Ben's to meet the needs and wishes of the young budding musicians, rather than stubbornly keeping to his own repertoire.

At the end of the tape, they talk awhile, and Ben offers the young musicians a soda. Listening to their conversation, it appears that in a few days, Duke Ellington will be coming to town with his orchestra to play at the Tivoli Gardens. Mercer Ellington had checked with Anders Stefansen to see if Ben was in town, because "The Guv'nor" wanted him to join them for the concert in Copenhagen on November 7 and in Malmö in Sweden three days later. Says Bent Kauling, "Mercer Ellington called from New York, Sunday evening before the concert in Copenhagen, to ask Ben to play with them. He was pleased to, and I promised to come over and pick him up, so we could meet the band at the airport. When I got over to his place at nine-thirty in the morning, Ben was already dressed in his newly shined shoes, ironed black pants, his good leather jacket, the good hat, white shirt with blue stripes, loosely knotted tie, and his hair conked. He was sharp and sober, and he wasn't sitting in his usual chair, but in the guest chair and facing the door."[54]

On the stage, Ben had borrowed a band uniform. From the television show of the two concerts that evening it is obvious that the jacket is a little bit tight as he sits in the saxophone group between Gonsalves and Harold Ashby. At the first concert he plays a two-chorus, routine solo in the opening tune, *C Jam Blues*. After *Rockin' in Rhythm*, Ellington announces Ben. Ben is unsure of what is going to happen until Ellington plays the introduction to *All Too Soon*, and Ben interprets it a little carefully and searchingly in short phrases. After the applause, he is on his way back to his chair, when Ellington sets a fast-paced *Cotton Tail*, and Ben goes back to the microphone and plays his old solo one more time. In his short solo, Ellington plays a little stride, bringing a radiant smile to Ben's face, and in the final B-part, Ben's statement is nice and confident. At the following concert, he is featured once again in *Cotton Tail*, but this time the tempo is too diabolically fast to produce anything interesting. However, it is followed by one of the high points of the evening, Ben's incredibly beautiful and emotional interpretation of *I Got It Bad and That Ain't Good*, a moving solo during which his own eyes turn watery at his playing.

Ben spent the last week of December and into the new year at the Jazzhus Montmartre before leaving for Oslo in Norway, where a weeklong booking waited at the Down Town Key Club, followed by a large concert at Chateau Neuf, likewise in Oslo, on January 12, 1972. The concert was in celebration of the twentieth anniversary of the Big Chief Jazz Band, and other guest acts included Papa Bue's Viking Jazzband, and the Dutch Swing College Band. Upon his return to Copenhagen, Ben wrote the following letter thanking Ove Stokstad:

Jan. 27, 72

Hi Ove—

Sorry I haven't written to you before now. I've been laid up with the flu.

I can never thank you enough for making the tape for me. It's wonderful.

I was in Oslo for a few days doing a jazz concert and The Down Town Key Club. Sure had a nice time, plus meeting the Crown Prince.

Sure would like to see you "ole buddy"—and please say hello to your family for me, and also bass man and his family.

So, take care, and I hope to see you soon.

Sincerely,

Ben

In Oslo, Ben undoubtedly didn't drink more than he usually did, but the story of his behavior toward the twenty-four-year-old Crown Prince Harald is highly questionable and seemingly made up. Papa Bue's trumpeter Keith Smith claims that when the bandleaders were introduced to Crown Prince Harald, who had attended the concert, Ben was drunk, and patted the crown prince on the shoulder, saying, "Ben Webster, King of the Tenors. Please to meet you, Prince!"[55] Back home, he had told Birgit Nordtorp about the event, and she remembers that he had been honored that the crown prince had taken the time to thank him for the concert. He had answered, "I thank *you*." Ben knew how to carry himself in dignified company, and it seems unlikely that he would make a fool of himself in front of royalty. He was no royalist, but he followed the events in the Danish royal family. In January 1972, he filmed King Frederik the Ninth's funeral procession from the windows of Bristol Music Center, and likewise the funeral ceremony at Roskilde Cathedral on his television.

In mid-January 1972, Ben and Dexter Gordon played together at the Jazzhus Montmartre. They repeated the collaboration in March on a tour to southern Jutland and northern West Germany with the Danish Radio Jazz Group. The extremely successful concert in Flensburg was recorded by the Danish Broadcasting Corporation. The next day, an enthusiastic reviewer wrote, "The surprise of the evening was the appearance on stage of tenor saxophonist Ben Webster. He is an enormous attraction, and displayed his huge talent in *Our Love Is Here to Stay* and *Old Folks.*"[56]

The music confirms the reviewer's point of view. The first tune shows Ben's great overview in a continuously building solo, climaxing in the concluding chorus. He swings absolutely splendidly, clearly enjoying the rhythm section immensely. Dexter Gordon's presence seems to stimulate him, and in *Perdido,* his statement is full of excellent phrases from the very first bars. His playing is fresh and never falls back into routine riffs.

Bassist Bo Stief, who was a member of the Danish Radio Jazz Group, played often with Ben during his last couple of years.

> Ben would sit in his chair in the kitchen [Jazzhus Montmartre] and tell us young musicians how a lot of things worked and what life was about. It was really serious, how we could deal with different situations and all. He was almost a kind of Buddha, a philosopher. He was wise about life, he had experienced a lot of hard things, but I also think he was happy to be here.
>
> All I can say is that Ben was one of the warmest and sweetest people I've ever met. He was very nice to us, whereas many of the other Americans could be hard on us. There were never any problems with Ben. He was never rude to us. Dexter Gordon was more the "I'm the bandleader and the star" type, but Ben would wait and see what happened. He didn't demand anything. He explained how he wanted the tune; introduction and tempo— "ping-ping-ping-ping." We considered ourselves very progressive, we liked Herbie Hancock and all that stuff, but Ben never said, "Don't play this" or "Don't play that." He was very progressive himself; he would say, "Oh, you play that way—that's fine."
>
> I heard a lot of people say that Ben didn't play well because he was getting old. But I don't remember ever thinking that Ben played badly. As long as the tempo wasn't too fast, he played well to the very last. His growl was really effective, and his timing was fantastic, cogent. And he was always perfectly in tune.
>
> There was so much power in his blues, which was rough and

potent with a lot of rhythmical things. Dexter's melodic lines were more complex than Ben's, but his rhythm was nowhere near as varied. I always looked forward to playing blues with Ben, because it had that fantastic swing. He always stayed solidly on the beat, while many other saxophonists soar on top.

The ballads were the best, also because he could play slow ballads. Many of the old swing musicians played medium-paced ballads, but Ben could play them way down where the beats were far apart. He created a certain mood; it was special when Ben played ballads. You find serenity, earnestness, plenty of time, it's beautiful, and very minimalistic. Ben's way of playing ballads doesn't exist any more. It died along with him. He taught me a lot about that, about being sombre in the slow tempi. If you're that serious about it, something happens, maybe even something painful. You become sad in a good way, and it becomes lyrical. Whenever we had played a ballad with Ben, we always had to sit for half a minute afterward to take a breather, and renew our energy, because he had pulled us through something painful, but something painful in a good way. Many jazz musicians lack the ability to create moods, but he could, and he had the *urge* to create moods.

I toured a lot with Ben, and sometimes with Ben and Dexter Gordon together. Dexter and Ben didn't compete. My impression was that they genuinely respected each other. Ben would drop by the Montmartre and sit in on Dexter's jobs and vice versa. You never see that kind of thing anymore.

In a way, I think Ben is a little underrated. It may be true that not as many have followed in his footsteps, as for example with Lester Young, but I still consider him one of the absolute greats. His sound fit anything; it was a universal sound. He based his playing on his sound, and he could hear everything, and followed the rhythm section. It was so very pretty, and contained so much.[57]

During long periods of 1972, Ben drank excessively, and consequently he and Birgit Nordtorp did not see each other very often. This may very well have been more of a problem for Ben than for Nordtorp, as he could have used her care. Niels-Henning Ørsted Pedersen offers an opinion on why so many jazz musicians drink. "The risk taken in a career like Ben's, Dexter Gordon's, and many others', is that they bare their emotions, and the audience expects them to do so," he explains.

> But by doing so, they reveal themselves for good and for bad. We receive the gift of presence, and are given the fantastic opportunity to experience someone with heartfelt emotions, and the sense that these are important to share. But at the same time, we have been allowed to see how much they have revealed. I also think that people like Ben were very lonesome, so how could he react? To pad the bared emotions again, they drank too much. Dexter had a heroin problem, Ben had a liquor problem. But put in context with what came out of their production, it's hard to see just how big a problem it was. Afterwards it could be said that apparently that was the price. Very few saxophonists have ever told as intimate a story as Ben did in a tune like *Danny Boy*. But apparently it was so close, in effect, to taking off your pants, that it almost embarrasses you, and then you have to hide a little afterwards, because you're a cool cat anyway. It's that double nature.
>
> Ben, Dexter Gordon, Bill Evans, and Chet Baker have given us a lot of things that cost them a lot in their personal lives. But don't think they were martyrs, because they made the choice themselves. Whenever I've—without comparing myself to them—told a story, as I felt it, and tried to get all the way down to the mundane thoughts which also are there, then it's hard to walk off stage afterwards and say, "Well hello there old chap, how are you?" because you have just been in a whole other place. I think I recognize that in all of those people.[58]

"Sometimes Ben would be so touched by his own playing that he cried," Ørsted Pedersen goes on.

> There is a wonderful story, which Niels Jørgen Steen can confirm. We were booked with the Danish Radio Concert Orchestra and the Radio Choir in Tivoli's concert hall, and Niels Jørgen Steen

was the conductor. The choir members are semiprofessionals; they can't practice in the daytime when they're at work, so they couldn't come until the late rehearsal. Ben didn't know about the choir. He was the soloist and sat in the front. In the afternoon, we practiced with the orchestra, and it was lovely, just fine. There was one place where the choir was going to come in, but Ben didn't know about it, so when we got to the concert, and the choir had arrived, they began singing. The very second they began to sing, Ben dropped the saxophone out of his mouth and began to cry, because it sounded so beautiful. That says a little about how close he was to the edge when he played. He protected himself by being gruff and a cool guy, but anybody who's heard him play knows that he had a very soft spot deep down, and at the same time, he could play very extroverted and growling. Allan Botschinsky described him very well by comparing him to a bull sniffing flowers, like Ferdinand the Bull.

"I was a journalist, and I didn't have to go to work until twelve or one in the afternoon," Wolsgaard-Iversen recalls,

and I would get back home around midnight, so Ben's and mine hours were more or less parallel. So I was also one of the people he could call. And that resulted in many long conversations. Sometimes he would call up and say, "Listen to this music!" and then he'd move the phone over to his record player and play Carl Nielsen's *Espansiva* conducted by Bernstein. And he wouldn't return to the phone until the record was over! I didn't get the chance to say that I knew it. No, he wanted me to hear *Espansiva* from beginning to end! Afterwards he would say, "It's fantastic. He can really write. Does Nielsen live here in Copenhagen, is he still alive?" "No, Ben, that's Carl Nielsen. He died years ago!" "Oh, what a shame. Oh! *Carl* Nielsen!" Then he knew who it was, but the record cover only said Nielsen.

Ben was friends with grocers, wholesalers, smugglers, cab drivers, counts, and barons. People waved to him when he walked down the street because he had been on television. He would fascinate people and he could get them to do anything for him. "Oh could you please help me with this . . ." He had a very winning personality, and women loved that old, fat man. He had a very good reputation.[59]

In the third week of April 1972, Johnny Griffin was booked at the Montmartre, and Ben and Dexter Gordon showed up. Griffin remembered that the evening proved very touching for him. "Ben and Dex were sitting at the bar, so naturally I pulled out my 'crips' [personal favorite musical tricks]. Ben came up to the bandstand and politely said, 'Let me see your horn, Itty Bitty.' 'Frog' played his butt off, and got the same sound from my horn as he does from his own! And to top it off, Dexter sat in the next set, used my horn and broke up the house. I was fit to be tied!"[60]

In early May, Ben took his first and only trip to Austria to play in Vienna with the amateur band Printer's Jazzband, quite a good mainstream band. Ben played with sparkle and warmth, and although he falls back on routine phrases in the fast *Sunday,* the quick pace does not seem to bother him. In Neal Hefti's slow blues *After Supper,* he plays two fine, homogenous, and well-rounded choruses, and in *Li'l Darling* his contribution is in fine accord with the gentle mood of the tune. After a concert in Germany, he traveled on to the Netherlands and a week's tour with Tete Montoliu's Trio. Ben was in fine form here as well. Bert Vuijsje reviewed the concert in Haarlem, and wrote that even though Ben was sixty-three, "There were absolutely no signs of old age at last night's concert. Webster played the repertoire with which he feels confident, with the élan of someone twenty years younger. As always, his ballad interpretations were irresistibly sensual, but he was also in great shape in the fast tunes—he ploughed through his choruses energetically with virile, growling sounds."[61]

Indeed, Webster sounds at his best on the recordings from Haarlem and Leiden, although he keeps his solos short. In Haarlem, he plays up a storm on *Sunday* and *In a Mellotone,* in a fantastic display of energy and intensity, and his interpretation of *I Got It Bad* is unbelievably beautiful, concluding on such a gentle and sensitive high note to be almost supernatural.

In late May, Ben was in Paris to play at the Jazz Festival d'Orly accompanied by George Arvanitas's trio. The concert was successful beyond all expectations. A reviewer wrote, "Finally Ben Webster entered the stage, unsure on his feet and out of breath. He sat down to play. But all this disappeared the moment he lifted the instrument to his lips." After a short description of his style, the review concludes, "Never before has old Ben played as sparklingly in France."[62]

While in Paris, on June 5, he recorded the album *Autumn Leaves* with George Arvanitas's trio, but this album is a disappointment. Although Arvanitas is a fine and inventive pianist, his and Ben's contributions are hampered by the somewhat rigid bassist who never manages to generate a swing in conjunction with the drummer. The best track is *Prelude to a Kiss,* played in duet with Arvanitas, but here the music is marred by poor recording technique. Ben's saxophone is placed in the background where it is almost impossible to hear his otherwise lovely interpretation of Ellington's tune. The ballad *You Better Go Now* is given a dreamy, gentle treatment that suits the tune, and Ben is heartfelt and involved on his own *Hal Blues,* but other than that, Ben's commitment is lacking.

The summer of 1972 brought more festivals, among others the Åhus Jazzfestival in southern Sweden on July 13, and the Pescara Jazz Festival in Italy later in the month. In Åhus, Ben was reunited with Clark Terry, and they played an excellent concert together accompanied by Kenny Drew, Red Mitchell, and American drummer Bobby Brooks, a resident of Copenhagen at the time. "The quintet played only Ellington music, an idea that was just as logical as it was popular," wrote *Orkester Journalen.* "Ben Webster was in a good mood, and played like the master he is on the playground of father Duke."[63]

Ben took the train directly to Italy and the Fourth International Jazz Festival in Pescara. He was booked on the festival's last evening, but when he failed to show up on time, plans were made to conclude the festival without him. Suddenly, when the curtain was about to fall and the audience were on their feet, the saxophonist came out from the backdrop. "And so he supplied an unexpected and triumphant finale, in which musicians fought to play, later returning to the Hotel Esplanade, where Ben's pay, which Mingus had received for playing instead of him, was presented to him in an atmosphere of 'embrassons nous,' resulting in everyone playing for the pleasure of one and all until the sun was high on the horizon."[64]

On the train to Italy, Ben traveled with the thirty-year-old Swedish vocalist Marlene Widmark, whom he had met the previous year, and she had been with him at the festival in Åhus as well. She moved in with Ben for a while, and filled in some of the vacuum left by Birgit Nordtorp in periods around this time. "The first time I met Ben Webster, he was playing with pianist Lars Sjösten in Stampen in Stockholm, and he was very tired," Widmark recalls. "So Sjösten said to me, 'Marlene, how about singing a song?' I did so, and it made Ben so happy, that he was recharged and played wonderfully all night. Since that day, we became friends for life, and he called me 'Benjamina.' I worked with him many times and accompanied him around Europe. It was wonderful to sing with Ben, because he made you feel so relaxed. He played like a warm wind. He could color the great songs and give them emotions that helped the music captivate you. He was a man of surprises, but he was exceptionally good to me in all ways."[65]

In recent years the Jazzhus Montmartre had changed its policy toward fewer long bookings. For Ben, this meant that he was offered more one-nighters, on which he usually was accompanied by pianist Ole Kock Hansen's trio with Bo Stief and Alex Riel, or Horace Parlan's trio with Hugo Rasmussen and the American drummer Jual Curtis. When not touring abroad, he usually played one night a week on a weekday. From one such evening that summer, one could read the following. "Despite Webster's age, his music is as alive as ever—and with a continuously growing authority. His absolute speciality is his ballads. Here, he is the unsurpassed interpreter, and his style is appreciated most—a slightly woolly tone with air on the side. At his performance Thursday, Webster was outstanding in the fast tempi as well, with a sharp and searing tone."[66]

Upon his return from Italy, Ben played a couple of jobs in the Jazzhus Montmartre, before traveling by train through central Europe again later in August. This time he was bound for Switzerland and a short tour with Clark Terry. Terry recalls, "Every time I would go to Europe I would see Frog. Many times we would change planes in Copenhagen Airport, so every time I had a big changeover I would call him and tell him to come out for a couple of hours, and he would jump in a taxi and come out to me. We loved to play together, and we did a little tour in Switzerland with the piano player Henri Chaix."[67] A review from the concert in Baden confirms that this, too, was a musically fruitful period for Ben.[68]

Back in Copenhagen, Ben was called in for sessions with the rock group Savage Rose. Three titles were recorded on September 25 and 26, the very beautiful ballad *What Do You Do Now,* given a superb interpretation by vocalist Anisette Koppel and supplied with a very compatible obbligato by Ben, and *Your Gift* and *The Dreamland,* on which Ben's obbligato likewise suits the song beautifully. His solo here is nice, but somewhat restrained.

The fall of 1972 brought on more tours. For a week around October 1, he visited various towns in southern Norway, and in early November, he was in Paris for another recording with Arvanitas, followed by a new visit to Switzerland. This time the second horn was Dexter Gordon, replacing Benny Carter, who was sick with the flu, and had caught a return flight to Los Angeles immediately after landing in Copenhagen's airport.

Soundwise, the recording with Arvanitas and his trio was much better this time. The session took place at La Maison de la Radio (the Radio Building) on November 4, 1972, with a live audience, and the recordings were later issued as *Ben Webster Live in Paris.* There are no surprises in the repertoire, and Ben plays fine, too. Of course, the finest moments are to be found in the two ballads *Old Folks* and *My Romance,* both given heartfelt interpretations, while *Perdido* offers vigorous playing. His two improvised choruses are filled with shakes, altissimo notes, and short, florid figures played rhythmically free, sometimes ending with an accentuation right on the beat.

A week before this tour, on October 29, the Newport Jazz Festival In Europe visited Tagskægget in Århus as the only Danish concert. Among the acts were Jimmy Smith, the Cannonball Adderley Quintet, the Elvin Jones Quartet, the Charles Mingus Sextet, the Giants of Jazz, fronted by Dizzy Gillespie, Kai Winding, and Sonny Stitt, and the Dave Brubeck Quartet with Gerry Mulligan as an added attraction. Ben was booked with Thomas Clausen, Bo Stief, and Alex Riel, and once again he was in great form. Bo Stief recalls the event clearly, because it was the first time he heard many of the big names. "It was absolutely fantastic," he remembers.

Ben played in the evening, and all the big names hung out and came to hear Ben, whom they respected greatly. Elvin Jones, who had never played with Ben before, sat in, and he played very carefully, no rumble and thunder, but very humble and respectful. We played *Come Rain or Come Shine,* which Thomas knew in Bill Evans's arrangement with a lot of exiting changes. And Ben wasn't much of a theoretician; he played everything by ear, he had amazing ears. But I never will forget that because he didn't play one note that sounded wrong in the context of Thomas's doctorate on how to harmonize *Come Rain or Come Shine.* And afterwards he said that it had been fun playing it again, because he hadn't played it in twenty-five years! It just shows his confident approach to his horn and to playing.[69]

A concert in Baden, Switzerland, on November 11, where Ben was teamed with Dexter Gordon, was recorded for the radio, and they performed three tunes together, *Perdido, Indiana,* and *In a Mellotone.* According to reviewers, Ben was in splendid form for this concert as well.[70] The music is still excellent; the drive, elasticity, and enthusiasm of the rhythm section, made up of Kenny Drew, Bo Stief, and Ed Thigpen, egged the two soloists on to great things. Ben builds his solos well, never falling through even in fast tempi; indeed, he engages in several smoking, sharp chases with Thigpen. He plays more inspired and emotionally than usual in the improvisations in the concluding choruses of *How Long Has This Been Going On?* and *My Romance.* The positive reviews were definitely well deserved.

After the job in Switzerland with Dexter Gordon, Ben continued to Barcelona in Spain, where he had a job and a recording session at the end of November with Tete Montoliu's trio. On the long train ride, Ben had a good time with a couple of his fellow passengers, and he was so drunk and noisy at the Spanish border that the authorities felt forced to take him off the train and detain him. He finally arrived the day after the job, and spent the interim until the recording session sightseeing. He used his eight-millimeter movie camera during a visit to the wonderful botanical garden Marimurta in Blanes on the Mediterranean coast a little north of Barcelona.

The album *Gentle Ben* was recorded in Barcelona on November 28, 1972. Once again, the rhythm section is not quite to Ben's liking. Although Montoliu holds back, refraining from steamrolling the soloist with his outstanding technique, the bassist and drummer are of the average European standard of the day, and their lack of drive is not inspiring to Ben. Consequently, his playing never rises above solid, and contains many standard phrases, as heard on the opening track, *Ben's Blues,* identical with *Go Home. My Nephew Bent* is a blues in B-flat minor taken at a medium slow tempo, in which Ben holds back and plays but a short solo. The concluding track, *Barcelona Shout,* is a twin of *Randle's Island,* and Ben is a little more involved here. However, as may be expected, the best details are in the ballads, *How Long Has This Been Going On?, Don't Blame Me,* and *The Man I Love,* although even they lack the depth he had demonstrated previously.

On his way back to Copenhagen from Spain, Ben stopped off in Hannover in Germany to play a concert on December 14 with Oscar Peterson's Trio with Niels-Henning Ørsted Pedersen and Tony Inzalaco. It was a moving and musically very satisfying reunion with Peterson. Fortunately, it was filmed. The footage shows a trio in extremely good form, and a no less effective Ben, despite the fact that he relies on many routine phrases and looks very tired when not playing. However, his weariness seems to disappear when he plays, and he expresses himself sharply, with bite and no unsteadiness in the fast *Sunday* and *Cotton Tail,* whereas his romantic and gentle side is expressed beautifully and fully in *I Got It Bad and That Ain't Good* and *Come Sunday.*

After concerts with the rock group Savage Rose on January 11 and 12, 1973, at Jazzhus Montmartre, Ben left for a two-week tour of Belgium, the Netherlands and Germany. In Belgium he met Milt Buckner for the last time. "He did a concert on January 29 in Antwerp with Michael Silva and Wild Bill Davis, for the Hot Club of Antwerp," says Buckner. "So we went, we sat up there. Wild Bill cooperated great with Ben. In the intermission we had some chicken and bread pudding. This was a funny night, because Ben was talking quite a bit and he ate up half that chicken. After the concert we went to some bar and we all sat in that little dining-room light and Wild Bill and Ben Webster got to talk about that time with Duke Ellington. And that was the funniest thing you ever heard."[71]

Ben was not quite as sharp and magnificent in Antwerp as he had otherwise been in recent months, because he lacked that last inspirational spark. At the following concerts he was accompanied by pianist Irv Rochlin's trio. Once again the bite was back, and his playing had more rhythmic attack and energy in the fast tunes, while the ballads were given more deeply felt interpretations.

Ben's mood was good during the tour. On recordings from Downtown in Düsseldorf in Germany, he is heard making a show of counting in by singing and counting at the same time, and he has enough surplus energy to sing along with Rochlin's solos. He had good reason to be satisfied with the rhythm section, which swings very well.

He spent the rest of February in Denmark, and then he set out with Dexter Gordon and Marlene Widmark for a tour of the Netherlands. Widmark remembers the Dutch tour. In Amsterdam, she sang with Ben at a jazz club, and recalls that one of his friends from Canada was there, and Ben stood up and played like a god.[72]

During this tour, Ben once again played as if his life depended on it. Gordon's presence is a positive influence on Ben, and they performed a couple of tunes together at the end of each evening, among them an extremely inspired *Lover Come Back to Me* and *Body and Soul* at the concert in Naaldwijk, which was privately recorded. Ben interprets *Body and Soul* with a great deal of tenderness before Gordon takes over. During Gordon's solo, the rhythm section changes over to the more advanced chords Gordon used when he recorded the tune for *The Panther,* which didn't appeal to Ben. In the beginning of the tour he concealed his displeasure, but on the last evening he scolded Gordon, accusing him of ruining the tune with the wrong chords. Gordon had not intended to insult Ben in any way, and felt bad about it. But for weeks afterward, whenever they met in the Jazzhus Montmartre, Ben would turn his back to Gordon and refuse to speak to him, regardless of how much Gordon tried to make contact. One evening, Gordon was sitting at the bar in the Montmartre, thinking that his and Ben's more than thirty-year friendship had ended, when Ben came in and threw a small box in his direction. It was a gold Cartier cigarette lighter, and he delivered it with the words, "But don't you ever do that again!"

At this time, at the urging of his physician, Dr. Backer, Ben had been off liquor for several months. The change led to improvements in his playing. Ben regained his presence and vitality, ideas and energy. Jesper Thilo says, "I believe that right up to the end, he could play 100 percent as well as when he was thirty to thirty-five. If only he was sober, there were no problems, even when I saw him lose his false teeth, which he was always complaining about. 'Arh,' he'd say and look deep into my eyes, 'never get old!' At the time he was around sixty, which isn't very old today, but he felt old. He didn't like getting old, because he had problems walking, and had to use a cane."[73]

Ben performed in Stockholm at Stampen's Fifth anniversary, a two-day celebration. He played on the first evening, March 19, with trumpeter Arne Ryskog, Teddy Wilson, Sture Nordin, and Ed Thigpen. Once again, Ben was in the mood for playing, if not quite as forcefully as during the previous concerts. On *I Cover the Waterfront*, Marlene Widmark sang with the group accompanied by Ben's beautiful obbligato, and Ben's following solo is a gem of lyrical phrasing. Afterward, a critic wrote, "Ben Webster was in better form than for a long time, completely sober, and consequently he occasionally sounded as he did in his heyday."[74]

The day after the job at Stampen, he took the train back to Copenhagen for a job at the Jazzhus Montmartre. There are various stories affiliated with his many jobs at this Copenhagen venue; Bent Kauling tells the following: "One evening some Germans were sitting right in front of Ben, talking constantly. Finally, he bent forward toward them and asked—and he could be extremely polite—'Have we played too loud?' And one of the Germans replied 'Yes!' Ben began howling with laughter. He thought that was hilarious."[75]

At another time, during one of Yusef Lateef's booking at the Jazzhus Montmartre, Ben showed up, and the two of them started talking about John Coltrane. Ben had listened to Coltrane quite a bit, and he felt sure that his playing was based on certain thoughts and ideas, but he could not quite figure out what they were. Lateef, who also knew Coltrane well, and had discussed theory with him, brought his saxophone out to the kitchen and demonstrated for Ben what Coltrane had practiced and figured out. "And sure enough," Ben said later to Hans Nymand, "there were certain exact ideas pertaining to how he wanted his music."[76]

Nils Winther from the SteepleChase label recorded many of

Ben's concerts at Jazzhus Montmartre that year, and they confirm his good form. There are stirring versions of *Willow Weep for Me* and *Old Folks*, on which his interpretations are magnificent, and in many of the fast tunes he holds on, playing cogently with many special rhythmical details in the relatively short phrases, ensuring that *Exactly Like You, Sunday, Set Call*, and *I Got Rhythm* swing splendidly. Many of the phrases are taken from his routine vocabulary, but they build a growing intensity to create a good story.

On March 27, Ben turned sixty-four, and the evening found him once again at the Jazzhus Montmartre. He had celebrated the day in his apartment earlier on. He received birthday cards from many of his friends and business connections, among them Peter Max Hansen from Tagskægget in Århus and Papa Bue's Viking Jazzband. Mule also sent him a card. Bent Kauling paid him a surprise visit, bringing him a gift Ben would never forget.

"I remember one of Ben's many stories," Kauling says.

There was this filthy rich lady who lived some place in the Deep South. She had read that a young local artist from the very same town had held a show in New York, and was praised highly as the new upcoming talent. So when he returns home, she calls him up and says, "Listen here, young man. I am a filthy rich lady, directly descended from General Custer, and in my dining room, there is a wall. Now on that wall there is a motif already, but I want you to cover it with your artistic interpretation of my great grandfather's last thoughts right before the battle at Little Big Horn. I am not at home, because I am going on a very expensive cruise around the world. But just pick up the key from the gardener." She goes on her cruise and returns six months later. When she opens the door to her dining room, she sees a picture of General Custer with his long blonde hair, a cow with a halo, and a whole bunch of Indians lying around screwing. She calls up the artist, somewhat piqued, and says, "Will you please come over here immediately and explain yourself!" And he tells her that Custer is standing there thinking, "Holy Cow! Where do all these fucking Indians come from!"

He told this story several times, so for his last birthday I gave him a big surprise. I had one of my friends, the painter Palle Rosenkrantz, paint a picture of what the wall might have looked like. So, I get up to Ben's place with the painting all wrapped up, and I leave it in the front hall and go in to say happy birthday. And then I tell him that I want to tell a story. I begin to tell Ben's story, the way he used to, and he interrupts me asking, "You been drinking?" "No, no, Ben," I answer and go on with the story. Ben stared at me, because I hadn't given him a present, and he couldn't understand that, because I would always bring a present. He just sat there, shaking his head, and I finish the story, and when I get to the place where the lady steps into the dining room, I go out to the front hall and get the painting. Ben unwraps it, and then he breaks up. He actually falls off his chair sobbing with laughter, and the other visitors laugh as well. Ben loved the painting and hung it in the place of honor. Afterwards, he called all his friends in New York and told them that his "nephew," as he called me, had gone crazy.[77]

In May, Benny Carter came to Denmark again, and as if that was not enough, he took Harry "Sweets" Edison along. Arnvid Meyer's orchestra toured Denmark from May 21 to May 31 with Carter, Edison, and Ben, and Richard Boone joined them for some of the jobs. Ben was again accompanied by Marlene Widmark. They traveled on their own, and for some reason Ben never showed up for the job in Skive. "Benny Carter couldn't take it," says Arnvid Meyer. "He was furious. But we continued the tour, and in Ålborg Ben showed up on his own. Suddenly he was there. I remember that after we had played a few tunes, Ben played a feature tune, and it was so emotional that we had tears rolling down our cheeks. We never chided him again. That was the sensitive Ben."[78]

Bent Kauling says of the first evening in Copenhagen that "it was in *Willow Weep for Me* that Ben demonstrated that he is a greater jazz artist than the other two. He may not be in as good physical shape, he gets out of breath, and his fingers don't always move fast enough, but he has something that lifts him above the other two."[79]

From the concert at the Holbæk Jazzklub on May 22, Ben's interpretation of *How Long Has This Been Going On?* is lovely with many emotional details in the last chorus, while *Sometimes I'm Happy* and *Keester Parade* find him playing call-and-response with himself in dynamically varied phrases.

After the tour, Ben took a train to the Netherlands, where he was to guest with the Metropole Orchestra at Breda Jazz Festival. He performed a very beautiful *That's All,* playing his last chorus an octave higher to produce an extremely moving effect, also due to his supple phrasing and divine sound, placed nice and clear in the recording.

In late July he had occasion to meet old friends again. On his way to the Molde Jazz Festival, pianist Eubie Blake stopped over in Copenhagen, where a television special was planned. Bassist Hugo Rasmussen was working elsewhere in the TV building that day, and he recalls,

> In a break I went over to the studio to watch. Then suddenly Ben came in because he wanted to say hello to Eubie, too. Pretty soon they took a break, and when Blake heard that Ben was there, he jumped up and ran down the stairs to Ben, who was sitting there with his cane. Right away, they started to talk about boxing, and they talked about all the old champions, going further and further back in time. Finally they were back at the turn of the century, when Eubie suddenly says, "Oh but that's long before you were born. You don't remember shit about that. Oh well, I have to play!" And he jumps up again. At the time, he was ninety, and Ben was around sixty, and he just sat there watching a man 50 percent his senior jump around like a gazelle, and he began crying and crying and said, "What is this?"[80]

"When Eubie Blake came, Ben acted like a schoolboy," Birgit Nordtorp recalls. "Blake and his wife lived at the Globetrotter Hotel, and we were invited out there for lunch. Ben was in a really good mood, and Blake talked and talked, while Ben just sat there listening like a schoolboy. He had this respect for old people, and Blake was ninety. Of course they spoke mainly about music and musicians, and I remember that they talked about Ellington at one point, and Blake asked Ben if that guy Ellington could play any piano, and naturally Ben confirmed that, yes, he did."[81]

A couple of days later, Clark Terry arrived in Copenhagen with his big band to perform two concerts at Jazzhus Montmartre, and naturally Ben showed up to see his old friends. "I was doing a tour with Clark Terry's Big Band," says Horace Parlan, "and we did a concert at the old Montmartre when Ben just walked in with his horn and came up. Ernie Wilkins had written an arrangement of the Duke Ellington tune called *All Too Soon*, and it was one of Ben's favorites. So he took out his horn and joined the band and played that number. It was incredible. I remember there were tears in people's eyes, and the whole room got totally quiet. It was quite an experience. I had a small cassette recorder, but I was so wrapped up in the way he was playing that I forgot to turn it on!"[82]

Clark Terry also has special memories of the event. Independently of Parlan, he too emphasizes this evening for Ben's emotional playing. "Frog came down to the gig and we coaxed him to sitting in. We had a beautiful arrangement of *All Too Soon*, and he played it so beautifully, and he also played *Cotton Tail*. I am still asking around for people who might have a tape of that. The guys in the band used to love Copenhagen so much. The ladies in Copenhagen are the most soulful people in the world, and the guys were fortunate enough to meet charming young ladies. So we used to call Copenhagen 'Koppin' Heaven'!"[83]

A month later, from his home in Bayside, N.Y., Terry wrote this little note to Ben, thanking him for the time in Copenhagen.[84] Ben received the letter just before leaving Copenhagen on what was to be his last tour.

> 8/24/73
>
> FAV'RIN'
>
> Made it back to the jungle O.K. Miss 'Koppin' Heaven' already!
>
> It sure was a gas to get to hang out with you for a while.
>
> Hope it's not too long before I get back over there again.
>
> Take care, Frog, and don't forget to stick some pork chops into your stomach every now and then.
>
> Give my best to Birritt (if that's the correct spelling).
>
> > Take care!!
> >
> > Love
> >
> > Clark Terry
> >
> > FAV'RIN'

In mid-August, Jimmy Rowles dropped by for an unannounced visit. He was touring Europe with Carmen McRae, and as the tour did not reach Denmark, Rowles begged leave for a few days in order to visit Ben.

"So there we are with a piano and pictures of my family all lined up, kids and everything," Rowles said.

> He was sitting in his chair and said, "S.H. [Shit House, their nickname for each other], play me that song that I like." It was *What Are You Doing The Rest Of Your Life.* I played it for him. I love that song. Then Ben said to me, "Give me an intro." I asked him, "Hey, Frog, play *Someone To Watch Over Me.*" I loved him to play that. Boy, he grabbed Betsy and played that sunuvabitch. Another one I used to make him play was *Danny Boy* in the key of D. It could make you cry, he loved Irish tunes. *Melancholy Baby,* oh, that's another one I loved to hear him play. He used to make me play the verse. He could never remember it.
>
> His wife [actually Birgit Nordtorp] came back the day I left, and all I remember is that Ben was in bad shape at the last. I didn't think Ben was going to go. The doctor was on his way over when I left. When I had to leave to meet Carmen, Ben hung out the window, still in his shorts, huge shoulders and chest bare, and waved and waved, and kept saying, "Come back, S.H. Come back and see me soon."[85]

Regardless of the joy they found in each other's company, the visit was a disaster for Ben. Until then, he had been on the wagon, and Birgit Nordtorp had arranged that he get vitamin B injections to repair some of the damage caused to his liver over the years. Rowles brought a lot of liquor with him, and neither was sober during his visit. Ben could not say no to his old friend, but he was in no condition for excessive drinking, and he never quite got over the physical regression. The last year had likewise seen a weakening of his mobility, and his overall physical condition was very bad. Bent Kauling and Birgit Nordtorp took Ben for a trip to the Copenhagen Zoo one summer's day, but he had so much trouble walking that he "walked from the main entrance to the lions, and had to sit down," remembers Kauling. "Then we went to see the monkeys, but after that he could walk no more, and finally we went home."[86]

"On a personal level, what I saw in his life, he was lonely and unhappy," says Ed Thigpen.

> In many ways he was a grown man, but he was still a child. A child of God, a child of his mama, a child of Ellington, and a child of the music, and in some cases lonely and unhappy. He grieved for the loss of the contact of older musicians, his friends and associations. I know, because I've seen it happen. When he left Ellington, he never left Ellington in spirit. The same happened with Jo Jones. He never left Basie and Walter Page in spirit. That was a family, it was a whole soul. But when you are not there physically, you miss it forever. They grew up in another time when people really kept in touch with one another over the years and had life experience together. Ben missed that very much, he really did. He didn't have that many to talk with anymore, and that was sad. Plus he was in another country; he was not in his homeland. But what do you do in your homeland when they didn't accept your work, your music? The acceptance and the respect they were getting here they didn't get at home. When I saw Ben at his apartment with those eyes, sleepy eyes, there was a certain sadness which I understand. He lived in a different time. But Denmark was good for him, though, because people was so open and he was working.[87]

On September 2, Birgit Nordtorp saw him off from Copenhagen's Central Station. Ben was on his way to a tour of Holland and Germany. The first stop was a concert in Leiden on September 6. Ben arrived in Amsterdam in plenty of time, and on the day of the first concert, he visited an exhibition of Kwint's paintings with Kwint, his wife Rens, and Johan van der Keuken. That evening, they drove in Kwint's car to Leiden, where Ben was to play at the Café Sociëteit De Twee Spieghels, a student hangout. Ben was accompanied by Irv Rochlin's Trio, and the evening was recorded. He played very emotionally this evening, occasionally almost furiously in the up-tempo tunes, *Pennies from Heaven, I Got Rhythm, Sunday, Just You, Just Me,* and *How High The Moon,* using many dynamic devices. It is as if he senses that this is to be his last performance. He interprets *My Romance* and *For All We Know* gently, dreamingly, and with extreme relaxation. But the evening was atypical because these were the only ballads. The concert was a physical and emotional exertion for Ben; toward the end he was exhausted, and did not even have the energy to play the final chorus of *Straight, No Chaser,* the last tune of the evening. His solo is very emotional and swings enormously, built up of short phrases and outbursts.

After the last tune, and following the applause, Ben addresses the audience, "Thank you! Now I will say to all of you youngsters what I heard when I was a kid from an old-timer. He said, 'Son, you're young and growing and I'm old and going. So have your fun while you can.' I repeat, you're young and growing and I'm old and going. So have your fun while you can."

The young audience seems to understand him, and they applaud. However, they have no way of knowing just how prophetic his short speech would be.

After the job, Kwint drove Ben through a foggy landscape to Hotel De Haas in Amsterdam. During the drive, Ben's condition worsened. He hardly sensed where he was, and upon their arrival at the hotel, he had to be helped up to his room. During the night, he became more ill; it took all his strength to call Birgit Nordtorp at noon the next day. "The telephone made funny fumbling noises," she says. "I knew it was him, and I thought he was drunk and got angry, saying we had tried so hard to keep him on the wagon, we gave him vitamin injections, etc. Afterwards, I was sorry I had talked like that to him."[88]

Later that afternoon, Kwint and Rens came by the hotel to visit Ben and found him sprawled out on the bed with one leg over the edge. The telephone was off the hook, and he could only mumble a few unintelligible sounds. While Rens called doctors and hospitals for help, Kwint took "Ol' Betsy" with him, and went out to cancel the evening's concert in Cologne. When finally, after hours of waiting, a doctor arrived, he immediately called an ambulance. Ben was admitted to Lucas Hospital, where he was examined and given the diagnosis of coronary thrombosis. He lost consciousness the same day and did not wake up until a couple of days later, Monday, September 10.

By this time, news had reached Birgit Nordtorp that Ben had been hospitalized, and she hurried to Amsterdam. "Ben could hardly speak when I saw him that afternoon in the hospital room. I had put on the red suit he gave me in London, and when he saw me in it, he said, 'Nørre Søgade' [where Ben had his apartment]. That was just about all he could say, and it was very moving for me."[89]

In Amsterdam, Nordtorp stayed with the Kwints. Ben's condition bettered slightly over the next week, but one side of his body was still paralyzed, and he had trouble speaking. He also had trouble breathing deeply, and Thursday morning, September 20, at 11:30 A.M., with Nordtorp by his side, he died of the ensuing pneumonia. Pianist Billy Moore, who lived in Copenhagen at the time, had helped Ben out during the last few years, checking his bookings, and making sure that he received royalty money due to him. Now he traveled to Amsterdam to help take care of things.

Ben lay in state at the hospital for friends and musicians to say their farewells, after which he was flown to Copenhagen. "I didn't have much say about the practical affairs after Ben died," says Nordtorp. "Ben hated flying, so we had discussed that his last trip shouldn't be by plane. I don't remember if it was a financial thing or what, but in the end he was put on a plane home. The idea was for him to be on the same plane as me, but as it turned out, he came on a later flight. So I waited in the airport, because I thought I had better be there when the coffin arrived."[90]

"By the time I got home with Ben's coffin and walked into his apartment, mattresses, everything were turned inside out, because they had been looking for a will," Nordtorp continues.

> Billy Moore took the lead, and he found someone to clean out the apartment, and I just had to say so if there was anything I wanted. But I only set foot in the apartment one last time, and that was for an auction they held one afternoon over some of his things. The things they didn't sell went on to an auctioneer.
>
> I hadn't expected Ben to die that early. I had expected him to live to be an old man, because his mother and aunt had been very old when they died, so naturally I expected him to as well.
>
> Steven Kwint visited Ben once, and he came to me, saying that he would like to inherit Ben's horn. Ben was sleeping, and when we were alone, I told him what Steven had asked. Ben said that in

that case, he'd better write it on the saxophone case, and so it turned out that Steven got the horn when Ben died. That was fine with me, but I'm not sure Billy Moore and everyone else back in Denmark were too happy about it.[91]

The ever faithful Mule had heard of Ben's death, and was already in Copenhagen when Nordtorp returned from Amsterdam. She attended the funeral at Bispebjerg Church on September 28. Priest and author Johannes Møllehave held the service, and on the organ Kenny Drew played *All Too Soon, Chelsea Bridge,* and *Come Sunday,* a few of Ben's favorite ballads, which he had given his most deeply felt and powerful interpretations. In his memorial speech, Møllehave said, in part,

> Ben Webster—I can see him now with his hat tilted back with the baggy skin beneath his eyes as puffed as his cheeks, his eyes closed, and the funny leak of breath often oozing out beside Betsy's mouthpiece, joining the conversation.
>
> I see him as the image of an oppressed people. A people to whom the freedom of expression in any other ways than music, songs, drums, horns has not been granted. Imagine a man who, submitting to society, says, "Well that's a deal, then—I am not allowed to speak freely, not allowed to say whatever occurs to me, not allowed to speak my mind. For people like me, there's no freedom of speech, only the freedom of blowing." Imagine such a man transforming his fortunes into expressions more perfect than those of any language. Expressions in which the happily inspired breath passing through the tenor sax and the leak of air oozing out beside the mouthpiece, "seen like the breath of a man breathing, now disappointed, now set free."[92]

After the service, there was a wake at the Jazzhus Montmartre, and later Ben's ashes were buried in the Assistens Churchyard in Nørrebro, not far from Ben's apartment, an old cemetery where Ben joined the company of many famous Danish people, including Hans Christian Andersen, Søren Kierkegaard, physicist Hans Christian Ørsted, and writer Martin Andersen Nexø. Several memorial concerts were held, the first on October 4, when Roy Eldridge was featured as a soloist with Arnvid Meyer's orchestra in the Jazzhus Montmartre.

Ben's personal belongings were spread to the wind, but when Kwint died unexpectedly in 1977, Ol' Betsy became the center of a true storm. In Denmark, the Ben Webster Foundation had been established in 1976 to administer the income from Ben's copyrights and record sales, as Ben had no heirs. Billy Moore, a member of the foundation board, wanted to bring Ol' Betsy back to Denmark, but in Holland, there were other plans. In 1979, after much lengthy correspondence, the saxophone went to the Institute of Jazz Studies at Rutgers University in Newark, New Jersey, which houses the world's largest collection of jazz as well as a museum exhibiting the instruments of many famous jazz musicians, including Lester Young's and Don Byas's saxophones, Roy Eldridge's and Miles Davis's trumpets, Eddie Condon's guitar, and many other objects. Ben had put Ol' Betsy in a new case, but Jesper Thilo was happy to donate the original case, and sent it off to its final destination.

Over the years, Ben's music has proved its great universal power, as it still appeals to people of all ages and ethnic heritage with its warmth, energy, and captivating sound. His sound was an inspiration and model for many of his instrumental colleagues, and its grandiose beauty has never been surpassed. John Coltrane was an avid admirer of Ben, and I will let his words conclude this chapter: "The sound of that tenor . . . I wish he'd show *me* how to make a sound like that."[93]

APPENDIX: BEN WEBSTER ON CD, DVD, AND VHS

The listings included here are not meant to be a complete survey, only a reference to recommended recordings. If the same recording can be found on both DVD and VHS, it is listed in the DVD section.

CD
A good survey of the first twenty years of Ben's career is the four-CD box Ben Webster, *Big Ben*, Properbox 37, covering 1931–51. Another fine set is the four-CD box Ben Webster, *Complete 1943–1951 Small Group Recordings*, Definitive DRCD 11189. None of the boxed sets includes alternative takes.

Here follows a list—mainly in chronological order—of CDs featuring Ben. If the title of the CD itself does not indicate the year of the performance, it is given in parentheses.

Blanche Calloway. *Blanche Calloway and Her Joy Boys*. Classics 783 (1931).

Bennie Moten. *Band Box Shuffle*. HEP CD1070/2 (1932).

Fletcher Henderson. *Fletcher Henderson and His Orchestra, 1932–1934*. Classics 535.

Fletcher Henderson. *Fletcher Henderson and His Orchestra, 1934–1937*. Classics 527.

Benny Carter. *The Complete Recordings, 1930–1940*. Vol. 1. Affinity CD AFS 1022–3 (1934).

Willie Bryant. *Willie Bryant and His Orchestra, 1935–1936*. Classics 768.

Billie Holiday. *Lady Day—the Complete Billie Holiday on Columbia, 1934–1944*. Columbia Legacy CXK 85470–11.

Cab Calloway. *Cab Calloway and His Orchestra, 1934–1937*. Classics 554.

Teddy Wilson. *His Piano and Orchestra, 1938–1939*. Jazz Unlimited JUCD 2068.

Teddy Wilson. *Teddy Wilson and His Orchestra, 1939–1940*. Classics 620.

Duke Ellington. *The Blanton-Webster Band*. RCA 74321 13181 2 (1940–42).

Duke Ellington. *The Duke at Fargo: Special Anniversary Edition*. Storyville STCD 8316/17 (1940).

Duke Ellington. *Jive Rhapsody*. Moon Records MCD084–2. Live recordings from June 12, 1940, February 16, June 2, and October 9, 1941.

Ray Nance. *When We're Alone: The Complete 1940–1949 Non-Ducal Violin Recordings*. AB Fable ABCD1–1014. Private recordings from autumn 1941, including Ben, Nance, and Blanton.

Duke Ellington. *At the Hurricane: Original 1943 Broadcasts.* Storyville 101 8359.

Duke Ellington. *The Duke Ellington Carnegie Hall Concerts, January 1943.* Prestige 2PCD 34004–2.

Duke Ellington. *At the Hollywood Empire: Original 1949 Transcriptions.* Storyville 101 8346.

Charlie Parker. *Charlie Parker Jam Session.* Verve 833 564–2 (1952).

Johnny Hodges. *The Complete 1941–1954 Small Group Sessions.* Vol. 4, *1952–53.* Blue Moon BMCD 1031.

Johnny Hodges. *The Complete 1941–1954 Small Group Sessions.* Vol. 5, *1954.* Blue Moon BMCD 1032.

Johnny Hodges. *The Complete Verve Johnny Hodges Small Group Sessions, 1956–1961.* Mosaic MD6–200.

Ben Webster. *Ben Webster and the Modern Jazz Quartet, 1953.* The Jazz Factory JFCD 22814.

Ben Webster. *King of the Tenors.* Verve 519 806–2 (1953).

Ben Webster. *Music for Loving: Ben Webster with Strings.* Verve 527 774–2 (1954–55). Sessions with music arranged by Billy Strayhorn and Ralph Burns.

Ella Fitzgerald. *Ella Fitzgerald Sings the Duke Ellington Songbook.* Verve 837 035–2 (1956).

Art Tatum. *Art Tatum—Ben Webster Quartet.* Pablo PACD-2405–431–2 (1956).

Buddy Bregman. *Swinging Kicks.* Verve 559 514–2 (1956).

Billie Holiday. *The Silver Collection.* Verve 823 449–2 (1956–57).

Billie Holiday. *Songs for Distingué Lovers.* Verve 539 056–2 (1957).

Woody Herman. *Songs for Hip Lovers.* Verve 559 872–2 (1957).

Red Norvo. *Just a Mood.* Bluebird RCA ND 86278 (1957).

Ben Webster. *The Soul of Ben Webster.* Verve 527 475–2. Sessions with Harry "Sweets" Edison, March 1957, and Johnny Hodges, April 1958.

Benny Carter. *Jazz Giant.* Contemporary OJCCD-167–2 (1957).

Bill Harris. *Bill Harris and Friends.* Fantasy OJCCD-083–2 (1957).

Ben Webster. *Soulville.* Verve 833 537–2 (1957).

Coleman Hawkins. *Coleman Hawkins Encounters Ben Webster.* Verve 521 427–2 (1957).

Rex Stewart and the Henderson All Stars. *The Big Reunion.* Fresh Sound FSR-CD 44 (1957).

Carmen McRae. *Birds of a Feather.* Verve 589 515–2 (1958).

Ben Webster. *Perdido.* Moon Records MCD 070–2 (1959–66).

Ben Webster. *Ben Webster and Associates.* Verve 543 302–2 (1959).

Jimmy Witherspoon. *The "Spoon" Concerts.* Fantasy FCD-24701–2 (1959).

Ben Webster. *Ben Webster Meets Oscar Peterson.* Verve 829 167–2 (1959).

Gerry Mulligan. *The Complete Gerry Mulligan Meets Ben Webster.* Verve 539 055–2 (1959).

Helen Humes. *Songs I Like to Sing.* Contemporary OJCCD-171–2 (1960).

Ben Webster. *At the Renaissance.* Contemporary OJCCD-390–2 (1960).

Ben Webster. *The Warm Moods.* Discovery DSCD 818 (1961). Session with strings and music arranged by Johnny Richards.

Richard "Groove" Holmes. *Groove.* Pacific Jazz CDP 7 94473–2 (1961).

Benny Carter. *BBB and Co.* Prestige Swingville OJCCD-758–2 (1962).

Ben Webster and Harry "Sweets" Edison. *Ben and Sweets*. CBS 460613–2 (1962).

Clark Terry Combo and Sextet. *Free and Oozy*. Blue Moon BMCD 3076 (1963).

Ben Webster and Joe Zawinul. *Soulmates*. Riverside OJCCD-109–2 (1963).

Ben Webster and Junior Mance Trio. *Live at Pio's*. Enja CD 2038–2 (1964).

Joe Williams. *Havin' a Good Time!* Hyena Records TMF 9331 (1964).

Ben Webster. *See You at the Fair*. Impulse GRP 11212 (1964).

Lionel Hampton. *You Better Know It!* Impulse GRP 11402 (1964).

Ben Webster. *At Ronnie Scott, 1964—The Punch*. Storyville 101 8373. Live recordings from London, December 11, 16, 18, and 31, 1964.

Ben Webster. *Plays Ballads—Plus 3 Bonus Tracks*. Storyville STCD 8319. Live recordings from London December 11 and 18, 1964, Copenhagen, April 18, 1968, Stockholm, August 13, 1969, Copenhagen, October 10 and November 11, 1969, April 18, 1970, and November 22, 1971.

Ben Webster. *At Montmartre*. Storyville 101 8347. Live recordings from January 21, 1965, and May 12, 1966.

Ben Webster. *At Jazzhus Montmartre*. Vol. 1. DA Music 874710–2. Live recordings from January 30 and 31, 1965.

Ben Webster. *At Jazzhus Montmartre*. Vol. 2. DA Music 874712–2. Live recordings from January 30 and 31, 1965.

Ben Webster. *In a Mellow Tone*. Ronnie Scott's Jazz House JACD 0071965. Live recordings from Ronnie Scott's Club May 14 and 15, 1965.

Ben Webster. *Black Lion Presents Ben Webster*. Black Lion BL 7607. Sessions from September 5, 13, 15, and 21, 1965, and April 27, 1967.

Duke Ellington. *Live at Jazz Festival at Cote D'Azur*. Verve 539 030–2 (1966).

Ben Webster. *Plays Duke Ellington—Plus 2 Bonus Tracks*. Storyville STCD 8320. Live recordings from Pori, July 1967, Copenhagen, October 10, November 11 and 27, 1969, November 22, 1971, and Åhus, July 13, 1972.

Ben Webster. *Ben and Buck*. Sackville SKCD 2–2037. Live recordings from Baden, June 3, 1967.

Ben Webster. *Ben and Buck: Live at Antwerp Jazz Club, Café Samson*. Storyville STCD 8245 (1967).

Ben Webster. *The Holland Sessions*. Blue Note 7243 8 57371 2. Sessions from January 12 and May 26, 1969, and live recordings from September 6, 1973.

Ben Webster and Dexter Gordon. *Tenor Titans*. Storyville STCD 8288. Live recordings from July 28, 1969, and March 23, 1972.

Ben Webster. *For the Guv'nor*. Affinity CD Charly 15. Sessions from May 26 and October 20, 1969.

Ben Webster. *Live at Stampen, Stockholm, 1969–1973*. Storyville 101 8361. Sessions from August 13, 1969, March 14, 1971, and March 19, 1973.

Ben Webster and Teddy Wilson. *Ben and Teddy*. Sackville SKCD 2–2056 (1970).

Ben Webster. *Wayfaring Webster*. Daybreak DB CHR 75023. Live recordings from September 2, 1970.

Ben Webster. *No Fool, No Fun: The Rehearsal Sessions*. Storyville STCD 8304 (1970).

Ben Webster. *With the Printers Jazzband*. RST Records RST-91529 (1972).

Ben Webster. *Live at the Haarlemse Jazz Club*. Limetree MCD 0040. Live recordings from May 9, 1972.

Ben Webster. *Autumn Leaves*. Futura Swing 06. Session from Paris, June 5, 1972.

Ben Webster. *Live in Paris 1972*. FCD 131. Session from November 4, 1972.
Ben Webster and Dexter Gordon. *Baden, 1972*. TCB Records 02102.
Ben Webster. *Gentle Ben*. Ensayo ENY-CD-3433. Session from November 28, 1972.

DVD

Duke Ellington. *The Centennial Collection*. Bluebird 82876 60091 2. This CD/DVD
   two-disk set contains eight of Ellington's short films, including the five from 1941
   with Ben Webster. Webster is seen soloing on *Hot Chocolate* ("Cotton Tail") and
   Jam Session ("C Jam Blues").
The Greatest Jazz Films Ever (Idem IDVD 1059). Contains "The Sound of Jazz," the
   famous TV broadcast from December 5, 1957. Ben Webster is seen with the
   Count Basie All Stars in "Fast and Happy Blues," "I Left My Baby," and "Dickie's
   Dream," and with Billie Holiday in "Fine And Mellow." Also available on Video
   Jazz 013KJ (60 min.). Furthermore, Ben is seen with his sextet in *Jazz from Studio
   61* (April 1959). This sequence is incomplete, as it only contains *Chelsea Bridge*
   and *Duke's Place* ("C Jam Blues"). The complete recording is on VHS (see
   below).
Jimmy Witherspoon/Ben Webster and Jimmy Rushing. Jazz Casual Idem IDVD 1002.
   Jazz Casual TV broadcast, January 2, 1962. Also available in VHS from
   Wea/Rhino.
Big Ben: Ben Webster in Europe. A film by Johan van der Keuken. Eforfilms 2869043
   (31 min.). This film from 1967 shows Ben in various surroundings, at the piano,
   at the billiard table, at the zoo, rehearsing with Don Byas, performing, etc.
Duke Ellington Masters—1971. Quantum Leap QLDVD 0253. TV broadcast Novem-
   ber 7, 1971 from the concert at the Tivoli Concert Hall, Copenhagen. Ben Webster is featured in "Cotton Tail," "All Too Soon," and "I Got It Bad." Also available in VHS.
Quiet Days in Clichy. Directed by Jens Jørgen Thorsen, 1970. Blue Underground,
   2004. Ben Webster is seen in a short segment at a nightclub playing "Blue
   Miller," recorded in September 1969.

VHS

The Brute and the Beautiful. Documentary directed by John Jeremy. Koch Entertainment, 1992 (110 min.). Contains interviews with several musicians and
   friends, and Ben Webster is seen playing in incomplete versions and in various
   settings, from Ellington in 1941 to Ellington in 1971.
Cab Calloway and His Orchestra *"Hi-De-Ho."* Milan Jazz Homevideo 791 286. Ben
   Webster is seen but not heard soloing in this movie soundtrack from 1937.
Jazz from Studio 61. Video Jazz Masters 010KJ (25 min.). Ben Webster Sextet play-
   ing "Mop Mop," "Chelsea Bridge," and "C Jam Blues," April 1959.
Jazz 625—Ben Webster. VIDJAZZ 10 (30 min.). Ben Webster filmed at the Marquee
   Club, London, December 1964, with the Stan Tracey Trio, playing "Sunday,"
   "Chelsea Bridge," "A Night in Tunisia" (with Ronnie Scott), "Over the Rain-
   bow," and "Perdido."
Teddy Wilson—on European Tour. VIDJAZZ 24. Ben Webster on a single track
   playing "Stardust," recorded in Copenhagen, November 14, 1969.

NOTES

CHAPTER 1

1. Where no other source is stated, all information on Ben Webster's family relations is taken from the census of 1930 and from Jeroen de Valk, *Ben Webster: His Life and Music* (Berkeley, Calif.: Berkeley Hills Books, 2001), originally published in Dutch in 1992. The Dutch version contains a useful family tree that unfortunately is not included in the English translation. De Valk had access to firsthand information from Ben's grand-cousin, Joyce Cockrell (1897–) and cousin Harley W. Robinson Jr. (1919–2001)—son of Blanche and Harley W. Robinson Sr. Both of them lived with Ben's family in Kansas City for separate periods; Joyce during Ben's childhood, and Harley from 1932 to 1937.

2. Mary Lou Williams, interview by John S. Wilson, 1973, Jazz Oral History Project, Institute of Jazz Studies, Rutgers University, Newark, N.J.

3. From the documentary *The Brute and the Beautiful* by John Jeremy, 1989.

4. Mary Lou Williams, interview. Williams might be right about the social status of Ben's family, but it has been impossible to confirm who were doctors and lawyers.

5. Jeremy, *The Brute and the Beautiful*.

6. Ibid. The film includes a photograph of Ben at the age of seven with his mother and stepfather. Information on his stepfather is from the census of 1930.

7. Henrik Iversen, "Big Ben," *Jazz Special* 45 (1999): 47.

8. Harley W. Robinson Jr. told de Valk that Agnes was one of the founders of the church, a fact that is hard to believe since the church dates back to the 1870s. However, Agnes may well have been on the board that rebuilt and modernized the church in the 1890s.

9. Tad Hershorn, ed., "The Conversational and Otherwise Art of Jimmy Rowles," unpublished manuscript, 28.

10. Whitney Balliett, "Fauntleroy and the Brute," *New Yorker,* August 15, 1983.

11. Jeremy, *The Brute and the Beautiful.*

12. Ben Webster, interview by Per Møller Hansen, 1971; used in part in the documentary *Big Ben,* shown on Danish television, November 1, 1971, and February 20, 1972.

13. Ben Webster, interview by Henrik Wolsgaard-Iversen, 1969. The interview was broadcast on Danish Radio in three parts on December 4 and 26, 1969, and January 4, 1970.

14. Hans J. Mauerer, ed., *The Pete Johnson Story* (Bremen: Humbug, 1965), 20.

15. Pete Johnson, letter to C. Q. Nägeli, Switzerland, June 1963. (Copy in authors possession.)

16. De Valk, *Ben Webster,* 13.

17. Stanley Dance, *The World of Duke Ellington* (New York: Charles Scribner's Sons, 1970), 232.

18. Linda Dahl, *Morning Glory: A Biography of Mary Lou Williams* (New York: Pantheon, 1999), 42.

19. Webster, interview by Wolsgaard-Iversen.

20. Birgit Nordtorp, interview by the author, October 18, 2002.

21. Ibid.

22. Bent Kauling, interview by the author, October 16, 2002.

23. Mary Lou Williams, interview.

24. De Valk, *Ben Webster,* 13–14.

25. Bert Vuijsje, *Jazzportretten* (Amsterdam: Van Gennep, 1983), 9. The postcard reads, "To my Former Pupil Bennie Webster from his former H.S. Teacher, A.T. Edwards 'Coach.'" The postcard states that Sumner was a senior high school and junior college with twelve hundred pupils and two music rooms.

26. Horace Henderson, interview by Tom McClusky, 1975, Jazz Oral History Project, Institute of Jazz Studies, Rutgers University, Newark, N.J.

27. Walter C. Allen, *Hendersonia* (Highland Park, N.J.: Walter C. Allen, 1973), 184.

28. Max Jones, *Talking Jazz* (London, Papermac, 1990), 80.

29. Rex Stewart, "The Frog and Me," *Down Beat,* June 1, 1967, 21; reprinted in Rex Stewart, *Jazz Masters of the Thirties* (New York: Macmillan, 1972).

30. Count Basie, *Good Morning Blues: The Autobiography of Count Basie as Told to Albert Murray* (New York: Random House, 1985), 86.

31. Webster, interview by Wolsgaard-Iversen.

32. Kauling, interview, October 16, 2002. Basie told the story to Kauling after Ben's death.

CHAPTER 2

1. Ross Russell, *Jazz Style in Kansas City and the Southwest* (Berkeley and Los Angeles: University of California Press, 1973), 238; Stewart, "The Frog and Me," 21.

2. Webster, interview by Wolsgaard-Iversen. In interviews, Ben often spoke of his grandmother rather than his aunt, causing some confusion, but of course he was referring to Mom.

3. Vuijsje, *Jazzportretten,* 10.

4. Walter Barnes Jr., "Hittin' High Notes," *Chicago Defender,* September 26, 1931, 7.

5. Interview with Albert "Budd" Johnson, 1975, Jazz Oral History Project, Institute of Jazz Studies, Rutgers University, Newark, N.J.

6. Webster, interview by Hansen.

7. Webster, interview by Wolsgaard-Iversen.

8. Webster, interview by Hansen.

9. Webster, interview by Wolsgaard-Iversen.

10. Douglas Henry Daniels, *Lester Leaps In: The Time and Life of Lester "Pres" Young* (Boston: Beacon Press, 2002), 107–8.

11. Webster, interview by Wolsgaard-Iversen.

12. Frank Büchmann-Møller, *You Just Fight for Your Life: The Story of Lester Young* (New York: Praeger, 1990), 22.

13. Webster, interview by Hansen.

14. "Ben Webster Speaking . . . ," *Crescendo* 3, no. 7 (1965): 22. Available online at www.jazzprofessional.com/interviews/BenWebster.htm.

15. Webster, interview by Wolsgaard-Iversen. The following years Theodore "Ted" Brinson played with, among others, King Oliver, the Blue Devils, and George E. Lee. Ben and Ted met again in 1934 in Andy Kirk's Clouds of Joy. Brinson was a member of the band from 1933 to 1939.

16. Russ Wilson, "Monterey Festival: Jazz Great Meets Fan Number One," unidentified newspaper clipping from early October 1959, vertical files, Institute of Jazz Studies, Rutgers University, Newark, N.J.

17. Ibid.

18. *Down Beat*, November 8, 1962, 49.

19. De Valk, *Ben Webster*, 25.

20. Dom Cerulli, "Ben Webster," *Down Beat*, June 26, 1958, 16.

21. *Chicago Defender*, February 22, 1930. Roderick Thompson later became more well known as Red "Dizzy" Thompson.

22. Ralph Ellison, *Shadow and Act* (New York: Vintage, 1972), 208, reprinted in *Keeping Time: Readings in Jazz History*, ed. Robert Walser (Oxford: Oxford University Press, 1999), 177. Ellison's memory is off by a few months. The year was 1930.

23. Albert "Budd" Johnson, interview.

24. John Shaw, "Ben Webster," *Jazz Journal*, November 1973, 2–3.

25. "Ben Webster Speaking."

26. Albert "Budd" Johnson, interview.

27. *Chicago Defender*, March 7, 1931.

CHAPTER 3

1. *Chicago Defender*, August 29, 1931.

2. Webster, interview by Wolsgaard-Iversen.

3. Cozy Cole, interview by Bill Kirchner, April 1980, Jazz Oral History Project, Institute of Jazz Studies, Rutgers University, Newark, N.J.

4. Not all discographers agree that Ben participated in all three sessions. Jan Evensmo, in his *History of Jazz Tenor Saxophone: Black Artists*, vol. 1, *1917–1934* (Oslo, 1996), suggests that Lawrence "Slim" Freeman was on the March 27 session. I don't agree with Evensmo. Though Freeman's sound was as dark as Ben's, he had a more legato approach and a far better developed technique than Ben at this time, as can be heard on Freeman's recordings with Andy Kirk and His Clouds of Joy from 1929 and 1930.

5. Webster, interview by Hansen.

6. Cole, interview.

7. *Pittsburgh Courier*, December 31, 1931. When reading the poll results, it must be remembered that the paper was read by the black community.

8. *Chicago Defender,* October 10, 1931.
9. Cole, interview.
10. Webster, interview by Wolsgaard-Iversen.
11. *Chicago Defender,* January 23, January 30, and February 13, 1932.
12. De Valk, *Ben Webster,* 19.
13. Basie, *Good Morning Blues,* 139.
14. Lars Bjorn with Jim Gallert, *Before Motown: A History of Jazz in Detroit, 1920–1960* (Ann Arbor: University of Michigan Press, 2001), 45.
15. Eddie Barefield, interview by Ira Gitler, 1978, Jazz Oral History Project, Institute of Jazz Studies, Rutgers University, Newark, N.J.
16. Basie, *Good Morning Blues,* 141.
17. Ibid., 143.
18. Barefield, interview.
19. Jones, *Talking Jazz,* 82.
20. The information is from Peter Broadbent's Charlie Christian Archive. Ben is mentioned as a member of the orchestra.
21. "Ben Webster Speaking," 22.
22. Mary Lou Williams, "Then Came Zombie Music," *Melody Maker,* May 8, 1954.
23. Mary Lou Williams, interview.
24. Hugo Rasmussen, interview by the author, January 24, 2002.
25. Dahl, *Morning Glory,* 93.
26. Andy Kirk, as told to Amy Lee, *Twenty Years on Wheels* (Oxford: Bayou Press, 1989), 79.
27. Basie, *Good Morning Blues,* 149.
28. Nat Shapiro and Nat Hentoff, eds., *Hear Me Talkin' to Ya: The Story of Jazz as Told by the Men Who Made It* (New York: Dover, 1966), 292–93.
29. Webster, interview by Hansen.
30. *Chicago Defender,* April 14 and June 16, 1934.
31. John Hammond, "The New and Greater Cab," *Melody Maker,* July 28, 1934. The article is dated New York, July 13.
32. John Hammond, "Nouvelle d'Amerique," *Jazz-Tango-Dancing,* September 1934.

CHAPTER 4
1. Max Jones, "Webster—'Rex could say a lot of things on cornet,'" *Melody Maker,* September 23, 1967.
2. Webster, interview by Wolsgaard-Iversen.
3. "Ben Webster Speaking," 22.
4. Russell Procope, interview by Chris Albertson, 1979, Jazz Oral History Project, Institute of Jazz Studies, Rutgers University, Newark, N.J.
5. Lawrence Lucie, interview by the author, New York, March 18, 2002.
6. Williams, "Then Came Zombie Music."
7. Mary Lou Williams, interview.
8. Webster, interview by Wolsgaard-Iversen.

9. Webster, interview by Hansen.

10. Lucie, interview.

11. Ibid.

12. Benny Carter, interview by the author, September 9, 2001.

13. "Russell Heads Apollo Theatre Revue," *New York Amsterdam News,* June 15, 1935.

14. Lucie, interview.

15. John Chilton, *Billie's Blues* (London: Quartet Books, 1975), 23.

16. Webster, interview by Wolsgaard-Iversen.

17. Webster, interview by Hansen.

18. The Ben Webster Collection, Music Department of the University Library of Southern Denmark, Odense.

19. Ben Webster, interview by Henry Whiston in London, April 20, 1971.

20. Doc Cheatham, *I Guess I'll Get the Papers and Go Home* (London: Cassell, 1995), 45.

21. Webster, interview by Wolsgaard-Iversen.

22. "Calloway Balks Whiteface Role," *New York Amsterdam News,* February 1, 1936.

23. Garvin Bushell, *Jazz from the Beginning* (Oxford: Bayou Press, 1988), 89.

24. Ibid.

25. Milt Hinton, interview by Tom Piazza, 1977, Jazz Oral History Project, Institute of Jazz Studies, Rutgers University, Newark, N.J.

26. Cheatham, *I'll Get the Papers,* 41.

27. Bushell, *Jazz from the Beginning,* 95–96.

28. "Cab 'Turns Down' an Invitation to Visit Disabled War Vets," *Pittsburgh Courier,* July 18, 1936.

29. Milt Hinton, interview by Billy Taylor, 1992, Jazz Oral History Project, Institute of Jazz Studies, Rutgers University, Newark, N.J.

30. Milt Hinton and David G. Berger, *Bass Line* (Philadelphia: Temple University Press, 1988), 72.

31. Hinton, interview by Taylor.

32. "Cab to Quit Cotton Club Next Month," *Pittsburgh Courier,* February 13, 1937.

33. Hinton and Berger, *Bass Line,* 110; Bushell, *Jazz from the Beginning,* 115.

34. Nordtorp, interview, October 18, 2002.

35. Hinton, interview by Piazza. In this and other interviews, as in his book, *Bass Line,* Hinton mistakenly claimed that Ben joined Ellington's orchestra right after Calloway's.

36. Allen, *Hendersonia,* 347.

37. Lucie, interview.

38. Jack B. Tenney, "Seagulls Take Hold of Local 47," *Metronome,* February 1938, 34. Tenney finishes by listing the whole orchestra's instrumentation, which makes his use of the word "combo" somewhat fuzzy, as the term is used to refer to small groups and not big bands.

39. Stanley Dance, *The World of Earl Hines* (New York: Scribner's, 1977), 250.

40. Lionel Hampton, "Swing," *Baltimore Afro-American,* April 1938, 10.

41. "These Musicians Changed Bands in May," *Down Beat,* June 1938, 11.

42. "Roy Eldridge and His Boys to Play at Savoy Ballroom," *Pittsburgh Courier,* August 6, 1938.

43. Roy Eldridge, interview by Dan Morgenstern, 1982–83, Jazz Oral History Project, Institute of Jazz Studies, Rutgers University, Newark, N.J.

44. An index of Selmer's serial numbers indicates that the first "Balanced Action" was produced in 1936. Its serial no. was 22650. In 1937 the factory began with no. 25600. "Balanced Action" was produced until 1948, when the "Super Action" model was introduced.

45. Ben visited the Selmer factory in 1971 and chose a couple of "Mark VI" models to bring home for trial. However, he never grew fond of them and soon returned to "Ol' Betsy."

46. Webster, interview by Wolsgaard-Iversen.

47. Ibid.

48. Billy Rowe, "Teddy Wilson Will Close Famous Door Engagement Sunday before Schedule," *Pittsburgh Courier,* May 15, 1939.

49. Johnny Simmen, "Teddy Wilson Orchestra, 1939–1940," *Coda,* December 1970, 31.

50. "Teddy Wilson's Orchestra Hitting Stride in Boston," *Pittsburgh Courier,* July 1, 1939.

51. "Teddy Wilson Scores Decisively at Apollo; Real Show Headliner," *Pittsburgh Courier,* August 5, 1939; "Teddy Wilson's Band Stirs Up Big Controversy," *New York Amsterdam News,* August 12, 1939.

52. Al Casey, interview by the author, March 17, 2002, in New York.

53. "Golden Gate Has Record Crowds," *New York Amsterdam News,* November 25, 1939.

54. Teddy Wilson, "Teddy Wilson Tells the 'Critics' Off!!" *Down Beat,* October 1, 1939, 2.

55. Cheatham, *I'll Get the Papers,* 52.

56. Simmen, "Teddy Wilson Orchestra, 1939–1940," 33.

CHAPTER 5

1. Vuijsje, *Jazzportretten,* 13.

2. Webster, interview by Wolsgaard-Iversen.

3. Duke Ellington, *Music Is My Mistress* (Garden City, N.Y.: Doubleday, 1973), 163.

4. Ibid., 164. In original signatures, Blanton spelled his first name as *Jimmie.* This form has been accepted in later years, and consequently I have maintained it in all further quotations.

5. "Ben Webster Speaking," 23.

6. Jeremy, *The Brute and the Beautiful.*

7. Webster, interview by Wolsgaard-Iversen.

8. Jeremy, *The Brute and the Beautiful.*

9. Webster, interview by Wolsgaard-Iversen.

10. Hinton, interview by Piazza.

11. Rex Stewart, *Boy Meets Horn,* ed. Claire P. Gordon (Ann Arbor: University of Michigan Press, 1991), 198.

12. Stewart, "The Frog and Me," 21–22.

13. Anne Judd, "Barney Goin' Easy," *Jazz Journal,* September 1967, 5.

14. Hershorn, "Art of Jimmy Rowles," 22–23.

15. David Hajdu, *Lush Life: A Biography of Billy Strayhorn* (New York: Farrar, Straus and Giroux, 1996), 90.

16. Hershorn, "Art of Jimmy Rowles," 27–28.

17. Hinton, interview by Piazza.

18. Webster, interview by Hansen.

19. Barrelhouse Dan, "Ellington Hits All-Time New High on 'Cotton Tail' Disc," *Down Beat,* June 27, 1940.

20. Hinton, interview by Piazza.

21. Hershorn, "Art of Jimmy Rowles," 26.

22. Dempsey J. Travis, *An Autobiography of Black Jazz* (Chicago: Urban Research Institute, 1983), 266.

23. Stanley Dance, "An Afternoon with Ben Webster," *Down Beat,* May 21, 1964, 14.

24. Jerry Valburn, "The Fargo Dance Date," booklet accompanying *The Duke at Fargo, 1940: Special 60th Anniversary Edition,* Storyville STCD 8316/17, p. 3.

25. William Strother, "After Fargo," ibid., 28.

26. Anne Kuebler, "The Duke at Fargo," ibid., 7.

27. Jack Towers, "Recording the Duke at Fargo, 1940," ibid., 32.

28. Ibid.

29. John Chilton, *Notes on the Music,* booklet included in *Giants of Jazz: Ben Webster,* Time-Life STL-J21, p. 42.

30. Webster, interview by Hansen.

31. Stuart Nicholson, *Reminiscing in Tempo: A Portrait of Duke Ellington* (Boston: Northeastern University Press, 1999), 236.

32. "Duke Ellington," *Down Beat,* October 15, 1941.

33. Wilma Cockrell, "Jam Session," *California Eagle,* June 26, 1941, 2B.

34. *Body and Soul* is on a few unreleased radio transcriptions from the Trianon Ballroom, Southgate, Calif., from May 1942.

35. "Ben Webster Takes Bride," *Down Beat,* April 1, 1942.

36. Gus Matzorkis, "Ben Webster," in booklet included in *Giants of Jazz: Ben Webster,* Time-Life STL-J21, 20.

37. Lee Young, interview by Patricia Willard, 1977, Jazz Oral History Project, Institute of Jazz Studies, Rutgers University, Newark, N.J.

38. Hal Holly, "Los Angeles Band Briefs," *Down Beat,* July 15, 1942, 12.

39. Matzorkis, "Ben Webster."

40. Hershorn, "Art of Jimmy Rowles," 23.

41. Jeremy, *The Brute and the Beautiful.*

42. Ibid.

43. Ibid.

44. Ulanov, "Duke Ellington," *Metronome,* September 1942.

45. Mary Lou Williams, interview.

46. Kauling, interview, October 16, 2002. Ben told the story to Kauling.

47. Hershorn, "Art of Jimmy Rowles," 60.

48. Dizzy Gillespie with Al Fraser, *To Be or Not to Bop* (Garden City, N.Y.: Doubleday, 1979), 218.

49. "Ben Webster Speaking."

50. Shapiro and Hentoff, *Hear Me Talkin'*, 356.

51. "Ben Webster Speaking."

52. Webster, interview by Wolsgaard-Iversen.

53. Teddy Reig with Edward Berger, *Reminiscing in Tempo: The Life and Times of a Jazz Hustler* (Metuchen, N.J.: Scarecrow Press, 1990), 7.

54. Jeremy, *The Brute and the Beautiful.*

55. Clark Terry, interview by the author, March 19 and 23, 2002.

56. Nicholson, *Reminiscing in Tempo*, 252.

57. Terry, interview.

58. Kauling, interview, October 16, 2002. Ben told these stories to Kauling.

59. Webster, interview by Hansen.

60. Webster, interview by Wolsgaard-Iversen.

CHAPTER 6

1. Webster, interview by Wolsgaard-Iversen.

2. Klaus Stratemann, *Ellington: Day by Day and Film by Film* (Copenhagen: Jazzmedia, 1992), 253. Stratemann offers no documentation for the date of August 13.

3. "Ben Webster Forms Unit," *Down Beat,* August 15, 1943.

4. Billy Taylor, interview by the author, August 28, 2002.

5. Webster, interview by Wolsgaard-Iversen.

6. Taylor, interview by the author.

7. Ibid.

8. Ibid.

9. Arnold Shaw, *52nd Street: The Street of Jazz* (New York: Da Capo Press, 1977), 161.

10. Taylor, interview by the author.

11. "Lee and Stan Shaw Interview—Part Two," interview by Bob Rusch, *Cadence,* August 1985, 11.

12. Ibid., 7.

13. "Ben Webster Speaking," 23.

14. Ibid., 24.

15. Hinton, interview by Piazza. A slightly different version of the story can be found in Hinton and Berger, *Bass Line,* 125–26.

16. Leonard Feather, "Coral's Girth of the Blues Is Dun & Bradstreet of Harlem," *Down Beat,* July 2, 1952, 6.

17. Gary Giddins, "Weatherbird: The Mile High Mainstream," *Village Voice,* October 8, 1985, 80.

18. "Lee and Stan Shaw Interview," 6. The piano player was Clyde Hart.

19. Webster, interview by Hansen.

20. "Honored at Carnegie Hall, Sunday Night," *New York Amsterdam News,*

April 8, 1944, 10. Esquire's 1945 *Jazz Book,* 117, also mentions the concert with Ben and Catlett among the many musicians.

21. *Down Beat,* August 1, 1944.

22. Travis, *Autobiography of Black Jazz,* 212.

23. Sadik Hakim, "Reflections of an Era—My Experiences with Bird and Prez," *Jazz Journal International,* August 1996, 17.

24. *New York Amsterdam News,* February 3 and February 10, 1945.

25. Hakim, "Reflections of an Era." Hakim does not remember the name of the proprietor correctly. He was Mike Westerman (Shaw, *52nd Street,* 321).

26. Webster, interview by Wolsgaard-Iversen.

27. Mark Gardner with Harvey Pekar, "Bill De Arango," *Jazz Journal,* July 1971, 25.

28. *New York Amsterdam News,* June 14, 1945.

29. A. B. Spellman, *Four Jazz Lives* (Ann Arbor: University of Michigan Press, 2004), 202–3.

30. *Kansas City . . . and All That's Jazz* (Kansas City: Kansas City Jazz Museum, 1999), 110.

31. Milt Buckner, interview by Kees Bakker, Willebroek, Belgium, mid–1970s. Buckner believed that the event occurred in 1944, although he was not absolutely sure about the year.

32. Donald L. Maggin, *Stan Getz: A Life in Jazz* (New York: William Morrow, 1996), 58–59.

33. Stanley Dance, *The World of Count Basie* (New York: Charles Scribner's Sons, 1980), 280.

34. Jeremy, *The Brute and the Beautiful.*

35. Kauling, interview, October 16, 2002.

36. Jeremy, *The Brute and the Beautiful.*

37. Tony Scott website: www.tonyscott.it.

38. "At Town Hall Feb. 9," *New York Amsterdam News,* February 9, 1946, 10.

39. The information on De Arango comes from *Down Beat,* February 25, 1946. Information in www.tonyscott.it states that Ben was picked up in Washington for a recording session with Tony Scott on March 6.

40. James Lester, *Too Marvelous for Words: The Life and Genius of Art Tatum* (New York: Oxford University Press, 1994), 181.

41. Jim Szantor, "Eddie Shaughnessy," *Down Beat,* April 12, 1973, 16.

42. *Jazz Record,* July 1946, informs us that Billy Taylor was part of the group in June–July. Sonny White's membership of Ben's band is documented by the session with Benny Carter on August 23, and David Griffiths, *Hot Jazz: From Harlem to Storyville* (Lanham, Md.: Scarecrow Press, 1998), 127, which states that he played with Ben during this period.

43. Nordtorp, interview, October 18, 2002. It has been impossible to find Mule's real name.

44. Dick Katz, interview by the author, January 28, 2003.

45. Webster, interview by Wolsgaard-Iversen.

46. Jack Egan, "Webster in Royal Return to Duke," *Down Beat,* December 1, 1948, 1.

47. Morroe Berger, Edward Berger, and James Patrick, *Benny Carter: A Life in American Music* (Metuchen, N.J.: Scarecrow Press, 1982), 2:142.

48. Richard Davis, interview by the author, September 16, 2002.

49. Peter Danson, "Charlie Rouse," *Coda* 187 (1982): 5.

50. Don DeMicheal, "Charlie Rouse—Artistry and Originality," *Down Beat*, May 25, 1961, 17.

CHAPTER 7

1. John S. Wilson, "The Street Just a Dead Alley Again," *Down Beat*, February 24, 1950, 1.

2. Nordtorp, interview, October 18, 2002.

3. *Kansas City . . . and All That's Jazz.*

4. Johnny Griffin, Danish Radio, March 27, 1999, from a show about the Ben Webster Award.

5. Ben Sidran, *Talking Jazz* (San Francisco: Pomegranate Artbooks, 1992), 84.

6. Ibid., 109.

7. Dance, *World of Count Basie*, 180.

8. Ibid., 192.

9. Harold Ashby, interview by the author, June 26, 2002.

10. Chip Deffaa, "Harold Ashby: Remembering Duke and Ben," *Mississippi Rag*, April 1985, 7.

11. Ibid.

12. Jeremy, *The Brute and the Beautiful.*

13. Billy Vera, "The Blues Was Alive and Well in Kansas City," liner notes to *Kansas City Blues 1940–49*, Capitol 7243 8 52047 2 2.

14. Dan Morgenstern, liner notes to *The Complete Ben Webster on EmArcy*, EmArcy 75J-3–4.

15. Hal Holly, "Two Coast Kids, 16 and 11, May Click on 1st Record," *Down Beat*, January 25, 1952, 13.

16. Charles Emgee, "Jazz Moves Underground in L.A. and Is Prospering," *Down Beat*, August 13, 1952, 8.

17. Ed Thigpen, interview by the author, September 12, 2002.

18. Preston Love, *A Thousand Honey Creeks Later* (Hanover, N.H.: Wesleyan University Press, 1997), 122.

19. Joe Darensbourg, *Telling It Like It Is* (New York: Macmillan, 1987), 126–27.

20. Hershorn, "Art of Jimmy Rowles," 22–23.

21. "Ben Webster to Snookie's NYC," *Down Beat*, December 12, 1952.

22. "Strictly Ad Lib. New York," *Down Beat*, February 25, 1953, 3.

23. Advertisements in *New York Amsterdam News*, May 2 and May 23, 1953.

24. Nat Hentoff, "Hail the Unsung," *Down Beat*, December 31, 1952, 6.

25. Chilton, *Notes on the Music*, 51.

26. Niels-Henning Ørsted Pedersen, interview by the author, October 8, 2001.

27. Nat Hentoff, "Some Fiery Jazz Heard as JATP Hits Carnegie," *Down Beat*, October 21, 1953, 3.

28. John Chilton, *Roy Eldridge: Little Jazz Giant* (London: Continuum, 2002), 196.

29. Burt Korall, *Drumming Men: The Heartbeat of Jazz* (New York: Schirmer Books, 1990), 85.

30. Harvey Sand, interview by the author, October 9, 2001. Sand was a waiter at Jazzhus Montmartre in Copenhagen and became one of Ben's best friends.

31. "Ben Webster Plays That Big Tenor," *Down Beat*, October 5, 1955, 12–13.

32. Ibid., 13.

33. Hajdu, *Lush Life*, 136.

34. Webster, interview by Wolsgaard-Iversen.

35. Webster, interview by Hansen.

36. Nat Hentoff, "Counterpoint," *Down Beat*, July 13, 1955, 12.

37. Steve Jordan with Tom Scanlan, *Rhythm Man: Fifty Years in Jazz* (Ann Arbor: University of Michigan Press, 1993), 107.

38. Jack Tracy, "Newport! Here's Your Complete Report on What Went On at the Huge Jazz Festival," *Down Beat*, August 24, 1955, 24.

39. Terkel, in Leon Forrest, "A Solo Long-Song: For Lady Day," *Callaloo* 16 (1993): 350.

40. Hershorn, "Art of Jimmy Rowles," 90–91.

41. Jeremy, *The Brute and the Beautiful*.

42. Oscar Peterson, *A Jazz Odyssey: The Life of Oscar Peterson*, ed. Richard Palmer (London: Continuum, 2002), 106.

43. Hershorn, "Art of Jimmy Rowles," 96.

44. Webster, interview by Hansen.

45. Webster, interview by Wolsgaard-Iversen.

46. Ibid.

47. Webster, interview by Hansen. Ben's memory failed him, because there are alternative takes of two of the seven tracks.

48. Webster, interview by Whiston.

49. *Down Beat*, May 16, 1957, 37.

50. Nordtorp, interview, October 18, 2002.

51. Terry, interview.

52. Buddy Collette with Steven Isoardi, *Jazz Generations: A Life in American Music and Society* (London: Continuum, 2000), 144.

53. Webster, interview by Wolsgaard-Iversen.

54. Ibid.

55. Peterson, *A Jazz Odyssey*, 215.

56. Bushell, *Jazz from the Beginning*, 123.

57. Horace Parlan, interview by the author, January 10, 2002.

58. Linda Dahl, *Stormy Weather* (London: Quartet Books, 1984), 200.

59. Rolontz, "Reviewed in Brief: Ella and Duke," *Billboard*, April 14, 1958, 7.

60. Dan Morgenstern, "Reports on Two Sessions," *Jazz Journal*, June 1958, 28.

61. Whitney Balliett, "Big Ben," *New Yorker*, January 19, 1963, 72–73.

62. Taylor, interview by the author.

63. Dan Morgenstern, interview by the author, January 21, 2003.

64. Don Gold and Dom Cerulli, "Newport," *Down Beat*, August 7, 1958, 16.

65. Bill Coleman, in a letter to C. Q. Nägeli, June 1963.

66. Francis Davis, liner notes to *The Soul of Ben Webster*, Verve 527 475–2.

67. Leonard Feather, "Big Ben: The Blindfold Test," *Down Beat,* November 27, 1958, 37.

68. Ibid.

69. Taylor, interview by the author.

CHAPTER 8

1. Steve Voce, "Scratching the Surface . . . ," *Jazz Journal International,* January 2001, 14.

2. Gene Lees, "The Monterey Festival. This One Was for Jazz," *Down Beat,* November 12, 1959, 23.

3. John Tynan, "The Bowl Fest," *Down Beat,* November 12, 1959, 19.

4. "Ben Webster Speaking," 24.

5. Chip Deffaa, "Jimmy Witherspoon," *JazzTimes,* January–February 1991, 53.

6. Jeremy, *The Brute and the Beautiful.*

7. Max Jones, "It's Still the Blues," *Melody Maker,* September 19, 1964, 6.

8. Phil Schaap, liner notes to *Gerry Mulligan Meets Ben Webster,* Verve 841 661–2.

9. Francis Davis, liner notes to *The Complete Gerry Mulligan Meets Ben Webster,* Verve 539 055–2.

10. Jeremy, *The Brute and the Beautiful.*

11. Hershorn, "Art of Jimmy Rowles," 91.

12. Don DeMicheal, "The Monterey Festival," *Down Beat,* November 9, 1961, 13.

13. Ralph J. Gleason, "When Ben Blew the Blues," *San Francisco Chronicle,* September 30, 1973.

14. Ibid.

15. Pete Welding, "First International Jazz Festival. Report from Washington," *Down Beat,* July 19, 1962, 20.

16. Bassist Roman Dylag was present and has sent me a photograph showing Ben and Coltrane seated with Polish musicians.

17. Shaw, "Ben Webster," 4.

18. Don DeMicheal, "Falling Angel? Monterey Jazz Festival Report," *Down Beat,* November 8, 1962, 13.

19. Ibid.

20. Gleason, "When Ben Blew the Blues."

21. DeMicheal, "Falling Angel?" 14.

22. Bob Hunter, "Ben Webster Still 'Blowing' Sweet Despite 'Father Time.'" *Chicago Daily Defender,* March 18, 1963, 16.

23. Parlan, interview.

24. Harvey Siders, "According to Webster, Jazz Means Individualism," *Boston Sunday Globe,* June 9, 1963, 75.

25. Terry, interview.

26. Bill Crow, letter to the author, September 14, 2002.

27. Dave Frishberg, letter to the author, January 6, 2003.

28. Richard Davis, interview by the author, September 16, 2002.

29. Hilton Jefferson, letter to C. Q. Nägeli, June 1963. (Copy in authors possession.)

30. Dan Morgenstern, "Big Ben in New York," *Jazz Journal*, January 1964, 5.
31. Ibid., 6.
32. Fred Miles, "FM Speaks," *Scoop USA*, August 31, 1963.
33. Howard Klein, "Fanfare: Part Four," *New York Times*, August 9, 1963.
34. William Bender, "Jazz Assessment at Lincoln Center," unidentified newspaper clipping from the Ben Webster Collection, Music Department, University Library of Southern Denmark, Odense.
35. Jeremy, *The Brute and the Beautiful*.
36. Peter Keepnews, liner notes to *Ben Webster and Joe Zawinul*. Milestone M-47056.
37. Ibid.
38. Anders Stefansen, interview by the author, May 29, 2001.
39. Morgenstern, interview by the author.
40. Jeremy, *The Brute and the Beautiful*.
41. Hunter, "Ben Webster Still Blowing."
42. Arnold Jay Smith, liner notes to *Carol and Ben*, Honey Dew HD 6608.
43. Ibid.
44. Dance, "Afternoon with Ben Webster," 14.
45. John S. Wilson, "Two Jazz Artists Play at Concert," *New York Times*, February 22, 1964.
46. Bill Crow, *From Birdland to Broadway: Scenes from a Jazz Life* (New York: Oxford University Press, 1992), 208.
47. Hinton, interview by Piazza. In the transcription of the interview, Jim & Andy's is mistakenly called Jim Anders. In an interview with Milt Hinton's widow, Mona, September 9, 2002, she told me that Jim often lent money to needy musicians, and that Ben and Hinton were regulars. Ben's collection reveals a series of slides taken by him of the bar and the regular customers. The building was demolished in an urban renewal plan in the late 1960s.
48. Ibid.
49. Don DeMicheal, "Newport," *Down Beat*, August 13, 1964, 30.
50. Balliett, "Fauntleroy and the Brute," 70–71.
51. Jeremy, *The Brute and the Beautiful*

CHAPTER 9
1. Ronnie Scott, *Some of My Best Friends Are Blues* (London: W. H. Allen, 1979), 82.
2. Max Jones, "Ben Webster Finally Makes It," *Melody Maker*, December 12, 1964, 6.
3. Ibid.
4. Max Jones, "It's Full Strength Webster," *Melody Maker*, December 19, 1964, 12.
5. John Fordham, *Jazz Man: The Amazing Story of Ronnie Scott and His Club* (London: Kylie Cathie, 1995), 102.
6. Ronnie Scott in a broadcast from Ronnie Scott's Club, London, with Ben Webster and Stan Tracey's Trio, recorded early January 1965, broadcast February 28, 1965.

7. Valerie Wilmer, "Warm and Websterish," *Jazzbeat* 2 (1965): 15.

8. Roman Dylag, letter to the author, July 5, 2002.

9. Hans Fridlund, *Aftonbladet* (Stockholm), January 6, 1965.

10. Rolf Dahlgren, "Hört på Cirklen," *Orkester Journalen,* January 1965, 17.

11. A copy of the contract between SBA and Herluf Kamp Larsen, Jazzhus Montmartre, December 19, 1964, indicates that Ben was paid one hundred dollars per night, after the booking agency took its share.

12. Erik Wiedemann, "Monmartres Big Ben," *Information* (Copenhagen), January 21, 1965.

13. Arnvid Meyer, "Webster—en uge efter," *Aktuelt* (Copenhagen), January 26, 1965.

14. Alex Riel, interview by the author, October 31, 2001.

15. Ørsted Pedersen, interview.

16. Henrik Wolsgaard-Iversen, interview by the author, October 16, 2002.

17. Lars Sjösten, interview by the author, September 7, 2001.

18. "Briljanta ballader med 'Big Ben' Webster," *Sundsvall Tidning* (Sundsvall), February 5, 1965.

19. Åke Lif, "Ben Webster i kyligt Sundsvall," *Dagbladet* (Sundsvall), February 5, 1965.

20. Arnvid Meyer, interview by the author, February 28, 2001.

21. Hans Nymand, interview by the author, April 3, 2001.

22. Randi Hultin, *Born under the Sign of Jazz* (London: Sanctuary, 1998), 247.

23. Tore Sandnæs, interview by the author, May 7, 2002.

24. *Jazz Magazine* (Paris), May 1965, 9.

25. Sjösten, interview.

26. Roman Dylag, letter to the author, July 5, 2002. *Lasse* is a nickname for *Lars;* the Lasse to whom Dylag refers is Lars Sjösten.

27. Jim Silvester, "Mainstream at the Festival Hall," *Jazz Journal,* June 1965, 11.

28. David Rosenthal, "Ben Webster in London," *Jazz Monthly,* July 1965, 23.

29. Benny Green, "Jazz," *The Observer* (London), May 23, 1965.

30. Fred Everet to Manfred Selchow in a letter accompanying the recordings from the South Bank Jazz Club, Grimsby, June 11, 1965.

31. Bruce Turner, *Hot Air, Cool Music* (London: Quartet Books, 1984), 167–68.

32. Stefansen, interview.

33. Sand, interview.

34. John Darville, interview by the author, March 1, 2001.

35. Niels Jørgen Steen, interview by the author, August 14, 2001.

36. Nymand, interview.

37. Rasmussen, interview.

38. Meyer, interview.

39. Stefansen, interview.

CHAPTER 10

1. Jeremy, *The Brute and the Beautiful.*

2. The documentary movie *Big Ben* by Johan van der Keuken (1967).

3. Cees Slinger, interview by the author, April 1, 2003.

4. Jeremy, *The Brute and the Beautiful.*

5. De Valk, *Ben Webster,* 147.

6. Ibid., 148–49.

7. Stefansen, interview.

8. Tore Sandnæs, interview by the author, April 7, 2003. *Liv* opened on Ben's birthday, March 27, 1967.

9. The episode is recounted by Bramsen in John Chilton, *The Song of the Hawk: The Life and Recordings of Coleman Hawkins* (Ann Arbor: University of Michigan Press, 1990), 369–70. Here Bramsen mentions the tune played by Ben and Hawkins as *You'd Be So Nice to Come Home To,* but a private tape of the show—unfortunately without any talking or announcements—reveals *Huneysuckle Rose.*

10. Max Jones, "Big Ben Still Chiming," *Melody Maker,* December 17, 1966, 20.

11. Max Jones, "Webster: Emigre Tenor Finds Europe to His Style," *Melody Maker,* January 7, 1967, 6.

12. Scott, *Some of My Best Friends Are Blues,* 84.

13. Quotations from "Ein Gigant des Jazz in der Aula: Ben Webster," *Badener Tagblatt* (Baden), February 2, 1967; and "Ben Webster spielte in Solothurn," *Das Volk* (Solothurn), February 1, 1967.

14. De Valk, *Ben Webster,* 153.

15. Ibid.

16. Bert Vuijsje, interview by the author, April 2, 2003. Vuijsje's review of the jam session with Noordijk, Byas, Tate, and Ben is from *Jazzwereld,* January 1968.

17. Max Jones, "Tenor of Jazz," *Melody Maker,* April 22, 1967, 6.

18. Steve Voce, "It Don't Mean a Thing," *Jazz Journal,* June 1967, 26.

19. Dance, *World of Count Basie,* 181.

20. Webster, interview by Whiston.

21. "Sensationelles Badener Jazzkonzert mit den Swing-Giganten Buck Clayton und Ben Webster," *Arbeiter-Zeitung* (Schaffhausen), June 8, 1967.

22. René Muttenzer, "Buck Clayton Meets Ben Webster," *National-Zeitung* (Basel), June 9, 1967.

23. All information on Ben's stay in Pori and Helsinki is from letters to the author from Seppo Lemponen, August 1 and 10, 2001, and May 28, 2003. Lemponen heard Ben in Pori, and he interviewed, among others, drummer Esko Rosnell about Ben's doings in Helsinki.

24. Joachim E. Berendt, "Jazz an einem Fjord im Sommer," *Jazz Podium,* September 1967, 254, and Jan Byrczyk, "Scandinavian Notebook," *Jazz Forum* (Warsaw), 1, no. 2 (1968): 65.

25. David Illingworth, "Ben Webster/Vi Redd," *Jazz Journal,* October 1967, 28.

26. Voce, "It Don't Mean a Thing," *Jazz Journal,* December 1967, 21.

27. Dave Green, interview by the author, November 22, 2001.

28. "Interview with Louis Moholo," *Wire* (London), March 1991, 37.

29. "Taking the A-Train," *Holland Herald* 2, no. 1 (1967): 33.

30. Albert McCarthy, "Newport All-Stars and Others," *Jazz Monthly,* December 1967, 6.

31. Voce, "It Don't Mean a Thing," *Jazz Journal,* December 1967, 21.

32. Hans Dulfer, interview by the author, April 2, 2003.

33. Vuijsje, interview.

34. Dan van Golberdinge, "Ben Webster in IJmuiden," *NJA Bulletin* 16 (1995): 25.

35. Ibid.

36. Derek Jewell, "Jazz," *Sunday Times* (London), January 7, 1968.

37. Hans Jacob Sahlertz, interview by the author, April 19, 2001.

38. Finn Ziegler, interview by the author, February 5, 2002.

39. Arnvid Meyer, "Tenorhuset," *Aktuelt* (Copenhagen), March 9, 1968.

40. Meyer, interview.

41. Yves Delubac, "Hier et avant-hier," *Jazz Magazine* (Paris), May 1968, 11.

42. Rasmussen, interview.

43. "Poland," *Down Beat,* July 11, 1968, 45.

44. Wesselin Nikolov, "Ben Webster and the Novi," *Jazz Forum* (Warsaw), 2, no. 3 (1968): 75–76, 78.

45. De Valk, *Ben Webster,* 187.

46. Heinz Baumeister, letter to the author, June 29, 2003.

47. Peter Verhagen, "'Hammerfeld Jazz Roermond' Festivals: Ben Webster," *NJA Bulletin* 47 (2003): 37.

48. Buckner, interview.

49. Dulfer, interview.

50. Laurie Henshaw, "Caught in the Act: Ben Webster," *Melody Maker,* December 7, 1968, 6.

51. Egbert de Bloeme, interview by the author, April 4, 2003.

52. Dulfer, interview.

53. "Expositie-Kwint bij Felison met jazz van Webster geopend," *IJmuider Courant* (Haarlem), March 31, 1969.

54. Jeremy, *The Brute and the Beautiful.* There was less racism in Europe than in the United States, but there was some in the countries with colonies abroad. With their large immigration from these colonies, you could therefore meet racism in large cities such as London, Paris, and Amsterdam.

CHAPTER 11

1. Klaus Albrectsen, "Hjemme hos Webster," *Politiken* (Copenhagen), April 10, 1969.

2. Wolsgaard-Iversen, interview by the author.

3. Ibid. In fact, Ben's first home of his own was the house he took over in Los Angeles from Mom and Mayme when they moved to the old-age home.

4. Webster, interview by Whiston.

5. Ibid.

6. Bertil Sundin, "Molde," *Orkester Journalen,* September 1969, 16.

7. Fletcher, "Jazz ute inne," *Orkester Journalen,* September 1969, 19.

8. Sjösten, interview.

9. Jens Jefsen, interview by the author, December 2, 2002.

10. Letter to Mary Lou Williams dated September 19, 1969, Mary Lou Williams Archive, Institute of Jazz Studies, Rutgers University, Newark, N.J.

11. Webster, interview by Whiston.

12. Darville, interview.

13. Bent Kauling, interview by the author, October 10, 2002.

14. Darville, interview.

15. Kauling, interview, October 10, 2002.

16. Barefield, interview.

17. Ole Just Astrup, "Minnesvärd konsert för Timme," *Orkester Journalen,* January 1970, 41.

18. Birgit Nordtorp, interview by the author, May 8, 2001.

19. Ibid.

20. Nordtorp, interview, October 18, 2002.

21. Wolsgaard-Iversen, interview by the author.

22. Christer Nilsson, "Nytt från Skåne," *Orkester Journalen,* March 1970, 16.

23. Jan Bruér, "Stor musikaktivitet i Uppsala," *Orkester Journalen,* April 1970, 14.

24. Sandnæs, interview, May 7, 2002.

25. Ove Stokstad, letter to the author, February 5, 2002.

26. Jesper Thilo, interview by the author, September 12, 2001.

27. Ibid.

28. Webster, interview by Whiston.

29. Chris Krenger, letter to the author, February 28, 2002.

30. Kauling, interview, October 10, 2002.

31. Max Jones, "Ben's Sax Roll Call," *Melody Maker,* August 22, 1970, 10.

32. Kauling, interview, October 10, 2002.

33. Slinger, interview.

34. Jesper Thilo, interview by the author.

35. The liner notes to *No Fool, No Fun,* Storyville STCD 8304, state mistakenly that Ben had just arrived from London. This is not true. He had returned from London almost two weeks earlier and had played at the Jazzhus Montmartre on October 21.

36. Kauling, interview, October 10, 2002.

37. Albrekt von Konow, "Indisponerad Webster," *Orkester Journalen,* February 1971, 7.

38. Bent Henius, "Dage med Webster," *Berlingske Tidende* (Copenhagen), March 7, 1971.

39. Kauling, interview, October 10, 2002.

40. Jenny Wilkins, interview by the author, December 12, 2001.

41. Arrigo Polillo, "3. Festival del jazz a Bergamo," *Musica Jazz,* May 1971, 18–19.

42. Buckner, interview.

43. Benny Green, "Webster's Way," *The Observer* (London), April 25, 1971.

44. Dave Green, interview.

45. Webster, interview by Whiston.

46. Jenny Armstrong, "Benny Carter in Denmark and Sweden," *Jazz Forum* (Warsaw), 15 (1972): 26.

47. Jean Levin, "Jazz en direct," *Jazz Magazine* (Paris), August 1971, 52.

48. Jesper Thilo, interview.

49. Undated letter, postmarked September 16, 1971, Mary Lou Williams Archive, Institute of Jazz Studies, Rutgers University, Newark, N.J.

50. Bjørn Alterhaug, letter to the author, January 31, 2001.

51. Ove Stokstad, letter to the author, February 5, 2002.

52. The recordings are in Norsk Jazzarkiv, Oslo.

53. Ben Besiakov, interview by the author, January 29, 2002.

54. Kauling, interview, October 10, 2002.

55. The full story is reproduced in De Valk, *Ben Webster*, 205–6, and in the liner notes to *Ben Webster in Europe*, Rarities 45. In autumn 2001, I wrote to His Royal Majesty King Harald, enquiring whether the story could be confirmed. An answer from the Royal Norwegian Court of November 21, 2001, states that the king has no such recollection, and that the story cannot be confirmed.

56. Hans Lyhne Møller, "En helt uforlignelig jazzkoncert," *Flensborg Avis*, March 24, 1972.

57. Bo Stief, interview by the author, September 17, 2001.

58. Ørsted Pedersen, interview.

59. Wolsgaard-Iversen, interview by the author.

60. Liner notes to *Ben Webster, Dexter Gordon, Baden 1972*, TCB Records 02102.

61. Bert Vuijsje, "Plezierige jazzavond," *Het Parool* (Amsterdam), May 10, 1972.

62. Denis Constant, "Orly," *Jazz Magazine* (Paris), 202 (1972): 30.

63. Lennart Östberg, "Åhus-festivalen svettig," *Orkester-Journalen*, October 1972, 14. In Denmark, Bobby Brooks usually played with the Bent Jædig–Richard Boone Quintet, but on January 15, 1972, he had played at the Jazzhus Montmartre in Kenny Drew's trio with Dexter Gordon and Ben. For a while he lived in Sweden, before finally settling in Holland. He should not be mistaken for another American, Billy Brooks, also a drummer, who also emigrated to Europe and now lives and teaches in Bern, Switzerland.

64. Gian Carlo Roncaglia, "A Pescara," *Musica Jazz*, October 1972, 17.

65. Marlene Widmark, interview by the author, September 14, 2001.

66. "Varm musik," *Land og Folk* (Copenhagen), July 22, 1972.

67. Terry, interview.

68. K. Korsunsky, "Jazz an einem Sommerabend," *Badener Tagblatt* (Baden), August 30, 1972.

69. Bo Stief, interview by the author, September 17, 2001. On December 15, 1954, Ben recorded *Come Rain or Come Shine* with strings.

70. "Jazz in der Aula: Zwei Konzerte in einem," *Badener Tagblatt* (Baden), November 15, 1972; and "Baden: Ben Webster und Dexter Gordon," *National-Zeitung* (Basel), November 17, 1972.

71. Buckner, interview.

72. Marlene Widmark, interview by the author, September 14, 2001.

73. Jesper Thilo, interview.

74. "Festligt femårsjubileum," *Orkester Journalen*, April 1973, 7.

75. Kauling, interview, October 10, 2002.

76. Nymand, interview.

77. Kauling, interview.

78. Meyer, interview.

79. Bent Kauling, "Swing-sot i Jazzhus Montmartre," *MM* 3 (1973): 19.
80. Rasmussen, interview.
81. Nordtorp, interview, October 18, 2002.
82. Parlan, interview.
83. Terry, interview.
84. The letter is in the Ben Webster Collection.
85. Hershorn, "Art of Jimmy Rowles," 126–27. Rowles and Ben called each other "S. H.," because at their first meeting—in Tacoma, Washington, in March 1940—one of Ben's first remarks to Rowles was, "How do you do? Which way to the shithouse?" See chapter 5.
86. Kauling, interview, October 10, 2002.
87. Ed Thigpen, interview by the author, September 12, 2001.
88. Nordtorp, interview.
89. Ibid.
90. Ibid.
91. Nordtorp, interview.
92. Mort Goode, liner notes to *Ben Webster and Sweets Edison: Ben and "Sweets,"* Columbia CK 40853.
93. Leonard Feather, "Blindfold Test: John Coltrane," *Down Beat,* February 19, 1959, 39. Available at http://www.downbeat.com/default.asp?sect=stories&subsect=story_detail&sid=814.

INDEX

Titles of songs, albums, movies, radio, TV shows, and so on are in italics. Webster's nicknames to his fellow musicians are given in quotation marks. If a town name occurs in the name of a club, hotel, and so on, the town is not mentioned in brackets as otherwise is the case. The Scandinavian æ/ä, ø/ö and å are alphabetized as a, o, and a respectively. Numbers in bold-faced type refer to pages 1–16 in the photo section.